*Raspberry-Glazed Ham, page 148*

*Creamy Green Bean Casserole,*
*page 205*

*Slow-Cooker Pumpkin Pie,*
*page 253*

"The *Fix-It and Forget-It* series is the country's bestselling crockpot cookbook series.

"The six books in the series compile edited versions of recipes contributed by everyday cooks and have sold more than nine million copies."
— *Publishers Weekly*

"The author who came in second to Rachael Ray in total foodie sales was Phyllis Pellman Good, who does not have a TV show."
— *Summary of Bestsellers*
*Publishers Weekly*

"One reason why the books are so popular is that they aren't intended for folks who dabble in cooking as a hobby or a whim.

"'The audience that I have in mind is those who have to cook every day of the week,' says Good."
— *Los Angeles Times*

"Good's books have sold more in the United States than the *combined* works of popular Food Network hosts Ina Garten, Giada De Laurentiis, and Jamie Oliver."
— *The New York Times*
*Front-page feature*

"One of the losses in our lives is that it's so hard to sit down at the dinner table, night after night, and have parents and children eating together," says Phyllis Pellman Good.

"With the slow cooker, you can prepare food early and bring everyone together at the table," she says. "It helps immensely."
— *The Associated Press*

# Fix-It and Forget-It

# Christmas Cookbook

# 600
## Slow Cooker Holiday Recipes

Phyllis
Pellman
Good

Good Books

Intercourse, PA 17534
800/762-7171
www.GoodBooks.com

Some of the recipes in *Fix-It and Forget-It Christmas Cookbook: 600 Slow Cooker Holiday Recipes*
first appeared in *Fix-It and Forget-It Recipes for Entertaining*,
published and copyrighted by Good Books, 2002.

Cover illustration and illustrations throughout the book by Cheryl Benner
Design by Cliff Snyder

**FIX-IT AND FORGET-IT® CHRISTMAS COOKBOOK: 600 SLOW COOKER HOLIDAY RECIPES**
Copyright © 2010 by Good Books, Intercourse, PA 17534

International Standard Book Number: 978-1-56148-701-1 (paperback edition)
International Standard Book Number: 978-1-56148-703-5 (hardcover gift edition)
International Standard Book Number: 978-1-56148-702-8 (comb-bound paperback edition)
Library of Congress Catalog Card Number: 2010026590

**Library of Congress Cataloging-in-Publication Data**
Good, Phyllis Pellman
  Fix-it and forget-it Christmas cookbook : 600 slow cooker holiday recipes / Phyllis
Pellman Good.
    p. cm.
  Includes index.
  ISBN 978-1-56148-701-1 (pbk. : alk. paper) -- ISBN 978-1-56148-702-8 (comb-bound
: alk. paper) -- ISBN 978-1-56148-703-5 (hardcover : alk. paper) 1. Electric cooking,
Slow. 2. Christmas cooking. I. Title.
  TX827.G634 2010
  641.5'686--dc22                                                      2010026590

# Table of Contents

# Welcome to Fix-It and Forget-It Christmas Cookbook

### It seemed like a good idea...

If you've invited your family or your special friends or neighbors to your home for a holiday meal, you might be caught somewhere between anticipation and dread right now.

Who doesn't like to have loved ones around the table, murmuring with delight about the food they've been eating? But which of us hasn't had panic nearly paralyze us on the way to that lovely moment?

### Running out...

Or maybe your energy and your cooking ideas left you before your holiday guests did? How do you prepare without running out of time—or graciousness?

Never fear. You absolutely can make holiday meals with ease and with pleasure!

### Beat the panic

Most of us prepare dozens of meals during the 60 days between early November and early January. Well, here are 600 *manageable* slow-cooker recipes— all from cooks who want to feast with their loved ones without being exhausted and frazzled.

*Phyllis Pellman Good*

## A bonus

Don't miss the "Ideas for Meaningful Holidays" and "Happy Hosting Tips," spread among the recipes. One more reason that this cookbook can quickly become your kitchen companion.

Thank you, all you wonderful cooks and hosts who so generously shared your holiday recipes and tips for happiness at this special time of year. And thank you, too, testers, for your care and comments. Each of you has demonstrated the wonder of hospitality.

## Make this cookbook your own

Most of the recipes in this collection are flexible and forgiving. You'll notice that most of them offer a range of cooking times; many of the recipes suggest optional ingredients.

Make this book your own. Write in it. Note the cooking time that worked for you. Star the recipe you liked. If you added or subtracted ingredients, write them in the neighboring column. Flip to the Index and put a big dot next to a recipe you especially liked. Then you can spot it at a glance when you're looking for cooking inspiration.

## One more thing

These recipes work at any time of the year! Don't restrict them to your holiday table.

# Christmas Smells

**Mary Kathryn Yoder**
Harrisonville, MO

*Prep. Time: 10 minutes*

***Ideal slow cooker size: 2-quart***

**4 cups water**
**rind of 1 lemon**
**rind of 1 orange**
**1-oz. box whole cloves**
**1-oz. box cinnamon sticks**
**2 bay leaves**

1. Pour water into 2-qt. slow cooker so it's half to ⅔ full.
2. Add all other ingredients. Stir well.
3. Cover. Turn cooker to High until mixture boils.
4. Remove lid. Reduce heat to Low. Let mixture simmer and fill your home with good smells. Add water as needed.

### Note:

*Do not leave your house with Christmas Smells cooking. This needs continual checking so it doesn't boil dry.*

# Tips for Using Your Slow Cooker: A Friendly Holiday Appliance

## 1. What to buy

- A good standard size for a household of four is a 4-quart slow cooker.

  But holiday-time may be the perfect opportunity to add to your slow-cooker collection. Because these babies are so absolutely useful and relieve so much hosting tension, I recommend:

  - *one large cooker (6- or 7-quart)*

    Then you're set for preparing sizable roasts, turkey breasts, chicken legs and thighs, or a big pot of soup.

  - *one or two medium cookers (4- or 5-quart)*

    Do your vegetables in these. Or if you're cooking for a smaller group, you can do your main dish in one or both of them. Don't forget that you can prepare brunch dishes or desserts in these, too.

  - *one or two small cookers (1½- 3-quart)*

    These are ideal for dips, breakfast fruit, dessert toppings, and more.

- Cookers which allow you to program "On," the length of the cooking time, and "Off," are convenient. If your model doesn't include that feature, you might want to get a digital appliance timer, which gives you that option. Make sure the timer is adequate for the electrical flow that your cooker demands.

- A baking insert, a cooking rack, a temperature probe, and an insulated carrying tote are all useful additions offered with some models. Or you can buy some of them separately by going to the manufacturers' websites.

## 2. Learn to know your slow cooker

- Some newer slow cookers cook at a very high temperature. You can check the temperature of your slow cooker this way:
    1. Place 2 quarts of water in your slow cooker.
    2. Cover. Heat on Low 8 hours.
    3. Lift the lid. Immediately check the water temp with an accurate thermometer.
    4. The temperature of the water should be 185°F. If the temperature is higher, foods may overcook and you should reduce the overall cooking time. If the temperature is lower, your foods will probably not reach a safe temperature quickly enough, and the cooker should be discarded.

## 3. Maximizing what a slow cooker does best

- Slow cookers tend to work best when they're ⅔ full. You many need to increase the cooking time if you've exceeded that amount, or reduce it if you've put in less than that.
- Cut the hard veggies going into your cooker into chunks of about equal size. In other words, make your potato and carrot pieces about the same size. Then they'll be done cooking at nearly the same time. Softer veggies, like bell peppers and zucchini, cook faster, so they don't need to be cut as small. But again, keep them similar in size to each other so they finish together.
- Because raw vegetables are notoriously tough customers in a slow cooker, layer them over the bottom and around the sides of the cooker, as much as possible. That puts them in more direct contact with the heat.
- There are consequences to lifting the lid on your slow cooker while it's cooking. To compensate for the lost heat, you should plan to add 15-20 minutes of cooking time for each time the lid was lifted off.

  On the other hand, moisture gathers in a slow cooker as it works. To allow that to cook off, or to thicken the cooking juices, take the lid off during the last half hour of cooking time.
- Use only the amount of liquid called for in a recipe. In contrast to an oven or a stovetop, a slow cooker tends to draw juices out of food and then harbor it.

Of course, if you sense that the food in your cooker is drying out, or browning excessively before it finishes cooking, you may want to add ½ cup of *warm* liquid to the cooker.

- Important variables to remember that don't show up in recipes:
  - *The fuller your slow cooker, the longer it will take its contents to cook.*
  - *The more densely packed the cooker's contents are, the longer they will take to cook.*
  - *The larger the chunks of meat or vegetables, the more time they will need to cook.*

## 4. Debunking the myths

- <u>You certainly can cook holiday-worthy dishes in a slow cooker!</u> These appliances can put out a meal at any level—elegant or comfortable.

*One hard-won piece of advice.* You'll notice that many of the recipes in this cookbook give a range of cooking times (for example, "Chicken a la Orange" on page 168 tells you to cook the dish 6-7 hours). Every slow cooker is different, so learn to know your cooker before you ask it to make your holiday turkey.

Do a test-run of a sample recipe, note the length of time it took to cook the dish to perfection, and then write that next to the recipe in this book. Make that experiment your baseline for judging the appropriate length of cooking time in your cooker for similar recipes. Now you can relax as you wait for your guests to arrive.

Two more reasons to put your cooker(s) to work during the holidays:

1. If your oven is full, use your slow cooker to relieve the space crunch.
2. When you want to avoid lots of last-minute work and enjoy your guests instead, make whatever you can in your slow cooker.

- Slow cookers are also *a handy year-round appliance.* They don't heat up a kitchen in warm weather. They allow you to escape to the pool or lake or lawn or gardens – so why not let them work for you when it's hot outdoors. A slow cooker fixes your dinner while you're at your child's soccer game, too.

- You can overdo food in a slow cooker. If you're tempted to stretch a recipe's 6-hour stated cooking time to 8 or 10 hours, you may be disappointed in your dinner. Yes, these cookers work their magic using slow, moist heat. Yes, many dishes cook a long time. But these outfits have their limits.

For example, chicken can overcook in a slow cooker. Especially boneless, skinless breasts. But legs and thighs aren't immune either. Once they go past the falling-off-the-bone stage, they are prone to move on to deeply dry.

Cooked pasta and sour cream do best if added late in the cooking process, ideally 10 minutes before the end of the cooking time if the cooker is on high; 30 minutes before the end of the cooking time if it's on low.

## 5. Safety

- A working slow cooker gets hot on the outside – and I mean the outer electrical unit as well as the inner vessel. Make sure that curious and unsuspecting children or adults don't grab hold of either part. Use oven mitts when lifting any part of a hot cooker.
- To prevent a slow cooker from bubbling over, either when its sitting still on a counter, or when its traveling to a carry-in dinner, fill the cooker only ⅔ full.

If you're going to exceed that limit, pull out your second slow cooker (what – you have only one?!) and divide the contents between them.

## 6. Adapting stove-top or oven recipes for a slow cooker

- Many stove-top and oven recipes can be adapted for a slow cooker. If you want to experiment, use these conversion factors:
  - *Low (in a slow cooker) = 200°F approximately (in an oven).*
  - *High (in a slow cooker) = 300°F approximately (in an oven).*
  - *In a slow cooker, 2 hours on Low = 1 hour, approximately, on High.*

# Appetizers, Snacks, and Spreads

## Creamy Artichoke Dip

**Jessica Stoner**
West Liberty, OH

*Makes 7-8 cups*

**Prep. Time: 15-20 minutes**
**Cooking Time: 1-1½ hours**
**Ideal slow cooker size: 3-qt.**

2 14-oz. cans water-packed artichoke hearts, coarsely chopped (drain one can; stir juice from other can into Dip)
2 cups (8 oz.) shredded, part-skim mozzarella cheese
8-oz. pkg. cream cheese, softened
1 cup grated Parmesan cheese
½ cup mayonnaise
½ cup shredded Swiss cheese
2 Tbsp. lemon juice
2 Tbsp. plain yogurt
1 Tbsp. seasoned salt

1 Tbsp. chopped, seeded jalapeño pepper
1 tsp. garlic powder
Dippers: tortilla chips

1  In slow cooker, combine artichoke hearts, cheeses, mayonnaise, lemon juice, yogurt, salt, jalapeño pepper, and garlic powder.
2  Cover. Cook on Low 1 hour, or until cheeses are melted and Dip is heated through.
3  Serve with tortilla chips.

**Variation:**
Add 2 10-oz. pkgs. frozen chopped spinach, thawed and squeezed dry, to Step 1.
**Steven Lantz**
Denver, CO

## Red Pepper-Cheese Dip

**Ann Bender**
Ft. Defiance, VA

*Makes 4-5 cups*

**Prep. Time: 10 minutes**
**Cooking Time: 2 hours**
**Ideal slow cooker size: 3-qt.**

2 Tbsp. olive oil
4-6 large red peppers, cut into 1" squares
crackers and/or pita bread
½ lb. feta cheese, crumbled

1. Pour oil into slow cooker. Stir in peppers.
2. Cover. Cook on Low 2 hours.
3. Serve on crackers or pita bread, topped with feta cheese.

# Ratatouille

**Barb Yoder**
Angola, IN

*Makes about 3½ cups*

**Prep. Time: 20-30 minutes**
**Cooking Time: 7-8 hours**
**Ideal slow cooker size: 4-qt.**

1½ cups chopped onion
6-oz. can tomato paste
1 Tbsp. olive oil
2 minced cloves garlic (1 tsp.)
1½ tsp. crushed dried basil
½ tsp. dried thyme
15-oz. can chopped tomatoes, with juice drained but reserved
1 large zucchini, halved lengthwise and sliced thin
salt and pepper to taste
slices of French bread *or* baguette

1. Mix all ingredients except bread in slow cooker.
2. Cover. Cook on Low 7-8 hours.
3. If mixture is stiffer than you wish, stir in some of reserved tomato juice.
4. Serve hot or cold on top of French bread or baguette slices.

# Hot Cheddar Mushroom Spread

**Amber Swarey**
Honea Path, SC

*Makes 3¼-½ cups*

**Prep. Time: 10 minutes**
**Cooking Time: 1-1½ hours**
**Ideal slow cooker size: 2-qt.**

1 cup mayonnaise
1 cup (4 oz.) shredded cheddar cheese
⅓ cup grated Parmesan cheese
2 4½-oz. cans sliced mushrooms, drained
half an envelope Ranch salad dressing mix
minced fresh parsley
assorted crackers

1. Combine mayonnaise, cheeses, mushrooms, and dressing mix in slow cooker.
2. Cover. Cook on Low 1 hour, or until cheeses are melted and Dip is heated through.
3. Sprinkle with parsley and serve with crackers.

# Nacho Dip

**Rose Hankins**
Stevensville, MD

*Makes 3-4 cups*

**Prep. Time: 5 minutes**
**Cooking Time: 3-4 hours**
**Ideal slow cooker size: 4-qt.**

4 cups (16 oz.) shredded cheddar cheese
14-oz. can diced tomatoes, drained, with juice reserved
7-oz. can chopped green chilies, drained
1 cup chopped onions
1 Tbsp. cumin
1 tsp. chili powder
1 tsp. hot pepper sauce
tortilla chips

1. Mix all ingredients except chips in slow cooker.
2. Cover. Cook on Low 3-4 hours.
3. Stir before serving. If Dip is stiffer than you like, stir in some of reserved tomato juice
4. Serve with tortilla chips for dipping.

*I like to keep a basket full of small gifts by the door to give to guests as they leave. These are simple gifts like home-made dip mixes in jars or freshly baked cookies, wrapped in colorful papers or gift bags. Sending friends home with a little something extra is a fun way to end a get-together.*
*Mary Rogers, Waseca, MN*

# Hot Chili Dip

**Lavina Hochstedler**
Grand Blanc, MI

**Anna Stoltzfus**
Honey Brook, PA

**Kathi Rogge**
Alexandria, IN

*Makes 5-6 cups*

*Prep Time: 5-10 minutes*
*Cooking Time: 1-2 hours*
*Ideal slow cooker size: 3-qt.*

24-oz. jar hot salsa
15-oz. can chili with beans
2 2¼-oz. cans sliced ripe
  olives, drained
12 ozs. mild cheese, cubed
tortilla chips

1. Combine all ingredients except tortilla chips in slow cooker.
2. Cover. Cook on Low 1-2 hours, or until cheese is melted, stirring halfway through.
3. Serve with tortilla chips.

# Hot Hamburger Dip

**Kristi See**
Weskan, KS

*Makes 7-8 cups*

*Prep. Time: 20 minutes*
*Cooking Time: 1-2 hours*
*Ideal slow cooker size: 2-qt.*

1 lb. ground beef
1 small onion, chopped
1 lb. Velveeta cheese,
  cubed
8-oz. can tomatoes and
  green chilies, undrained
2 tsp. Worcestershire sauce
½ tsp. chili powder
1 tsp. garlic powder
½ tsp. pepper
10¾-oz. can tomato soup
10¾-oz. can cream of
  mushroom soup
corn chips
little barbecued smokies

1. Brown ground beef and onions in skillet. Drain off drippings. Place beef and onions in slow cooker.
2. Add remaining ingredients, except corn chips and smokies, and stir well.
3. Cover. Simmer until cheese is melted.
4. Serve with corn chips and little barbecued smokies.

# Cheesy Hot Bean Dip

**John D. Allen**, Rye, CO

*Makes 4-5 cups*

*Prep. Time: 10 minutes • Cooking Time: 2 hours*
*Ideal slow cooker size: 2-qt.*

16-oz. can refried beans
1 cup salsa
2 cups (8 oz.) shredded
  Jack and cheddar
  cheeses, mixed
1 cup sour cream
3-oz. pkg. cream
  cheese, cubed
1 Tbsp. chili powder
¼ tsp. ground cumin
tortilla chips

1. Combine all ingredients except chips in slow cooker.
2. Cover. Cook on High 2 hours. Stir 2-3 times during cooking time.
3. Serve warm from cooker with chips.

Note:
   This bean dip is a favorite of ours. Once you start on it, it's hard to leave it alone.
   We have been known to dip into it even when it's cold.

# Creamy Taco Dip

**Nanci Keatley**
Salem, OR

*Makes 7-8 cups*

**Prep. Time: 15 minutes**
**Cooking Time: 1-2 hours**
**Ideal slow cooker size: 4-qt.**

8-oz. pkg. cream cheese,
   softened
1 cup sour cream
¾ cup mayonnaise
1 lb. ground beef
1 envelope taco seasoning
12-oz. jar salsa
2 cups (8 oz.) shredded
   cheddar cheese
garnishes: 4 cups lettuce,
   shredded; 2 medium
   tomatoes, chopped; 1
   small onion, chopped
tortilla chips

1. In good-sized mixing
bowl, mix together cream
cheese, sour cream, and
mayonnaise. Spread in bottom
of lightly greased slow cooker.
2. Brown ground beef in
skillet, breaking up clumps of
meat with a wooden spoon as
it browns. Drain off drippings.
3. Mix taco seasoning and
salsa into browned meat.
Spoon mixture over cream
cheese mixture in slow
cooker.
4. Sprinkle shredded
cheddar over top.
5. Cover. Cook on Low
1-2 hours, or until cheese is
melted.
6. Serve with lettuce,
tomatoes, onions, and tortilla
chips.

# TNT Dip

**Sheila Plock**
Boalsburg, PA

*Makes 8 cups*

**Prep. Time: 15 minutes**
**Cooking Time: 1-1¼ hours**
**Ideal slow cooker size: 3-qt.**

1½ lbs. ground beef
10¾-oz. can cream of
   mushroom soup
half a stick (4 Tbsp.)
   butter, melted
1 lb. Velveeta, cubed
1 cup salsa
2 Tbsp. chili powder
tortilla chips and/or corn
   chips
party rye bread

1. Brown ground beef in
skillet. Drain off drippings.
Place browned beef in slow
cooker.
2. Add all remaining
ingredients, except chips and
bread, to slow cooker. Mix
well.
3. Cover. Cook on High
1-1¼ hours, or until cheese is
melted. If you're at home, stir
occasionally during cooking.
4. Serve with tortilla chips,
corn chips, and/or party rye
bread.

**Variation:**
   To change the balance
of flavors, use only 1 lb.
browned ground beef and add
1½ cups salsa.

**Note:**
   *My son has hosted a Super
Bowl party for his college*

*friends at our house the past
two years. He served this Dip
the first year, and the second
year it was requested.*
   *His friends claim it's the best
Dip they've ever eaten. With a
bunch of college kids it disappears quickly.*

# Hot Beef Dip

**Paula Showalter**
Weyers Cave, VA

*Makes about 3 cups*

**Prep. Time: 15 minutes**
**Cooking Time: 2-3 hours**
**Ideal slow cooker size: 2-qt.**

2 8-oz. pkgs. cream cheese,
   softened
2 cups (8 oz.) mild cheddar
   cheese, grated
1 green bell pepper,
   chopped fine
1 small onion, chopped
   fine
¼ lb. chipped dried beef,
   shredded
assortment of crackers

1. Combine cheeses in slow
cooker.
2. Fold in pepper, onions,
and beef.
3. Cover. Cook on Low 2-3
hours.
4. Serve hot with crackers.

**Variation:**
   For more kick, add a few
finely diced chili peppers to
Step 2.

# Taco Appetizer

**Annie C. Boshart**
Lebanon, PA

*Makes 8 cups*

**Prep. Time: 15-30 minutes**
**Cooking Time: 30-60 minutes**
**Ideal slow cooker size: 3-qt.**

½ lb. lean ground beef
½ lb. hot Italian sausage
1 large onion, finely
    chopped
salt to taste
2 tsp. hot pepper sauce, *or*
    more or less to taste
2 16-oz. cans refried beans
4-oz. can chopped green
    chilies, drained
2-3 cups (8-12 oz.) grated
    Monterey Jack cheese
¾ cup hot, *or* mild, taco
    sauce
tortilla chips *or* corn chips
garnishes: chopped
    tomatoes, chopped green
    onions, chopped ripe
    olives, smashed ripe
    avocado, sour cream

1. In skillet, sauté meats with onion until browned. Drain off drippings. Season meat with salt and hot pepper sauce to taste.
2. Meanwhile, spread refried beans in lightly greased slow cooker.
3. Spoon browned meat over refried beans.
4. Top with chopped chilies.
5. Sprinkle with grated cheese.
6. Pour taco sauce on top of cheese. (Do not stir.)

7. Heat in slow cooker for 30-60 minutes on Medium High, or until Dip is heated through.
8. Serve with chips and garnishes.

# Cheesy Sausage Dip

**Marissa Pinon**
Rio Rancho, NM

**Cynthia Morris**
Grottoes, VA

*Makes 4-5 cups*

**Prep. Time: 15-25 minutes**
**Cooking Time: 30-60 minutes**
**Ideal slow cooker size: 3- to 4-qt.**

1 lb. loose sausage
14½-oz. can Rotel
    tomatoes—hot, medium,
    *or* mild
2 lbs. Velveeta, *or* 3 8-oz.
    blocks cream cheese, cut
    into 1" squares
chips and/or tortilla scoops

1. Brown sausage in skillet, breaking up clumps of meat as it browns. Drain off drippings.
2. Transfer sausage to slow cooker. Stir in tomatoes and cheese cubes.
3. Cover. Cook on Low until melted, stirring occasionally.
4. Once cheese melts, turn slow cooker to "Keep Warm" or Low setting. Serve with chips or tortilla scoops.

# Bacon Cheese Dip

**Genelle Taylor**
Perrysburg, OH

*Makes 6 cups*

**Prep. Time: 10-20 minutes**
**Cooking Time: 2 hours or less**
**Ideal slow cooker size: 3-qt.**

2 8-oz. pkgs. cream cheese,
    cubed
4 cups shredded sharp
    cheddar cheese
1 cup half-and-half
2 tsp. Worcestershire sauce
1 tsp. dried minced onion
1 tsp. prepared mustard
16 bacon strips, cooked
    and crumbled
tortilla chips and/or
    French bread slices

1. Combine first six ingredients in slow cooker.
2. Cover. Cook on Low 2 hours, or until cheeses are melted. Stir occasionally if you're home and able to do so.
3. Just before serving, stir in bacon.
4. Serve warm with tortilla chips and/or French bread.

# Cheesy Spinach and Bacon Dip

**Amy Bauer**
New Ulm, MN

*Makes 3½ cups*

*Prep. Time: 15 minutes*
*Cooking Time: 1 hour*
*Ideal slow cooker size: 3-qt.*

10-oz. pkg. frozen chopped spinach, thawed and squeezed dry
1 lb. Velveeta, *or your choice of soft cheese, cut into ½" cubes*
3-oz. pkg. cream cheese, softened
14½-oz. can Rotel diced tomatoes and green chilies, undrained
8 slices bacon, cooked crisp and crumbled
crackers and/or chips

1. Combine all ingredients except bacon, crackers and chips in slow cooker.
2. Cover. Heat on Low 1 hour, or until cheeses have melted and Dip is heated through. Stir occasionally if you're around to do so.
3. Just before serving, stir in crumbled bacon.
4. Serve warm with crackers and/or chips.

Variation:
This is also tasty with half a package of spinach.

# Creamy Pizza Dip

**Rosalie Buckwalter**
Narvon, PA

*Makes 4½ cups*

*Prep. Time: 15-20 minutes*
*Cooking Time: 2-4 hours*
*Ideal slow cooker size: 3-qt.*

8-oz. pkg. cream cheese, cubed and softened
¾ cup salad dressing, *or* mayonnaise (regular *or* light)
1 cup shredded mozzarella cheese
8 oz. sliced pepperoni, chopped
2 ripe plum tomatoes, chopped
10 large, black olives, chopped
4 crusty Italian rolls, toasted if you wish, and then cut into ½" cubes and/or crackers

1. Mix all ingredients, except rolls and crackers for dipping, in slow cooker.
2. Cover. Cook on High 2-4 hours, or until cheese is melted and Dip is heated through.
3. Turn on Low to keep warm while serving.
4. Remove cover. Allow to cool slightly before serving with rolls and/or crackers for dipping.

# Cheese Pizza Fondue

**Annie C. Boshart**
Lebanon, PA

*Makes 6-7 cups*

*Prep. Time: 30 minutes*
*Cooking Time: 1¼ hours*
*Ideal slow cooker size: 2-qt.*

1 lb. ground beef
½ cup chopped onions
3 8-oz. cans pizza sauce with cheese
1 Tbsp. cornstarch
¾ tsp. oregano
¼ tsp. garlic powder
1 cup shredded mozzarella cheese
2 cups shredded cheddar cheese
cubed French bread, tortilla chips, crackers

1. Brown ground beef and onion in skillet. Stir frequently with wooden spoon, breaking up clumps of meat. When brown, drain off drippings. Spoon meat and onion into slow cooker.
2. Add pizza sauce, cornstarch, oregano, and garlic powder to slow cooker. Stir into meat mixture.
3. Cover. Cook on Low 1 hour, or until mixtures bubbles and thickens. Stir occasionally if you're able to.
4. Add cheese gradually, stirring well until it melts.
5. Serve hot with bread cubes, chips, and/or crackers for dipping.

**Tester's Idea:**

I served this to my family as a main dish for supper. I made angel-hair pasta and we put the fondue over it as a sauce. We loved it! I also offered breadsticks for dipping into the sauce.

# Meatless Pizza Fondue

**Virginia Graybill**
Hershey, PA

*Makes 4 cups*

**Prep. Time: 5 minutes**
**Cooking Time: 3 hours**
**Ideal slow cooker size: 3-qt.**

29-oz. jar meatless
 spaghetti sauce
2 cups (8 oz.) shredded
 mozzarella cheese
¼ cup shredded Parmesan
 cheese
2 tsp. dried oregano
1 tsp. dried minced onion
¼ tsp. garlic powder
1 lb. unsliced loaf Italian
 bread, cut into cubes

1. Combine spaghetti sauce, cheeses, oregano, onion, and garlic powder in slow cooker.
2. Cover. Cook on Low 3 hours, or until cheese is melted and sauce is hot.
3. Serve with bread cubes.

**Note:**

*Each Christmas season, we have an evening set aside for a fondue meal. This recipe is always a hit.*

**Note from Tester:**

I had some leftover sauce that I served as a topping for steamed cauliflower. My family loved it!

# Slow Cooker Reuben Dip

**Allison Ingels**
Maynard, IA

*Makes 5 cups*

**Prep. Time: 10 minutes**
**Cooking Time: 3-4 hours**
**Ideal slow cooker size: 3-qt.**

8 oz. sour cream
2 8-oz. pkgs. cream cheese,
 softened
8-oz. can sauerkraut,
 drained
3 2½-oz. pkgs. dried corned
 beef, finely chopped
6-oz. pkg. shredded Swiss
 cheese
rye crackers and/or rye
 party bread

1. Combine all ingredients except crackers and/or bread in slow cooker.
2. Cover. Heat on Low 3-4 hours, or until cheeses are melted.
3. Serve from cooker with rye crackers or rye party bread.

*I like to set up an appetizer table so that I don't feel as pressured if I'm running a little late with my meal. I try to make appetizers that can be prepared ahead and quickly set out.* Kristine Martin, Newmanstown, PA

# Cranberry Meatballs

**Char Hagner**
Montague, MI

*Makes about 50-60 meatballs*

**Prep. Time: 30-45 minutes**
**Cooking Time: 2 hours**
**Ideal slow cooker size: 3- to 4-qt.**

## Meatballs:

**2 lbs. ground beef**
**⅓ cup parsley flakes**
**2 Tbsp. soy sauce**
**½ tsp. garlic powder**
**2 Tbsp. minced onion**
**1 cup cornflake crumbs**
**2 eggs**
**½ cup ketchup**

## Sauce:

**1 can jellied cranberry**
**sauce**
**12-oz. bottle chili sauce**
**2 Tbsp. brown sugar**
**1 Tbsp. lemon juice**

1. In a large mixing bowl, combine Meatball ingredients until well mixed.

2. Form into 50-60 Meatballs and put in lightly greased 9x13 baking pan.

3. Bake at 350 degrees for about 30 minutes, or until Meatballs are cooked through. (Cut one open to test.)

4. While meatballs are baking, combine Sauce ingredients in saucepan. Heat over low heat until jellied sauce and brown sugar melt. Stir frequently.

5. Place baked Meatballs in slow cooker. Pour Sauce over Meatballs, making sure that all are covered in Sauce if you've layered them into the cooker.

6. Cover. Cook on Low 2 hours, or until Sauce is bubbly.

7. Turn slow cooker to Warm and serve with toothpicks.

Variations:

1. Use 1 lb. ground beef and 1 lb. ground pork instead of 2 lbs. ground beef.

2. Use 10¾-oz. can condensed tomato soup, mixed with 1 tsp. prepared mustard, instead of chili sauce.
**Jane Geigley**
Honey Brook, PA

3. Here's an alternative meatball recipe:
**2 egg whites**
**2 lbs. ground turkey**
**2 green onions with tops, sliced**
**4 tsp. grated orange peel**
**2 tsp. reduced-sodium soy sauce**
**½ tsp. black pepper**
**⅛ tsp. cayenne pepper,** *optional*

Follow Steps 1-3 above, and then continue with rest of recipe.
**Mary Ann Bowman**
East Earl, PA

# Buffalo Chicken Dip

**Gail Skiff**
Clifton Park, NY

*Makes 3-4 cups*

**Prep. Time: 30-40 minutes**
**Cooking Time: 1 hour**
**Ideal slow cooker size: 2- to 3-qt.**

**8-oz. pkg. cream cheese, softened**
**½-¾ cup bleu cheese dressing**
**½ cup bleu cheese crumbles**
**½ cup buffalo wing sauce (I use Anchor Bar Buffalo Wing Sauce)**
**1 lb. boneless skinless chicken breasts, cooked and shredded**
**celery sticks and/or your favorite chips**

1. Mix cream cheese, dressing, blue cheese crumbles, and sauce in slow cooker.

2. Stir in chicken.

3. Cover. Heat on Low 1 hour, or until cheeses melt and Dip is heated through. Stir several times during the hour if you're home and able to do so.

4. Serve warm with celery sticks and/or your favorite chips.

*Keep it simple. Too many different items, especially finger foods, are a lot of work. A few (3-4) very nice items will be remembered and enjoyed.*
*Carol Findling, Carol Stream, IL*

# Sweet Chili Chicken Bites

**Nanci Keatley**
Salem, OR

*Makes 4 cups*

*Prep. Time: 10 minutes*
*Cooking Time: 4-6 hours*
*Ideal slow cooker size: 4-qt.*

**4 lbs. boneless skinless chicken breasts**

**1 bottle Asian sweet chili sauce (we use May Ploy brand)**

1. Cut chicken into bite-size pieces. Place in slow cooker.
2. Pour bottle of sauce over chicken. Stir together well.
3. Cover. Cook on Low 4-6 hours, or until chicken is fully cooked.
4. Serve with toothpicks.

**Tester's Idea**
This is also good as a main dish served over cooked rice.

# Hot Crab Dip

**Cassandra Ly**
Carlisle, PA
**Miriam Nolt**
New Holland, PA

*Makes 6-7 cups*

*Prep. Time: 10-15 minutes*
*Cooking Time: 3-4 hours*
*Ideal slow cooker size: 3-qt.*

**½ cup milk**
**⅓ cup salsa**
**3 8-oz. pkgs. cream cheese, cubed**
**2 8-oz. pkgs. imitation crabmeat, flaked**
**1 cup thinly sliced green onions**
**4-oz. can chopped green chilies, drained**
**assorted crackers and/or bread cubes**

1. Grease interior of slow cooker.
2. Combine milk and salsa in slow cooker.
3. Stir in cream cheese, crabmeat, onions, and chilies.
4. Cover. Cook on Low 3-4 hours, stirring every 30 minutes if you're home and able to do so.
5. Serve with crackers and/or bread.

# Sweet and Sour Chicken Wings

**Irma H. Schoen**, Windsor, CT

*Makes 6-8 servings*

*Prep. Time: 15 minutes • Cooking Time: 7 hours*
*Ideal slow cooker size: 3- to 4-qt.*

**1½ cups sugar**
**1 cup cider vinegar**
**½ cup ketchup**
**1 chicken bouillon cube**
**2 Tbsp. soy sauce**
**¼ tsp. salt,** *optional*
**¼ tsp. pepper,** *optional*
**16 chicken wings**
**¼ cup cornstarch**
**½ cup cold water**

1. On stove in medium-sized saucepan, mix together sugar, vinegar, ketchup, bouillon cube, soy sauce, and salt and pepper if you wish.
2. Bring to a boil over medium heat. Stir to dissolve sugar and bouillon cube.
3. Put wings in slow cooker. Pour sauce over wings.
4. Cover. Simmer on Low 6½ hours, or until wings are tender but not dry.
5. A few minutes before end of cooking time, combine water and cornstarch in a small bowl. When smooth, stir gently into wings and sauce.
6. Cover. Simmer on High until liquid thickens, about 30 minutes.
7. To serve, keep cooker turned to Low. Stir occasionally.

# Cheese and Crab Dip

**Donna Lantgen**, Rapid City, SD

*Makes 5 cups*

*Prep. Time: 10 minutes • Cooking Time: 2 hours*
*Ideal slow cooker size: 2-qt.*

3 8-oz. pkgs. cream
  cheese, softened
2 6-oz. cans crabmeat,
  drained
1 can broken shrimp,
  drained

6 Tbsp. finely chopped
  onions
1 tsp. horseradish
½ cup toasted almonds,
  broken
assorted crackers and/or
  bread cubes

1. Combine all ingredients, except crackers and/or bread cubes, in slow cooker.
2. Cover. Cook on Low 2 hours.
3. Serve with crackers or bread cubes.

Variation:
  Add 2 tsp. Worcestershire sauce to Step 1 for added zest.
  **Dorothy VanDeest** • Memphis, TN

# Liver Paté

**Barbara Walker**
Sturgis, SD

*Makes 1½ cups paté*

*Prep. Time: 10-15 minutes*
*Cooking Time: 4-5 hours*
*Cooling Time: 1-2 hours*
*Ideal slow cooker size: 1½-qt.*

1 lb. chicken livers
½ cup dry wine
1 tsp. instant chicken
  bouillon granules
1 tsp. minced fresh, *or* dry,
  parsley
1 Tbsp. instant minced
  onion

¼ tsp. ground ginger
½ tsp. seasoning salt
1 Tbsp. soy sauce
¼ tsp. dry mustard
half a stick (4 Tbsp.)
  butter, softened
1 Tbsp. brandy
crackers and/or toast cubes

1. In slow cooker, combine all ingredients except butter, brandy, crackers, and/or toast cubes.
2. Cover. Cook on Low 4-5 hours. Let stand in liquid until cool.
3. Drain. Place in blender or food grinder.
4. Add butter and brandy. Process until smooth.
5. Serve with crackers and/or toast cubes.

# Snack Mix

**Yvonne Boettger**
Harrisonburg, VA

*Makes 14 cups*

*Prep. Time: 10 minutes*
*Cooking Time: 2 hours*
*Ideal slow cooker size: 5-qt.*

8 cups Chex cereal, of any
  combination
6 cups from the
  following: pretzels,
  snack crackers, goldfish,
  Cheerios, nuts, bagel
  chips, toasted corn
¾ stick (6 Tbsp.) butter,
  melted
2 Tbsp. Worcestershire
  sauce
1 tsp. seasoning salt
½ tsp. garlic powder
½ tsp. onion salt
½ tsp. onion powder

1. Combine 14 cups of dry ingredients in slow cooker.
2. In a mixing bowl, combine butter and seasonings.
3. Pour over dry ingredients in slow cooker. Toss until well mixed.
4. Cover. Cook on Low 2 hours, stirring every 30 minutes.

Variation:
  To liven up the Snack Mix a bit more, increase Worcestershire sauce to 4 Tbsp. and add a dash of Tabasco sauce.
  **Dorothy van Deest**
  Memphis, TN

# Spicy Party Mix

**Sharon Miller**
Holmesville, OH

*Makes 13 cups*

*Prep. Time: 15 minutes*
*Cooking Time: 3-4 hours*
*Ideal slow cooker size: 4- to 5-qt.*

¾ stick (6 Tbsp.) butter, melted
1-oz. packet taco seasoning mix
¾ tsp. ground cinnamon
⅛-¼ tsp. cayenne, depending on your taste preferences
2 cups pecan halves
2 cups roasted cashews, unsalted
2 cups walnut halves
2 cups whole almonds, unblanched
3 cups goldfish, *or* bite-size cheese, crackers
2 cups pretzel nuggets *or* sticks

1. Mix butter and seasonings in slow cooker.
2. Add all remaining ingredients and toss together gently.
3. Cook uncovered on Low 3-4 hours, stirring every 30 minutes until nuts are toasted. Turn off heat.
4. Serve from slow cooker with large spoon, or pour into big serving bowl.

Tip:
You can make this a day before your party. Just be sure to store it in an airtight container.

# Christmas Sugared Walnuts

**Lavina Hochstedler**
Grand Blanc, MI

*Makes 3-4 cups*

*Prep. Time: 10 minutes*
*Cooking Time: 2-3 hours*
*Ideal slow cooker size: 2- to 3-qt.*

1 lb. walnut pieces
1 stick (8 Tbsp.) unsalted butter, melted
½ cup confectioners sugar
1½ tsp. ground cinnamon
¼ tsp. ground ginger
¼ tsp. ground allspice
⅛ tsp. ground cloves

1. In slow cooker, stir walnuts and butter together until combined.
2. Add confectioners sugar, stirring to coat nuts evenly.
3. Cover. Cook on High 15 minutes. Then reduce heat to Low.
4. Cook uncovered, stirring occasionally until nuts are coated with a crisp glaze, about 2 hours.
5. Transfer nuts to a serving bowl.
6. In a small bowl, combine spices. Sift over nuts, stirring to coat evenly.
7. Cool nuts completely before serving.

# Caramel Peanut Butter Dip

**Genelle Taylor**
Perrysburg, OH

*Makes about 1½ cups*

*Prep. Time: 20 minutes*
*Ideal slow cooker size: 1-qt.*

30 caramels, unwrapped
1-2 Tbsp. water
¼ cup, plus 2 Tbsp., creamy peanut butter
¼ cup finely crushed peanuts, *optional*
sliced apples, unpeeled

1. In a microwave-safe bowl, microwave caramels and water for 1 minute on High. Stir. Microwave 1 minute more, or until smooth.
2. Add peanut butter and mix well. Microwave 30 seconds on High, or until smooth.
3. Stir in peanuts if you wish.
4. Transfer to a 1-qt. slow-cooker. Turn to Warm while serving.
5. Serve with sliced apples.

Note:
Red and green apples look very festive for the holiday season.

*Have a popcorn and cranberry stringing party.*
*Lena Sheaffer, Port Matilda, PA*

# Chunky Sweet Spiced Apple Butter

**Jennifer Freed**
Harrisonburg, VA

*Makes 4 cups*

*Prep. Time: 20 minutes*
*Cooking Time: 8 hours*
*Ideal slow cooker size: 2- to 3-qt.*

4 cups (about 1¼ lbs.) peeled, chopped Granny Smith apples
¾ cup packed dark brown sugar
2 Tbsp. balsamic vinegar
half a stick (4 Tbsp.) butter, *divided*
1 Tbsp. ground cinnamon
½ tsp. salt
¼ tsp. ground cloves
1½ tsp. vanilla

1. Combine apples, sugar, vinegar, 2 Tbsp. butter, cinnamon, salt, and cloves in slow cooker.
2. Cover. Cook on Low 8 hours.
3. Stir in remaining 2 Tbsp. butter and vanilla.
4. Cool completely before serving, storing, or giving away.

# Pumpkin Butter

**Emily Fox**
Bethel, PA

*Makes approximately 6½ cups*

*Prep. Time: 5-10 minutes*
*Cooking Time: 11-12 hours*
*Ideal slow cooker size: 3-qt.*

6 cups pumpkin purée
2¾ cups light brown sugar
2½ tsp. pumpkin pie spice

1. Mix pumpkin purée, brown sugar, and pumpkin pie spice together in slow cooker.
2. Cook *uncovered* on Low for 11-12 hours, depending on how thick you'd like the butter to be. Cool.
3. Serve on bread or rolls for seasonal eating.

Note:
Refrigerate or freeze until ready to use.

Tip from Tester:
You could replace 3 cups pumpkin purée with 3 cups applesauce for a different twist on pumpkin butter.

# Pear Butter

**Betty Moore**
Plano, IL

*Makes 2-3 pints*

*Prep. Time: 15 minutes*
*Cooking Time: 11-13 hours*
*Ideal slow cooker size: 4-qt.*

10 large pears (about 4 lbs.)
1 cup orange juice
2½ cups sugar
1 tsp. ground cinnamon
1 tsp. ground cloves
½ tsp. ground allspice

1. Peel and quarter pears. Place in slow cooker.
2. Cover. Cook on Low 10-12 hours. Drain. Discard liquid.
3. Mash or purée pears. Add remaining ingredients. Mix well and return to slow cooker.
4. Cover. Cook on High 1 hour.
5. Place in hot sterile jars and process, following the instructions of your canning equipment. Allow to cool undisturbed for 24 hours.

*Use Christmas cookie-baking time as an opportunity to teach your children about how to measure ingredients, break eggs, and pour milk. Share your special cooking secrets. For example, I keep two knives or narrow spatulas in hot water while frosting cookies. When one gets sticky, I'm prepared with a fresh hot knife.* *Orpha Herr, Andover, NY*

# Breakfast and Brunch Dishes

## Western Omelet Casserole

**Mary Louise Martin**, Boyd, WI
**Jan Mast**, Lancaster, PA

*Makes 10 servings*

**Prep. Time: 15 minutes**
**Cooking Time: 4-6 hours**
**Ideal slow cooker size: 5-qt.**

**32-oz. bag frozen hash brown potatoes,** *divided*
**1 lb. cooked ham, cubed,** *divided*
**1 medium onion, diced,** *divided*
**1½ cups shredded cheddar cheese,** *divided*
**18 eggs**
**1½ cups milk**
**1 tsp. salt**
**1 tsp. pepper**

1. Layer one-third each of frozen potatoes, ham, onion, and cheese in bottom of slow cooker. Repeat 2 times.

2. Beat together eggs, milk, salt, and pepper in a large mixing bowl. Pour over mixture in slow cooker.

3. Cover. Cook on Low 4-6 hours.

**Note:**

This is a great breakfast, served along with orange juice and fresh fruit.

## Eggs 'n' Spinach

**Shirley Unternahrer**
Wayland, IA

*Makes 8 servings*

**Prep. Time: 20 minutes**
**Cooking Time: 1½-8 hours**
**Ideal slow cooker size: 6-qt.**

**1 lb. sausage with bacon (Farmland offers this)**
**1½ 10-oz. pkgs. frozen spinach, thawed and squeezed dry**
**⅓ cup, plus 2 Tbsp., grated Parmesan cheese,** *divided*
**8 eggs**
**⅛ tsp. black pepper, ground** *or* **cracked**

1. Sauté sausage with bacon in skillet until browned. Drain off half the drippings.

2. Coat interior of slow cooker with cooking spray. Place sausage and reserved drippings in slow cooker.

3. Stir spinach into slow cooker.

4. Stir in ⅓ cup Parmesan cheese.

5. Break eggs directly onto mixture in slow cooker. Be careful not to break yolks. Do not stir.

6. Cover. Cook on High 1½ hours, or on Low up to 8 hours (you can turn it on right before you go to bed).

7. Sprinkle with pepper and 2 Tbsp. Parmesan cheese before serving.

# Breakfast Skillet

**Sue Hamilton**
Minooka, IL

*Makes 4-5 servings*

***Prep. Time: 15 minutes***
***Cooking Time: 2½-6 hours***
***Ideal slow cooker size: 3½-qt.***

3 cups milk
5½-oz. box au gratin
    potatoes
1 tsp. hot sauce
5 eggs, lightly beaten
1 Tbsp. prepared mustard
4-oz. can sliced
    mushrooms, drained
8 slices bacon, fried and
    crumbled
1 cup cheddar cheese,
    shredded

    1. Combine milk, au gratin-sauce packet, hot sauce, eggs, and mustard in slow cooker until well blended.
    2. Stir in dried potatoes, drained mushrooms, and bacon.
    3. Cover. Cook on High 2½-3 hours, or on Low 5-6 hours.
    4. Sprinkle cheese over top. Cover and let stand a few minutes until cheese melts.

# Apple Oatmeal

**Sheila Plock**
Boalsburg, PA

*Makes 6-8 servings*

***Prep. Time: 15 minutes***
***Cooking Time: 6 hours***
***Ideal slow cooker size: 5-qt.***

3-4 apples, peeled and
    sliced
½ cup brown sugar
1 tsp. nutmeg
1 tsp. cinnamon
¼ stick (2 Tbsp.) butter
½ cup walnuts
3 cups uncooked rolled
    oats
6 cups milk

    1. Layer apples in bottom of slow cooker.
    2. Sprinkle with brown sugar, nutmeg, and cinnamon.
    3. Dot with butter.
    4. Scatter walnuts evenly over top.
    5. Layer oatmeal over fruit and nuts.
    6. Pour milk over oatmeal. Stir together until well blended.
    7. Cover. Cook on Low 6 hours.

Note:
    Wake up to the smell of freshly baked apple pie!

# Slow-Cooker Oatmeal

**Betty B. Dennison**
Grove City, PA

*Makes 2 servings*

***Prep. Time: 5 minutes***
***Cooking Time: 6-8 hours***
***Ideal slow cooker size: 1½-qt.***

1 cup uncooked rolled oats
2 cups water
salt
⅓-½ cup raisins
¼ tsp. ground nutmeg
¼ tsp. ground cinnamon

    1. Combine all ingredients in slow cooker.
    2. Cover. Cook on Low 6-8 hours.
    3. Eat warm with milk and brown sugar.

# Oatmeal Morning

**Barbara Forrester Landis**
Lititz, PA

*Makes 6 servings*

**Prep. Time: 5 minutes**
**Cooking Time: 2½-6 hours**
**Ideal slow cooker size: 3-qt.**

1 cup uncooked steel cut
  oats
1 cup dried cranberries
1 cup walnuts
½ tsp. salt
1 Tbsp. cinnamon
4 cups liquid – milk,
  water, *or* combination of
  the two

1. Combine all dry ingredients in slow cooker. Stir well.
2. Pour in liquid ingredient(s). Mix together well.
3. Cover. Cook on High 2½ hours or on Low 5-6 hours.

Variation:

If you wish, substitute fresh or dried blueberries, or raisins, for the dried cranberries.

# Fruit and Grains Breakfast Cereal

**Jean Butzer**
Batavia, NY

**Katrina Eberly**
Wernersville, PA

*Makes 10 servings*

**Prep. Time: 10 minutes**
**Cooking Time: 6-7 hours**
**Ideal slow cooker size: 5-qt.**

5 cups water
2 cups uncooked whole-
  grain cereal of your
  choice
1 medium apple, peeled
  and chopped
1 cup unsweetened apple
  juice
¼ cup dried apricots,
  chopped
¼ cup dried cranberries
¼ cup raisins
¼ cup chopped dates
2-4 Tbsp. maple syrup,
  according to your
  preference for
  sweetness
1 tsp. cinnamon
½ tsp. salt

1. Combine all ingredients in slow cooker.

2. Cover. Cook on Low 6-7 hours, or until fruits and grain are as soft as you like them.

Note:

*This hearty breakfast dish reminds me of the old-fashioned oatmeal that was a winter staple in our country kitchen many years ago. My dad would put it on to cook before he went to the barn to milk cows. It would be cooked to perfection by the time he was done with chores and ready for breakfast.*

**Jean Butzer**
Batavia, NY

*Our local historical museum hosts an annual "Wonderland of Trees," inviting organizations to decorate a tree for display. Our quilt guild decorates one with homemade fabric ornaments and fabric garlands. A kitchen shop uses kitchen notions—whisks, measuring spoons, etc. The garden club does one in a gardening theme. There are usually 20-30 trees on display from November through December for the public to enjoy.*
*Jean Butzer, Batavia, NY*

# Hot Wheatberry Cereal

**Rosemarie Fitzgerald**
Gibsonia, PA

*Makes 4 servings*

*Prep. Time: 5 minutes*
*Soaking Time: 8 hours*
*Cooking Time: 10 hours*
*Ideal slow cooker size: 3-qt.*

1 cup dry wheatberries
5 cups water
butter
milk
honey

1. Rinse and sort berries. Cover with water and soak 8 hours in slow cooker.
2. Cover. Cook on Low overnight (or up to 10 hours).
3. Drain, if needed. Serve hot with honey, milk, and butter.

### Variation:

Eat your hot wheatberries with raisins and maple syrup as a variation.

### Note:

Wheatberries can also be used in pilafs or grain salads. Cook as indicated, drain, and cool.

# Mexican-Style Grits

**Mary Sommerfeld**
Lancaster, PA

*Makes 10-12 servings*

*Prep. Time: 10 minutes*
*Cooking Time: 2-6 hours*
*Ideal slow cooker size: 3-qt.*

1½ cups instant grits
1 lb. Velveeta cheese, cubed
½ tsp. garlic powder
2 4-oz. cans diced chilies, drained
1 stick (8 Tbsp.) butter, cut in chunks

1. Prepare grits according to package directions.
2. Stir in cheese, garlic powder, and chilies, until cheese is melted.
3. Stir in butter. Pour into greased slow cooker.
4. Cover. Cook on High 2-3 hours, or on Low 4-6 hours.

# Cornmeal Mush

**Betty Hostetler**
Allensville, PA

*Makes 15-18 servings*

*Prep. Time: 5-10 minutes*
*Cooking Time: 4-7 hours*
*Ideal slow cooker size: 4-qt.*

2 cups cornmeal
2 tsp. salt
2 cups cold water
6 cups hot water
2 sticks (½ lb.) butter, *optional*

1. Combine cornmeal, salt, and cold water in greased slow cooker.
2. Stir in hot water, stirring until well blended.
3. Cover. Cook on High 1 hour. Stir well. Cook on Low 3-4 hours. (Or cook on Low 5-6 hours, stirring once every hour during the first 2 hours.)
4. Serve hot with butter alongside for those who want to add a chunk to their individual servings. Or serve warm with milk and syrup.

### Variations:

1. Pour cooked cornmeal mush into loaf pans. Chill until set (several hours or overnight). Cut into ½"-thick slices.
2. Dredge each slice in flour. Melt butter in large skillet. Fry slices in butter, being careful not to crowd the skillet or mush will steam and not brown. When the first side is well browned, flip each slice to brown the other side.

3. Serve slices for breakfast with maple syrup, bacon, sausage, or ham and eggs.

4. Mush is much like polenta. It is also delicious topped with chili for a lunch or supper.

**Note:**

*When we lived on the farm, Mother would prepare boiled mush for the evening meal.*

*The rest she poured into pans and fried for supper the next evening. I adapted this recipe for the slow cooker several years ago when Mother was living with us and I needed to go to work.*

# Breakfast Apple Cobbler

**Anona M. Teel**
Bangor, PA

*Makes 6-8 servings*

**Prep. Time: 15 minutes**
**Cooking Time: 2-9 hours**
**Ideal slow cooker size: 3½- to 4-qt.**

**8 medium apples, cored, peeled, sliced**
**¼ cup sugar**
**dash of cinnamon**
**juice of 1 lemon**
**half a stick (4 Tbsp.) butter, melted**
**2 cups granola**

1. Combine all ingredients in slow cooker.

2. Cover. Cook on Low 7-9 hours (while you sleep), or on High 2-3 hours (after you're up in the morning).

# Hot Applesauce Breakfast

**Colleen Konetzni**
Rio Rancho, NM

*Makes 8 servings*

**Prep. Time: 15 minutes**
**Cooking Time: 8-10 hours**
**Ideal slow cooker size: 3½-qt.**

**10 apples, peeled and sliced**
**½-1 cup sugar, according to the sweetness of the apples and your taste preference**
**1 Tbsp. ground cinnamon**
**¼ tsp. ground nutmeg**

1. Combine all ingredients in slow cooker.

2. Cover. Cook on Low 8-10 hours (while you're asleep?).

*Serving suggestion: This is yummy over oatmeal or mixed with vanilla yogurt. Or serve it over pancakes or waffles.*

**Variation:**

Add chopped nuts for an extra treat, either before cooking or before serving.

# Breakfast Prunes

**Jo Haberkamp**
Fairbank, IA

*Makes 6 servings*

**Prep. Time: 10 minutes**
**Cooking Time: 8-10 hours**
**Ideal slow cooker size: 2-qt.**

**2 cups orange juice**
**¼ cup orange marmalade**
**1 tsp. ground cinnamon**
**¼ tsp. ground cloves**
**¼ tsp. ground nutmeg**
**1 cup water**
**12-oz. pkg. pitted dried prunes (1¾ cups)**
**2 thin lemon slices**

1. Combine orange juice, marmalade, cinnamon, cloves, nutmeg, and water in slow cooker.

2. Stir in prunes and lemon slices.

3. Cover. Cook on Low 8-10 hours, or overnight.

4. Serve warm as a breakfast food, or warm or chilled as a side dish with a meal later in the day.

**Variation:**

If you prefer more citrus flavor, eliminate the ground cloves and reduce the cinnamon to ½ tsp. and the nutmeg to ⅛ tsp.

# Boston Brown Bread

**Jean Butzer**
Batavia, NY

*Makes 3 loaves*

*Prep. Time: 15-20 minutes*
*Cooking Time: 4 hours*
*Ideal slow cooker size: large*
*enough to hold 3 cans upright*

3 16-oz. vegetable cans, cleaned and emptied
½ cup rye flour
½ cup yellow cornmeal
½ cup whole wheat flour
3 Tbsp. sugar
1 tsp. baking soda
¾ tsp. salt
½ cup chopped walnuts
½ cup raisins
1 cup buttermilk*
⅓ cup molasses

1. Spray insides of vegetable cans, and one side of 3 6"-square pieces of foil, with nonstick cooking spray. Set aside.
2. Combine rye flour, cornmeal, whole wheat flour, sugar, baking soda, and salt in a large bowl.

3. Stir in walnuts and raisins.
4. Whisk together buttermilk and molasses in a separate bowl. Add to dry ingredients. Stir until well mixed. Spoon into prepared cans.
5. Place one piece of foil, greased side down, on top of each can. Secure foil with rubberbands or cotton string. Place upright in slow cooker.
6. Pour boiling water into slow cooker to come halfway up sides of cans. (Make sure foil tops do not touch boiling water).
7. Cover cooker. Cook on Low 4 hours, or until skewer inserted in center of bread comes out clean.
8. To remove bread, lay cans on their sides. Roll and tap gently on all sides until bread releases. Cool completely on wire racks.
9. Serve with butter or cream cheese.

* To substitute for buttermilk, pour 1 Tbsp. lemon juice into a 1-cup measure. Add enough milk to fill the cup. Let stand 5 minutes before mixing with molasses.

# Dulce Leche (Sweet Milk)

**Dorothy Horst**
Tiskilwa, IL

*Makes 2½ cups*

*Prep. Time: 5 minutes*
*Cooking Time: 2 hours*
*Ideal slow cooker size: large*
*enough to hold 2 cans upright*

2 14-oz. cans sweetened condensed milk

1. Place unopened cans of milk in slow cooker. Fill cooker with warm water so that it comes above the cans by 1½-2 inches.
2. Cover cooker. Cook on High 2 hours.
3. Cool unopened cans.
4. When opened, the contents should be thick and spreadable. Use as a filling between 2 cookies or crackers.

Note:
*When on a tour in Argentina, we were served this at breakfast time as a spread on toast or thick slices of bread. We were also presented with a container of prepared Dulce Leche as a parting gift to take home. This dish sometimes appears on Mexican menus.*

# Soups, Stews, and Chilis

## Hearty Bean and Vegetable Soup

**Jewel Showalter**
Landisville, PA

*Makes 6-8 servings*

**Prep. Time: 20-25 minutes**
**Cooking Time: 6-8 hours**
**Ideal slow cooker size: 5-qt.**

2 medium onions, sliced
2 garlic cloves, minced
2 Tbsp. olive oil
8 cups chicken, *or*
  vegetable, broth
1 small head cabbage,
  chopped
2 large red potatoes, chopped
2 cups chopped celery
2 cups chopped carrots
4 cups corn
2 tsp. dried basil
1 tsp. dried marjoram
¼ tsp. dried oregano
1 tsp. salt
½ tsp. pepper
2 15-oz. cans navy beans,
  drained

1. Sauté onions and garlic in oil in skillet. Transfer to large slow cooker.
2. Add remaining ingredients  Mix together well.
3. Cover. Cook on Low 6-8 hours.

**Variation:**
  Add 2-3 cups cooked and cut-up chicken 30 minutes before serving if you wish.

**Note:**
  *I discovered this recipe after my husband's heart attack. It's a great nutritious soup using only a little fat.*

*Invite friends over. Have everyone bring a slow-cooker soup. Set all of the slow cookers around the counter with labels on each one. It's a great way to sample lots of different kinds of soups. (You can assign a different recipe to each person if you're concerned about having duplicates.)*
*Nancy Wagner Graves, Manhattan, KS*

# Minestrone

**Bernita Boyts**
Shawnee Mission, KS

*Makes 8-10 servings*

*Prep. Time: 15 minutes*
*Cooking Time: 4-9 hours*
*Ideal slow cooker size: 3½- to 4-qt.*

1 large onion, chopped
4 carrots, sliced
3 ribs celery, sliced
2 garlic cloves, minced
1 Tbsp. olive oil
6-oz. can tomato paste
14½-oz. can chicken, beef,
 *or* vegetable, broth
24-oz. can pinto beans,
 undrained
10-oz. pkg. frozen green
 beans
2-3 cups chopped cabbage
1 medium zucchini, sliced
8 cups water
2 Tbsp. parsley
2 Tbsp. Italian spice
1 tsp. salt, *or* more
½ tsp. pepper
¾ cup dry acini di pepe
 (small round pasta)
grated Parmesan, *or*
 Asiago, cheese

1. Sauté onion, carrots,
celery, and garlic in oil in
skillet until tender.
2. Combine all ingredients,
except pasta and cheese, in
slow cooker.
3. Cover. Cook 4-5 hours
on High or 8-9 hours on Low.
4. Add pasta 1 hour before
cooking is complete.
5. Top individual servings
with cheese.

# Zesty Minestrone

**Lavina Hochstedler**
Grand Blanc, MI

*Makes 8 servings*

*Prep. Time: 15 minutes*
*Cooking Time: 3-6 hours*
*Ideal slow cooker size: 3- to 4-qt.*

¼ cup zesty Italian
 dressing
1 onion, chopped
1 rib celery, chopped
1 carrot, peeled and
 chopped
14½-oz. can diced
 tomatoes, with juice
10-oz. can kidney beans,
 rinsed and drained
2 14-oz. cans vegetable
 broth
2 cups water
1 tsp. Italian seasonings
1½ cups small shell
 macaroni, uncooked
½ cup grated Parmesan
 cheese

1. Heat dressing in large
skillet on medium-high heat.
Add onions, celery, and
carrots.
2. Cook 2 minutes, or
until crisp-tender, stirring
occasionally. Spoon into slow
cooker.
3. Stir in tomatoes, beans,
broth, water, and seasonings.
4. Cover. Cook on Low 6
hours or on High 3 hours.
5. Stir in macaroni 30
minutes before end of cooking time.
6. Sprinkle individual
servings with cheese.

**Variation:**
 White beans or garbanzo
beans work just as well as
kidney beans. Substitute if
you wish.

# Slow-Cooker
# Bean Soup

**Betty B. Dennison**
Grove City, PA

*Makes 6 servings*

*Prep. Time: 30 minutes*
*Cooking Time: 8-9 hours*
*Ideal slow cooker size: 6-qt., or
 2 4- to 5-qt.*

3 15-oz. cans pinto beans,
 undrained
3 15-oz. cans great northern
 beans, undrained
4 cups chicken, *or*
 vegetable, broth
3 potatoes, peeled and
 chopped
4 carrots, sliced
2 celery ribs, sliced
1 large onion, chopped
1 green bell pepper,
 chopped
1 sweet red pepper,
 chopped, *optional*
2 garlic cloves, minced
1 tsp. salt, *or* to taste
¼ tsp. pepper, *or* to taste
1 bay leaf, *optional*
½ tsp. liquid barbecue
 smoke, *optional*

1. Empty beans into
6-qt. slow cooker, or divide
ingredients between 2 4- or
5-qt. cookers.

2. Cover. Cook on Low while preparing vegetables.

3. Add remaining ingredients and mix well.

4. Cover. Cook on Low 8-9 hours, or until vegetables are as tender as you like.

*Serving suggestion: Serve with tossed salad, **Italian bread**, or **cornbread**.*

Note:

*This is a stress-free recipe when you're expecting guests, but you're not sure of their arrival time. Slow-Cooker Bean Soup can burble on Low heat for longer than its appointed cooking time without being damaged.*

# Great Northern Bean Soup

**Alice Miller**
Stuarts Draft, VA

*Makes 6-8 servings*

*Prep. Time: 15-20 minutes*
*Cooking Time: 3 hours*
*Ideal slow cooker size: 3-qt.*

2 1-lb. cans great northern beans, rinsed and drained
1-lb. can stewed, *or* diced, tomatoes, including juice
1-2 Tbsp. brown sugar
½ cup green bell peppers, chopped
½ cup red bell peppers, chopped

1. Put beans, tomatoes, and brown sugar into slow cooker. Stir until well mixed.

2. Cover. Cook on High 2½ hours.

3. Stir chopped red and green peppers into Soup.

4. Cover. Cook on High 30 more minutes.

# Southwestern Bean Soup with Cornmeal Dumplings

**Melba Eshleman**
Manheim, PA

*Makes 4 servings*

*Prep. Time: 20 minutes*
*Cooking Time: 4½-12½ hours*
*Ideal slow cooker size: 5-qt.*

15½-oz. can red kidney beans, rinsed and drained
15½-oz. can black beans, pinto beans, *or* great northern beans, rinsed and drained
3 cups water
14½-oz. can Mexican-style stewed tomatoes
10-oz. pkg. frozen whole-kernel corn, thawed
1 cup sliced carrots
1 cup chopped onions
4-oz. can chopped green chilies, drained
2 Tbsp. instant beef, chicken, *or* vegetable, bouillon granules
1-2 tsp. chili powder
2 cloves garlic, minced

Dumplings:
⅓ cup flour
¼ cup yellow cornmeal
1 tsp. baking powder
dash of salt
dash of pepper
1 egg white, beaten
2 Tbsp. milk
1 Tbsp. oil

1. Combine all Soup ingredients in slow cooker.

2. Cover. Cook on Low 10-12 hours or on High 4-5 hours.

3. Make Dumplings by mixing together flour, cornmeal, baking powder, salt, and pepper in a large bowl.

4. Combine egg white, milk, and oil in a separate bowl. Add to flour mixture. Stir with fork until just combined.

5. At end of Soup's cooking time, turn slow cooker to High. Drop Dumpling mixture by rounded teaspoonfuls to make 8 mounds atop the soup.

6. Cover. Cook for 30 minutes. Do not lift lid during that time!

# Back-on-Track Soup

**Barbara Forrester Landis**
Lititz, PA

*Makes 8 servings*

*Prep. Time: 20 minutes*
*Cooking Time: 3-5 hours*
*Standing Time: 15 minutes*
*Ideal slow cooker size: 5-qt.*

1 Tbsp. olive oil
2-4 cloves garlic, minced, depending on how much you like garlic
2 bay leaves
2 15-oz. cans pinto, *or* kidney, beans, rinsed and drained
2 lbs. potatoes cut into ½" pieces
8 cups vegetable broth
1 box frozen chopped spinach, thawed and squeezed dry
salt and pepper to taste

1. Combine everything except spinach, salt, and pepper in slow cooker.
2. Cover. Cook on High 3 hours or on Low 5 hours.
3. Fifteen minutes before serving, stir in spinach.
4. Cover cooker and allow to stand 15 minutes. Taste, then add salt and pepper to enhance flavoring.
5. If you wish, use a potato masher to partially mash and thicken the Soup.

Note:
This is a great Soup for getting back to healthy eating after holiday feasting. No punishment here!

# Many-Bean Soup

**Trudy Kutter**
Corfu, NY

*Makes 12 servings*

*Prep. Time: 15 minutes*
*Cooking Time: 8¼-10¼*
*Ideal slow cooker size: 6-qt*

20-oz. pkg. dried 15-bean soup mix, *or* 2¼ cups dried beans of your choice
5 14½-oz. cans chicken, *or* vegetable, broth
2 cups chopped carrots
1½ cups chopped celery
1 cup chopped onions
2 Tbsp. tomato paste
1 tsp. Italian seasoning
½ tsp. pepper
14½-oz. can diced tomatoes

1. Combine all ingredients except tomatoes in slow cooker.
2. Cover. Cook on Low 8-10 hours, or until beans are tender.
3. Stir in tomatoes.
4. Cover. Cook on High 10-20 minutes, or until soup is heated through.

*Serving suggestion: Serve with **bread** and **salad**.*

# Blessing Soup

**Alix Nancy Botsford**
Seminole, OK

*Makes 8-10 servings*

*Prep. Time: 20 minutes*
*Soaking Time: 8 hours, or overnight*
*Cooking Time: 4-12 hours*
*Ideal slow cooker size: 4- to 5-qt.*

2 cups mixed dried beans—10-18 different kinds, if you can find them!
2-2½ qts. water
1 cup diced ham
1 large onion, chopped
1 garlic clove, minced
juice of 1 lemon
14½-oz. can Italian tomatoes, chopped
½ cup chopped sweet red peppers
½ cup chopped celery
2 carrots, thinly sliced
1 tsp. salt
1 tsp. pepper

1. Wash beans. Discard any stones. Place in slow cooker. Cover with water and soak 8 hours or overnight.
2. Drain water off beans.
3. Add 2-2½ qts. water to drained beans. Cook on High 2 hours.
4. Combine all remaining ingredients with beans in slow cooker.
5. Add more water if necessary so that everything is just covered with water.
6. Cover. Cook on High 4-6 hours or on Low 8-12 hours, or until beans and

other vegetables are tender but not mushy.

Note:

*During one January that was especially dismal, I invited many friends, most of whom didn't know each other, to my home. I put on a video about rose gardens around the world. Then I made this soup and a fresh bread crouton that could be eaten on top of the soup and tossed a large salad.*

# Garbanzo Souper

**Willard E. Roth**
Elkhart, IN

*Makes 6 servings*

*Prep. Time: 20 minutes*
*Soaking Time: 8 hours, or overnight*
*Cooking Time: 6 hours*
*Ideal slow cooker size: 4-qt.*

1 lb. dry garbanzo beans
4 oz. raw baby carrots, cut in halves
1 large onion, diced
3 ribs celery, cut in 1" pieces
1 large green bell pepper, diced
½ tsp. dried basil
½ tsp. dried oregano
½ tsp. dried rosemary
½ tsp. dried thyme
2 28-oz. cans vegetable broth
1 broth can of water
8-oz. can tomato sauce
8 oz. prepared hummus
½ tsp. sea salt

1. Place beans in slow cooker. Cover with water. Soak 8 hours, or overnight.
2. Drain off water. Return soaked beans to slow cooker.
3. Add carrots, onion, celery, and green pepper.
4. Sprinkle with basil, oregano, rosemary, and thyme.
5. Add broth and water.
6. Cover. Cook on High 6 hours, or until beans and vegetables are tender but not over-cooked.
7. Half an hour before serving, stir in tomato sauce, hummus, and salt. Continue cooking until hot.

*Serving suggestion: Serve with **Irish soda bread** and **lemon curd**.*

Note:

*A fine meal for vegetarians on St. Patrick's Day!*

# Russian Red Lentil Soup

**Naomi E. Fast**
Hesston, KS

*Makes 8 servings*

*Prep. Time: 15 minutes*
*Cooking Time: 3¾-4¾ hours*
*Ideal slow cooker size: 3½- to 4-qt.*

1 Tbsp. oil
1 large onion, chopped
3 cloves garlic, minced
½ cup diced, dried apricots
1½ cups dried red lentils
½ tsp. cumin
½ tsp. dried thyme
3 cups water
2 14½-oz. cans chicken, *or* vegetable, broth
14½-oz. can diced tomatoes
1 Tbsp. honey
¾ tsp. salt
½ tsp. coarsely ground black pepper
2 Tbsp. chopped fresh mint
1½ cups plain yogurt

1. Combine all ingredients except mint and yogurt in slow cooker.
2. Cover. Heat on High until soup starts to simmer.
3. Turn to Low and cook 3-4 hours, or until lentils and vegetables are tender.
4. Add mint and dollop of yogurt to each individual bowl of soup.

# Lentil Soup

Tina Snyder
Manheim, PA

*Makes 10 servings*

*Prep. Time: 15 minutes*
*Cooking Time: 8 hours*
*Ideal slow cooker size: 3½-qt.*

4 cups hot water
14½-oz. can tomatoes
¼ cup tomato juice
3 medium potatoes, peeled
   and diced
3 carrots, thinly sliced
1 onion, chopped
1 rib celery, sliced
1 cup dry lentils
2 garlic cloves, minced
2 bay leaves
4 tsp. curry powder
1½ tsp. salt
sour cream

1. Combine all ingredients except sour cream in slow cooker.
2. Cover. Cook on Low 8 hours.
3. Serve with sour cream on top of individual servings and crusty bread as a go-along.

# Black Bean and Tomato Soup

Sue Tjon
Austin, TX

*Makes 6 servings*

*Prep. Time: 10-15 minutes*
*Soaking Time: 8 hours, or*
  *overnight*
*Cooking Time: 8 hours*
*Ideal slow cooker size: 4-qt.*

1-lb. bag dry black beans
2 10-oz. cans Rotel tomatoes
1 medium onion, chopped
1 medium green bell
  pepper, chopped
1 Tbsp. minced garlic
14½-oz. can chicken, *or*
  vegetable, broth
water
Cajun seasoning to taste

1. Place beans in slow cooker. Cover with water and soak for 8 hours or overnight.
2. Drain well. Add tomatoes, onions, pepper, garlic, and broth to beans in slow cooker.
3. Add water just to cover all ingredients.
4. Stir in Cajun seasoning to taste.
5. Cover. Cook on High 8 hours.
6. Mash some of the beans before serving for a thicker consistency.

*Serving suggestion: Serve over **rice** or in **black bean tacos.***

Tip:
Leftovers freeze well.

# Black Bean and Ham Soup

Janie Steele
Moore, OK

*Makes 5-6 qts., or about*
*18 servings*

*Prep. Time: 20 minutes*
*Soaking Time: 8 hours, or*
  *overnight*
*Cooking Time: 7½-10 hours*
*Ideal slow cooker size: 6-qt. or*
  *2 4- to 5-qt.*

4 cups dry black beans
5 qts. water
ham bone, ham pieces, *or*
  ham hocks
3 bunches green onions,
  sliced thin
4 bay leaves
1 Tbsp. salt
¼-½ tsp. pepper
3 cloves minced garlic
4 celery ribs, chopped
3 large onions, chopped
10½-oz. can consommé
1 stick (8 Tbsp.) butter
2½ Tbsp. flour
1 cup Madeira wine, *optional*
chopped parsley

1. In 6-qt. slow cooker, soak beans in 5 qts. water for 8 hours or overnight.
2. Rinse. Drain. Pour beans back into slow cooker, or divide between 2 4- or 5-qt. cookers.
3. Add ham, green onions, bay leaves, salt, pepper, garlic, celery, and onions. Pour in consommé. Add water to cover vegetables and meat. Stir well

4. Cover. Cook on High 1½-2 hours. Reduce heat to Low and cook 6-8 hours.

5. Remove ham bones and bay leaves. Cut ham off bones and set meat aside

6. Force vegetable mixture through sieve, if you wish.

7. Taste and adjust seasonings, adding more salt and pepper if needed. Return cooked ingredients and cut-up ham to cooker.

8. In saucepan, melt butter. Stir in flour until smooth. Stir into soup to thicken and enrich.

9. Prior to serving, add wine to heated soup mixture if you wish. Garnish with chopped parsley.

# Party Bean Soup

**Jo Haberkamp**
Fairbank, IA

*Makes 9 servings*

*Prep. Time: 10 minutes*
*Cooking Time: 20-22 hours*
*Ideal slow cooker size: 5-qt.*

1 cup dry navy beans
1 qt. water
1 lb. smoked, *or* plain, ham hocks
1 cup chopped onions
½ cup chopped celery
1 garlic clove, minced
8-oz. can tomatoes, cut up
2 14½-oz. cans chicken broth
⅛ tsp. salt
⅛ tsp. pepper
1 cup (4 oz.) shredded cheddar cheese
1 Tbsp. dried parsley flakes

1. Place beans and water in slow cooker.

2. Cover. Cook on Low 12 hours.

3. Add ham hocks, onions, celery, garlic, tomatoes, chicken broth, salt, and pepper.

4. Cover. Cook on Low 8-10 more hours.

5. Add cheese and parsley just before serving. Stir until cheese is melted.

# Red and Green Bean Soup

**Carol Duree**
Salina, KS

*Makes 6-8 servings*

*Prep. Time: 15 minutes*
*Cooking Time: 6¼-8¼ hours*
*Ideal slow cooker size: 4-qt.*

1 lb. dry navy beans
6 cups boiling water
1 cup sliced carrots
½ cup chopped onion
1½-2 lbs. ham hocks
salt and pepper to taste
1-2 cups chopped kale, spinach, *or* chard
½ cup roasted red peppers, chopped
Parmesan cheese, grated

1. Rinse beans; then place in slow cooker.

2. Add all other ingredients except kale, red peppers, and cheese.

3. Cover. Cook on Low 6-8 hours, or until beans are tender but not mushy.

4. Ten minutes before serving, add kale and peppers. Cover and continue to cook 10 more minutes.

5. Sprinkle Parmesan cheese on top of individual servings.

# Navy Bean Soup

**Lucille Amos**
Greensboro, NC

*Makes 8 servings*

**Prep. Time: 5-10 minutes**
**Soaking Time: 8 hours, or**
**overnight**
**Cooking Time: 5-12 hours**
**Ideal slow cooker size: 2- to 3-qt.**

**2 cups dry navy beans**
**1 cup chopped onions**
**1 bay leaf**
**1 tsp. salt**
**1 tsp. pepper**
**½ lb. ham, chopped**

1. Place dry beans in slow cooker. Cover with water. Allow to soak 8 hours, or overnight.

2. Drain off water. Add all remaining ingredients to beans in slow cooker.

3. Add water to cover.

4. Cover. Cook on Low 10-12 hours or on High 5-6 hours.

5. Remove bay leaf and serve.

# Navy Bean and Bacon Chowder

**Ruth A. Feister**
Narvon, PA

*Makes 6 servings*

**Prep. Time: 15 minutes**
**Soaking Time: 8 hours, or**
**overnight**
**Cooking Time: 7¼-9¼ hours**
**Ideal slow cooker size: 5-qt.**

**1½ cups dry navy beans**
**2 cups cold water**
**8 slices bacon, cooked and**
**crumbled**
**2 medium carrots, sliced**
**1 rib celery, sliced**
**1 medium onion, chopped**
**1 tsp. dried Italian**
**seasoning**
**⅛ tsp. pepper**
**46-oz. can chicken broth**
**1 cup milk**

1. Place beans in cooker. Add 2 cups cold water. Soak 8 hours, or overnight.

2. Drain off any water. Add all remaining ingredients, except milk, to beans in slow cooker.

3. Cover. Cook on Low 7-9 hours, or until beans are crisp-tender.

4. Place 2 cups cooked bean mixture into blender. (Cover lid of blender with heavy towel and hold it on tightly. Hot ingredients can blow the lid off as you run the blender.) Process until smooth.

5. Return blended beans to slow cooker.

6. Add milk. Cover and heat on High 10 minutes.

*Serving suggestion: Serve with crusty **French bread** and additional **herbs** and **seasonings** for diners to add as they wish.*

*Bauer 24-Day Countdown to Christmas: Our family hangs a string of our own stockings in our living room each December. There are three of us, so we each choose eight socks and hang them using clothes pins. Each morning we take turns checking a sock for a surprise. We may find a small gift or something as simple as a note that says "Will cook supper for Mom tonight." We have fun thinking of unique ideas for each other, and before you know it, Christmas is here.*

*Amy Bauer, New Ulm, MN*

# Cassoulet Chowder

**Miriam Friesen**
Staunton, VA

*Makes 8-10 servings*

*Prep. Time: 1¾ hours*
*Refrigeration Time: 4-8 hours*
*Cooking Time: 4-10 hours*
*Ideal slow cooker size: 5-qt.*

1¼ cups dry pinto beans
4 cups water
12-oz. pkg. brown-and-
    serve sausage links,
    cooked and drained
2 cups cubed cooked
    chicken
2 cups cubed cooked ham
1½ cups sliced carrots
8-oz. can tomato sauce
¾ cup dry red wine
½ cup chopped onions
½ tsp. garlic powder
1 bay leaf

1. Combine beans and
water in large saucepan.
Bring to boil. Reduce heat
and simmer 1½ hours.
2. Allow cooked beans to
cool. Refrigerate beans and
liquid 4-8 hours.
3. Combine all ingredients
in slow cooker.
4. Cover. Cook on Low 8-10
hours or on High 4 hours.
5. If Chowder seems too
thin, remove lid during last
30 minutes of cooking time to
allow some liquid to cook off.
6. Remove bay leaf before
serving.

# Polish Sausage Bean Soup

**Janie Steele**
Moore, OK

*Makes 10 servings*

*Prep. Time: 15 minutes*
*Soaking Time: 8 hours, or*
*    overnight*
*Cooking Time: 9-9½ hours*
*Ideal slow cooker size: 6-qt.*

1-lb. pkg. dry great northern
    beans
28-oz. can whole tomatoes
2 8-oz. cans tomato sauce
2 large onions, chopped
3 cloves garlic, minced
1 tsp. salt
¼-½ tsp. pepper, according
    to your taste preference
3 celery ribs, sliced
bell pepper, sliced
large ham bone, *or* ham hock
1-2 lbs. smoked sausage
    links, sliced

1. Place beans in 6-qt. slow
cocker. Cover with water and
soak 8 hours, or overnight.
2. Rinse and drain. Return
beans to cooker and cover
with water again.
3. Combine all other
ingredients, except sausage,
with beans in slow cooker.
4. Cover. Cook on High
1-1½ hours. Reduce to Low
and cook 7 hours.
5. Remove ham bone or
hock and debone. Stir ham
pieces back into soup.
6. Add sausage links.
7. Cover. Cook on Low 1
mcre hour.

# Grandma's Barley Soup

**Andrea O'Neil**
Fairfield, CT

*Makes 10-12 servings*

*Prep. Time: 10 minutes*
*Cooking Time: 6-8 hours*
*Ideal slow cooker size: 4- to 5-qt.*

2 smoked ham hocks
4 carrots, sliced
4 potatoes, cubed
1 cup dry lima beans
1 cup tomato paste
1½-2 cups cooked barley
salt, if needed

1. Combine all ingredients
in slow cooker, except salt.
2. Cover with water.
3. Cover. Simmer on Low
6-8 hours, or until both ham
and beans are tender.
4. Debone ham hocks and
return cut-up meat to soup.
5. Taste before serving.
Add salt if needed.

**Tip:**
   If you want to reduce the
amount of meat you eat, this
dish is flavorful using only 1
ham hock.

# Split Pea Soup

**Janette Anderson**
Sedalia, MO

*Makes 6-8 servings*

**Prep. Time: 20 minutes**
**Cooking Time: 8-11 hours**
**Ideal slow cooker size: 5- to 6-qt.**

1 *or* 2 ham hocks
1 lb. (2 cups) dry split peas
2 carrots, sliced
1 onion, diced
2 ribs celery, diced
¼ tsp. pepper
1 tsp. salt
3 potatoes, diced
1 qt. water
1 qt. chicken broth

1. Place ham hock(s) in slow cooker.

2. Add remaining ingredients and stir well.

3. Cover. Cook on Low 8-10 hours, or until ham and split peas are tender.

4. Remove ham bone. Allow to cool until it's possible to handle it.

5. Debone and cut up meat. Stir meat back into soup.

6. For creamier soup, cook an hour or so longer. Stir occasionally to prevent sticking.

**Variations:**

1. Add 14½-oz. can diced tomatoes with juice in Step 2.

**Holly Schwartz**
Lac Du Flambeau, WI

2. Instead of ham hocks, use 1 lb. smoked kielbasa, sliced. Stir into Soup in Step 2.

**Nathan LeBeau**
Rapid City, SD

# White Marrow Bean Soup

**Becky Frey**
Lebanon, PA

*Makes 8 servings*

**Prep. Time: 30 minutes**
**Cooking Time: 4-5 hours**
**Ideal slow cooker size: 5-qt.**

2 qts. cooked marrow
  beans, *or* your choice
  of cooked white beans,
  undrained
1 cup onions, chopped
1 cup cooked ham,
  chopped
1 cup celery, chopped
3 cups potatoes, peeled
  and diced
2 qts. ham broth
parsley to taste
salt to taste
pepper to taste

1. Put beans, onions, ham, celery, potatoes, broth, and seasonings in slow cooker.

2. Cover. Cook on High 4-5 hours, or until potatoes are soft.

**Tip:**

You can use dried beans in the recipe if you have time to soak and cook them before following the instructions above.

**Note from Tester:**

*I would add a finely chopped jalapeño pepper to the Soup 1 hour before the end of cooking time. And I would add ¼ cup chopped red bell pepper and ¼ cup chopped green bell pepper to the Soup, just before serving it.*

*Before your main meal, serve a bowl of your favorite homemade soup. Don't forget your soup tureen. Your guests will feel special. Why have a soup tureen and not use it?*
*Leona M. Slabaugh, Apple Creek, OH*

# Rice & Bean Soup

**Sharon Easter**
Yuba City, CA

*Makes 6 servings*

*Prep. Time: 10 minutes*
*Cooking Time: 3½-4 hours*
*Ideal slow cooker size: 5-qt.*

½ lb. loose Italian sausage,
   hot *or* sweet
2 32-oz. boxes chicken, *or*
   vegetable, broth
28-oz. can diced tomatoes
½ tsp. salt
¼ tsp. pepper
½ tsp. dried oregano
1 cup long-grain rice,
   uncooked
15-oz. can white beans,
   rinsed and drained
1 cup diced celery
4 carrots, sliced

1. Brown sausage in skillet.
Drain off drippings.
2. Put all ingredients in
slow cooker. Stir until well
blended.
3. Cover. Cook on Low 2
hours. Stir Soup.
4. Cover and cook an additional 1½-2 hours on Low, or
until vegetables and rice are
tender, but not mushy.

# Mexican Rice and Bean Soup

**Esther J. Mast**
East Petersburg, PA

*Makes 6 servings*

*Prep. Time: 15-20 minutes*
*Cooking Time: 6 hours*
*Ideal slow cooker size: 4- to 5-qt.*

½ cup chopped onions
⅓ cup chopped green bell
   peppers
1 garlic clove, minced
1 Tbsp. oil
4-oz. pkg. thinly sliced, *or*
   chipped, dried beef
18-oz. can tomato juice
15½-oz. can red kidney
   beans, undrained
1½ cups water
½ cup long-grain rice,
   uncooked
1 tsp. paprika
½-1 tsp. chili powder
½ tsp. salt
dash of pepper

1. Cook onions, green
peppers, and garlic in oil
in skillet until vegetables
are tender but not brown.
Transfer to slow cooker.
2. Tear beef into small
pieces and add to slow
cooker.
3. Add remaining ingredi-
ents. Mix well.
4. Cover. Cook on Low 6
hours. Stir before serving.

*Serving suggestion: Serve
with **relish tray** and **cornbread**, **home-canned fruit**,
and **cookies**.*

**Note:**
*This is a recipe I fixed often
when our sons were growing up.
We have all enjoyed it in any
season of the year.*

# Green Beans and Ham Soup

**Loretta Krahn**
Mountain Lake, MN

*Makes 6 servings*

*Prep. Time: 15 minutes*
*Cooking Time: 4¼-6¼ hours*
*Ideal slow cooker size: 5- to 6-qt.*

1 meaty ham bone, *or* 2
   cups cubed ham
1½ qts. water
1 large onion, chopped
2-3 cups cut-up green
   beans
3 large carrots, sliced
2 large potatoes, peeled
   and cubed
1 Tbsp. parsley
1 Tbsp. summer savory
½ tsp. salt
¼ tsp. pepper
1 cup cream, *or* milk

1. Combine all ingredients
except cream in slow cooker.
2. Cover. Cook on High 4-6
hours.
3. Remove ham bone. Cut
off meat and return to slow
cooker.
4. Turn to Low. Stir in
cream or milk. Heat through
and serve.

# Green Beans and Sausage Soup

**Bernita Boyts**
Shawnee Mission, KS

*Makes 5-6 servings*

*Prep. Time: 20-25 minutes*
*Cooking Time: 7-10 hours*
*Ideal slow cooker size: 4- to 5-qt.*

⅓ lb. link sausage, sliced,
  *or* bulk sausage
1 medium onion, chopped
2 carrots, sliced
2 ribs celery, sliced
1 Tbsp. olive oil
5 medium potatoes, cubed
10-oz. pkg. frozen green
  beans
2 14½-oz. cans chicken
  broth
2 broth cans water
2 Tbsp. chopped fresh
  parsley, *or* 2 tsp. dried
  parsley
1-2 Tbsp. chopped fresh
  oregano, *or* 1-2 tsp. dried
  oregano
1 tsp. Italian spice
salt to taste
pepper to taste

1. Brown sausage in skillet.
Stir frequently for even
browning.
2. Remove meat from skil-
let and place in slow cooker.
Reserve drippings.
3. Sauté onion, carrots, and
celery in skillet drippings
until tender.
4. Place sautéed vegetables
in slow cooker, along with all
remaining ingredients. Mix
together well.

5. Cover. Cook on High 1-2
hours and then on Low 6-8
hours.

**Variation:**

If you like it hot, add
ground red pepper or hot
sauce just before serving, or
offer to individual eaters to
add to their own bowls.

# Broccoli and Cauliflower Soup

**Wafi Brandt**
Manheim, PA

*Makes 4-6 servings*

*Prep. Time: 15 minutes*
*Cooking Time: 4¼ hours*
*Ideal slow cooker size: 3-qt.*

16-oz. bag frozen broccoli
  and cauliflower
¼ stick (2 Tbsp.) butter
½ Tbsp. dried onion
2 cups water
2 chicken bouillon cubes
4 Tbsp. flour
2 cups milk, *divided*
½ tsp. Worcestershire
  sauce
½ tsp. salt
1 cup grated cheddar
  cheese
chopped chives
parsley

1. Put broccoli and cauliflower, butter, onion, water,
and bouillon cubes in slow
cooker.

2. Cover. Cook on High 4
hours.
3. When broccoli and cauliflower are soft, mix flour and
1 cup milk together in a jar
with a tight-fitting lid. Cover
jar and shake vigorously until
flour dissolves and mixture is
smooth.
4. Pour milk mixture into
vegetables and stir. The soup
will soon thicken.
5. Then stir in Worcestershire sauce, salt, and cheese.
6. When cheese is melted,
stir in last cup of milk. Allow
to heat through before serving.
7. Sprinkle chives and
parsley over top of each
individual serving bowl.

# Broccoli, Potato, and Cheese Soup

**Ruth Shank**
Gridley, IL

*Makes 6 servings*

*Prep. Time: 20-25 minutes*
*Cooking Time: 4 hours*
*Ideal slow cooker size: 4-qt.*

2 cups cubed, *or* diced,
  potatoes
3 Tbsp. chopped onion
10-oz. pkg. frozen broccoli
  cuts, thawed
¼ stick (2 Tbsp.) butter,
  melted
1 Tbsp. flour
2 cups cubed Velveeta
  cheese
½ tsp. salt
5½ cups milk

1. Cook potatoes and onion in boiling water in saucepan until potatoes are crisp-tender. Drain. Place in slow cooker.

2. Add remaining ingredients. Stir together.

3. Cover. Cook on Low 4 hours.

# Cheesy Broccoli Soup

Dede Peterson, Rapid City, SD

*Makes 4 servings*

*Prep. Time: 15 minutes*
*Cooking Time: 5-6 hours*
*Ideal slow cooker size: 3-qt.*

1 lb. frozen chopped broccoli, thawed

1 lb. Velveeta cheese, cubed
10¾-oz. can cream of celery soup
14½-oz. can chicken, *or* vegetable, broth
dash of pepper
dash of salt

1. Combine ingredients in slow cooker.

2. Cover. Cook on Low 5-6 hours.

# Carrot Ginger Soup

Jean Harris Robinson, Pemberton, NJ

*Makes 8-10 servings*

*Prep. Time: 30 minutes • Cooking Time: 3½-4½ hours*
*Ideal slow cooker size: 5-qt.*

2 Tbsp. olive oil
3 lbs. carrots, peeled and thinly sliced
2 Tbsp. chopped gingerroot
2 Tbsp. minced green onion
3 ribs celery, chopped
49½-oz. can chicken broth
1-3 tsp. kosher salt
1 tsp. ground pepper
2 Tbsp. honey
¼ stick (2 Tbsp.) butter
1 cup heavy cream

1. Pour olive oil into slow cooker. Swirl to cover bottom of cooker.

2. Add carrots, ginger, onion, and celery.

3. Pour in broth. Add salt, pepper, honey, and butter. Stir to mix all ingredients well.

4. Cover. Cook on High 3-4 hours, or until carrots are soft.

5. Pulse with an immersion blender to purée.

6. Stir in one cup heavy cream. Heat Soup 15-20 minutes until heated through, but don't let it boil. Serve immediately.

Note:

*I was first introduced to this Soup at one of my quilt guild's regular meetings. Even the professed carrot-haters loved it.*

# Ham and Broccoli Chowder

Rachel Olinger
Parkesburg, PA

*Makes 6 servings*

*Prep. Time: 10 minutes*
*Cooking Time: 7 hours*
*Ideal slow cooker size: 4-qt.*

2 Tbsp. flour
12-oz. can evaporated milk
2 cups diced ham
1 pkg. frozen chopped broccoli
¼ cup minced onion
1 cup grated Swiss cheese
2 cups water
1 cup light cream

1. Mix flour and milk in slow cooker until smooth.

2. Add all additional ingredients except cream.

3. Cover. Cook on Low 7 hours.

4. Before serving, stir in cream and heat through.

# Curried Carrot Soup

**Ann Bender**
Ft. Defiance, VA

*Makes 6-8 servings*

**Prep. Time: 20 minutes**
**Cooking Time: 2 hours**
**Ideal slow cooker size: 3-qt.**

1 garlic clove, minced
1 large onion, chopped
2 Tbsp. oil
1 Tbsp. butter
1 tsp. curry powder
1 Tbsp. flour
4 cups chicken, *or*
　vegetable, broth
6 large carrots, sliced
¼ tsp. salt
¼ tsp. ground red pepper,
　*optional*
1½ cups plain yogurt, *or*
　light sour cream

1. In skillet cook minced garlic and onion in oil and butter until vegetables are limp but not brown.
2. Add curry and flour. Cook 30 seconds. Pour into slow cooker.
3. Add chicken broth and carrots. Mix together well.
4. Cover. Cook on High for about 2 hours, or until carrots are soft.
5. Purée mixture in blender. Hold top on tightly with a thick towel. (The heat tends to push the lid of the blender off.)
6. Return to slow cooker and add seasoning. Keep warm until ready to serve.
7. Add a dollop of yogurt or sour cream to each serving.

# Corn Chowder

**Betty Moore**
Plano, IL

*Makes 4-6 servings*

**Prep. Time: 20-30 minutes**
**Cooking Time: 6 hours**
**Ideal slow cooker size: 4-qt.**

2½ cups milk
14¾-oz. can cream-style
　corn
10¾-oz. can cream of
　mushroom soup
1¾ cups frozen corn
1 cup frozen shredded
　hash brown potatoes
1 cup cooked ham, diced
1 medium-large onion,
　diced
¼ stick (2 Tbsp.) butter
2 tsp. parsley flakes
salt and pepper to taste

1. Combine all ingredients in slow cooker.
2. Cover and cook on Low 6 hours.

**Note from Tester:**
*I would garnish each individual bowl of soup with diced red and green bell peppers. Looks like the holidays!*

**Variations:**
1. Replace ham with 8 slices bacon, cooked and crumbled. Add just before serving in order to keep the bacon crisp.
2. Stir ½ tsp. Worcestershire sauce in with Step 1.
**Orpha Herr**
Andover, NY

# Green Chile Corn Chowder

**Kelly Evenson**
Pittsboro, NC

*Makes 8 servings*

**Prep. Time: 15 minutes**
**Cooking Time: 7¼-8¼ hours**
**Ideal slow cooker size: 4-qt.**

16-oz. can cream-style corn
3 potatoes, peeled or not,
　and diced
2 Tbsp. chopped fresh
　chives
4-oz. can diced green
　chilies, drained
2-oz. jar chopped
　pimentos, drained
½-¾ cup chopped cooked
　ham
2 10½-oz. cans chicken
　broth
salt to taste
pepper to taste
Tabasco sauce to taste
1 cup milk
shredded Monterey Jack
　cheese

1. Combine all ingredients except milk and cheese in slow cooker.
2. Cover. Cook on Low 7-8 hours or until potatoes are tender.
3. Stir in milk. Heat until hot.
4. Top individual servings with cheese.

# Chicken Corn Soup

**Moreen Weaver**
Bath, NY

*Makes 8-10 servings*

*Prep. Time: 1 hour*
*Cooking Time: 4-5 hours*
*Ideal slow cooker size: 5- to 6-qt.*

4-5 lbs. chicken leg
  quarters
3 qts. water
1 tsp. salt
1½ cups chopped celery
1 medium onion, chopped
4 cups fresh, *or* frozen,
  corn
3 chicken bouillon cubes
pepper to taste
12-oz. bag fine noodles,
  uncooked

1. If you wish, remove skin from chicken. Put chicken in large stockpot. Add salt and water. Cover and cook until tender.

2. Remove chicken. Allow to stand until cool enough to debone. Meanwhile, strain broth and pour into slow cooker.

3. Remove chicken from bones and cut in small pieces. Place in slow cooker.

4. Stir celery, onion, corn, bouillon, and pepper into slow cooker.

5. Cover. Cook on Low 4-5 hours.

6. Fifteen minutes before end of cooking time, stir in noodles.

Note:
*My mother-in-law makes this recipe every Christmas. It just wouldn't be Christmas without it!*

# Red French Onion Soup

**Marilyn Mowry**
Irving, TX

*Makes 6-8 servings*

*Prep. Time: 10-15 minutes*
*Cooking Time: 4-5 hours*
*Ideal slow cooker size: 3- to 4-qt.*

5 large red onions
¼ stick (2 Tbsp.) butter
1 cup dry red wine
4 cups beef broth
½ tsp. dried thyme
2 Tbsp. fresh chopped
  parsley
French baguette
½ cup grated Swiss cheese

1. Cut onions into thin slices. Add with butter to cooker.

2. Turn to High. As butter melts, stir into onions.

3. Add wine, broth, thyme, and parsley. Stir well.

4. Cover. Cook 4-5 hours on Low, or until onions are tender.

5. Prepare bread toppers 30 minutes before Soup is finished cooking. Slice French bread into 1"-thick slices. Lay slices on a baking sheet. Bake 10 minutes at 350 degrees, or until bread is dry and crisp.

6. Sprinkle cheese over each slice of warm bread.

7. To serve, float a cheesy bread topper on top of each bowl of soup.

Variations:
1. Add 1½ tsp. Worcestershire sauce to Step 3.

2. Place cheese on top of bread slices before baking. Then broil them to make the cheese brown and bubble. Watch carefully so the cheese doesn't burn.

3. Instead of Swiss cheese, use ⅓ cup grated mozzarella mixed with ¼ cup grated Parmesan cheese.

**Lucille Amos**
Greensboro, NC

**Betty Drescher**
Quakertown, PA

Note:
*This is a handy recipe at holiday-time when you need to do last-minute shopping.*

# Onion Soup

**Lucille Amos**
Greensboro, NC

*Makes 10 servings*

*Prep. Time: 30 minutes*
*Cooking Time: 4-5 hours*
*Ideal slow cooker size: 4- to 5-qt.*

6 large onions
1 stick (8 Tbsp.) butter
6 10½-oz. cans beef broth
1½ tsp. Worcestershire
  sauce
pepper to taste
10 ½"-thick slices French
  bread
shredded mozzarella
  cheese and Parmesan
  cheese, shredded

1. In large skillet or saucepan, sauté onions in butter until tender. Do not brown. Transfer to slow cooker.
2. Add broth, Worcestershire sauce, and pepper.
3. Cover. Cook on Low 4-5 hours or until onions are very tender.
4. Top each serving with French bread and cheese.

# Creamy Potato Soup

**Janeen Troyer**
Fairview, MI

*Makes 6-8 servings*

*Prep. Time: 30 minutes*
*Cooking Time: 3¼-3½ hours*
*Ideal slow cooker size: 4-qt.*

3 cups chopped potatoes,
  peeled or unpeeled
1 cup water
½ cup chopped celery
½ cup chopped carrots
¼ cup chopped onions
2 cubes chicken, *or*
  vegetable, bouillon
1 tsp. parsley
½ tsp. salt
¼ tsp. pepper
1½ cups milk
2 Tbsp. flour
½ lb. cheese, your choice,
  shredded

1. Combine potatoes, water, celery, carrots, onion, bouillon, parsley, salt, and pepper in slow cooker.
2. Cover. Cook on High 3 hours, or until vegetables are tender.
3. In a jar with a tight-fitting lid, add milk to flour. Cover tightly and shake until flour dissolves in milk. When smooth, add mixture to vegetables in cooker. Stir well.
4. Cover. Cook on High another 15-30 minutes, or until soup is thickened and smooth. Stir occasionally to prevent lumps from forming.
5. Add cheese. Stir until melted.

**Note from Tester:**
  *For the Christmas holidays, garnish individual soup bowls with fresh parsley and chopped red bell peppers.*

# Ham and Potato Chowder

**Penny Blosser**
Beavercreek, OH

*Makes 5 servings*

*Prep. Time: 10 minutes*
*Cooking Time: 8 hours*
*Ideal slow cooker size: 4-qt.*

5-oz. pkg. scalloped potatoes
  sauce mix from potato pkg.
1 cup cooked ham, cut into
  narrow strips
4 cups chicken broth
1 cup chopped celery
⅓ cup chopped onions
salt to taste
pepper to taste
2 cups half-and-half
⅓ cup flour

1. Combine potatoes, sauce mix, ham, broth, celery, onions, salt, and pepper in slow cooker.
2. Cover. Cook on Low 7 hours.
3. Combine half-and-half and flour in small bowl. Gradually stir into slow cooker, blending well.
4. Cover. Cook on Low up to 1 hour, stirring occasionally until thickened.

# Creamy Tomato Soup

**Susie Shenk Wenger**
Lancaster, PA

*Makes 4 servings*

*Prep. Time: 10-15 minutes*
*Cooking Time: 3-4 hours*
*Ideal slow cooker size: 3-qt.*

29-oz. can tomato sauce,
  *or* crushed tomatoes,
  *or* 1 qt. home-canned
  tomatoes, chopped
1 small onion, chopped
1-2 carrots, sliced thin
2 tsp. brown sugar
1 tsp. Italian seasoning
¼ tsp. salt
¼ tsp. pepper
1 tsp. freshly chopped
  parsley
½ tsp. Worcestershire
  sauce
1 cup heaving whipping
  cream
croutons, preferably
  homemade
freshly grated Parmesan
  cheese

1. Combine tomato sauce, onions, carrots, brown sugar, Italian seasoning, salt, pepper, parsley, and Worcestershire sauce in slow cooker.
2. Cover. Cook on Low 3-4 hours, or until vegetables are soft.
3. Cool Soup a bit. Purée with immersion blender.
4. Add cream and blend lightly again.
5. Serve hot with croutons and Parmesan as garnish.

**Tip:**
This recipe can be easily doubled.

# Butternut Squash and Apple Soup

**Tina Hartman**
Lancaster, PA

*Makes 25-28 1-cup servings*

*Prep. Time: 30-60 minutes*
*Cooking Time: 1-2 hours*
*Ideal slow cooker size: 8-qt.*

¼ stick (2 Tbsp.) unsalted
  butter
2 Tbsp. olive oil
4 cups chopped yellow
  onions
2 Tbsp. mild curry powder
5 lbs. butternut squash (2
  large ones)
1½ lbs. sweet apples
2 tsp. salt
½ tsp. ground pepper
2 cups water
2 cups apple cider, *or* juice

1. Warm butter, olive oil, onions, and curry powder in large stockpot over low heat on stove until onions are tender (15 to 20 minutes).
2. Peel squash and remove seeds. Cut squash into chunks.
3. Peel, core, and cut apples into about 8 wedges each.
4. Add squash, apples, salt, pepper, and water to pot. Cook until soft enough to purée.
5. Purée or process with a food processor.
6. Pour entire mixture into slow cooker. Add apple cider or juice.
7. Cover. Cook on Low 1-2 hours. Serve hot from the cooker.

**Note:**
*This recipe is actually from my friends Brittany Leffler and Brian McKee. (They should get credit for it!) They host a cookie-exchange party every Christmas, and they serve this and chili. The rest of us bring the cookies. It is wonderful.*

*We have an old holiday storybook which my mother used to read to us children. It's pretty battered, but it's a family treasure. One year my sister crafted and painted a special box for it, and now whoever hosts Christmas (we take turns) gets to keep the book until the following Christmas, when it's always the first gift opened.*

*Carol L. Miller, Lockport, NY*

# Naturally Colorful Vegetable Soup

**Darla Sathre**
Baxter, MN

*Makes 6 servings*

*Prep. Time: 20-30 minutes*
*Cooking Time: 9-11 hours*
*Ideal slow cooker size: 4-qt.*

15-oz. can whole-kernel
   corn, undrained
2 cups frozen peas
16-oz. can kidney beans,
   undrained
14½-oz. can diced tomatoes
   with juice
15-oz. can tomato sauce
½ lb. baby carrots, halved
   lengthwise
1 onion, chopped
6 cloves garlic, thinly
   sliced
2 tsp. Italian seasoning
1 tsp. dried marjoram
1 tsp. dried basil

   1. Put all ingredients into
slow cooker. Stir well.
   2. Cover. Cook on High 1-2
hours. Then cook on Low 8-9
hours, or until carrots and
onions are as tender as you
like them.

# Cream of Pumpkin Soup

**Nanci Keatley**
Salem, OR

*Makes 4-6 servings*

*Prep. Time: 10-15 minutes*
*Cooking Time: 2-3 hours*
*Ideal slow cooker size: 4-qt.*

1 Tbsp. butter, melted
1 large onion, diced fine
32-oz. box vegetable stock
16-oz. can solid-pack
   pumpkin
1 tsp. salt
¼ tsp. cinnamon
¼ tsp. freshly ground
   nutmeg
⅛ tsp. ground ginger
⅛ tsp. ground cloves
⅛ tsp. ground cardamom
¼ tsp. freshly ground
   pepper
1½ cups half-and-half
1 cup heavy cream
chopped chives

   1. Mix butter and onion in
slow cooker.
   2. Add stock, pumpkin, salt,
and other seasonings. Mix well.
   3. Cover. Cook on Low 2-3
hours.

# Peanut Butter Pumpkin Soup

**Carol L. Miller**, Lockport, NY

*Makes 8-10 servings*

*Prep. Time: 15 minutes \* • Cooking Time: 6 hours*
*Ideal slow cooker size: 4-qt.*

¼ stick (2 Tbsp.) butter
4 cups canned pumpkin
2 cups cooked puréed
   sweet potatoes, *or*
   butternut squash
1 cup smooth peanut
   butter
6 cups chicken broth
1 tsp. black pepper
¼ tsp. salt
croutons for garnish,
   *optional*
crumbled cooked bacon
   for garnish, *optional*

   1. Place butter, pumpkin, sweet potatoes or squash,
peanut butter, broth, pepper, and salt in slow cooker.
   2. Cover. Cook on Low 6 hours, stirring well after first 2
hours.
   3. Serve with croutons or crumbled bacon as garnishes if
you wish.

   *If you have to make your own puréed sweet potatoes
or squash, add another hour to the Prep Time. Use 2 large
sweet potatoes, or a medium-sized butternut squash, in
order to get the 2 cups mashed.

4. Add half-and-half and cream.

5. Cover. Cook on Low 1 hour, or until heated through.

6. Garnish individual serving bowls with chives.

# Savory Cheese Soup

**Diane Eby**
Holtwood, PA
**Dorothy Lingerfelt**
Stonyford, CA

*Makes 4-5 servings*

*Prep. Time: 20 minutes*
*Cooking Time: 8-9 hours*
*Ideal slow cooker size: 5-qt.*

3 14½ -oz. cans chicken
   broth
1 small onion, chopped
1 large carrot, chopped
1 celery rib, chopped
¼ cup chopped sweet red
   bell pepper
¼ stick (2 Tbsp.) butter
1 tsp. salt
½ tsp. pepper
⅓ cup flour
⅓ cup cold water
8-oz. pkg. cream cheese,
   softened and cubed
2 cups shredded cheddar
   cheese
croutons, popcorn,
   crumpled bacon, sliced
   green onions, *optional*

1. In a slow cooker, combine chicken broth, onion, carrot, celery, sweet pepper, butter, salt, and pepper.

2. Cover and cook on Low 7-8 hours.

3. In a jar with a tight-fitting lid, combine flour and water. Put on lid and shake vigorously until mixture is smooth and without lumps. Stir into soup.

4. Cover. Cook on High 30 minutes, or until soup has thickened. Stir every 10 minutes or so to prevent lumps from forming.

5. Stir in cream cheese and cheddar cheese until blended.

6. Cover. Cook on Low until cheeses melt and Soup is heated through.

7. Serve with the toppings that you wish.

# Easy Cheese Soup

**Nancy Wagner Graves**
Manhattan, KS

*Makes 4 servings*

*Prep. Time: 5-10 minutes*
*Cooking Time: 4-6 hours*
*Ideal slow cooker size: 3½-qt.*

2 10¾-oz. cans cream of
   mushroom, *or* cream of
   chicken, soup
1 cup beer, *or* milk
1 lb. cheddar cheese, grated
1 tsp. Worcestershire sauce
¼ tsp. paprika
croutons

1. Combine all ingredients except croutons in slow cooker.

2. Cover. Cook on Low 4-6 hours.

3. Stir thoroughly 1 hour before serving to make sure cheese is well distributed and melted.

4. Serve topped with croutons or in bread bowls.

*I have made fabric bags for my friends. They each know which one is theirs (the bags are all different). I get them back every year at the end of the holiday season, ready to use again the next year. It sure saves on wrapping paper.*
*Sharon Easter, Yuba City, CA*

# Aunt Thelma's Homemade Soup

**Janice Muller**
Derwood, MD

*Makes 10-12 servings*

**Prep. Time: 10 minutes**
**Cooking Time: 4½-6½ hours**
**Ideal slow cooker size: 6-qt.**

7 cups water
4 chicken, *or* vegetable, bouillon cubes
1 cup thinly sliced carrots
1 lb. frozen peas
1 lb. frozen corn
1 lb. frozen lima beans
1 bay leaf
¼ tsp. dill seed
28-oz. can whole tomatoes
1 cup diced raw potatoes
1 cup chopped onions
2-3 tsp. salt
½ tsp. dried basil
¼ tsp. pepper
2 Tbsp. cornstarch
¼ cup cold water

1. Combine all ingredients except cornstarch and ¼ cup water in slow cooker.
2. Cover. Simmer on High 4-6 hours, or until vegetables are tender.
3. Thirty minutes before end of cooking time, mix cornstarch and cold water together in a small bowl until smooth.
4. Remove 1 cup broth from cooker and mix with cornstarch-water. When smooth, stir into soup.
5. Cover and continue cooking another half hour, or until soup thickens slightly.

*Serving suggestion: A loaf of fresh **Italian bread** goes well with a hot bowl of this soup.*

**Note:**
*My aunt always makes this in the winter and freezes an extra batch for unexpected guests. I converted the recipe to slow-cooker use a few years ago, but I think of her whenever I make it.*

# Diet Soup Unlimited

**Eileen Lehman**
Kidron, OH

*Makes 6 servings*

**Prep. Time: 15 minutes**
**Cooking Time: 4-8 hours**
**Ideal slow cooker size: 3½- to 4-qt.**

4 cups water
2 cups tomato juice
2 beef, *or* vegetable, bouillon cubes
1 Tbsp. soy sauce, *optional*
2 tsp. sugar, *optional*
1 cup sliced cabbage
2 carrots, sliced
1 celery rib, sliced
1 onion, sliced
2 cups frozen green beans
1 tsp. salt
pepper to taste

1. Combine all ingredients in slow cooker.
2. Cover. Cook on Low 4-8 hours, or just until vegetables are as tender as you like them.

**Variation:**
Add fresh mushrooms, if you like, after the first 2 hours of cooking.

**Note:**
*After the holidays this tasty, low-calorie soup is a welcome meal. It improves in flavor the longer it cooks.*

# The Soup

**Joanne Kennedy**
Plattsburgh, NY

*Makes 8 servings*

**Prep. Time: 20 minutes**
**Cooking Time: 9 hours**
**Ideal slow cooker size: 5- to 6-qt.**

2 14½-oz. cans vegetable broth
2 vegetable boullion cubes
4 cups water
1 qt. canned tomatoes
3-4 garlic cloves, minced
1 large onion, chopped
1 cup chopped celery
2 cups chopped carrots
1 small zucchini, cubed
1 small yellow squash, cubed
2 tsp. fresh basil
1 tsp. fresh parsley
pepper to taste
3 dashes Tabasco sauce

# Norma's Vegetarian Chili

### Kathy Hertzler, Lancaster, PA

*Makes 8-10 servings*

*Prep. Time: 20 minutes • Cooking Time: 8½ hours*
*Ideal slow cooker size: 5-qt.*

2 Tbsp. oil
2 cups minced celery
1½ cups chopped green
   bell pepper
1 cup minced onions
4 garlic cloves, minced
5½ cups stewed
   tomatoes
2 1-lb. cans kidney
   beans, undrained
1½-2 cups raisins
¼ cup wine vinegar

1 Tbsp. chopped
   parsley
2 tsp. salt
1½ tsp. dried oregano
1½ tsp. cumin
¼ tsp. pepper
¼ tsp. Tabasco sauce
1 bay leaf
¾ cup cashews
1 cup grated cheese,
*optional*

1. Combine all ingredients except cashews and cheese in slow cooker.
2. Cover. Simmer on Low 8 hours. Add cashews and simmer 30 minutes more.
3. Garnish individual servings with grated cheese.

1. Combine all ingredients in slow cooker.
2. Cover. Cook on Low 9 hours, or until vegetables are as tender as you like them.

Variation:
Add cooked pasta after soup is done cooking.

*When guests visit I provide a set of slippers for each one to keep their feet toasty and more comfortable. I invite them to keep them when they leave.*

*Donna Conto, Saylorsburg, PA*

# Wintertime Vegetable Chili

### Maricarol Magill
### Freehold, NJ

*Makes 6 servings*

*Prep. Time: 20 minutes*
*Cooking Time: 6-8 hours*
*Ideal slow cooker size: 6-qt.*

1 medium butternut
   squash, peeled and
   cubed
2 medium carrots, peeled
   and diced
1 medium onion, diced
3 tsp.—3 Tbsp. chili
   powder, depending upon
   how hot you like your
   chili
2 14-oz. cans diced
   tomatoes
4¼-oz. can chopped mild
   green chilies, drained
1 tsp. salt, *optional*
1 cup vegetable broth
2 16-oz. cans black beans,
   drained and rinsed
sour cream, *optional*

1. In slow cooker, layer all ingredients, except sour cream, in order given.
2. Cover. Cook on Low 6-8 hours, or until vegetables are as tender as you want.
3. Stir before serving.
4. Top individual servings with dollops of sour cream.

*Serving suggestion: Serve with crusty **French bread**.*

# Your-Choice-of-Vegetables Soup

**Dawn Day**
Westminster, CA

*Makes 6-8 servings*

*Prep. Time: 10 minutes*
*Cooking Time: 6 hours*
*Ideal slow cooker size: 4- to 5-qt.*

4 cups vegetable, beef, *or*
  chicken stock
4 cups vegetables (use
  any or all of corn, peas,
  carrots, broccoli, green
  beans, cauliflower,
  mushrooms), either fresh
  *or* frozen
leftover cooked meat, cut
  in small pieces, *or* 1 lb.
  cubed beef, browned in
  oil in skillet
15-oz. can chopped
  tomatoes
1 bay leaf
¼ cup uncooked long-
  grain rice *or* small pearl
  barley, *or* ½ cup cooked
  orzo *or* small shells

1. Combine all ingredients
in slow cooker except rice,
barley, or pasta.
2. Cover. Cook on Low 6
hours.
3. One hour before end of
cooking time, stir in rice or
barley. Or 30 minutes before
end of cooking time, stir in
cooked pasta.

**Note:**
*Serve with rolls and a salad
for a great comfort meal.*

# Homemade Vegetable Soup

**Audrey Romonosky**
Austin, TX

*Makes 6-8 servings*

*Prep. Time: 15 minutes*
*Cooking Time: 6-8 hours*
*Ideal slow cooker size: 4-qt.*

1 lb. stewing meat, cut into
  pieces
1 bay leaf
1 small onion, diced
3 carrots, sliced
2 ribs celery, sliced
2-3 potatoes, diced
14½-oz. can stewed
  tomatoes, cut up
8-oz. can tomato sauce
¼ cup frozen corn
½ cup frozen green beans
¼ cup frozen peas
¼ cup chopped cabbage
salt to taste
pepper to taste

1. Combine all ingredients
in slow cooker. Add water to
cover ingredients.
2. Cover. Cook on Low
6-8 hours, or until meat and
vegetables are as tender as
you like them.

# Stay-in-Bed Stew

**Janie Steele**
Moore, OK

**Judy Newman**
St. Mary's, Ontario, Canada

*Makes 6 servings*

*Prep. Time: 20 minutes*
*Cooking Time: 5-6 hours*
*Ideal slow cooker size: 3-qt.*

1 lb. chuck stewing meat
1 large onion, chunked
2 potatoes, peeled and
  diced large
4 carrots, peeled and sliced
10¾-oz. can tomato soup
½ soup can water
dash of pepper
½ tsp. salt
1 bay leaf
1 cup frozen peas

1. Put all ingredients
except peas in slow cooker.
2. Cover. Cook on Low 5-6
hours, or until vegetables are
as tender as you like them.
3. Add peas ½ hour before
serving.
4. Remove bay leaf before
serving.

# Beef Dumpling Soup

Barbara Walker
Sturgis, SD

*Makes 5-6 servings*

*Prep. Time: 10-15 minutes*
*Cooking Time: 4½-6½ hours*
*Ideal slow cooker size: 4-qt.*

1 lb. beef stewing meat, cubed
1 envelope dry onion soup mix
6 cups hot water
2 carrots, peeled and shredded
1 celery rib, finely chopped
1 tomato, peeled and chopped
1 cup buttermilk biscuit mix
1 Tbsp. finely chopped parsley
6 Tbsp. milk

1. Place meat in slow cooker. Sprinkle with onion soup mix. Pour water over meat.
2. Add carrots, celery, and tomato.
3. Cover. Cook on Low 4-6 hours, or until meat is tender.
4. Combine biscuit mix and parsley in bowl. Stir in milk with fork until moistened. Drop dumplings by teaspoonfuls into cooker.
5. Cover. Cook on High 30 minutes.

Variation:
Increase flavor of broth by adding 2 cloves garlic, ½ tsp. dried basil, and ¼ tsp. dill weed in Step 2.

# Easy Hamburger Vegetable Soup

Winifred Paul
Scottdale, PA

*Makes 8-10 servings*

*Prep. Time: 20 minutes*
*Cooking Time: 8-10 hours*
*Ideal slow cooker size: 5-qt.*

1 lb. ground beef
oil
1 cup chopped onions
15-oz. can kidney beans, *or* butter beans, undrained
1 cup sliced carrots
¼ cup long-grain rice, uncooked
1 qt. stewed tomatoes
3½ cups water
5 beef bouillon cubes
1 Tbsp. parsley flakes
1 tsp. salt
⅛ tsp. pepper
¼ tsp. dried basil
1 bay leaf

1. Brown ground beef in skillet in oil if needed. Stir frequently to break up clumps of meat. Cook until meat is no longer pink. Drain off drippings.
2. Place meat in cooker, along with all other ingredients.
3. Cover. Cook on Low 8-10 hours.

Tip:
Add more herbs and additional seasonings for zestier flavor in Step 2.

# Ruth's Ground Beef Vegetable Soup

Ruth Ann Penner
Hillsboro, KS

*Makes 6 servings*

*Prep. Time: 15 minutes*
*Cooking Time: 8-10 hours*
*Ideal slow cooker size: 5-qt.*

1 lb. ground beef
1½ qts. water
¾ cup chopped celery
1 cup chopped carrots
1 large onion, chopped
2 cups cubed potatoes
1½ tsp. salt
½ cup long-grain rice, uncooked
¼ tsp. pepper
10¾-oz. can tomato soup

1. Crumble ground beef into slow cooker. Add water.
2. Add remaining ingredients except soup. Mix together well.
3. Cover. Cook on Low 8-10 hours.
4. Add soup 30 minutes before serving and stir through.

# Beef Barley Soup

**Michelle Showalter**
Bridgewater, VA

*Makes 10-12 servings*

**Prep. Time:** *15 minutes*
**Cooking Time:** *4-10 hours*
**Ideal slow cooker size:** *6-qt.*

1 lb. ground beef
1½ qts. water
1 qt. canned tomatoes,
   stewed, crushed, *or* whole
3 cups sliced carrots
1 cup diced celery
1 cup diced potatoes
1 cup diced onions
¾ cup quick-cooking barley
3 tsp. beef bouillon granules,
   *or* 3 beef bouillon cubes
2-3 tsp. salt
¼ tsp. pepper

1. Brown ground beef in skillet in oil if needed. Stir frequently to break up clumps of meat. When meat is no longer pink, drain off drippings.

2. Place meat in cooker, along with all other ingredients. Mix together well.

3. Cover. Cook on Low 8-10 hours or on High 4-5 hours.

*Serving suggestion: Serve with fresh* **bread** *and* **cheese cubes**.

**Variation:**

You may use pearl barley instead of quick-cooking barley. Cook it in a saucepan according to package directions, and add halfway through Soup's cooking time.

# Easy Veggie-Beef Soup

**Rebecca Plank Leichty**
Harrisonburg, VA

*Makes 6-8 servings*

**Prep. Time:** *20 minutes*
**Cooking Time:** *4-8 hours*
**Ideal slow cooker size:** *5-qt.*

1 lb. ground beef, *or* 2 cups
   stewing beef
2 cups sliced carrots
1 lb. frozen green beans,
   thawed
14½-oz. can corn, drained,
   *or* 16-oz. bag frozen corn,
   thawed
28-oz. can diced tomatoes
3 cups beef, *or* veggie,
   broth
3 tsp. instant beef bouillon
2 tsp. Worcestershire sauce
1 Tbsp. sugar
1 Tbsp. minced onion
10¾-oz. can cream of
   celery soup

1. If using ground beef, place in skillet with a bit of oil if needed. Brown, stirring frequently to break up clumps. When no longer pink, drain off drippings.

2. Place meat in slow cooker.

3. Add all remaining ingredients except celery soup. Mix well.

4. Stir in soup.

5. Cover. Cook on Low 7-8 hours or on High 4 hours.

6. If using stewing meat, shred and mix through soup just before serving.

*Serving suggestion: Serve with freshly baked* **bread** *and homemade* **jam**.

**Note:**

*Two modern-day conveniences —the slow cooker and bread machine—allow me to prepare tasty meals without too much last-minute dashing around. Utilizing both gives me time to plan table settings and decorations, too.*

*Make sure your invitations inform your guests about whether your party is informal or formal. It's really uncomfortable to be over-dressed at an informal party or vice versa.*

Anita Troyer, Fairview, MI

# Hamburger Soup

**Naomi Ressler**
Harrisonburg, VA
**Kay Magruder**
Seminole, OK

*Makes 8 servings*

*Prep. Time: 20 minutes*
*Cooking Time: 3-10 hours*
*Ideal slow cooker size: 4-qt.*

1½ lbs. ground beef
oil
1 medium onion, chopped
1 cup sliced carrots
1 cup sliced celery
1 cup sliced cabbage
6-oz. can tomato paste
2 tsp. Worcestershire sauce
2-3 cups beef broth,
   depending upon how
   thick or thin you like
   your soup

1. Brown ground beef in skillet in oil if needed. Stir frequently in order to break up clumps of meat. When beef is no longer pink, drain off drippings.
2. Combine beef, onions, carrots, celery, and cabbage in slow cooker.
3. Combine tomato paste, Worcestershire sauce, and broth in bowl. When blended, pour into slow cooker. Mix with other ingredients.
4. Cover. Cook on Low 8-10 hours or on High 3-4 hours.

Variation:
Stir in ¼ tsp. black, *or* cayenne, pepper and 2 bay leaves in Step 3 for added flavor.

# Ground Beef Soup

**Nadine L. Martinitz**
Salina, KS

*Makes 6-8 servings*

*Prep. Time: 15-20 minutes*
*Cooking Time: 7-9 hours*
*Ideal slow cooker size: 4- to 5-qt.*

1 lb. ground beef
1 medium onion, chopped
1 Tbsp. oil
15½-oz. can great northern
   beans, undrained
15-oz. can tomato sauce
1½-2 tomato-sauce cans
   water
2 large potatoes, cubed
14½-oz. can tomatoes
1 tsp. salt

1. Brown ground beef and onions in oil in skillet. Stir frequently, breaking up clumps of meat. When meat is no longer pink, drain off drippings.
2. Place beef and onions in slow cooker. Stir in remaining ingredients.
3. Cook on High 1 hour, and then on Low 6-8 hours.

*Serving suggestion: Serve with **grilled cheese sandwiches.***

# Hamburger Vegetable Soup

**Joyce Shackelford**
Green Bay, WI

*Makes 8-10 servings*

*Prep. Time: 20 minutes*
*Cooking Time: 8-9 hours*
*Ideal slow cooker size: 5-qt.*

1 lb. ground chuck
1 onion, chopped
2 garlic cloves, minced
oil
4 cups V-8 juice
14½-oz. can stewed
   tomatoes
2 cups cole slaw mix
2 cups frozen green beans
2 cups frozen corn
2 Tbsp. Worcestershire
   sauce
1 tsp. dried basil
½ tsp. salt
¼ tsp. pepper

1. Brown beef, onion, and garlic in skillet in oil. Stir frequently to break up clumps of meat. When meat is no longer pink, drain off drippings.
2. Transfer beef and vegetables to slow cooker.
3. Add all remaining ingredients and combine.
4. Cover. Cook on Low 8-9 hours, or until vegetables are as tender as you like them.

# Snowmobile Soup

**Jane Geigley**
Honey Brook, PA

*Makes 4-6 servings*

**Prep. Time: 20 minutes**
**Cooking Time: 3-4 hours**
**Ideal slow cooker size: 4- to 6-qt.**

1 lb. ground beef
1 small onion, chopped
5 large potatoes, julienned
   like French fries (you
   can leave the skins on)
10¾-oz. can cream of
   mushroom soup
1 soup can milk
2 lbs. shredded cheddar
   cheese
1 tsp. salt
¼ tsp. pepper

1. Brown beef in skillet.
Stir frequently to break up
clumps. When meat is no
longer pink, drain off all but
2 Tbsp. drippings.
2. Place browned beef in
slow cooker.
3. Sauté onion in drippings
in skillet until softened.
4. Stir onions, potatoes,
soup, milk, cheese, salt, and
pepper into meat in slow
cooker.
5. Cover. Cook on High 3-4
hours, or until potatoes are as
soft as you like them.

# Taco Soup with Corn

**Suzanne Slagel**
Midway, OH

*Makes 6-8 servings*

**Prep. Time: 15 minutes**
**Cooking Time: 4-6 hours**
**Ideal slow cooker size: 5- to 6-qt.**

1 lb. ground beef
1 large onion, chopped
oil
16-oz. can Mexican-style
   tomatoes
16-oz. can ranch-style
   beans
16-oz. can whole-kernel
   corn, undrained
16-oz. can kidney beans,
   undrained
16-oz. can black beans,
   undrained
16-oz. jar picante sauce
corn, *or* tortilla, chips
sour cream
shredded cheddar cheese

1. Brown meat and onions
in skillet in oil if needed.
Stir frequently to break up
clumps of meat. When meat
is no longer pink, drain off
drippings.
2. Place meat and onions
in slow cooker. Add other
vegetables and picante sauce.
Stir well.
3. Cover. Cook on Low 4-6
hours.

*Serving suggestion: Serve
with **corn** or **tortilla chips**,
**sour cream**, and **shredded
cheese** as toppings.*

# Taco Soup with Hominy

**Sue Tjon**
Austin, TX

*Makes 8 servings*

**Prep. Time: 15 minutes**
**Cooking Time: 4 hours**
**Ideal slow cooker size: 6-qt.**

1 lb. ground beef
oil
1 envelope dry ranch
   dressing mix
1 envelope dry taco
   seasoning mix
3 12-oz. cans Rotel
   tomatoes, undrained
2 24-oz. cans pinto beans,
   undrained
24-oz. can hominy,
   undrained
14½-oz. can stewed
   tomatoes, undrained
1 onion, chopped
2 cups water

1. Brown meat in skillet
in oil if needed. Stir frequently to break up clumps
of meat. When meat is no
longer pink, drain off drippings.
2. Spoon meat into slow
cooker. Add all remaining
ingredients. Mix well.
3. Cover. Cook on Low
4 hours.

*Serving suggestion: Line
each individual soup bowl with
**tortilla chips**. Then ladle Taco
Soup on top and sprinkle with
**grated cheese**.*

**Tip:**

Increase or decrease the amount of water you add to make the dish either stew-like or soup-like.

# Slow-Cooker Chili

**Kay Magruder**
Seminole, OK

*Makes 8-10 servings*

*Prep. Time: 25 minutes*
*Cooking Time: 6-12 hours*
*Ideal slow cooker size: 6-qt.*

3 lbs. stewing meat
2 cloves garlic, minced
¼ tsp. pepper
½ tsp. cumin
¼ tsp. dry mustard
7½-oz. can jalapeño relish
1 cup beef broth
1-1½ onions, chopped, according to your taste preference
½ tsp. salt
½ tsp. dried oregano
1 Tbsp. chili powder
7-oz. can green chilies, chopped
14½-oz. can stewed tomatoes, chopped
15-oz. can tomato sauce
2 15-oz. cans red kidney beans, rinsed and drained
2 15-oz. cans pinto beans, rinsed and drained

1. Combine all ingredients except kidney and pinto beans in slow cooker.
2. Cover. Cook on Low 10-12 hours or on High 6-7 hours. Add beans halfway through cooking time.

*Serving suggestion: Serve with* **Mexican cornbread**.

# Chili Con Carne Supreme

**Jane Geigley**
Honey Brook, PA

*Makes 8 servings*

*Prep. Time: 30-35 minutes*
*Cooking Time: 2 hours*
*Ideal slow cooker size: 4-qt.*

2 lbs. ground beef
2 Tbsp. olive oil
2 garlic cloves, minced, *optional*
2 medium onions, chopped
1 green bell pepper, chopped
3 beef bouillon cubes
1 cup boiling water
1½ tsp. salt
2 Tbsp. chili powder
1 tsp. ground cumin
2 tsp. dried oregano
¼ tsp. ground cinnamon
⅛ tsp. cayenne pepper
2 16-oz. cans stewed, *or* diced, tomatoes with liquid
15½-oz. can kidney beans, undrained

1. Brown ground beef in large skillet in oil. Stir frequently to break up clumps. When no longer pink, reserve drippings. Spoon meat into slow cooker.
2. In skillet drippings, sauté garlic, onions, and green peppers over low heat until onions are tender. Spoon veggies into slow cooker.
3. Dissolve bouillon cubes in boiling water. Pour into slow cooker.
4. Add rest of ingredients to slow cooker. Stir together until well mixed.
5. Cover. Cook on Low 2 hours.

*We always have chili on Christmas Eve. We all enjoy a no-stress meal.*
*Nancy Wagner Graves, Manhattan, KS*

# Our Favorite Chili

**Ruth Shank**
Gridley, IL

*Makes 10-12 servings*

*Prep. Time: 20 minutes*
*Cooking Time: 4-10 hours*
*Ideal slow cooker size: 5-qt.*

1½ lbs. ground beef
¼ cup chopped onions
1 rib celery, chopped
oil
29-oz. can stewed tomatoes
2 15½-oz. cans red kidney
   beans, undrained
2 16-oz. cans chili beans,
   undrained
½ cup ketchup
1½ tsp. lemon juice
2 tsp. vinegar
1½ tsp. brown sugar
1½ tsp. salt
1 tsp. Worcestershire sauce
½ tsp. garlic powder
½ tsp. dry mustard powder
1 Tbsp. chili powder
2 6-oz. cans tomato paste

1. Brown ground beef,
onions, and celery in skillet
in oil if needed. Stir frequently to break up clumps of
meat. When meat is no longer
pink, drain off drippings.
2. Place meat and veg-
etables in slow cooker. Add
all remaining ingredients.
Mix well.
3. Cover. Cook on Low 8-10
hours or on High 4-5 hours.

*Serving suggestion: Serve*
*with fresh warm **cornbread***
*and slices of **Colby** or*
***Monterey Jack cheese.***

# Slow-Cooked Chili

**Jean A. Shaner**
York, PA

*Makes 10 servings*

*Prep. Time: 20 minutes*
*Cooking Time: 8-10 hours*
*Ideal slow cooker size: 5-qt.*

2 lbs. ground beef
oil
2 16-oz. cans kidney beans,
   rinsed and drained
2 14½-oz. cans diced
   tomatoes
8-oz. can tomato sauce
2 onions, chopped
1 green bell pepper,
   chopped
2 garlic cloves, minced
2 Tbsp. chili powder
2 tsp. salt
1 tsp. pepper
shredded cheddar cheese

1. Brown ground beef in
skillet in oil if needed. Stir
frequently to break up clumps
of meat. When no longer
pink, drain off drippings.
2. Spoon meat into slow
cooker. Add all other ingredients to cooker, except cheese.
Stir together well.
3. Cover. Cook on Low 8-10
hours.
4. Ladle chili into indi-
vidual bowls and top with
cheese just before serving.

# Chili Soup

**Glenna Fay Bergey**
Lebanon, OR

*Makes 5 qts.*

*Prep. Time: 25 minutes*
*Cooking Time: 2-6 hours*
*Ideal slow cooker size: 2 4- to*
   *5-qt.*

3 lbs. ground beef
¾ cup chopped onions
2 Tbsp. celery flakes
2 tsp. salt
1 Tbsp. chili powder, *or*
   more, according to your
   taste preferences
oil
3 15-oz. cans kidney beans,
   drained
1 qt. tomato juice
2 10¾-oz. cans tomato soup
1 cup ketchup
¼ cup brown sugar

1. Brown meat, onions, and
seasonings in large skillet in
oil if needed. Stir frequently
to break up clumps of meat.
When meat is no longer pink,
drain off drippings.
2. Transfer mixture to slow
cooker. Stir in all remaining
ingredients.
3. Divide between 2 4- or
5-qt. slow cookers. (This is a
large recipe!)
4. Cover. Cook on High 2
hours or on Low 4-6 hours.

*Serving suggestion: Serve*
*with **cornbread**.*

# Country Auction Chili Soup

**Clara Newswanger**
Gordonville, PA

*Makes 20 servings*

*Prep. Time: 25 minutes*
*Cooking Time: 4-8 hours*
*Ideal slow cooker size: 6-qt.*

1½ lbs. ground beef
¼ cup chopped onions
oil
½ cup flour
1 Tbsp. chili powder
1 tsp. salt
6 cups water
2 cups ketchup
⅓ cup brown sugar
3 15½-oz. cans kidney
    beans, undrained

1. Brown ground beef and onions in skillet in oil if needed. Stir frequently to break up clumps of meat. When no longer pink, drain off drippings.
2. Spoon meat mixture into slow cooker. Stir flour into meat and onions. Add seasonings.
3. Slowly stir in water. Add ketchup, brown sugar, and beans.
4. Cover. Cook on High 4 hours or on Low 8 hours.

# Hot and Good Chili

**Rose Hankins**
Stevensville, MD

*Makes 12 servings*

*Prep. Time: 20 minutes*
*Cooking Time: 4-10 hours*
*Ideal slow cooker size: 5-qt.*

1 lb. ground beef
oil
1 cup chopped onions
1 cup chopped celery
1 cup chopped green bell
    peppers
28-oz. can tomatoes,
    broken up
14-oz. can tomato sauce
2 14-oz. cans kidney
    beans, undrained
2 Tbsp. chili powder
1 Tbsp. garlic powder
1 Tbsp. hot sauce

1. Brown beef in skillet in oil if needed. Stir frequently, breaking up clumps of meat. When meat is no longer pink, transfer meat to slow cooker. Reserve drippings
2. Sauté onions, celery, and green peppers in drippings until just wilted. Drain and transfer to slow cooker.
3. Stir in remaining ingredients.
4. Cover. Cook on High 4-5 hours or on Low 8-10 hours.

# Slowly Cooked Chili

**Beatrice Martin**
Goshen, IN

*Makes 6-8 servings*

*Prep. Time: 20 minutes*
*Cooking Time: 5-12 hours*
*Ideal slow cooker size: 4-qt.*

2 lbs. ground beef, *or* turkey
oil
15½-oz. can kidney beans,
    undrained
3 cups tomato juice
3 Tbsp. chili powder
1 tsp. minced garlic
1 envelope dry onion soup
    mix
½-1 tsp. salt, according to
    taste
¼ tsp. pepper

1. Brown ground beef or turkey in skillet in oil if needed. Stir frequently, breaking up clumps of meat. When meat is no longer pink, drain off drippings.
2. Place browned meat in cooker. Stir in all remaining ingredients with meat.
3. Cover. Cook on Low 10-12 hours or on High 5-6 hours.

*Serving suggestion: Serve in soup bowls with **crackers**, or over **rice**.*

Tip:
    This chili freezes well.

*Have everyone bring a dish of food, plus its printed recipe to share.*
        *Nancy Wagner Graves, Manhattan, KS*

# Three-Bean Chili

**Chris Kaczynski**
Schenectady, NY

*Makes 8-10 servings*

*Prep. Time: 25 minutes*
*Cooking Time: 8-10 hours*
*Ideal slow cooker size: 6-qt. or
2 4- to 5-qt.*

2 lbs. ground beef
2 medium onions, diced
oil
16-oz. jar medium salsa
2 envelopes dry chili
  seasoning
2 16-oz. cans red kidney
  beans, drained
2 16-oz. cans black beans,
  drained
2 16-oz. cans white kidney,
  *or* garbanzo, beans
  drained
28-oz. can crushed tomatoes
16-oz. can diced tomatoes
2 tsp. sugar

1. Brown beef and onions
in skillet in oil if needed. Stir
frequently, breaking up clumps
of meat. When beef is no longer
pink, drain off drippings.
2. Spoon beef into slow
cooker. Add all remaining
ingredients to beef.
3. Cover. Cook on Low 8-10
hours.

*Serving suggestion: Serve
with **chopped raw onion** and/
or **shredded cheddar cheese**
as toppings.*

**Tip:**
This recipe can be cut
in half without injuring its

flavor if you don't have a
single cooker, or multiple
cookers, large enough to
handle the full amount.

# Hearty Chili

**Joylynn Keener**
Lancaster, PA

*Makes 8 servings*

*Prep. Time: 20-25 minutes*
*Cooking Time: 8 hours*
*Ideal slow cooker size: 5-qt.*

1 onion, chopped
2 ribs celery, chopped
1 lb. ground beef
oil
2 14-oz. cans kidney
  beans, undrained
14-oz. can pinto beans,
  undrained
14-oz. can diced tomatoes
2 14-oz. cans tomato sauce
1 green bell pepper, chopped
1 Tbsp. sugar
1 tsp. salt
1 tsp. dried thyme
1 tsp. dried oregano
1 Tbsp. chili powder, *or* to
  taste

1. Brown onion, celery, and
beef in skillet in oil if needed.
Stir frequently to break up
clumps of meat. When meat
is no longer pink, drain off
drippings.
2. Spoon meat into slow
cooker. Stir in all remaining
ingredients, mixing well.
3. Cover. Cook on Low 8
hours.

# So Easy Chili

**Sue Graber**
Eureka, IL

*Makes 4 servings*

*Prep. Time: 15 minutes*
*Cooking Time: 4-6 hours*
*Ideal slow cooker size: 3½-qt.*

1 lb. ground beef
1 onion, chopped
oil
15-oz. can chili, with *or*
  without beans
14½-oz. can diced tomatoes
  with green chilies, *or*
  with basil, garlic, and
  oregano
1 cup tomato juice
chopped onion
grated cheddar cheese

1. Brown ground beef
and onion in skillet in oil,
if needed. Stir frequently to
break up clumps of meat.
When meat is no longer pink,
drain off drippings.
2. Spoon meat into slow
cooker.
3. Stir in chili, diced
tomatoes, and tomato juice.
4. Cover. Cook on Low 4-6
hours.

*Serving suggestion: Serve
with **onions** and **cheese** as
toppings for individual servings.*

**Tips:**
1. This chili is a good
consistency for serving over
rice.
2. For a thicker chili, add 4-6
oz. tomato paste 20 minutes
before end of cooking time.

# The Chili Connection

**Anne Townsend**
Albuquerque, NM

*Makes 6 servings*

**Prep. Time: 15-20 minutes**
**Cooking Time: 3-5 hours**
**Ideal slow cooker size: 3½-qt.**

1½ lbs. ground beef
1 cup chopped onions
oil
28-oz. can tomatoes, chopped
15-oz. can kidney beans, undrained
1 Tbsp. brown, *or* granulated, sugar
2-4 tsp. chili powder, according to your taste preference
1 tsp. salt

1. Brown ground beef and onions in skillet in oil if needed. Stir frequently to break up clumps of meat. When meat is no longer pink, drain off drippings.
2. Spoon meat and onions into slow cooker. Stir in all other ingredients.
3. Cover. Cook on Low 3-5 hours.

Variation:

In order to have a thicker chili, stir in a 6-oz. can tomato paste in Step 2.

Tips:

*An assortment of toppings can take the place of a salad with this chili. I usually offer chopped onions, tomatoes, grated cheddar cheese, picante sauce, and, when avocados are in season, guacamole.*

*Cornbread or refrigerated twist rolls sprinkled with garlic salt are delicious. Either chocolate or apple cake with ice cream makes a happy ending.*

*This is a fun informal party dish which connects the guests as they get involved in selecting their favorite toppings.*

*As a frequently enjoyed dish, this recipe has stood the test of time. Our children thought it was delicious when they were young and now they enjoy preparing it for their own families.*

# Extra Easy Chili

**Jennifer Gehman**
Harrisburg, PA

*Makes 4-6 servings*

**Prep. Time: 5-10 minutes**
**Cooking Time: 3-8 hours**
**Ideal slow cooker size: 4-qt.**

1 lb. ground beef, *or* turkey
1 envelope dry chili seasoning mix
16-oz. can chili beans in sauce
2 28-oz. cans crushed, *or* diced, tomatoes seasoned with garlic and onion

1. Crumble meat into slow cooker.
2. Stir in remaining ingredients.

3. Cover. Cook on High 3-4 hours or on Low 6-8 hours. Stir halfway through cooking time.

*Serving suggestion: Serve over **white rice**, topped with **shredded cheddar cheese** and **chopped raw onions**.*

Note:

*I decided to make this Chili recipe one year for Christmas. Our family was hosting other family members—and we had had guests for about a week prior to Christmas.*

*Needless to say, I was tired of cooking so this seemed easy enough. It was so nice to put the ingredients in the slow cooker and let it cook all day long. Not only did the Chili warm us up on a cold day, but it was a welcomed change from the traditional Christmas meal. It has been my tradition ever since!*

# Grandma's Chili

Beverly Flatt-Getz
Warriors Mark, PA

*Makes 8 servings*

*Prep. Time: 20 minutes*
*Cooking Time: 4 hours*
*Ideal slow cooker size: 5-qt.*

1 large onion, chopped
2 lbs. ground beef
oil
28-oz. can stewed tomatoes
16-oz. can dark kidney
  beans, undrained
15-oz. can chili with beans
10¾-oz. can tomato soup
1 tsp. K.C. Masterpiece
  BBQ sauce
¼ tsp. garlic salt
¼ tsp. garlic powder
¼ tsp. onion salt
¼ tsp. chili powder
pinch of sugar

1. Brown onion and beef
in skillet in oil, if needed.
Stir meat frequently to make
sure it's browning evenly, but
leave meat in larger chunks.
When meat is no longer pink,
drain off drippings.

2. Spoon meat and onion
into slow cooker. Stir in
remaining ingredients.

3. Cover. Cook on High 4
hours.

*Serving suggestion: Serve*
*with **crackers**, **rolls**, **butter**,*
*and **apple crisp** with **whipped***
***topping**.*

Note:
*When the grandchildren*
*come to visit from five different*
*states, they always ask for*
*Grandma's Chili. I just made*
*up the recipe. Now I'm afraid to*
*change it!*

# Hearty Potato Chili

Janice Muller
Derwood, MD

*Makes 8 servings*

*Prep. Time: 20-25 minutes*
*Cooking Time: 4 hours*
*Ideal slow cooker size: 5-qt.*

1 lb. ground beef
oil
½ cup chopped onions
½ cup chopped green bell
  pepper
1 Tbsp. poppy seeds,
  *optional*
1 tsp. salt
½ tsp. chili powder
1 pkg. au gratin, *or*
  scalloped, potato mix
1 cup hot water
15-oz. can kidney beans,
  undrained
16-oz. can stewed tomatoes
4-oz. can mushroom
  pieces, undrained

1. Brown ground beef
in skillet in oil, if needed.
Stir frequently, breaking up
clumps of meat. When meat
is no longer pink, spoon into
slow cooker. Reserve drippings.

2. Sauté onions and green
peppers in drippings until
softened.

3. Place sautéed vegetables,
along with all other ingredients in slow cooker. Mix
together well.

4. Cover. Cook on High
4 hours, or until liquid is
absorbed and potatoes are
tender.

# Spicy Chili

Deborah Swartz
Grottoes, VA

*Makes 4-6 servings*

*Prep. Time: 20 minutes*
*Cooking Time: 2-3 hours*
*Ideal slow cooker size: 3½-qt.*

½ lb. sausage, either cut in
  thin slices or removed
  from casings
½ lb. ground beef
½ cup chopped onions
½ lb. fresh mushrooms,
  sliced
⅛ cup chopped celery
⅛ cup chopped green bell
  peppers
1 cup salsa
16-oz. can tomato juice
6-oz. can tomato paste
½ tsp. sugar
½ tsp. salt
½ tsp. dried oregano
½ tsp. Worcestershire
  sauce
¼ tsp. dried basil
¼ tsp. pepper

1. Brown sausage, ground
beef, and onions in skillet.
Stir frequently to break up
clumps of meat.

2. During last 3 minutes of

browning, add mushrooms, celery, and green peppers. Continue cooking; then drain off drippings.

3. Spoon meat and sautéed vegetables into cooker. Stir in remaining ingredients.

3. Cover. Cook on High 2-3 hours.

Variations:

Add any or all of the following to Step 3:

1 tsp. chili powder
1 tsp. ground cumin
15-oz. can black beans, undrained
15-oz. can whole-kernel corn, undrained

# M&T's Chili

**Sherry Conyers**
McPherson, KS

*Makes 4 servings*

*Prep. Time: 20 minutes*
*Cooking Time: 5-6 hours*
*Ideal slow cooker size: 5-qt.*

1 lb. ground beef
½ lb. sausage links, sliced
1 envelope Williams chili seasoning
2 10-oz. cans Mexican tomatoes
15-oz. can chili with no beans
2 10-oz. cans Rotel tomatoes
1-lb. can refried beans
¼ cup diced onions

1. Brown beef and sliced sausage in skillet. Stir frequently to break up clumps of beef. When meat is no longer pink, drain off drippings.

2. Spoon meats into cooker. Stir in all additional ingredients.

3. Cover. Cook on Low 5-6 hours.

Variation:

If you want a soupier and less spicy chili, add a 1-lb. can of stewed tomatoes or 2 cups tomato juice in Step 2.

# Black Bean Chili Con Carne

**Janie Steele**
Moore, OK

*Makes 18 1-cup servings*

*Prep. Time: 25-30 minutes*
*Soaking Time: 8 hours, or overnight*
*Cooking Time: 8 hours*
*Ideal slow cooker size: 6-qt. or 2 4- to 5-qt. cookers*

1 lb. dry black beans
3 lbs. ground beef
oil
2 large onions, chopped
1 green bell pepper, chopped
3 cloves garlic, minced
2 tsp. salt
1 tsp. pepper
6-oz. can tomato paste
3 cups tomato juice, *or* more
1 tsp. celery salt

1 Tbsp. Worcestershire sauce
1 tsp. dry mustard
cayenne pepper to taste
cumin to taste
3 Tbsp. chili powder

1. Place beans in slow cooker. Cover with water. Soak 8 hours or overnight.

2. Rinse beans and drain. Return soaked beans to slow cooker.

3. Brown ground beef in batches in large skillet in oil, if needed. Stir frequently to break up clumps of meat. When beef is no longer pink, drain off drippings.

4. Spoon meat into slow cooker with beans.

5. Mix in all remaining ingredients.

6. Cover. Cook on Low 8 hours.

*Serving suggestion: Serve over **salad greens** or wrapped in **tortillas**, topped with **lettuce** and **grated cheese**.*

# Beef Tortellini Soup

**Char Hagner**
Montague, MI

*Makes 6 servings*

*Prep. Time: 30 minutes*
*Cooking Time: 8 hours*
*Ideal slow cooker size: 4- to 5-qt.*

1 lb. ground beef
oil

28-oz. can stewed, *or* diced, tomatoes
10½-oz. can condensed French onion soup
9-oz. pkg. frozen green beans
9-oz. pkg. cheese tortellini
1 tsp. dried basil
1 medium zucchini, chopped
½-¾ tsp. salt
¼ tsp. pepper
3½ cups water

1. Brown beef in a skillet in oil, if needed. Stir frequently to break up clumps.

When meat is no longer pink, drain off drippings.

2. Place meat in slow cooker. Stir in all other ingredients.

3. Cover. Cook on Low 8 hours.

# Sausage, Tomato, Spinach Soup

**Wendy B. Martzall**, New Holland, PA

*Makes 6-8 servings*

*Prep. Time: 15-20 minutes • Cooking Time: 5 hours*
*Ideal slow cooker size: 3- to 4-qt.*

½ lb. loose pork, *or* turkey, sausage
1 medium onion, chopped
1 small green bell pepper, chopped
28-oz. can diced tomatoes
2 14½-oz. cans beef broth
8-oz. can tomato sauce
½ cup picante sauce
1½ tsp. sugar
1 tsp. dried basil
½ tsp. dried oregano
10-oz. pkg. frozen spinach, thawed and squeezed dry
½-¾ cup shredded mozzarella cheese

1. Brown sausage with onions and peppers in skillet. (If you use turkey sausage, you'll probably need to add 1-2 Tbsp. oil to the pan.) Stir frequently, breaking up clumps of meat. When meat is no longer pink, drain off drippings.

2. Spoon meat and vegetables into slow cooker.

3. Add all remaining ingredients except spinach and cheese. Stir until well blended.

4. Cover. Cook on Low 4¾ hours.

5. Stir spinach into Soup. Cover and continue cooking on Low another 15 minutes.

6. Top each individual serving with a sprinkling of mozzarella cheese.

# Sausage Tortellini Soup

**Susie Shenk Wenger**
Lancaster, PA

*Makes 12-15 servings*

*Prep. Time: 20-25 minutes*
*Cooking Time: 4-5 hours*
*Ideal slow cooker size: 4-qt.*

2 lbs. sweet Italian sausage, casings removed
2-3 cups carrots, diced
1 large onion, diced
3 small zucchini, cubed
1½ cups fresh, *or* frozen, sweet corn
1 large can diced petite tomatoes with garlic and olive oil
2 10¾-oz. cans tomato soup
2 soup cans water
1 large can tomato purée
1 family-sized bag of 3-cheese frozen tortellini, cooked according to package directions
shredded cheese of your choice

1. In large skillet, brown sausage, stirring frequently to break up meat. Drain off

all but 2 Tbsp. drippings. Put sausage in slow cooker.

2. Sauté carrots and onions in sausage drippings just until softened.

3. Add carrots, onions, zucchini, corn, tomatoes, tomato soup, water and tomato purée to slow cooker. Stir until well mixed.

4. Cover. Cook on High 1 hour. Stir.

5. Cover. Cook on Low 3 hours, or until vegetables are softened.

6. Just before serving, stir in cooked tortellini.

*Serving suggestion: Serve steaming hot with **shredded cheddar cheese** sprinkled over each individual bowl of soup.*

Note:

*Because we have three ovens in our home, we host a day-after-Thanksgiving cookie-bake every year at our house. Extended family join in, and we have all the ovens going full-time. This soup is always the lunch for this event. It's the fuel to keep the bakers going through the day, and it doesn't require oven space.*

# Vegetable Pork Soup

**Naomi Ressler**
Harrisonburg, VA

*Makes 6 servings*

*Prep. Time: 25-30 minutes*
*Cooking Time: 6-7 hours*
*Ideal slow cooker size: 4-qt.*

1-lb. pork tenderloin, cut into bite-sized pieces
1 tsp. garlic powder
2 tsp. oil
28-oz. can diced tomatoes
4 medium carrots, cut into bite-sized pieces
2 medium potatoes, peeled or unpeeled, cubed
14½-oz. can chicken broth
¼ cup quick-cooking tapioca
2 bay leaves
1 Tbsp. Worcestershire sauce
1 Tbsp. honey
1 tsp. dried thyme
¼ tsp. salt
¼ tsp. pepper
⅛ tsp. nutmeg

1. Sprinkle pork with garlic powder. In large skillet, brown pork in oil.

2. Transfer meat to slow cooker.

3. Stir remaining ingredients into pork.

4. Cover. Cook on Low 6-7 hours, or just until pork and vegetables are tender.

5. Discard bay leaves before serving.

# Pork Chile

**Carol Duree**
Salina, KS

*Makes 4-5 servings*

*Prep. Time: 15 minutes*
*Cooking Time: 4-8 hours*
*Ideal slow cooker size: 4-qt.*

1½-2 lbs. boneless pork ribs, *or* other cut of pork
2 14½-oz. cans fire-roasted diced tomatoes
1, *or* 2 4¼-oz. cans diced green chili peppers, drained
½ cup chopped onion
1, *or* 2 cloves garlic, minced
salt and pepper to taste
1 Tbsp. chili powder, *or* to taste

1. Layer ingredients into slow cooker in order given.

2. Cover. Cook on High 4 hours or on Low 6-8 hours, or until pork is tender but not dry.

3. Cut up or shred meat. Stir through chile and serve.

Notes:

1. You can serve this as soup, but we especially like it over rice.

2. You can add a 1-lb. can of your favorite chili beans 30 minutes before end of cooking time.

# Black-Eyed Pea Chili

**Lena Mae Janes**
Lane, KS

*Makes 10 servings*

*Prep. Time: 20-30 minutes*
*Cooking Time: 2 hours*
*Ideal slow cooker size: 5- to 6-qt.*

1 lb. loose pork sausage
1 medium onion, chopped
½ cup celery chopped
4 15-oz. cans black-eyed peas, undrained
14-oz. can diced tomatoes, undrained
10-oz. can diced tomatoes with green chilies, undrained
2 Tbsp. chili powder

1. Cook sausage in skillet until no longer pink, stirring frequently. Drain sausage on paper towel.
2. Discard all but 2 Tbsp. pan drippings. To these drippings, add onion and celery. Cook until translucent, stirring frequently.
3. Place peas, tomatoes, tomatoes with green chilies, cooked onions and celery, sausage, and chili powder in slow cooker. Stir well.
4. Cover. Cook on High until all ingredients are hot, about an hour. Then turn cooker to Low and cook 1 more hour.

*Serving suggestion:* **Corn-bread sticks** *are a great accompaniment to this Chili.*

**Note:**
*Black-Eyed Pea Chili, slow-cooked, is a New Year's must for our household. Black-eyed peas bring good luck, you know!*

# Asian Pork Soup

**Judi Manos**
West Islip, NY

*Makes 6 servings*

*Prep. Time: 20 minutes*
*Cooking Time: 4-10 hours*
*Ideal slow cooker size: 4-qt.*

1 lb. ground pork, chicken, or turkey
1 garlic clove, minced
oil
2 medium carrots, cut into julienne strips
4 medium green onions, cut into 1" pieces
1 garlic clove, minced
¼ cup soy sauce
½ tsp. gingerroot, chopped
⅛ tsp. pepper
49½-oz. can chicken broth
1 cup sliced mushrooms
1 cup bean sprouts

1. Cook meat with garlic in skillet in oil, if needed. Stir frequently to break up clumps of meat. When meat is no longer pink, drain off drippings.
2. Spoon meat and garlic into slow cooker. Stir in all other ingredients except mushrooms and sprouts.
3. Cover. Cook on Low 7-9

hours or on High 3-4 hours.
4. Stir in mushrooms and bean sprouts.
5. Cover. Cook on Low 1 more hour.

**Variation:**
For added flavor to the meat, add ⅛ tsp. five-spice blend to Step 2.

# Lentil Soup with Ham Bone

**Rhoda Atzeff**
Harrisburg, PA

*Makes 6-8 servings*

*Prep. Time: 15 minutes*
*Cooking Time: 8-9 hours*
*Ideal slow cooker size: 4-qt.*

1 lb. dry lentils, washed and drained
1 celery rib, chopped
1 large carrot, grated
½ cup chopped onions
1 bay leaf
¼ tsp. dried thyme
7-8 cups water
1 ham bone, ½ lb. thinly sliced kielbasa, *or* ½ lb. hot smoked sausage, sliced
¼-½ tsp. crushed red hot pepper flakes
pepper to taste
salt to taste

1. Combine all ingredients except pepper and salt in slow cooker.
2. Cover. Cook on Low 8-9 hours, or until meat and lentils are tender.

3. Remove bay leaf and ham bone. Allow ham bone to cool. Then dice meat from bone and return to cooker.

4. Season to taste with pepper and salt.

*Serving suggestion: Serve alone, or over **rice** with **grated cheese** on top.*

# Everyone's Hungry Soup

**Janie Steele**
Moore, OK

*Makes 20-25 servings*

**Prep. Time: 45 minutes**
**Cooking Time: 8-10 hours**
**Ideal slow cooker size: 2 6- to 7-qt. cookers**

6 thick slices bacon
3 lbs. boneless beef stewing meat, cubed
1 lb. boneless pork, cubed
3 14½-oz. cans stewed, *or* diced, tomatoes
10-oz. can Rotel tomatoes with chilies
3 celery ribs, chopped
3 large onions, chopped
garlic to taste
salt to taste
pepper to taste
½ cup Worcestershire sauce
2 Tbsp. chili powder
2 cups water
6-8 medium potatoes, peeled and cubed
1 lb. carrots, sliced
15-oz. can peas, undrained
14½-oz. can green beans, undrained
15¼-oz. can corn, undrained
1 lb. cut-up okra, *optional*

1. Fry bacon in skillet until crisp. Remove bacon, but reserve drippings. Crumble bacon and divide between 2 large (6-qt. or larger) slow cookers.

2. Brown stewing beef and pork in skillet in bacon drippings. Drain off drippings.

3. Divide beef and pork between two cookers.

4. In a large bowl, combine all remaining ingredients and mix well. Divide between slow cookers.

5. Stir each cooker's ingredients well. Cover. Cook on Low 8-10 hours.

*Serving suggestion: Serve with loaves of **homemade bread** or pans of **cornbread**.*

# Hamburger Sausage Soup

**Esther Becker**
Gordonville, PA

*Makes 4-6 servings*

**Prep. Time: 20-25 minutes**
**Cooking Time: 8-10 hours**
**Ideal slow cooker size: 5-qt.**

1 lb. ground beef
1 lb. Polish sausage, sliced
½ tsp. seasoning salt
¼ tsp. dried oregano
¼ tsp. dried basil
1 envelope dry onion soup mix
6 cups boiling water
16-oz. can diced tomatoes
1 Tbsp. soy sauce
½ cup sliced celery
¼ cup chopped celery leaves
1 cup pared, sliced carrots
1 cup uncooked macaroni

1. Brown ground beef and sausage in skillet. Stir frequently, breaking up clumps of beef. When meats are no longer pink, drain off drippings.

2. Place meats in slow cooker. Add seasoning salt, oregano, basil, and onion soup mix to cooker.

3. Stir in boiling water, tomatoes, and soy sauce.

4. Add celery, celery leaves, and carrots. Stir well.

5. Cover. Cook on Low 8-10 hours.

6. One hour before end of cooking time, stir in dry macaroni.

*Serving suggestion: Serve with **cornbread** or **corn muffins**.*

# Delicious Sausage Soup

**Karen Waggoner**
Joplin, MO

*Makes 4 servings*

*Prep. Time: 15-20 minutes*
*Cooking Time: 4-5 hours*
*Ideal slow cooker size: 5-qt.*

1 lb. spicy Italian sausage
5½ cups chicken broth
½ cup heavy cream
3 carrots, grated
4 potatoes, sliced, *or* cubed
4 cups kale, chopped
½ tsp. salt
½ tsp. crushed red pepper flakes

1. Slice sausage into thin pieces, or squeeze out of casings. Place in skillet. Cook, stirring frequently to brown all sides. When no more pink remains in meat, drain off drippings.
2. Place meat in slow cooker. Add broth, cream, and vegetables.
3. Sprinkle spices over top.
4. Cover. Cook on High 4-5 hours, stirring occasionally if you're home and able to do so.

# Spicy Sausage Soup

**Janie Steele**
Moore, OK

*Makes 8-10 servings*

*Prep. Time: 25 minutes*
*Cooking Time: 6-8 hours*
*Ideal slow cooker size: 5-qt.*

1 lb. ground beef
1 lb. bulk spicy sausage, casings removed
half a large onion, chopped
2 cups chopped carrots
2 cups chopped celery
1 green, *or* red, bell pepper, chopped, *optional*
2 tsp. salt, *or* to taste
¼ tsp. pepper, *or* to taste
1 tsp. dried oregano, *or* to taste
2 *or* 3 garlic cloves, minced
14½-oz. can stewed tomatoes with chilies
14½-oz. can green beans
¼ tsp. chili powder
1 cup instant rice, uncooked

1. Combine beef, sausage, and onions in a large bowl. Form into balls. Place in slow cooker.
2. Place all remaining ingredients, except rice, in another large bowl. Stir together well.
3. Stir vegetable mixture and meatballs together gently so as not to break up the meatballs.
4. Cover. Cook on Low 6-8 hours. Stir in rice 20 minutes before serving.

*Serving suggestion: Serve with **rolls** or **cornbread**.*

# Sauerkraut-Sausage Bean Soup

**Bonnie Goering**
Bridgewater, VA

*Makes 8-10 servings*

*Prep. Time: 10 minutes*
*Cooking Time: 2-3 hours*
*Ideal slow cooker size: 4-qt.*

3 15-oz. cans white beans, undrained
16-oz. can sauerkraut, drained and rinsed
1 lb. link sausage, sliced thin
¼ cup brown sugar
½ cup ketchup

1. Combine all ingredients in slow cooker.
2. Cover. Cook on High 2-3 hours.

*Serving suggestion: Serve with **cornbread**, **applesauce**, and/or **cole slaw**.*

Tip:

Add some tomato juice or water if you prefer a thinner soup.

# Jambalaya

**Mary Ann Lefever**
Lancaster, PA

*Makes 10-12 servings*

*Prep. Time: 30 minutes*
*Cooking Time: 2-3 hours*
*Ideal slow cooker size: 4- to 5-qt.*

1 lb. hot, *or* mild, Italian
    sausage, removed from
    casings
½ cup chopped celery
1 cup chopped onion
½ cup chopped green bell
    pepper
1 tsp. minced garlic
16-oz. can chopped, *or*
    diced, tomatoes
12-oz. can chicken broth
6-oz. can tomato juice
½ cup long-grain rice,
    uncooked
¼ tsp. black pepper
14 drops hot pepper sauce,
    *or* to taste, *optional*
1 chicken breast, cooked,
    cut into small pieces, *or*
    2 cups leftover cooked
    turkey
½ lb. uncooked medium
    shrimp, peeled

1. Brown sausage in skillet
with celery and onions,
breaking up sausage as it
cooks. When the meat is no
longer pink, drain off drippings.

2. Spoon meat, celery, and
onion into slow cooker.

3. Add green pepper, garlic,
tomatoes, broth, tomato juice,
rice, pepper, and hot sauce
if you wish to cooker. Stir
together well.

4. Cover. Cook on Low
2-3 hours, or until rice has
cooked tender.

5 Five minutes before
end of cooking time, stir in
cooked chicken and shrimp.

6. Cover and cook 5 more
minutes.

*Serving suggestion: Serve
with plenty of cooked rice.*

Note:
This has become our
traditional Christmas dish
ever since we stopped doing a
big sit-down meal. With family coming at different times
during the day, a slow-cooker
Jambalaya is perfect.

# White Chicken Chili

**Jewel Showalter**
Landisville, PA

*Makes 6-8 servings*

*Prep. Time: 25 minutes*
*Cooking Time: 3½-5 hours*
*Ideal slow cooker size: 5-qt.*

2 whole skinless chicken
    breasts
6 cups water
2 chopped onions
2 garlic cloves, minced
1 Tbsp. oil
2-4 4¼-oz. cans chopped
    green chilies, drained,
    depending on your taste
    preference
1-2 diced jalapeño peppers
2 tsp. ground cumin

1½ tsp. dried oregano
¼ tsp. cayenne pepper
½ tsp. salt
3-lb. can navy beans,
    undrained
1-2 cups shredded cheese
sour cream
salsa

1. Place chicken in slow
cooker. Add 6 cups water.

2. Cover. Cook on Low
3-4 hours, or until chicken is
tender but not dry.

3. Remove chicken from
slow cooker. When cool
enough to handle, cube and
set aside.

4. Sauté onions and garlic
in oil in skillet. Add chilies,
jalapeño peppers, cumin,
oregano, pepper, and salt.
Sauté 2 minutes. Transfer to
broth in slow cooker.

5. Add navy beans.

6. Cover. Cook on Low
30-60 minutes.

7. Right before serving add
chicken and cheese.

8. Serve topped with sour
cream and salsa.

*Serving suggestion: Corn-
bread and/or corn chips are
good go-alongs with this Chili.*

Variation:
If you want to use dried
beans, use 3 cups navy
beans. Cover with water in
saucepan, soaking overnight.
In the morning, drain and
cover with fresh water. Cook
in saucepan over low heat,
7-8 hours, or until tender.
Drain off excess moisture and
stir into chicken and broth.

# White Chili

**Rebecca Plank Leichty**
Harrisonburg, VA

*Makes 6-8 servings*

**Prep. Time: 15 minutes**
**Cooking Time: 4-10 hours**
**Ideal slow cooker size: 5-qt.**

15-oz. can chickpeas,
  *or* garbanzo beans,
  undrained
15-oz. can small northern
  beans, undrained
15-oz. can pinto beans,
  undrained
1 qt. frozen corn, *or* 2 1-lb.
  bags frozen corn
1½ cups shredded cooked
  chicken
2 Tbsp. minced onion
1 red bell pepper, diced
3 tsp. minced garlic
3 tsp. ground cumin
½ tsp. salt
½ tsp. dried oregano
2 15-oz. cans chicken broth

1. Combine all ingredients
in slow cooker.
2. Cover. Cook on Low 8-10
hours or on High 4-5 hours.

*Serving suggestion: Serve*
*with warmed **tortilla chips***
*topped with melted **cheddar***
***cheese**.*

Variation:
  For more zip, add 2 tsp.
chili powder, or one or more
chopped jalapeño peppers, to
Step 1.

# Italian Chicken Chili

**Betty K. Drescher**, Quakertown, PA

*Makes 8 servings*

**Prep. Time: 20-30 minutes • Cooking Time: 6¾ hours**
**Ideal slow cooker size: 5-qt.**

½ lb. loose Italian
  sausage, hot, *or* sweet
1 tsp. olive oil
1 lb. boneless, skinless
  chicken breasts,
  uncooked and cut into
  1" cubes
28-oz. can crushed
  tomatoes, undrained
28-oz. can diced tomatoes,
  undrained
15-oz. can white kidney,
  *or* cannellini, beans,
  rinsed and drained
2 celery ribs, chopped
1 cup onions, chopped
1 small red bell pepper,
  chopped
½ cup chicken broth
2 Tbsp. chili powder
2 tsp. dried oregano
2 tsp. minced garlic
2 tsp. dried thyme
1 medium zucchini, diced
1 cup sliced fresh
  mushrooms
¼ cup minced fresh
  parsley
shredded Italian cheese
  blend, *optional*

1. In large skillet, cook sausage in oil over medium heat.
Stir frequently to break up clumps. Cook until no longer
pink. Drain off drippings.
2. Transfer sausage to slow cooker. Stir in chicken,
crushed and diced tomatoes, beans, celery, onion, red bell
pepper, broth, chili powder, oregano, garlic, and thyme.
3. Cover. Cook on Low 6 hours.
4. Stir in zucchini and mushrooms.
5. Cover. Cook on High 45 minutes.
6. Sprinkle with parsley.
7. Serve individual bowls of soup with shredded Italian
cheese blend, if you wish.

# Chicken Sausage Fennel Soup

**Jean Harris Robinson**
Pemberton, NJ

*Makes 12-14 cups*

*Prep. Time: 20 minutes*
*Cooking Time: 4-5 hours*
*Ideal slow cooker size: 4- to 5-qt.*

1 stick (8 Tbsp.) butter
¾ cup flour
2 fennel bulbs cut into large strips (plus some fennel fronds, chopped)
3 celery ribs, chopped
1 medium onion, chopped
2 Tbsp. olive oil
8 cups chicken stock
½ lb. loose mild turkey sausage
3 cups cooked and diced chicken breast
salt and pepper to taste

1. Melt butter in a small skillet. Blend in flour. Cook over medium heat just until roux turns golden. Stir frequently so mixture doesn't stick. Set aside.

2. In a larger skillet, sauté fennel, celery, and onion in olive oil for 10 minutes. Spoon vegetables into slow cooker.

3. Stir chicken stock into slow cooker. Turn cooker on High.

4. Sauté sausage in skillet, breaking up into small pieces with a wooden spoon, just until cooked through. Drain off drippings. Add meat to cooker.

5. Stir in chopped chicken. Cover cooker.

6. When Soup begins to bubble, add roux, stirring constantly until it dissolves into the Soup.

7. Cover cooker. Turn back to Low and cook 4 hours.

# Apple Chicken Stew

**Lorraine Pflederer**
Goshen, IN

*Makes 4 servings*

*Prep. Time: 30-40 minutes*
*Cooking Time: 4-5 hours*
*Ideal slow cooker size: 5-qt.*

4 medium potatoes, cubed
4 medium carrots, cut ¼"-thick slices
1 medium red onion, halved and sliced
1 celery rib, thinly sliced
1½ tsp. salt
¾ tsp. dried thyme
½ tsp. pepper
¼-½ tsp. caraway seeds
2 lbs. boneless, skinless chicken breasts, cubed
2 Tbsp. olive, *or* vegetable, oil
1 large tart apple, peeled and cubed
1¼ cups apple cider, *or* juice
1 Tbsp. cider vinegar
1 bay leaf
minced fresh parsley

1. Layer potatoes, carrots, onion, and celery into slow cooker.

2. In a small bowl, combine salt, thyme, pepper, and caraway seeds. Sprinkle half over vegetables.

3. In a skillet, sauté chicken in oil just until lightly browned. Drain off drippings.

4. Transfer chicken to slow cooker. Top with cubed apple.

5. In another small bowl, combine apple cider and vinegar. Pour over chicken and apple.

6. Sprinkle with remaining salt mixture. Lay bay leaf on top.

7. Cover. Cook on High 4-5 hours, or until vegetables are tender and chicken juices run clear.

8. Discard bay leaf. Stir before serving.

9. Sprinkle individual serving bowls with parsley.

*If you've made a thick slow-cooker stew or chili, you can serve it in individual hard rolls. Cut the top off each roll. Hollow out the bottom, leaving a half inch of bread inside. Spoon about a cup of the stew or chili into each roll, just before serving.*

*Jean M. Butzer, Batavia, NY*

# Santa Fe Chicken Soup

**Sherry Conyers**
McPherson, KS

*Makes 6-8 servings*

*Prep. Time: 30 minutes if using
cooked chicken, or 4½-5½
hours if using uncooked chicken*
*Cooking Time: 3-4 hours*
*Ideal slow cooker size: 6-qt.*

**4 whole chicken breasts,
cooked\* and shredded**
**1 small onion, diced**
**15¼-oz. can whole-kernel
corn, undrained**
**24-oz. can pinto beans,
undrained**
**14½-oz. can diced
tomatoes, undrained**
**10-oz. can Rotel tomatoes,
undrained**
**1 lb. Velveeta cheese,
cubed**
**¼ cup milk**

1. Place chicken and onions
in slow cooker.
2. Add corn, beans,
tomatoes, cubed cheese, and
milk. Stir together well.
3. Cover. Cook on Low
3-4 hours, or until cheese is
melted. Try not to let soup
boil.

\*To prepare cooked
chicken in a slow cooker
for this recipe, see "White
Chicken Chili," on page 65 of
this cookbook. Follow Steps
1-3 of the instructions, but
increase water to 8 cups and
cooking time to 4-5 hours

on Low, or until chicken is
tender but not dry.

# Pixie's Chicken Stew

**Janice Muller**
Derwood, MD

*Makes 8-10 servings*

*Prep. Time: 15 minutes*
*Cooking Time: 5-6 hours*
*Ideal slow cooker size: 5- to 6-qt.*

**2-3-lb. chicken**
**2 qts. water**
**1 pkg. dry chicken noodle
soup**
**2 chicken bouillon cubes**
**15-oz. can whole-kernel
corn, undrained**
**1 Tbsp. onion flakes**
**½ tsp. dried thyme,** *or*
**according to your taste
preference**

1. Place chicken in slow
cooker. Add water.
2. Cover. Cook on High 3-4
hours. Cool.
3. Strain broth into con-
tainer and reserve.
4. When chicken is cool
enough to handle, debone.
Return cut-up meat and
strained broth to slow cooker.
5. Stir in all remaining
ingredients.
6. Cover. Cook on High 2
hours.

**Tip:**
I've found that if I make
this a day ahead so that it can

sit overnight in the refrigerator, it's easy to skim the fat
off the top.

**Note:**
*Pixie invited friends in for
soup after long walks in the
snow. She always served this
with fresh bread in front of a
roaring fire. Pixie finished these
meals by offering us a plate of
chocolate fudge. Life couldn't
get any better.*

# Chicken Noodle Soup

**Jennifer J. Gehman**
Harrisburg, PA

*Makes 6-8 servings*

*Prep. Time: 5-10 minutes*
*Cooking Time: 4-8 hours*
*Ideal slow cooker size: 5-qt.*

**2 cups uncooked cubed
chicken, dark,** *or* **white
meat**
**15¼-oz. can corn,** *or* **2 cups
frozen corn**
**1 cup green beans,** *or* **peas\***
**10 cups water**
**10-12 chicken bouillon
cubes**
**3 Tbsp. bacon drippings**
**½ pkg. dry Kluski (or other
very sturdy) noodles**

1. Combine all ingredients
except noodles in slow
cooker.
2. Cover. Cook on High
4-6 hours or on Low 6-8
hours.

3. Two hours before end of cooking time, stir in noodles.

*Serving suggestion: Serve with potato rolls and butter or grilled cheese sandwiches.*

*If using green beans, stir in during Step 1. If using peas, stir into slow cooker just 20 minutes before end of cooking time.

# Matzoh Ball Soup

**Audrey Romonosky**
Austin, TX

*Makes 6 servings*

*Prep. Time: 30 minutes*
*Chilling Time: 20 minutes*
*Cooking Time: 2-6 hours*
*Ideal slow cooker size: 2-qt.*

2 eggs
2 Tbsp. oil
2 Tbsp. water
½ cup matzoh meal*
1 tsp. salt, *optional*
1½ qts. water
32-oz. can chicken broth

1. Lightly beat eggs, oil, and 2 Tbsp. water together in a good-sized bowl.
2. Add matzoh meal and salt. Mix well.
3. Cover and refrigerate 20 minutes.
4. Bring 1½ qts. water to boil in saucepan.
5. Wet hands. Roll chilled matzoh mixture into 1" balls.
6. Drop into boiling water and cook 20 minutes. Using a slotted spoon, remove from water. Drain. (Cooked balls can be stored in refrigerator for up to 2 days.)
7. Pour chicken broth into slow cooker. Add matzoh balls.
8. Cover. Cook on High 2-3 hours or on Low 5-6 hours.

*Finely crushed matzoh may be substituted.

Note:
I made this soup for an ethnic luncheon at work. Everyone enjoyed it. Matzoh ball soup is traditionally served on the Jewish holiday of Passover. It is also tasty all year-round.

# Pumpkin Black-Bean Turkey Chili

**Rhoda Atzeff**
Harrisburg, PA

*Makes 10-12 servings*

*Prep. Time: 20 minutes*
*Cooking Time: 7-8 hours*
*Ideal slow cooker size: 5-qt.*

1 cup chopped onions
1 cup chopped yellow bell pepper
3 garlic cloves, minced
2 Tbsp. oil
1½ tsp. dried oregano
1½-2 tsp. ground cumin
2 tsp. chili powder
2 15-oz. cans black beans, rinsed and drained
2½ cups chopped cooked turkey
16-oz. can pumpkin
14½-oz. can diced tomatoes
3 cups chicken broth

1. Sauté onions, yellow pepper, and garlic in oil in skillet for 8 minutes, or until soft.
2. Stir in oregano, cumin, and chili powder. Cook 1 minute. Transfer to slow cooker.
3. Stir in remaining ingredients.
4. Cover. Cook on Low 7-8 hours.

*Host a soup bar with everyone bringing their favorite soup or stew.*
*Amber Swarey, Honea Path, SC*

# Turkey Green Chili Chowder

**Colleen Konetzni**
Rio Rancho, NM

*Makes 12 servings*

*Prep. Time: 45 minutes*
*Cooking Time: 6 hours*
*Ideal slow cooker size: 6-qt.*

1 cup chopped celery
1 cup chopped onion
¼ stick (2 Tbsp.) butter
3 cups chopped cooked
   turkey
4 cups turkey broth
4 potatoes, peeled, *or*
   unpeeled, and cubed
½ cup green chili, chopped
½ cup cubed cheese, your
   choice
2 cans creamed corn
2 cups milk

1. In a skillet, sauté celery and onion in butter until vegetables soften and begin to brown.
2. Place sautéed vegetables, turkey, broth, potatoes, chili, cheese, corn, and milk in slow cooker.
3. Cover. Cook on High 6 hours, or until potatoes are soft.
4. If you wish, mash the Chowder a few times with a potato masher to make it thicker.
5. Turn slow cooker to Low until time to serve.

# Turkey Frame Soup

**Joyce Zuercher**
Hesston, KS

*Makes 6-8 servings*

*Prep. Time: 40 minutes*
*Cooking Time: 3-4 hours*
*Ideal slow cooker size: 6-qt.*

2-3 cups cooked and cut-up
   turkey*
3 qts. turkey broth
1 onion, diced
½-¾ tsp. salt, *or* to taste
16-oz. can chopped
   tomatoes
1 Tbsp. chicken bouillon
   granules
1 tsp. dried thyme
⅛ tsp. pepper
1½ tsp. dried oregano
4 cups chopped fresh
   vegetables —any
   combination of sliced
   celery, carrots, onions,
   rutabaga, broccoli,
   cauliflower, mushrooms,
   and more
1½ cups uncooked noodles

1. Place turkey, broth, onion, salt, tomatoes, bouillon granules, thyme, pepper, oregano, and vegetables into slow cooker. Stir.
2. Cover. Cook on Low 3-4 hours, or until vegetables are nearly done.
3. Fifteen to 30 minutes before serving time, stir in noodles. Cover. Cook on Low. If noodles are thin and small, they'll cook in 15 minutes or less. If heavier, they may need 30 minutes to become tender.
4. Stir well before serving.

*If you've got a big turkey frame, and you know it's got some good meaty morsels on it, here's what to do. Break it up enough to fit into your Dutch oven. Add 3 qts. water, 1 onion, quartered, and 2 tsp. salt. Cover, and simmer 1½ hours. Remove turkey bones from Dutch oven and allow to cool. Then debone and chop meat coarsely. Discard bones and skin. Strain broth. Begin with Step 1 above!

*Picking a color theme and re-purposing everyday items makes holiday decorating easy. Fill glass flower vases with candy (red, green, white) and tie red ribbons around knobs and handles. Your kitchen will look festive without losing work space.*
*Susan Tjon, Austin, TX*

# Turkey Mushroom Soup

**Lois Stoltzfus**
Honey Brook, PA

*Makes 6-8 servings*

*Prep. Time: 20-30 minutes*
*Cooking Time: 6-9 hours*
*Ideal slow cooker size: 4-qt.*

2 cups cooked turkey
2 qts. turkey broth (add
    water if necessary to
    reach 2 quarts)
2 cups carrots, chopped
1 cup celery, chopped
2 cups potatoes, cubed
1 small onion, chopped
1 cup long-grain rice,
    uncooked
1 tsp. garlic salt
¼ tsp. pepper
1 tsp. dried parsley
10¾-oz. cream of
    mushroom soup

1. Place all ingredients except cream of mushroom soup in slow cooker.
2. Cover. Cook on Low 6-9 hours, or until potatoes and rice are as tender as you like them.
3. Add cream of mushroom soup during last hour of cooking time.

Note:
*This recipe, with some changes, comes from an old cookbook first published in 1950. The quote at the end of the recipe said, "A grand end to a noble bird!"*

# Turkey Meatball Soup

**Mary Ann Lefever**
Lancaster, PA

*Makes 8 servings*

*Prep. Time: 30 minutes*
*Cooking Time: 8 hours*
*Ideal slow cooker size: 5- to 6-qt.*

4-5 large carrots, chopped
10 cups chicken broth
¾ lb. escarole, washed and
    cut into bite-size pieces
1 lb. ground turkey,
    uncooked
1 medium onion, chopped
2 large eggs, beaten
½ cup Italian bread
    crumbs
½ cup freshly grated
    Parmesan, plus more for
    serving
1 tsp. salt
¼ tsp. pepper

1. In slow cooker, combine carrots and chicken broth.
2. Stir in escarole.
3. Cover. Cook on Low 4 hours.
4. Combine turkey, onion, eggs, bread crumbs, ½ cup Parmesan cheese, salt, and pepper in good-sized bowl. Mix well and shape into 1" balls. Drop carefully into soup.
5. Cover cooker. Cook on Low 4 more hours, or just until meatballs and vegetables are cooked through.
6. Serve hot sprinkled with extra Parmesan cheese.

Variation:
If you wish, you can substitute 3 cups cut-up, cooked turkey for the ground turkey meatballs.

# Turkey Chili

**Reita F. Yoder**
Carlsbad, NM

*Makes 6-8 servings*

*Prep. Time: 10 minutes*
*Cooking Time: 6-8 hours*
*Ideal slow cooker size: 4- to 5-qt.*

2 lbs. ground turkey
16-oz. can pinto, *or* kidney,
    beans
2 cups fresh, *or* canned,
    tomatoes, chopped
2 cups tomato sauce
1 garlic clove, minced
1 small onion, chopped
16-oz. can Rotel tomatoes
1-oz. pkg. Williams chili
    seasoning

1. Crumble ground turkey into slow cooker.
2. Add remaining ingredients. Mix well.
3. Cover. Cook on Low 6-8 hours.

# Chilly Chili

**Alix Nancy Botsford**
Seminole, OK

*Makes 6-8 servings*

**Prep. Time:** *15 minutes*
**Soaking Time:** *6-8 hours, or overnight*
**Cooking Time:** *3-11 hours*
**Ideal slow cooker size:** *3½-qt.*

2 cups dry beans of your choice
1 tsp. salt
1 large onion, chopped
1 lb. ground turkey
2 tsp. minced garlic
2 Tbsp. olive oil
1 tsp. salt
2 celery ribs, chopped
1 green bell pepper, diced
10-oz. can tomatoes and green chilies

1. Wash beans and remove any stones. Place beans in slow cooker and cover with water. Soak 6-8 hours, or overnight.
2. Drain off water. Return beans to cooker and cover with fresh water.
3. Stir in 1 tsp. salt.
4. Cover. Cook on High 2-3 hours, or until a bean can be crushed with a fork.

5. Drain off all but 1-2 cups liquid.
6. While beans are cooking, place onion, turkey, and garlic in oil in skillet over medium heat. Stir frequently, breaking up clumps of meat. When meat is no longer pink, drain off drippings.
7. Place meat and vegetables in slow cooker.
8. Add 1 tsp. salt, celery, and green pepper. Stir in tomatoes.
9. Cover. Cook on Low 1-8 hours, or until vegetables are as tender as you like them.

*Serving suggestion: Serve with slices of **cheese** and **crackers**.*

Note:

This is a good meal for guests—or when we're all working outdoors and need our meal to be ready when we come in, like during early spring when we're getting the garden ready.

# Smoked Salmon Corn Chowder

**Sandra Haverstraw**
Hummelstown, PA

*Makes 8-10 servings*

**Prep. Time:** *30 minutes*
**Cooking Time:** *4½-5½ hours*
**Ideal slow cooker size:** *5- to 6-qt.*

1 large onion, chopped
½ cup chopped celery
⅓ cup chopped red bell pepper
¼ stick (2 Tbsp.) butter
3 cups peeled, cubed potatoes, cooked
2 cups chicken broth
15-oz. can creamed corn
16-oz. bag frozen corn
½ tsp. salt, *optional*
½ tsp. ground black pepper
2 tsp. dried dill weed
2 oz. smoked salmon, chopped
1 cup whole milk
1 cup shredded cheddar cheese
½ tsp. hot pepper sauce, *optional*
1 cup sour cream, *optional*

1. In medium skillet, sauté onion, celery, and red bell pepper in butter until soft.
2. Mix sautéed vegetables, cooked potatoes, chicken broth, creamed corn, frozen corn, salt if you wish, pepper, dill, and smoked salmon in slow cooker.
3. Cover. Cook on High 1 hour.

*When relatives from far come and stay, we make special sleep-over accommodations. We move the cars out of our 3 car garage and put some furniture in. We even make it warm and cozy with lights, an electric space heater, and an electric fireplace.*
*Annie C. Boshart, Lebanon, PA*

4. Reduce heat to Low and cook 3-4 hours.

5. One half hour prior to serving, add milk and cheese, and hot pepper sauce and sour cream if you wish, to Chowder in slow cooker.

6. Cover and continue cooking 25-30 minutes, or until cheese has melted and chowder is fully heated.

Note:

*Our family always goes to Christmas Eve Services, and we enjoy corn chowder on our return home. During a trip to Alaska, I was served a delicious corn chowder with smoked salmon. Now I've added that to our favorite recipe.*

*The rest of the menu for our Christmas Eve Buffet: cold steamed shrimp with cocktail sauce, cocktail meatballs in a small slow cooker, fresh vegetables with Ranch dip, assorted cheeses and crackers. Plus hot mulled cider or wine in a large slow cooker. And, of course, coconut cake, fruit, and cookies.*

# Corn and Shrimp Chowder

**Naomi E. Fast**, Hesston, KS

*Makes 6 servings*

*Prep. Time: 20 minutes • Cooking Time: 3-4 hours*
*Ideal slow cooker size: 3½-qt.*

4 slices bacon, diced
1 cup chopped onions
2 cups diced, unpeeled
  red potatoes
2 10-oz. pkgs. frozen corn
1 tsp. Worcestershire
  sauce
½ tsp. paprika
½ tsp. salt
⅛ tsp. pepper
2 6-oz. cans shrimp
2 cups water
¼ stick (2 Tbsp.) butter
12-oz. can evaporated milk
chopped chives

1. Fry bacon in skillet until lightly crisp. Add onions to drippings and sauté until transparent. Using slotted spoon, transfer bacon and onions to slow cooker.

2. Add remaining ingredients to cooker, except milk and chives. Stir together well.

3. Cover. Cook on Low 3-4 hours.

4. Add milk and chives 30 minutes before end of cooking time.

*Serving suggestion: Serve with **broccoli salad**.*

Note:

*I learned to make this recipe in a 7th-grade home economics class. It made an impression on my father who liked seafood very much. The recipe calls for canned shrimp, but I often increase the taste appeal with extra cooked shrimp.*

Variation:

*I frequently use frozen hash brown potatoes for speedy preparation. There is no difference in the taste.*

# Wonderful Clam Chowder

**Carlene Horne**
Bedford, NH

*Makes 4-6 servings*

*Prep. Time: 10-15 minutes*
*Cooking Time: 4-5 hours*
*Ideal slow cooker size: 3½-qt.*

2 12-oz. cans evaporated milk
1 evaporated milk can of water
1 small onion, chopped
2 small potatoes, diced
2 6-oz. cans whole clams, undrained
6-oz. can minced clams, undrained
2 Tbsp. cornstarch
¼ cup water

1. Combine all ingredients except clams, cornstarch, and ¼ cup water in slow cooker.

2. Cover. Cook on Low 3-4 hours, or until vegetables are tender, or nearly so.

3. One hour before end of cooking time, stir clams with their juice into slow cooker.

4. Immediately following that, mix cornstarch and ¼ cup water together in small bowl. When smooth, stir into soup. Stir until soup thickens.

5. Cover and continue cooking another 50 minutes or so.

# Clam Chowder

**Ruth Shank**
Gridley, IL

*Makes 8-12 servings*

*Prep. Time: 15 minutes*
*Cooking Time: 2-3 hours*
*Ideal slow cooker size: 4-qt.*

2 10¾-oz. cans cream of potato soup
10¾-oz. can cream of celery soup
2 6½-oz. cans minced clams, drained
3 slices bacon, diced and fried
1 soup can of water
1 small onion, minced
1 Tbsp. fresh parsley
dash of dried marjoram
1 Tbsp. Worcestershire sauce
pepper to taste
2 soup cans of milk

1. Combine all ingredients, except 2 soup cans of milk, in slow cooker.

2. Cover. Cook on Low 2-3 hours.

3. Twenty minutes before end of cooking time, stir in milk. Continue cooking until heated through.

# Oyster Stew

**Nadine Martinitz**
Salina, KS

*Makes 6 servings*

*Prep. Time: 20 minutes*
*Ideal slow cooker size: 4-qt.*

1 cup celery, chopped
3 Tbsp. butter
1 tsp. Worcestershire sauce
2 8-oz. cans whole stewing oysters with their juices
4 cups hot milk, *or* 2 cups milk and 2 cups light cream
salt & pepper
sherry, *optional*
paprika

1. In a large skillet, simmer celery in butter until tender.

2. Add Worcestershire sauce and oysters with their juices. Heat just until oysters begin to curl.

3. Place oyster mixture in slow cooker. Add milk and salt and pepper to taste. Season with sherry if you wish.

4. Keep hot in slow cooker turned on Low until time to serve.

5. Serve steaming in bowls, garnished with a sprinkling of paprika.

*One night during December the children like to sleep by the Christmas tree.*
*Karen Sauder, Adamstown, PA*

# Beef Main Dishes

## Spicy Beef Roast

**Karen Ceneviva**
Seymour, CT

*Makes 8-10 servings*

*Prep. Time: 15-20 minutes*
*Cooking Time: 4-10 hours*
*Ideal slow cooker size: 4- to 5-qt.*

1-2 Tbsp. cracked black
    peppercorns
2 cloves garlic, minced
3 lbs. round tip roast, *or*
    brisket, trimmed of fat
3 Tbsp. balsamic vinegar
¼ cup reduced-sodium soy
    sauce
2 Tbsp. Worcestershire
    sauce
2 tsp. dry mustard

1. Rub cracked pepper and garlic onto roast. Put roast in slow cooker.
2. Make several shallow slits in top of meat.

3. In a small bowl, combine remaining ingredients. Spoon over meat.
4. Cover. Cook on Low 8-10 hours or on High 4-5 hours, just until meat is tender but not dry.

Note:
*Once when I had made this roast for friends, my son said—in front of all the guests— "Mom, you always cook so well and you have a smile while you're doing it." That's the kind of comment you don't forget. And this roast is that good!*

## Wine Tender Roast

**Rose Hankins**
Stevensville, MD

*Makes 8-10 servings*

*Prep. Time: 10 minutes*
*Cooking Time: 8-10 hours*
*Ideal slow cooker size: 4- to 5-qt.*

2½-3-lb. chuck roast
1 cup thinly sliced onion
½ cup chopped apple,
    peeled, *or* unpeeled
3 cloves garlic, chopped
1 cup red wine
salt and pepper

1. Put roast in slow cooker. Layer onions, apples, and garlic on top of roast.
2. Carefully pour wine over roast without disturbing its toppings.
3. Sprinkle with salt and pepper.
4. Cover. Cook on Low 8-10 hours, or until meat is tender but not dry.

# Plum Roast

**Shirley Unternahrer**
Wayland, IA

*Makes 8 servings*

*Prep. Time: 10-15 minutes*
*Cooking Time: 6-8 hours*
*Ideal slow cooker size: 6-qt.*

3½-4-lb. beef roast, any cut
12-oz. can cola
½-¾ tsp. salt
1 large onion, sliced
1 rib celery, sliced
1 whole clove garlic
2 cups fresh, *or* canned,
   plums, cut up

1. Layer first six ingredients into slow cooker in order.
2. Cover. Cook on High 6-8 hours, or just until roast is tender but not dry.
3. Add plums (including juice if they're canned) for last hour of cooking. Cover.

# Machaca Beef

**Jeanne Allen**, Rye, CO

*Makes 10-12 servings*

*Prep. Time: 5-7 minutes • Cooking Time: 10-12 hours*
*Ideal slow cooker size: 3½-qt.*

1½-lb. beef roast
1 large onion, sliced
4-oz. can chopped green
   chilies, undrained
2 beef bouillon cubes
1½ tsp. dry mustard
½ tsp. garlic powder
1 tsp. seasoning salt
½ tsp. pepper
1 cup salsa

1. Combine all ingredients except salsa in slow cooker. Add just enough water to cover meat.
2. Cover cooker and cook on Low 10-12 hours, or until beef is tender but not dry. Drain and reserve liquid.
3. Shred beef using two forks to pull it apart.
4. Combine beef, salsa, and enough of reserved liquid to have the consistency you want.
5. Use as filling for burritos, chalupas, quesadillas, or tacos.

Note:
*After living in New Mexico for the past 30 years, I get homesick for New Mexican cuisine now that I live in Colorado. I keep memories of New Mexico alive by cooking foods that remind me of home.*

# Cranberry Brisket

**Roseann Wilson**
Albuquerque, NM

*Makes 5-6 servings*

*Prep. Time: 10-15 minutes*
*Cooking Time: 8-10 hours*
*Ideal slow cooker size: 5-qt.*

2½-lb. beef brisket
½ tsp. salt
¼ tsp. pepper

16-oz. can whole berry
   cranberry sauce
8-oz. can tomato sauce
½ cup chopped onion
1 Tbsp. prepared mustard

1. Rub brisket with salt and pepper. Place in slow cooker.
2. Combine cranberry sauce, tomato sauce, onion, and mustard in a mixing bowl. Spoon over brisket, being careful not to disturb seasoning on meat.
3. Cover. Cook on Low 8-10 hours, or until meat is tender but not dry.
4. Remove brisket. Slice thinly across grain. Skim fat from juices. Serve juices with brisket.

# Smoked Beef Brisket

**Joy Martin**
Myerstown, PA

*Makes 4-5 servings*

*Prep. Time: 10-12 minutes*
*Cooking Time: 8-9 hours*
*Ideal slow cooker size: 3- to 4-qt.*

2½ lbs. beef brisket
1 Tbsp. liquid smoke
1 tsp. salt
½ tsp. pepper
½ cup chopped onion
½ cup ketchup
2 tsp. prepared Dijon mustard
½ tsp. celery seed

1. Cut brisket in half. Rub both pieces with liquid smoke, salt, and pepper.
2. Place brisket halves in slow cooker. Top with onion.
3. In a small bowl, combine ketchup, mustard, and celery seed. Spread over meat.
4. Cover. Cook on Low 8-9 hours, or until meat is tender but not dry.
5. Remove brisket and keep warm.
6. Transfer cooking juices to a blender. Cover and process until smooth. (Cover lid of blender with thick towel and hold it on tightly while using.) Serve juices with brisket.

# Salsa Chuck Roast

**Hazel L. Propst**
Oxford, PA

*Makes 6 servings*

*Prep. Time: 15 minutes*
*Cooking Time: 7-8 hours*
*Ideal slow cooker size: 5-qt.*

3-4-lb. chuck, *or round,* roast
1 Tbsp. oil
1 pkg. dry onion soup mix
2 cups water
1 cup salsa

1 Brown meat in skillet in oil on both sides. Place in slow cooker.
2. Add remaining ingredients to drippings in pan. Simmer 2-3 minutes. Pour over roast in slow cooker.
3. Cover. Cook on Low 7-8 hours.

*Serving suggestion: This is a good topping for **noodles** or **rice**, along with the roast's rich broth.*

# Melt-in-Your-Mouth Mexican Meat Dish

**Marlene Bogard**, Newton, KS

*Makes 6 servings*

*Prep. Time: 15 minutes*
*Cooking Time: 8-10 hours*
*Ideal slow cooker size: 4-qt.*

4-lb. chuck roast
1 tsp. salt
1 tsp. pepper
2 Tbsp. oil
1 onion, chopped
1 tsp. chili powder
1 tsp. garlic powder
1¼ cups diced green chili peppers
½ cup chipotle salsa
¼ cup hot pepper sauce
water
flour, *optional*

1. Season roast with salt and pepper. Sear on all sides in oil in skillet. Place in slow cooker.
2. In a bowl, mix together remaining ingredients, except water, and spoon over meat.
3. Pour water down along side of the cooker (so as not to wash off the topping) until roast is ⅓ covered.
4. Cover cooker. Cook on High 6 hours. Reduce to Low and cook 2-4 more hours, or until meat falls apart but doesn't dry out.
5. Thicken hot sauce with several Tbsp. flour, if you like, in the slow cooker.

*Serving suggestion: This highly seasoned meat is perfect for **shredded beef Mexican tacos** and **burritos**.*

# Apple and Onion Beef Pot Roast

**Betty K. Drescher**
Quakertown, PA

*Makes 8-10 servings*

**Prep. Time: 20 minutes**
**Cooking Time: 5-6 hours**
**Ideal slow cooker size: 4-qt.**

3-lb. boneless beef roast,
  cut in half
oil
1 cup water
1 tsp. seasoning salt
½ tsp. soy sauce
½ tsp. Worcestershire
  sauce
¼ tsp. garlic powder
1 large tart apple,
  quartered
1 large onion, sliced
2 Tbsp. cornstarch
2 Tbsp. water

1. Brown roast on all sides in oil in skillet. Transfer to slow cooker.
2. Add water to skillet. Stir with wooden spoon to loosen browned bits. Pour over roast.
3. Sprinkle with seasoning salt, soy sauce, Worcestershire sauce, and garlic powder.
4. Top with apple and onion.
5. Cover. Cook on Low 5-6 hours.
6. Remove roast and onion. Let stand 15 minutes.
7. To make gravy, pour juices from roast into saucepan and simmer until reduced to 2 cups.
8. Combine cornstarch and water until smooth in small bowl.
9. Stir into beef broth. Bring to boil. Cook and stir 2 minutes, or until thickened.
10. Slice pot roast and serve with gravy.

# There's-No-Easier Roast Beef

**Sue Pennington**
Bridgewater, VA

*Makes 6-8 servings*

**Prep. Time: 5 minutes**
**Cooking Time: 6-8 hours**
**Ideal slow cooker size: 4-qt.**

12-oz. bottle barbecue
  sauce, *divided*
3-4-lb. beef roast

1. Pour half of barbecue sauce into bottom of slow cooker.
2. Add roast. Top with remaining barbecue sauce.
3. Cover. Cook on Low 6-8 hours.
4. Slice roast and serve with sauce.

**Variation:**
Use an 18-oz. bottle of barbecue sauce if you prefer a juicier outcome.

# 8-Hour Tangy Beef

**Mary Martins**
Fairbank, IA

*Makes 6-8 servings*

**Prep. Time: 5 minutes**
**Cooking Time: 8-9 hours**
**Ideal slow cooker size: 4-qt.**

3½-4-lb. beef roast
12-oz. can ginger ale
1½ cups ketchup

1. Put beef in slow cooker.
2. Blend ginger ale and ketchup together in a good-sized bowl. Pour over roast.
3. Cover. Cook on Low 8-9 hours.

*Serving suggestion: Shred with 2 forks and serve on buns. Or break up into chunks and serve over rice, potatoes, or pasta.*

**Variations:**
1. This recipe produces a lot of juice. You can add chopped onions, potatoes, and green beans in Step 2, if you want. Or stir in sliced mushrooms and/or peas 30 minutes before the end of the cooking time.
2. For a tangier finished dish, add chili powder or cumin, along with black pepper, in Step 2.

# Beef Roast in Beer

**Evelyn Page**
Riverton, WY

*Makes 5-6 servings*

*Prep. Time: 5 minutes*
*Marinating Time: 8 hours*
*Cooking Time: 6-8 hours*
*Ideal slow cooker size: 3-qt.*

2-3-lb. beef roast
12-oz. can beer
1 onion, sliced

1. Place roast in slow cooker. Poke all over surface with fork.
2. Pour beer over roast. Cover. Refrigerate 8 hours.
3. Add sliced onion to top of roast.
4. Cover. Cook on Low 6-8 hours.

**Variations:**
1. Brown roast in oil in skillet on top and bottom before placing in cooker.
2. Mix together 1 cup cider vinegar and 2 Tbsp. Worcestershire sauce in slow cooker. Marinate roast in mixture in refrigerator for 2-4 hours. When ready to cook roast, either discard marinade, or add other ingredients to it.
3. To thicken broth, mix together ¼ cup flour and 1 cup water until smooth. Twenty minutes before end of cooking time, remove roast from cooker. Stir flour paste into beef broth in cooker until smooth. Return roast to cooker and continue cooking. When finished, cut roast into chunks and serve with gravy.

# Italian Beef Au Jus

**Carol Sherwood**
Batavia, NY

*Makes 8 servings*

*Prep. Time: 5 minutes*
*Cooking Time: 8 hours*
*Ideal slow cooker size: 4- to 5-qt.*

3-5-lb. boneless beef roast
4-5-oz. pkg. au jus mix
1 pkg. Italian salad
    dressing mix
14½-oz. can beef broth
half a soup can water

1. Place beef in slow cooker.
2. Combine remaining ingredients in bowl. Pour over roast.
3. Cover. Cook on Low 8 hours.

*Serving suggestion: Slice meat and spoon onto hard rolls with straining spoon to make sandwiches. Or shred with 2 forks and serve over noodles or rice in broth thickened with flour.*

**Tip:**
To thicken broth, mix 3 Tbsp. cornstarch into ¼ cup cold water in small bowl. Stir until smooth. Remove ½ cup beef broth from cooker and blend into cornstarch-water. Stir back into broth in cooker, stirring until smooth. Cook 10-15 minutes on High until broth reaches gravy consistency.

# Saucy Italian Roast

**Sharon Miller**
Holmesville, OH

*Makes 8-10 servings*

*Prep. Time: 5-10 minutes*
*Cooking Time: 8-9 hours*
*Ideal slow cooker size: 4-qt.*

3-3½-lb. boneless rump
    roast
½ tsp. salt
½ tsp. garlic powder
¼ tsp. pepper
4½-oz. jar mushroom
    pieces, drained
1 medium onion, diced
14-oz. jar spaghetti sauce
¼-½ cup beef broth

1. Cut roast in half.
2. Combine salt, garlic powder, and pepper in a small bowl. Rub over both halves of roast. Place in slow cooker.
3. Top with mushrooms and onions.
4. Combine spaghetti sauce and broth in a good-sized bowl. Spoon over roast, being careful not to disturb toppings and seasonings covering it.
5. Cover. Cook on Low 8-9 hours.

*Serving suggestion: Slice roast. Serve in sauce over pasta.*

# Simply Super Supper

**Anne Townsend**
Albuquerque, NM

*Makes 4 servings*

**Prep. Time: 10 minutes**
**Cooking Time: 7-8 hours**
**Ideal slow cooker size: 3- to 4-qt.**

2 ribs celery, sliced
3 carrots, cut in strips
2 potatoes, cubed
2 onions, coarsely chopped
2-lb. beef roast
1 pkg. dry onion soup mix
1 Tbsp. liquid smoke
1½ cups water

1. Place vegetables in slow cooker.
2. Place roast on top of vegetables.
3. Sprinkle with dry soup mix.
4. Combine liquid smoke and water in a small bowl. Pour over roast.
5. Cover. Cook on Low 7-8 hours, or until vegetables are tender.

*Serving suggestion: Slice meat and serve with **cole slaw** and **French bread**. **Lemon pie** makes a nice finish.*

Note:
*This is a welcoming dinner to come home to because the house smells so yummy as you walk in. And the wonderful aroma lingers.*

# Sunday Roast Beef

**Beverly Flatt-Getz**
Warriors Mark, PA

*Makes 8 servings*

**Prep. Time: 15 minutes**
**Cooking Time: 8½-10½ hours**
**Ideal slow cooker size: 4-qt.**

4 potatoes, peeled and quartered
½ cup peeled small onions
1 cup carrot chunks
4-lb. beef chuck roast
1 Tbsp. olive oil
1 pkg. George Washington Seasoning
½ tsp. onion salt
½ tsp. minced garlic
½ tsp. garlic salt
1 cup water
few drops Worcestershire sauce
1 Tbsp. cornstarch
½ cup cold water

1. Place potatoes, onions, and carrots in bottom of slow cooker.
2. Sear beef on all sides in olive oil in skillet. Add to vegetables in slow cooker.
3. Sprinkle with seasonings.
4. Pour water around roast.
5. Cover. Cook on Low 8-10 hours.

6. Remove meat and vegetables from juice. Season juice with Worcestershire sauce.
7. Dissolve cornstarch in cold water in a small bowl. Stir into slow cooker. Cook on High until thick and bubbly. Serve with juice alongside.

Note:
*When I was growing up we often had this for Sunday lunch after church. Mom put it in the oven very early. I adapted the recipe for making it in a slow cooker.*

# Bavarian Beef

**Naomi E. Fast**
Hesston, KS

*Makes 6 servings*

**Prep. Time: 15 minutes**
**Cooking Time: 6½-7½ hours**
**Ideal slow cooker size: 4-qt.**

3-3½-lb. boneless beef chuck roast
oil
3 cups sliced carrots
3 cups sliced onions
2 large kosher dill pickles, chopped

*Every year I buy a new game for the whole extended family to play after dinner. Some we've especially enjoyed are Pictionary, Guesstures, Family Feud, etc.*

*Marsha Sabus, Fallbrook, CA*

1 cup sliced celery
½ cup dry red wine, *or*
beef broth
⅓ cup German-style
mustard
2 tsp. coarsely ground
black pepper
2 bay leaves
¼ tsp. ground cloves
⅓ cup flour
1 cup water

1. Brown roast on both
sides in oil in skillet. Transfer
to slow cooker.
2. Distribute carrots,
onions, pickles and celery
around roast in slow cooker.
3. Combine wine, mustard,
pepper, bay leaves, and cloves
in a bowl. Pour over ingredients in slow cooker.
4. Cover. Cook on Low
6-7 hours, or until meat and
vegetables are tender but not
dry or mushy.
5. Remove meat and
vegetables to large platter.
Cover to keep warm.
6. Mix flour with 1 cup
water in bowl until smooth.
Turn cooker to High. Stir in
flour-water paste, stirring
continually until broth is
smooth and thickened. Serve
with broth alongside.

*Serving suggestion: Try
serving this over* **noodles** *or*
**spaetzle.**

# Sauerbraten

**Leona M. Slabaugh**
Apple Creek, OH

*Makes 8-10 servings*

*Prep. Time: 10-20 minutes*
*Marinating Time: 8 hours, or*
*overnight*
*Cooking Time: 5-7 hours*
*Ideal slow cooker size: 6-qt.*

1 cup cider vinegar
¾ cup red wine vinegar
2 tsp. salt
½ tsp. black pepper
6 whole cloves
2 bay leaves
1 Tbsp. mustard seeds
3½-lb. boneless top round
roast, tied
20 gingersnaps (about 5 oz.),
crushed

1. Combine vinegars, salt,
pepper, cloves, bay leaves,
and mustard seeds in a large
bowl.
2. Place roast in bowl.
Spoon marinade over it.
3. Cover roast in marinade
and refrigerate overnight,
turning once.
4. Place roast and mari-
nade in slow cooker.
5. Cover. Cook on High 5
hours or on Low 7 hours, or
until meat is tender but not
dry.
6. Remove roast to platter
and keep warm.
7. Strain liquid from slow
cooker. Stir crushed gingersnaps into liquid until well
blended.
8. Slice roast and serve
with sauce alongside.

# Beef Pot Roast

**Nancy Wagner Graves**
Manhattan, KS

*Makes 6-8 servings*

*Prep. Time: 10 minutes*
*Cooking Time: 6-7 hours*
*Ideal slow cooker size: 4-qt.*

4-5-lb. beef chuck roast
1 garlic clove, cut in half
salt to taste
pepper to taste
1 carrot, chopped
1 rib celery, chopped
1 small onion, sliced
¾ cup sour cream
3 Tbsp. flour
½ cup dry white wine

1. Rub roast with garlic.
Season with salt and pepper.
Place in slow cooker.
2. Add carrots, celery, and
onion.
3. Combine sour cream,
flour, and wine in a small
bowl. Pour into slow cooker.
4. Cover. Cook on Low 6-7
hours.

# Pot-Roast Complete

Naomi E. Fast, Hesston, KS

*Makes 6-8 servings*

*Prep. Time: 15 minutes • Cooking Time: 6½-7½ hours*
*Ideal slow cooker size: 4-qt.*

3-3½-lb. arm roast,
  boneless
2 large onions, sliced
½ cup brown sugar
⅓ cup soy sauce
⅓ cup cider vinegar
2 bay leaves
2-3 garlic cloves, minced
1 tsp. grated fresh ginger,
  or ¼ tsp. ground ginger

1 cup julienned carrots,
  matchstick size, *or*
  baby carrots
2 cups sliced button
  mushrooms
2-3 cups fresh spinach
  leaves, *or* 2 10-oz. pkgs.
  frozen spinach, thawed
  and squeezed dry
2 Tbsp. cornstarch

1. Place meat in slow cooker. Top with onions.
2. Combine brown sugar, soy sauce, and vinegar in a small bowl. Spoon over beef.
3. Scatter bay leaves, garlic, and ginger over roast.
4. Cover. Cook on Low 6-7 hours.
5. Spread carrots, mushrooms, and spinach over beef.
6. Cover. Cook on High 20 minutes.
7. In small bowl, mix cornstarch with ½ cup broth from slow cooker. Return to slow cooker.
8. Cover. Cook 10 minutes more.

*Serving suggestion: Serve over **rice**.*

Note:

*I can't count how many times I have used this recipe over the last 15-20 years as a guest meal.*

# Spicy Short Ribs

Joan Terwilliger
Lebanon, PA

*Makes 4-6 servings*

*Prep Time: 30 minutes*
*Cooking Time: 6 hours*
*Ideal slow-cooker size: 4- to 6-qt.*

8 bone-in beef short ribs
15-oz. can crushed
  tomatoes
3 Tbsp. tomato paste
2-3 Tbsp. hot pepper jam,
  *or* horseradish jam
6 cloves garlic, peeled
¾ tsp. dried rosemary,
  crushed
1 Tbsp. dried minced
  onions
½ tsp ground ginger
¼ cup dry red wine

1. Broil ribs 6 inches from heat until browned, 5-10 minutes per side.
2. Place ribs in slow cooker.
3. Combine remaining ingredients in mixing bowl. Pour over ribs. (If you've had to stack them, lift the top layer and spoon sauce over bottom layer.)
4. Cover. Cook on Low 6 hours.
5. Spoon off fat before serving.

# Slow-Cooked Short Ribs

**Jean A. Shaner**
York, PA

**Barbara L. McGinnis**
Jupiter, FL

*Makes 12 servings*

*Prep. Time: 35 minutes*
*Cooking Time: 9-10 hours*
*Ideal slow cooker size: 6-qt.*

⅔ cup flour
2 tsp. salt
½ tsp. pepper
4-4½ lbs. boneless beef
 short ribs, *or* 6-7 lbs.
 bone-in beef short ribs
oil, *or* butter
1 large onion, chopped
1½ cups beef broth
¾ cup wine, *or* cider
 vinegar
½-¾ cup packed brown
 sugar, according to your
 taste preference
½ cup chili sauce
⅓ cup ketchup
⅓ cup Worcestershire
 sauce
5 garlic cloves, minced
1½ tsp. chili powder

1. Combine flour, salt, and pepper in plastic bag. Add ribs, a few at a time, and shake to coat.
2. Brown meat in small amount of oil, or in butter, in batches in skillet. Transfer to slow cooker. Reserve drippings in skillet.
3. Combine remaining ingredients in skillet. Cook, stirring up browned drippings, until mixture comes to a boil. Pour over ribs.
4. Cover. Cook on Low 9-10 hours.
5. Debone and serve.

*Serving suggestion: Serve over **rice** or **noodles**.*

**Tip:**

It is ideal to cook these ribs one day in advance of serving. Refrigerate for several hours or overnight. Remove layer of congealed fat before serving.

# Beef Ribs with Sauerkraut

**Rosaria Strachan**
Fairfield, CT

*Makes 8-10 servings*

*Prep. Time: 10 minutes*
*Cooking Time: 3-8 hours*
*Ideal slow cooker size: 6-qt.*

3-4 lbs. beef short ribs
32-oz. bag, *or* 27-oz. can,
 sauerkraut, drained
2 Tbsp. caraway seeds
¼ cup water

1. Put ribs in 6-qt. slow cooker.
2. Place sauerkraut and caraway seeds on top of ribs.
3. Pour in water.
4. Cover. Cook on High 3-4 hours or on Low 7-8 hours.

*Serving suggestion: These need **mashed potatoes** to complete the meal!*

**Variation:**

If you really enjoy sauerkraut, double the amount of sauerkraut, and divide the recipe between 2 4- or 5-qt. cookers.

*Christmas is all year for me. Most of the gifts I give are homemade. This year I made six kinds of jelly, apple butter, chow-chow, and bread-and-butter pickles. This works well for people like me who are on a limited income. Plus I can be done early and share gifts from the heart.*

*Janet Batdorf, Harrisburg, PA*

# Ribs and Limas

**Miriam Friesen**
Staunton, VA

*Makes 6 servings*

*Prep. Time: 25 minutes*
*Cooking Time: 5½-12½ hours*
*Ideal slow cooker size: 6-qt.*

3 lbs. beef short ribs
2 Tbsp. oil
1 onion, chopped
4 carrots, sliced
¼ cup packed brown sugar
2 Tbsp. flour
2 tsp. dry mustard
1½ tsp. salt
¼ tsp. pepper
1¼ cups water
¼ cup cider vinegar
1 large bay leaf, broken in half
10-oz. pkg. frozen lima beans, *or* peas

1. Cut ribs into serving-size pieces. Brown ribs in large skillet in batches in oil.
2. Place onions and carrots in slow cooker. Add ribs.
3. In a mixing bowl, combine brown sugar, flour, mustard, salt, and pepper. Stir in water and vinegar until smooth. Pour over ribs. Push bay leaf pieces into liquid.
4. Cover. Cook on High 5-6 hours or on Low 10-12 hours.
5. Stir in lima beans.
6. Cover. Cook on High 20-30 minutes.
7. Remove bay leaf before serving.

*Serving suggestion: We like this with a **citrus salad** and **crusty rolls**.*

# Tender Texas-Style Steaks

**Janice Muller**
Derwood, MD

*Makes 4-6 servings*

*Prep. Time: 5 minutes*
*Cooking Time: 6 hours*
*Ideal slow cooker size: 3-qt.*

6 ½-¾-lb. steaks, *or* chops
1 cup brown sugar
1 cup ketchup
salt to taste
pepper to taste
few dashes of Worcestershire sauce

1. Lay steaks in bottom of slow cooker.
2. Combine brown sugar and ketchup in a mixing bowl. Pour over steaks
3. Sprinkle with salt and pepper and a few dashes of Worcestershire sauce.
4. Cover. Cook on High 3 hours and on Low 3 hours, or until meat is fork tender but not dry.

*Serving suggestion: Serve with **wide egg noodles**, **green beans**, and **applesauce**.*

Tip:

I spoon some of the juice from the cooker over the noodles. Sometimes I stir 2-4 Tbsp. flour into the hot broth (after lifting the meat onto a platter) until it becomes smooth. By cooking it a few more minutes, the broth thickens into a gravy.

# Swiss Steak

**Marie Shank**
Harrisonburg, VA

*Makes 6-8 servings*

*Prep. Time: 5 minutes*
*Cooking Time: 3-10 hours*
*Ideal slow cooker size: 4-qt.*

2-lb. round steak, cut into serving pieces
1 tsp. salt
½ tsp. pepper
1 large onion, sliced, *or* 1 pkg. dry onion soup mix
16-oz. can tomatoes

1. Combine all ingredients in slow cooker.
2. Cover. Cook on Low 6-10 hours or on High 3-4 hours, just until meat is fork tender.

Tip:

You may want to omit the salt if you use the onion soup mix.

# Savory Pepper Steak

**Grace W. Yoder**
Harrisonburg, VA

*Makes 6 servings*

*Prep. Time: 15 minutes*
*Cooking Time: 8-10 hours*
*Ideal slow cooker size: 4-qt.*

1½-lb. beef round steak,
   cut ½" thick
¼ cup flour
½ tsp. salt
⅛ tsp. pepper
1 medium onion, chopped,
   *or* sliced
1 garlic clove, minced
2 large green bell peppers,
   sliced in ½" strips,
   *divided*
29-oz. can whole tomatoes
1 Tbsp. beef flavor base, *or*
   1 beef bouillon cube
1 Tbsp. soy sauce
2 tsp. Worcestershire
   sauce
3 Tbsp. flour
3 Tbsp. water

1. Cut beef into strips about 1" wide.

2. In a large bowl, combine ¼ cup flour, salt, and pepper. Toss with beef until well coated. Place in slow cooker.

3. Add onions, garlic, and half the green pepper slices. Mix well.

4. In the large bowl, combine tomatoes, beef base, soy sauce, and Worcestershire sauce. Pour into slow cooker.

5. Cover. Cook on Low 8-10 hours.

6. One hour before serving, turn to High and stir in remaining green pepper strips.

7. Combine 3 Tbsp. flour and water in a small bowl to make a smooth paste. Stir into slow cooker. Cover. Cook until thickened, about 10 minutes.

*Serving suggestion: This is a good topping for **cooked rice**.*

# Three-Pepper Steak

**Renee Hankins**
Narvon, PA

*Makes 10 servings*

*Prep. Time: 30 minutes*
*Cooking Time: 5-8 hours*
*Ideal slow cooker size: 4- to 5-qt.*

3 bell peppers—one red,
   one orange, and one
   yellow pepper (or any
   combination of colors),
   cut into ¼"-thick slices
2 garlic cloves, sliced
1 large onion, sliced
1 tsp. ground cumin
½ tsp. dried oregano
1 bay leaf
3½-lb. beef flank steak,
   cut in ¼-½"-thick slices
   across the grain
salt to taste
14½-oz. can diced tomatoes
   in juice
jalapeño chilies, sliced,
   *optional*

1. Place sliced peppers, garlic, onion, cumin, oregano, and bay leaf in slow cooker. Stir gently to mix.

2. Put steak slices on top of vegetable mixture. Season with salt.

3. Spoon tomatoes with juice over top. Sprinkle with jalapeño pepper slices if you wish. Do not stir.

4. Cover. Cook on Low 5-8 hours, depending on your slow cooker. Check after 5 hours to see if meat is tender. If not, continue cooking until tender but not dry.

*Serving suggestion: We love this served over **noodles**, **rice**, or torn **tortillas**.*

## Stuffed Flank Steak

Renee Baum
Chambersburg, PA

*Makes 6 servings*

*Prep. Time: 30 minutes*
*Cooking Time: 4½-5½ hours*
*Ideal slow cooker size: 4- to 5-qt.*

8-oz. pkg. crushed
　cornbread stuffing
1 cup chopped onion
1 cup chopped celery
¼ cup minced fresh
　parsley
2 eggs
1¼ cups beef broth
5⅓ Tbsp. (⅓ cup) butter,
　melted
½ tsp. seasoned salt,
　*optional*
½ tsp. pepper
1½ lbs. flank steak

1. Combine stuffing, onion, celery, and parsley in large bowl.

2. In a small bowl, beat eggs. Stir in broth and butter. Pour over stuffing mixture. Sprinkle with seasoned salt if you wish, and pepper. Stir well.

3. Pound steak to ¼"- thickness.

4. Spread 1½ cups stuffing mixture over steak. Roll up, starting with short side. Tie with string.

5. Place steak in slow cooker.

6. Wrap remaining stuffing tightly in foil and place on top of rolled steak.

7. Cover. Cook on Low 4½-5½ hours, or until meat thermometer reaches 165 degrees.

8. Remove string before slicing.

Note:

If you have a helpful butcher, ask him/her to pound the steak for you.

## Fruited Flank Steak

Ruth A. Feister
Narvon, PA

*Makes 6 servings*

*Prep. Time: 10 minutes*
*Cooking Time: 6-8 hours*
*Ideal slow cooker size: 3-qt.*

1½-2-lb. flank steak
salt to taste
pepper to taste
14½-oz. can mixed fruit,
　*or your choice of canned*
　fruit
1 Tbsp. salad oil
1 Tbsp. lemon juice
¼ cup teriyaki sauce
1 tsp. vinegar
1 garlic clove, minced

1. Sprinkle steak with salt and pepper. Place in slow cooker.

2. Drain fruit, saving ¼ cup syrup. Set fruit aside.

3. In a small bowl, combine ¼ cup reserved syrup with remaining ingredients. Pour over steak.

4. Cover. Cook on Low 6-8 hours, or just until meat is tender but not dry.

5. Add drained fruit during last 15 minutes of cooking time.

6. Lift meat from cooker onto platter. Using sharp knife slice across the grain, making thin slices. Spoon fruit over meat.

*Serving suggestion: Top off this meal by serving the steak and fruit with **baked rice**.*

*Sometime between Christmas and New Year's we have a neighborhood dinner which we follow with singing hymns or Christmas songs. One neighbor brings her autoharp and another brings her accordion.*

*Sara Kinsinger, Stuarts Draft, VA*

# Slow Cooker Beef with Mushrooms

**Grace W. Yoder**, Harrisonburg, VA

*Makes 6 servings*

*Prep. Time: 10 minutes*
*Cooking Time: 7-8 hours*
*Ideal slow cooker size: 3-qt.*

2 medium onions, thinly
　sliced
½ lb. mushrooms, sliced,
　*or* 2 4-oz. cans sliced
　mushrooms, drained
2½-lb. beef flank, *or* round,
　steak
salt to taste
pepper to taste
1 Tbsp. Worcestershire sauce
1 Tbsp. oil
paprika to taste

1. Place sliced onions and mushrooms in slow cooker.
2. Score top of meat about ½" deep in diamond pattern.
3. Season with salt and pepper. Rub in Worcestershire sauce and oil. Sprinkle top with paprika.
4. Place meat on top of onions.
5. Cover. Cook on Low 7-8 hours, or until meat is tender but not dry.
6. To serve, cut beef across grain in thin slices. Top with mushrooms and onions.

Variation:
　Add 1 Tbsp. lemon juice to Worcestershire sauce and oil in Step 3.

**Genelle Taylor**
Perrysburg, OH

# Barbecued Chuck Steak

**Rhonda Burgoon**
Collingswood, NJ

*Makes 4 servings*

*Prep. Time: 10 minutes*
*Cooking Time: 3-5 hours*
*Ideal slow cooker size: 3-qt.*

1½-lb. boneless chuck
　steak, 1½" thick
1 clove garlic, minced
¼ cup wine vinegar
1 Tbsp. brown sugar
1 tsp. paprika
2 Tbsp. Worcestershire
　sauce
½ cup ketchup
1 tsp. salt
1 tsp. prepared mustard
¼ tsp. black pepper

1. Cut beef on diagonal across the grain into 1"-thick slices. Place in slow cooker.
2. Combine remaining ingredients in a bowl. Pour over meat. Stir to mix.
3. Cover. Cook on Low 3-5 hours.

# Pigs in Blankets

**Linda Sluiter**
Schererville, IN

*Makes 4-6 servings*

*Prep. Time: 15 minutes*
*Cooking Time: 8 hours*
*Ideal slow cooker size: 4-qt.*

2-3-lb. round steak, cut
　about 1" thick
1 lb. bacon
1 cup ketchup
¾ cup brown sugar
1 cup water
half a yellow onion,
　chopped

1. Cut steak into strips 1" thick x 3" long.
2. Lay a bacon strip down, then a strip of beef on top of the bacon slice. Roll up and secure with toothpick. Place in slow cooker.
3. Combine remaining ingredients in a bowl. Pour over meat roll-ups.
4. Cover. Cook on High 8 hours.

# Corned Beef

**Elaine Vigoda**
Rochester, NY

*Makes 8 servings*

*Prep. Time: 15 minutes*
*Cooking Time: 7-12 hours*
*Ideal slow cooker size: 5- to 6-qt.*

3 large carrots, cut into
   chunks
1 cup chopped celery
1 tsp. salt
½ tsp. pepper
1 cup water
3-4-lb. corned beef
1 large onion, cut into
   pieces
half a small head of
   cabbage, cut in wedges
4 potatoes, peeled and
   chunked

1. Place carrots, celery,
seasonings, and water in
slow cooker. Stir together.
2. Add beef. Cover with
onions.
3. Cover. Cook on Low
8-10 hours or on High 5-6
hours.
4. Lift corned beef out
of cooker and add cabbage
and potatoes, pushing them
to bottom of slow cooker.
Return beef to cooker.
5. Cover. Cook on High
2 hours, or until vegetables
are as tender as you like
them.
6. Remove corned
beef. Cool and slice on the
diagonal.
7. Serve surrounded by
vegetables.

**Variations:**
1. Scatter 10-12 pepper-
corns over corned beef and
onions in Step 2.
**Rosaria Strachan**
Fairfield, CT

2. In a bowl, mix together
1 cup water, ½ cup brown
sugar, 1 Tbsp. prepared mustard, and a dash of ground
cloves. Spread over beef in
Step 4, just before cooking on
High 2 more hours.
**Shirley Sears**
Tiskilwa, IL

# Apple and Brown Sugar Corned Beef

**Mary Seielstad**
Sparks, NV

*Makes 8-10 servings*

*Prep. Time: 10 minutes*
*Cooking Time: 6-12 hours*
*Ideal slow cooker size: 6-qt. or*
*2 4- to 5-qt. cookers*

2½-3-lb. corned beef
   brisket
8 small red potatoes
3 medium carrots, peeled
   and sliced
1 large onion, cut in 6-8
   pieces
1 small head cabbage, cut
   in chunks
1 qt. apple juice
1 cup brown sugar
1 Tbsp. prepared mustard

1. Place meat, potatoes,
carrots, onion, and cabbage
in 6-qt. slow cooker, or divide
between 2 4- to 5-qt. cookers.
2. Combine apple juice,
brown sugar, and mustard
in a bowl. Pour into slow
cooker(s).
3. Cover. Cook on High
6-6½ hours or on Low 10-12
hours, or until vegetables and
meat are tender.
4. Remove meat and
vegetables from slow cooker.
Thinly slice meat across the
grain. Serve topped with
vegetables.

*Serving suggestion: We love
to eat this with* **cornbread**.

**Tip:**
If potatoes are not small,
quarter them before placing
in slow cooker.

# Home-Style Beef Cubes

**Dorothy Horst**
Tiskilwa, IL

*Makes 8-10 servings*

*Prep. Time: 10 minutes*
*Cooking Time: 7-12 hours*
*Ideal slow cooker size: 5-qt.*

½ cup flour
1 tsp. salt
⅛ tsp. pepper
4 lbs. beef cubes
½ cup chopped shallots, *or*
   green onions
2 4-oz. cans sliced
   mushrooms, drained, *or*
   ½ lb. fresh mushrooms,
   sliced

14½-oz. can beef broth
1 tsp. Worcestershire sauce
2 tsp. ketchup
¼ cup water
3 Tbsp. flour

1. In a large bowl, combine ½ cup flour, salt, and pepper. Toss beef in flour mixture to coat. Place in slow cooker.

2. Cover with onions and mushrooms.

3. Combine broth, Worcestershire sauce, and ketchup in a bowl. Pour into slow cooker. Mix everything together well.

4. Cover. Cook on Low 7-12 hours, or until beef is as tender as you like.

5. One hour before serving, make a smooth paste of water and 3 Tbsp. flour in a small bowl. Stir into slow cooker. Cover and continue cooking until broth thickens.

*Serving suggestion: This is a treat served over hot **buttered noodles**.*

# Fruited Beef Tagine

**Naomi E. Fast**
Hesston, KS

*Makes 6-8 servings*

*Prep. Time: 20 minutes*
*Cooking Time: 5-6 hours*
*Ideal slow cooker size: 4-qt.*

2 lbs. beef, cut into 2" cubes
1 Tbsp. oil
4 cups sliced onions
2 tsp. ground coriander
1½ tsp. ground cinnamon
¾ tsp. ground ginger
14½-oz. can beef broth, plus enough water to equal 2 cups
16 ozs. pitted prunes
salt to taste
fresh ground pepper to taste
juice of one lemon

1. Brown beef cubes in oil in skillet. Do in batches so beef browns and doesn't steam. As you finish browning, place beef in slow cooker. Reserve drippings.

2. Sauté onions in drippings until lightly browned, adding more oil if needed. Add to slow cooker.

3. Add remaining ingredients, except lemon juice.

4. Simmer on Low 5-6 hours, adding lemon juice during the last 10 minutes.

*Serving suggestion: This recipe, accompanied with a tossed **green salad** and **rolls**, makes a complete meal.*

**Variations:**

1. Mix in a few very thin slices of lemon rind to add flavor and eye appeal.

2. You can substitute lamb cubes for the beef.

# Salsa Beef

**Sarah Niessen**
Akron, PA

*Makes 5-6 servings*

*Prep. Time: 15 minutes*
*Cooking Time: 6-8 hours*
*Ideal slow cooker size: 5- to 6-qt.*

2-2½ lbs. beef, cut in bite-sized cubes
1 Tbsp. oil
16-oz. jar salsa
8-oz. can tomato sauce
2 garlic cloves, minced
2 Tbsp. brown sugar
1 Tbsp. soy sauce
1 cup canned tomatoes

1. Brown beef in skillet in oil. Do it in batches so beef browns and doesn't steam. As you finish a batch, place browned cubes in slow cooker.

2. Stir in remaining ingredients.

3. Cover. Cook on Low 6-8 hours.

*Serving suggestion: I usually serve this over **rice**.*

**Variation:**

For added flavor, use Italian tomato sauce.

# Beef Mushroom Casserole

**Susan Stephani Smith**
Monument, CO

*Makes 12 servings*

*Prep. Time: 10 minutes*
*Cooking Time: 4½-5½ hours*
*Ideal slow cooker size: 5-qt.*

4 lbs. lean beef sirloin, cut into 1" cubes
2 10¾-oz. cans cream of mushroom soup
2 pkgs. dry onion soup mix
¼-1 tsp. pepper, according to your taste preference
½ tsp. salt
1-2 cups red Burgundy wine, *optional*
1½ lbs. fresh mushrooms, quartered
¼ cup sour cream, *optional*

1. Combine all ingredients except wine, mushrooms, and sour cream in slow cooker.
2. Cover. Cook on Low 4-5 hours, stirring occasionally if you're home and able to do so.
3. Stir in mushrooms and wine. Cook 30 minutes longer.
4. Ten minutes before end of cooking time, stir in sour cream if you wish.

*Serving suggestion: This is a treat served over **egg noodles**.*

# Easy Stroganoff

**Vicki Dinkel**
Sharon Springs, KS

*Makes 6-8 servings*

*Prep. Time: 5 minutes*
*Cooking Time: 6½-8½ hours*
*Ideal slow cooker size: 4-qt.*

10¾-oz. can cream of mushroom soup
14½-oz. can beef broth
1 lb. beef stewing meat, *or* round steak, cut in 1" pieces
1 cup sour cream
2 cups cooked noodles

1. Combine soup and broth in slow cooker.
2. Stir in meat.
3. Cover. Cook on High 3-4 hours. Reduce heat to Low and cook 3-4 hours, or just until beef is fork tender.
4. Stir in sour cream.
5. Stir in noodles.
6. Cook on High 20 minutes, or just until Stroganoff is hot throughout.

*Serving suggestion: A **vegetable** or **salad** and some crispy **French bread** make good additions to the meal.*

Note:
*Since I'm in school part-time and work two part-time jobs, this nearly complete meal is great to come home to. It smells wonderful when I open the door.*

# Garlic Beef Stroganoff

**Sharon Miller**
Holmesville, OH

*Makes 6-8 servings*

*Prep. Time: 10-15 minutes*
*Cooking Time: 7-8 hours*
*Ideal slow cooker size: 4-qt.*

2 tsp. beef bouillon granules
2 4½-oz. jars sliced mushrooms, drained, with juice reserved
1 cup mushroom juice, with boiling water added to make a full cup
10¾-oz. can cream of mushroom soup
1 large onion, chopped
3 garlic cloves, minced
1 Tbsp. Worcestershire sauce
1½-2-lb. boneless round steak, cut into thin strips
2 Tbsp. oil
8-oz. pkg. cream cheese, cubed and softened

1. Dissolve bouillon in mushroom juice/water mixture in slow cooker.
2. Stir in mushrooms, soup, onion, garlic, and Worcestershire sauce.
3. Sauté beef in oil in skillet. Transfer to slow cooker and stir into sauce.
4. Cover. Cook on Low 7-8 hours. Turn off heat.
5. Stir in cream cheese until smooth.

*Serving suggestion: You'll love this served over **noodles**.*

# Beef Burgundy

Joyce Kaut, Rochester, NY

*Makes 6 servings*

*Prep. Time: 30 minutes • Cooking Time: 3¼-4¼ hours*
*Ideal slow cooker size: 3- to 4-qt.*

2 slices bacon, cut in squares
2 lbs. sirloin tip, *or* round, steak, cubed
¼ cup flour
½ tsp. salt
¼ tsp. seasoning salt
¼ tsp. dried marjoram
¼ tsp. dried thyme
¼ tsp. pepper
1 garlic clove, minced
1 beef bouillon cube, crushed
1 cup burgundy wine
¼ lb. fresh mushrooms, sliced
1-1½ cups ketchup
2 Tbsp. cornstarch, *optional*
2 Tbsp. cold water, *optional*

1. Cook bacon in skillet until crisp and browned. Remove bacon, reserving drippings.
2. Coat beef with flour and brown on all sides in bacon drippings. (Don't crowd the skillet so the beef browns rather than steams.)
3. Combine steak, bacon drippings, bacon, seasonings and herbs, garlic, bouillon, and wine in slow cooker.
4. Cover. Cook on Low 4 hours (or 3 hours, if you've browned the beef well in Step 2), or until beef is just tender.
5. Stir in mushrooms and ketchup.
6. Dissolve cornstarch in water in a small bowl. Stir into slow cooker—if sauce is not as thick as you wish.
7. Cover. Cook on High 15 minutes, until sauce thickens.

*Serving suggestion: Try serving this over **noodles**.*

# Italian Beef Stew

Kathy Hertzler
Lancaster, PA

*Makes 4-6 servings*

*Prep. Time: 30 minutes*
*Cooking Time: 6½ hours*
*Ideal slow cooker size: 4-qt.*

2 Tbsp. flour
2 tsp. chopped fresh thyme
1 tsp. salt
¼-½ tsp. freshly ground pepper
2¼ lbs. beef stewing meat, cubed
3 Tbsp. olive oil
1 onion, chopped
1 cup tomato sauce
1 cup beef stock
1 cup red wine
3 garlic cloves, minced
2 Tbsp. tomato paste
2 cups frozen peas, thawed but not cooked
1 tsp. sugar

1. Spoon flour into small dish. Season with thyme, salt, and pepper. Add beef cubes and coat evenly.
2. Heat oil in slow cooker on High. Add floured beef and brown on all sides.
3. Stir in remaining ingredients except peas and sugar.
4. Cover. Cook on Low 6 hours.
5. Add peas and sugar. Cook an additional 30 minutes, or until beef is tender and peas are warm.

# Dawn's Mushroom Beef Stew

**Dawn Day**
Westminster, CA

*Makes 8-10 servings*

*Prep. Time: 20 minutes*
*Cooking Time: 6-7½ hours*
*Ideal slow cooker size: 3- to 4-qt.*

1 lb. sirloin, cubed
2 Tbsp. flour
oil
1 large onion, chopped
2 garlic cloves, minced
½ lb. button mushrooms, sliced
2 ribs celery, sliced
2 carrots, sliced
3-4 large potatoes, cubed
2 tsp. seasoning salt
14½-oz. can beef stock, *or* 2 bouillon cubes dissolved in 1⅔ cups water
½-1 cup good red wine

1. Dredge sirloin in flour and brown in oil in skillet. Reserve drippings. Place meat in slow cooker.
2. Sauté onion, garlic, and mushrooms in drippings just until soft. Add to meat.
3. Stir in all remaining ingredients.
4. Cover. Cook on Low 6 hours. Test to see if vegetables are tender. If not, continue cooking on Low for another 1-1½ hours.

# Tempting Beef Stew

**Patricia Howard**
Albuquerque, NM

*Makes 10-12 servings*

*Prep. Time: 10 minutes*
*Cooking Time: 10-12 hours*
*Ideal slow cooker size: 5-qt.*

2-3 lbs. beef stewing meat
3 carrots, sliced thin
1-lb. pkg. frozen green peas with onions
1-lb. pkg. frozen green beans
16-oz. can whole, *or* stewed, tomatoes
½ cup beef broth
½ cup white wine
½ cup brown sugar
4 Tbsp. instant tapioca
½ cup bread crumbs
2 tsp. salt
1 bay leaf
pepper to taste

1. Combine all ingredients in slow cooker.
2. Cover. Cook on Low 10-12 hours, or until meat and vegetables are as tender as you wish.

*Serving suggestion: Serve over **noodles**, **rice**, **couscous**, or **biscuits**.*

**Tip:**
Prepare this Tempting Beef Stew before your guests arrive. Give yourself time to relax instead of panicking in a last-minute rush.

**Variation:**
In place of tapioca, thicken stew with ¼ cup flour dissolved in ⅓-½ cup water. Mix in and turn cooker to High. Cover and cook for 15-20 minutes.

# Beef Stew with Wine

**Andrea O'Neil**
Fairfield, CT

*Makes 8-10 servings*

*Prep. Time: 20 minutes*
*Cooking Time: 9-10 hours*
*Ideal slow cooker size: 4-qt.*

1 lb. stewing meat, cubed
oil
2 onions, quartered
4 carrots, sliced
4-5 potatoes, cubed
28-oz. can crushed tomatoes
½ cup wine
1 pkg. dry onion soup mix
1 cup water
2 tsp. salt
¾ tsp. pepper
3 Tbsp. cornstarch
¼ cup water

1. Brown beef cubes in skillet in oil.
2. Place browned beef in slow cooker. Add all other ingredients except cornstarch and ¼ cup water. Stir to combine.
3. Cover. Cook on Low 9-10 hours.
4. Ten minutes before

# Beef Stew with Shiitake Mushrooms

Kathy Hertzler, Lancaster, PA

*Makes 4-6 servings*

**Prep. Time: 10 minutes • Cooking Time: 8-9 hours**
**Ideal slow cooker size: 5-qt.**

12 new potatoes, cut into quarters
½ cup chopped onions
8-oz. pkg. baby carrots
3-4-oz. pkg. fresh shiitake mushrooms, sliced, *or* 2 cups regular white mushrooms, sliced
16-oz. can whole tomatoes
14½-oz. can beef broth
½ cup flour
1 Tbsp. Worcestershire sauce
1 tsp. salt
1 tsp. sugar
1 tsp. dried marjoram leaves
¼ tsp. pepper
1 lb. beef stewing meat, cubed

1. Combine all ingredients except beef in slow cooker.
2. Stir in beef.
3. Cover. Cook on Low 8-9 hours. Stir well before serving.

serving, stir cornstarch into water in a small bowl until smooth. Stir into hot Stew.

Variation:
For added zest, add ½ tsp. Old Bay Seasoning and 1 rib celery, diced, in Step 2.

## Best Ever Beef Stew

**Barbara Walker**
Sturgis, SD

*Makes 6 servings*

**Prep. Time: 15 minutes**
**Cooking Time: 6-7 hours**
**Ideal slow cooker size: 4- to 5-qt.**

2 cups water
1 pkg. beef stew mix
2 lbs. stewing meat, cubed
3 15-oz. cans whole new potatoes, *or* 3 lbs. fresh new potatoes
1 cup sliced celery
10-12 small white onions, peeled
1-1½ cups sliced carrots
8 oz. fresh mushrooms, whole, *or* sliced

1. Combine water and beef stew mix in slow cooker.
2. Place meat in slow cooker.
3. Stir in remaining ingredients.
4. Cover. Cook on High 6-7 hours, or until meat and vegetables are as tender as you like.

*I put up a small tree in my kitchen and decorate it with my mother's old cookie cutters and some of her recipe cards. I enjoy it while I'm in the kitchen during the holidays—which is a lot of time!*

*Carol L. Miller, Lockport, NY*

# Tomato-y Beef Stew

**Janie Steele**
Moore, OK

*Makes 6-8 servings*

**Prep. Time:** *15 minutes*
**Cooking Time:** *8 hours*
**Ideal slow cooker size:** *5- to 6-qt.*

5 lbs. stewing meat, cubed
2 onions, chopped
14½-oz. can chopped
   tomatoes
10¾-oz. can tomato soup
5-6 carrots, sliced
5-6 potatoes, peeled and
   cubed
1 cup sliced celery
1 bell pepper, sliced
2 tsp. salt
½ tsp. pepper
2 cloves minced garlic

1. Combine all ingredients in slow cooker.
2. Cover. Cook on Low 8 hours.

*Serving suggestion: Since this is a nearly complete meal, I usually add only warm **bread** or **cornbread** to round it out.*

Tip:
   This recipe is very adaptable. You can reduce the amount of meat and increase the vegetables as you wish.

---

# After-Work Stew

**Vera M. Kuhns**
Harrisonburg, VA

*Makes 5 servings*

**Prep. Time:** *15-20 minutes*
**Cooking Time:** *8-9 hours*
**Ideal slow cooker size:** *3- to 4-qt.*

1½ lbs. beef, cut into 1½"
   cubes
oil
3 medium-sized potatoes,
   pared and cubed
4 medium-sized carrots,
   quartered
2 celery ribs, sliced
2 medium-sized onions,
   sliced
2 tsp. salt
½ tsp. dried basil
½ tsp. pepper
10¾-oz. can tomato soup
half a soup can water

1. Brown beef cubes in oil in skillet. Do in batches so that beef browns and doesn't steam. Drain off drippings. Return beef to skillet.
2. Meanwhile, layer potatoes, carrots, celery, and onions in slow cooker.
3. Mix browned beef in skillet with salt, basil, and pepper, stirring up any browned bits in the skillet.
4. Place seasoned beef on top of vegetables.
5. Combine soup and water in a bowl. Pour over ingredients in slow cooker.
6. Cover. Cook on Low 8-9 hours, or just until vegetables and meat are tender.

---

# Easy Beef Stew

**Janie Steele**
Moore, OK

*Makes 14-18 servings*

**Prep. Time:** *25 minutes*
**Cooking Time:** *10-11 hours*
**Ideal slow cooker size:** *2 4-qt. cookers*

2-3 lbs. beef, cubed
16-oz. pkg. frozen green
   beans, *or* mixed
   vegetables
16-oz. pkg. frozen corn
2 lbs. carrots, chopped
1 large onion, chopped
4 medium potatoes, peeled
   and chopped
10¾-oz. can tomato soup
10¾-oz. can celery soup
10¾-oz. can mushroom
   soup
bell pepper chopped,
   *optional*
16-oz. pkg. frozen peas

1. Combine all ingredients except peas in 2 4-qt. slow cookers. This is a very large recipe.
2. Cover. Cook on Low 10-11 hours, or until beef and vegetables are as tender as you like them.
3. Fifteen minutes before end of cooking time, stir in peas.

# New Mexico Stew

**Helen Kenagy**
Carlsbad, NM

*Makes 8 servings*

**Prep. Time: 15 minutes**
**Cooking Time: 8½-10½ hours**
**Ideal slow cooker size: 5-qt.**

salt to taste
pepper to taste
2 lbs. stewing meat, *or*
    steak, cubed, *divided*
1 Tbsp. oil
5-6 potatoes, cubed, *divided*
6-8 carrots, diced, *divided*
other vegetables of your
    choice, diced, *divided*
1-2 4¼-oz. cans chopped
    green chilies, undrained,
    *divided*
1½ lbs. raw pork sausage,
    crumbled, *divided*

1. Salt and pepper stewing meat. Brown in oil in skillet.
2. Place half the stewing meat in bottom of slow cooker. Sprinkle with salt and pepper.
3. Layer half the vegetables and chilies over beef. Sprinkle with salt and pepper.
4. Crumble half the sausage over top. Sprinkle with salt and pepper.
5. Repeat layering until all ingredients are used.
6. Cover. Cook on High until ingredients begin to boil. Then turn cooker to Low for 8-10 hours. Do not lift lid and do not stir during cooking.

*Serving suggestion: With such a complete dish, all you need to add is a **green salad** and **fresh bread** if you wish.*

# Hungarian Beef Stew

**Esther Becker**
Gordonville, PA

*Makes 6 servings*

**Prep. Time: 15 minutes**
**Cooking Time: 10-12 hours**
**Ideal slow cooker size: 4-qt.**

2 lbs. beef cubes
1 onion, chopped
2 medium potatoes, peeled
    and cubed
2 carrots, sliced
10-oz. pkg. frozen lima
    beans
2 tsp. parsley
½ cup beef broth
2 tsp. paprika
1 tsp. salt
16-oz. can diced tomatoes

1. Combine beef, onion, potatoes, carrots, lima beans, and parsley in slow cooker.
2. Combine remaining ingredients in a bowl. Pour into slow cooker.
3. Cover. Cook on Low 10-12 hours.

*Serving suggestion: This is a great meal, especially when served with a **tossed salad** and **homemade rolls**.*

# Hungarian Barley Stew

**Naomi E. Fast**
Hesston, KS

*Makes 8 servings*

**Prep. Time: 20 minutes**
**Cooking Time: 5 hours**
**Ideal slow cooker size: 5-qt.**

1½ lbs. beef cubes
2 Tbsp. oil
2 large onions, diced
1 medium-sized green bell
    pepper, chopped
28-oz. can whole tomatoes
½ cup ketchup
⅔ cup dry small pearl
    barley
1 tsp. salt
½ tsp. pepper
1 Tbsp. paprika
10-oz. pkg. frozen baby
    lima beans
3 cups water
1 cup sour cream

1. Brown beef cubes in oil in skillet. Add onions and green peppers. Sauté until no longer crispy. Pour into slow cooker.
2. Stir in remaining ingredients except sour cream.
3. Cover. Cook on High 5 hours.
4. Stir in sour cream before serving.

*Serving suggestion: This goes well with **cabbage slaw**.*

# Wash-Day Stew

**Naomi E. Fast**
Hesston, KS

*Makes 8-10 servings*

**Prep. Time: 10 minutes**
**Cooking Time: 6-7 hours**
**Ideal slow cooker size: 5-qt.**

1½-2 lbs. lean lamb, *or* beef, cubed
2 15-oz. cans garbanzo beans, drained
2 15-oz. cans white beans, drained
2 medium onions, peeled and quartered
1 qt. water
1 tsp. salt
1 tomato, peeled and quartered
1 tsp. turmeric
3 Tbsp. fresh lemon juice
8-10 pita bread pockets

1. Combine all ingredients except pita bread in slow cooker.
2. Cover. Cook on High 6-7 hours.
3. Lift stew from cooker with a strainer spoon and stuff in pita bread pockets.

**Note:**

*I learned to prepare this nutritious meal from a student from Iran, who was attending graduate school at the University of Nebraska. Fatimeh explained to me that her family prepared this dish every wash day.*

*Very early in the morning, they made a fire in a large rock-lined pit outside. Then they placed a large covered kettle, filled with the above ingredients, over the coals to cook slowly all day. At the end of a day of doing laundry, the food was ready with a minimum of preparation.*

*Of course, they started with dry garbanzos and white beans, presoaked the night before.*

*They served this Wash-Day Stew spooned into pita bread and ate it with their hands.*

# Potluck Beef Barbecue Sandwiches

**Carol Sommers**
Millersburg, OH

*Makes 16 servings*

**Prep. Time: 5-10 minutes**
**Cooking Time: 6½-8¾ hours**
**Ideal slow cooker size: 5-qt.**

4-lb. beef chuck roast
1 cup brewed coffee, *or* water
1 Tbsp. apple cider, *or* red-wine, vinegar
1 tsp. salt
½ tsp. pepper
14-oz. bottle ketchup
15-oz. can tomato sauce
1 cup sweet pickle relish
2 Tbsp. Worcestershire sauce
¼ cup brown sugar

1. Place roast, coffee, vinegar, salt, and pepper in slow cooker.
2. Cover. Cook on High 5-8 hours, or until meat is very tender.
3. Pour off cooking liquid. Shred meat with two forks.
4. Add remaining ingredients. Stir well.
5. Cover. Cook on High 30-45 minutes. Reduce heat to Low for serving.

# Barbara Jean's Junior Beef

**Barbara Jean Fabel**
Wausau, WI

*Makes 8 servings*

**Prep. Time: 10 minutes**
**Cooking Time: 5-6 hours**
**Ideal slow cooker size: 4-qt.**

3½-5-lb. beef roast
½ tsp. salt
½ tsp. cayenne pepper
½ tsp. black pepper
1 tsp. seasoned salt
1 medium onion, chopped
1 qt. dill pickle juice
4 dill pickles, chopped
8 hamburger rolls
½ lb. fresh mushrooms, sliced and sautéed
2 cups grated cheddar, *or* Swiss, cheese

1. Combine all ingredients except rolls, mushrooms, and cheese in slow cooker.
2. Cover. Cook on High 4-5 hours.
3. Shred meat using two forks. Reduce heat to Low and cook 1 hour, or until meat is very tender.

4. Serve on hamburger buns with sautéed, sliced, fresh mushrooms and grated cheddar or Swiss cheese.

# Ranch Hand Beef

**Sharon Timpe**
Mequon, WI

*Makes 10-12 servings*

**Prep. Time: 10 minutes**
**Cooking Time: 4-9 hours**
**Ideal slow cooker size: 4-qt.**

**3-3½-lb. boneless beef chuck roast**
**1 cup thinly sliced onions**
**10¾-oz. can cream of celery soup**
**4-oz. can sliced mushrooms, drained**
**12-oz. can beer**
**½ cup ketchup**
**1 large bay leaf**
**½ tsp. salt**
**¼ tsp. lemon pepper**
**2 Tbsp. chopped fresh parsley, *or* 1½ tsp. dried parsley**

1. Place roast in slow cooker.
2. Combine remaining ingredients in a large bowl. Pour over roast.
3. Cover. Cook on Low 7-9 hours or on medium setting 4-6 hours, until meat is tender.
4. Remove bay leaf.
5. Shred roast with two forks. Mix meat through sauce.

*Serving suggestion: This works well two ways: served on **buns** as sandwiches, or over cooked **noodles**.*

*Or, to give this dish a Mexican theme, serve the beef over **tortilla chips** or **fritos** and have bowls of shredded **lettuce**, diced **avocado**, sliced **green onions**, sliced ripe **olives**, **sour cream**, diced **tomatoes**, and shredded **cheese** for garnishing the meat.*

### Variation:

If you prefer a thicker sauce, stir 2 Tbsp. cornstarch into ¼ cup water. When smooth, stir into hot sauce in cooker, 15 minutes before serving.

# Beef Barbecue Sandwiches

**Melba Eshleman**
Manheim, PA

*Makes 12-16 servings*

**Prep. Time: 10 minutes**
**Refrigeration Time: 8-10 hours**
**Cooking Time: 10-12 hours**
**Ideal slow cooker size: 4-qt.**

**3-4-lb. beef roast (bottom round or rump is best)**
**½ cup water**
**½ cup ketchup**
**1 tsp. chili powder**
**1½ Tbsp. Worcestershire sauce**
**2 Tbsp. vinegar**
**1 tsp. salt**
**1 Tbsp. sugar**
**1 tsp. dry mustard**
**1 medium onion, finely chopped**
**½ cup water**

1. The night before serving, place roast in slow cooker with ½ cup water.
2. Cover. Cook on Low 10-12 hours.
3. Also the night before serving, combine remaining ingredients (except rolls) and refrigerate 8-10 hours.
4. In the morning, shred roast with fork and return to cooker. Pour remaining ingredients over top. Mix together.
5. Heat on Low until lunch or suppertime.

*Serving suggestion: Serve on **kaiser rolls**.*

# Easy Roast Beef Barbecue

**Rose Hankins**
Stevensville, MD

*Makes 12-16 servings*

*Prep. Time: 10 minutes*
*Cooking Time: 12 hours*
*Ideal slow cooker size: 4-qt.*

3-4-lb. beef roast
12-oz. bottle barbecue
  sauce
½ cup water
½ cup ketchup
½ cup chopped onions
½ cup chopped green
  pepper

1. Combine ingredients in slow cooker.
2. Cover. Cook on Low 12 hours.
3. Shred meat using 2 forks. Mix thoroughly through sauce.

*Serving suggestion: This is enough Barbecue to serve on 12-16 **sandwich rolls**. Offer **cole slaw** as a side dish, or as an additional sandwich filler.*

# Herby Beef Sandwiches

**Jean A. Shaner**
York, PA

*Makes 10-12 servings*

*Prep. Time: 5 minutes*
*Cooking Time: 7-8 hours*
*Ideal slow cooker size: 4-qt.*

3-4-lb. boneless beef chuck
  roast
3 Tbsp. fresh basil, *or* 1
  Tbsp. dried basil
3 Tbsp. fresh oregano, *or* 1
  Tbsp. dried oregano
1½ cups water
1 pkg. dry onion soup mix

1. Place roast in slow cooker.
2. Combine basil, oregano, and water in a bowl. Pour over roast.
3. Sprinkle with onion soup mix.
4. Cover. Cook on Low 7-8 hours.
5. Shred meat with fork. Stir sauce through shredded meat.

*Serving suggestion: I like to serve these on crusty **Italian rolls**. This amount of beef fills 10-12 rolls.*

# Hot Beef Sandwiches

**Evelyn L. Ward**
Greeley, CO

*Makes 10 servings*

*Prep. Time: 5-10 minutes*
*Cooking Time: 8-10 hours*
*Ideal slow cooker size: 4-qt.*

3 lbs. beef chuck roast
1 large onion, chopped
¼ cup vinegar
1 clove garlic, minced
1-1½ tsp. salt
¼-½ tsp. pepper

1. Place meat in slow cooker. Top with onions.
2. Combine vinegar, garlic, salt, and pepper in a bowl. Pour over meat, but don't disturb the onions.
3. Cover. Cook on Low 8-10 hours.
4. Drain broth but save for dipping.
5. Shred meat.

Note:

I volunteer with Habitat for Humanity. I don't do construction, but I provide lunch sometimes for work crews. These sandwiches are a favorite. I make the most colorful tossed salad that I can and serve seasonal fresh fruit and pie along with the sandwiches.

# Middle Eastern Sandwiches (for a crowd)

**Esther Mast**
East Petersburg, PA

*Makes 10-16 sandwiches*

**Prep. Time: 50 minutes**
**Cooking Time: 6¼-8¼ hours**
**Ideal slow cooker size: 4-qt.**

4 lbs. boneless beef, *or*
  venison, cut in ½"
  cubes
4 Tbsp. cooking oil
2 cups chopped onions
2 garlic cloves, minced
1 cup dry red wine
6-oz. can tomato paste
1 tsp. dried oregano
1 tsp. dried basil
½ tsp. dried rosemary
2 tsp. salt
dash of pepper
¼ cup cornstarch
¼ cup cold water
pita pocket breads
2 cups shredded lettuce
1 large tomato, seeded and
  diced
1 large cucumber, seeded
  and diced
8-oz. carton plain yogurt

1. Brown meat, 1 lb. at a
time, in skillet in 1 Tbsp. oil.
As you finish one batch, place
browned beef in slow cooker.
Reserve drippings.
2. Sauté onions and garlic
in drippings until tender. Add
to meat.
3. Stir in wine, tomato
paste, oregano, basil, rosemary, salt, and pepper.

4. Cover. Cook on Low 6-8
hours.
5. Turn cooker to High.
Combine cornstarch and
water in small bowl until
smooth. Stir into meat
mixture. Cook until bubbly
and thickened, stirring
occasionally.
6. Split pita breads to make
pockets. Fill each with meat
mixture, lettuce, tomato,
cucumber, and yogurt.

*Serving suggestion: All you
need to top this off is **salad** or
**applesauce**.*

# Ground Beef Stroganoff

**Janie S. Canupp**
Millersville, MD

*Makes 5-6 servings*

**Prep. Time: 30 minutes**
**Cooking Time: 3 hours**
**Ideal slow cooker size: 5-qt.**

2 lbs. ground beef
2 medium onions, chopped
2 cloves garlic, minced
4-oz. can sliced
  mushrooms, drained
1-1½ tsp. salt
¼ tsp. black pepper
1 cup beef broth, *or* 1
  bouillon cube dissolved
  in 1 cup water
3 Tbsp. tomato paste, *or*
  ketchup
1½ cups sour cream
¼ cup flour

1. Brown beef in large
skillet. Stir frequently to
break up clumps.
2. When meat is no longer
pink, add onions, garlic, and
mushrooms. Sauté until onion
is tender. Put mixture into
slow cooker.
3. In a small bowl, mix
together salt, pepper, broth,
and tomato paste. Stir into
beef mixture in slow cooker.
4. Cover. Cook on Low 2½
hours.
5. Meanwhile, combine
sour cream and flour in
a small bowl until well
blended. Stir into slow
cooker.
6. Cover. Cook 30 more
minutes, or until Stroganoff is
thickened and bubbly.

*Serving suggestion: Serve
over buttered **noodles** or **rice**.*

Variation:
Instead of beef broth or
bouillon cube dissolved in
water, use 10¾-oz. can cream
of chicken soup in Step 3.
**Bonnie L. Miller**
Louisville, OH

# Christmas Meat Loaf

**Wafi Brandt**
Manheim, PA

*Makes 4-6 servings*

*Prep. Time: 25 minutes*
*Cooking Time: 4 hours*
*Ideal slow cooker size: 4-qt.*

Meat Loaf:

2 eggs
1 envelope dry onion soup mix
½ cup seasoned bread crumbs
¼ cup chopped dried cranberries
1 tsp. parsley
1½ lbs. ground beef

Sauce:

16-oz. can whole berry cranberry sauce
¾ cup ketchup
½ cup beef broth
3 Tbsp. brown sugar
3 Tbsp. finely chopped onion
2 tsp. cider vinegar

1. Mix all Meat Loaf ingredients together in a good-sized bowl. Shape into loaf and place in lightly greased slow cooker.
2. Mix Sauce ingredients together in another bowl. Pour over meat.
3. Cover. Cook on High 4 hours.
4. Allow to stand 10 minutes before lifting out of cooker and slicing.

**Tip from Tester:**
After slicing and arranging the Meat Loaf on a platter, I ladled the Sauce over the slices. There was more Sauce than fit on the platter, so I put the remainder in a dish to pass. Then individuals could add more to their slices as a condiment. We loved it!

# Meat Loaf

**Colleen Heatwole**
Burton, MI

*Makes 8 servings*

*Prep. Time: 15 minutes*
*Cooking Time: 4-10 hours*
*Ideal slow cooker size: 4-qt.*

2 lbs. ground beef
2 eggs
⅔ cup dry quick oats
1 envelope dry onion soup mix
½-1 tsp. liquid smoke
1 tsp. ground mustard
½ cup ketchup, *divided*

1. Combine ground beef, eggs, dry oats, dry soup mix, liquid smoke, ground mustard, and all but 2 Tbsp. ketchup in large bowl. Shape into loaf and place in slow cooker.
2. Top with remaining ketchup.
3. Cover. Cook on Low 8-10 hours or on High 4-6 hours.

Variation:
For a special topping for the Meat Loaf, make your own Sauce:

26-oz. can, *or* 2 10¾-oz. cans, mushroom soup
6-10 fresh mushrooms, diced
1 Tbsp. onion flakes
half soup can water
¼ tsp. salt
⅛ tsp. pepper

Combine Sauce ingredients in a bowl. Pour over Meat Loaf in Step 2 instead of ketchup.

**Betty B. Dennison**
Grove City, PA

# Magic Meat Loaf

**Carolyn Baer**
Conrath, WI

*Makes 6 servings*

*Prep. Time: 20 minutes*
*Cooking Time: 9-11 hours*
*Ideal slow cooker size: 4-qt.*

1 egg, beaten
¼ cup milk
1½ tsp. salt
2 slices bread, crumbled
1½ lbs. ground beef
half a small onion, chopped
2 Tbsp. chopped green bell peppers
2 Tbsp. chopped celery
ketchup
green pepper rings
4-6 potatoes, cubed
3 Tbsp. butter, melted

1. Combine egg, milk, salt, and bread crumbs in large bowl. Allow bread crumbs to soften.

2. Add meat, onions, green peppers, and celery. Shape into loaf and place off to the side in slow cooker.

3. Top with ketchup and green pepper rings.

4. Toss potatoes with melted butter in a good sized bowl. Spoon into cooker alongside meat loaf.

5. Cover. Cook on High 1 hour, and then on Low 8-10 hours, or until meat and vegetables are as tender as you want them.

# Gourmet Meat Loaf

**Anne Townsend**
Albuquerque, NM

*Makes 8 servings*

*Prep. Time: 25 minutes*
*Cooking Time: 8-12 hours*
*Ideal slow cooker size: 4-qt.*

**2 medium potatoes, cut in strips**

Meat loaf:
**2 lbs. ground beef**
**½ lb. bulk sausage**
**1 onion, finely chopped**

**2-3 cloves garlic, minced, according to your taste preference**
**½ cup ketchup**
**¾ cup crushed saltines**
**2 eggs**
**2 tsp. Worcestershire sauce**
**2 tsp. seasoning salt**
**¼ tsp. pepper**

Sauce:
**½ cup ketchup**
**¼ cup brown sugar**
**1½ tsp. dry mustard**
**½ tsp. ground nutmeg**

1. Place potatoes in bottom of slow cooker.

2. Combine Meat Loaf ingredients in a large bowl. Form into loaf and place on top of potatoes.

3. Combine Sauce ingredients in a separate bowl. Spoon over Meat Loaf.

4. Cover. Cook on Low 8-12 hours.

Tip:
The potatoes take longer to cook than the meat so make sure you allow enough time.

Note:
*My husband has this at the top of his list of favorite Meat Loaf recipes.*

# Cheese Meat Loaf

**Mary Sommerfeld**
Lancaster, PA

*Makes 8 servings*

*Prep. Time: 15 minutes*
*Cooking Time: 6-8 hours*
*Ideal slow cooker size: 4-qt.*

**2 lbs. ground chuck, *or* ground beef**
**2 cups shredded sharp cheddar, *or* American, cheese**
**1 tsp. salt**
**1 tsp. dry mustard**
**¼ tsp. pepper**
**½ cup chili sauce**
**2 cups crushed cornflakes**
**2 eggs**
**½ cup milk**

1. Combine all ingredients in a large bowl. Shape into loaf. Place in greased slow cooker.

2. Cover. Cook on Low 6-8 hours.

*Serving suggestion: Slice and serve with your favorite **tomato sauce** or **ketchup**.*

Variation:
Before baking, surround meat loaf with quartered potatoes, tossed lightly in oil.

*Our out-of-state relatives always bring gifts specifically made in their states to share with others.*

*Annie C. Boshart, Lebanon, PA*

# Festive Meatballs

### Jean Butzer
Batavia, NY

*Makes 5-7 servings*

*Prep. Time: 20 minutes*
*Cooking Time: 2¾-3¾ hours*
*Ideal slow cooker size: 4-qt.*

1½ lbs. ground beef
4½-oz. can deviled ham
⅔ cup evaporated milk
2 eggs, beaten slightly
1 Tbsp. grated onion
2 cups soft bread crumbs
1 tsp. salt
¼ tsp. allspice
¼ tsp. pepper
¼ cup flour
¼ cup water
1 Tbsp. ketchup
2 tsp. dill weed
1 cup sour cream

1. Combine beef, ham, milk, eggs, onion, bread crumbs, salt, allspice, and pepper in large bowl. Shape into 2" meatballs. As you finish making a ball, place it in the slow cooker.

2. Cover. Cook on Low 2½-3½ hours. Turn to High.

3. In a bowl, dissolve flour in water until smooth. Stir in ketchup and dill weed. Add to meatballs, stirring gently.

4. Cook on High 15-20 minutes, or until slightly thickened.

5. Turn off heat. Stir in sour cream.

*Serving suggestion: Serve over **rice** or **pasta**.*

# Easy Meatballs

### Carlene Horne
Bedford, NH

*Makes 10-12 servings*

*Prep. Time: 5 minutes*
*Cooking Time: 4-5 hours*
*Ideal slow cooker size: 5-qt.*

2 10¾-oz. cans cream of mushroom soup
2 8-oz. pkgs. cream cheese, softened
4-oz. can sliced mushrooms, undrained
1 cup milk
2-3 lbs. frozen meatballs

1. Combine soup, cream cheese, mushrooms, and milk in slow cooker.

2. Stir in meatballs.

3. Cover. Cook on Low 4-5 hours.

*Serving suggestion: Serve over **noodles**.*

# Swedish Meat Balls

### Zona Mae Bontrager
Kokomo, IN

*Makes 6-8 servings*

*Prep. Time: 35 minutes*
*Cooking Time: 4¼-5¼ hours*
*Ideal slow cooker size: 4- to 5-qt.*

1 lb. ground beef
½ lb. ground pork
½ cup minced onions

¾ cup fine dry bread crumbs
1 Tbsp. minced parsley
1 tsp. salt
⅛ tsp. pepper
½ tsp. garlic powder
1 Tbsp. Worcestershire sauce
1 egg
½ cup milk
¼ cup oil

Gravy:
¼ cup flour
¼ tsp. salt
¼ tsp. garlic powder
⅛ tsp. pepper
1 tsp. paprika
2 cups boiling water
¾ cup sour cream

1. In a large bowl, combine meats, onions, bread crumbs, parsley, salt, pepper, garlic powder, Worcestershire sauce, egg, and milk.

2. Shape into balls the size of a walnut. Brown in batches in oil in skillet. As you finish a batch, place browned Meatballs in slow cooker. Reserve drippings in skillet.

3. Cover. Cook on High 10-15 minutes.

4. Meanwhile, make Gravy by stirring flour, salt, garlic powder, pepper, and paprika into hot drippings in skillet.

5. Stir in water and sour cream, stirring continually over medium heat until Gravy thickens. Pour over meatballs.

6. Cover. Reduce heat to Low. Cook 4-5 hours.

*Serving suggestion: Serve over **rice** or **noodles**.*

# Italian Meatball Subs

**Bonnie Miller**
Louisville, OH

*Makes 6-7 servings*

*Prep. Time: 45 minutes*
*Cooking Time: 4-6 hours*
*Ideal slow cooker size: 4- to 5-qt.*

2 eggs, beaten
¼ cup milk
½ cup dry bread crumbs
2 Tbsp. grated Parmesan
  cheese
1 tsp. salt
¼ tsp. pepper
⅛ tsp. garlic powder
1 lb. ground beef
½ lb. bulk pork sausage

Sauce:
15-oz. can tomato sauce
6-oz. can tomato paste
1 small onion, chopped
½ cup chopped green bell
  pepper
½ cup red wine, *or* beef
  broth
⅓ cup water
2 garlic cloves, minced
1 tsp. dried oregano
1 tsp. salt
½ tsp. pepper
½ tsp. sugar

1  Make Meatballs by combining eggs and milk in a large bowl. Add bread crumbs, cheese, and seasonings. Add meats.

2. Mix well. Shape into 1" balls. Broil or sauté in batches until brown in non-stick skillet. As you finish a batch, place Meatballs in slow cooker.

3. Combine Sauce ingredients in a good-sized bowl. Pour over Meatballs. (Make sure Meatballs on the bottom of the cooker are covered with Sauce, too.)

4. Cover. Cook on Low 4-6 hours.

*Serving suggestion: Serve on* **rolls,** *along with* **creamy red potatoes, salad, and dessert.**

# Arlene's BBQ Meatballs

**Arlene Groff**
Lewistown, PA

*Makes 12 servings*

*Prep. Time: 35 minutes*
*Cooking Time: 4 hours*
*Ideal slow cooker size: 5-qt.*

2 lbs. ground beef
2 eggs
1 small onion, chopped
¼ cup milk
1½ cup crushed crackers
  (equal to one packaged
  column of saltines)
1 tsp. prepared mustard
1 tsp. salt
½ tsp. pepper
oil
1½ cups tomato juice
⅓ cup vinegar
1 Tbsp. soy sauce
1 Tbsp. Worcestershire
  sauce
¾ cup brown sugar
2 Tbsp. cornstarch
1 tsp. prepared mustard

1. Combine beef, eggs, onion, milk, crackers, 1 tsp. mustard, salt, and pepper in a large bowl. Form into small balls.

2. Brown in batches in oil in skillet. As you finish a batch, place Meatballs in slow cooker.

3. Combine remaining ingredients in a good-sized bowl. Pour over Meatballs, making sure that all are covered with sauce.

4. Cover. Cook on Low 2 hours. Stir well. Cook an additional 2 hours on Low.

*We enjoy gathering for a simple meal with friends. We roast hot dogs in the fire place and everyone brings something they have on hand. The meal usually ends up well balanced even though unplanned.*

*Karen Sauder, Adamstown, PA*

# Cocktail Meatballs

**Kathy Purcell**
Dublin, OH

*Makes 10-12 servings*

*Prep. Time: 50 minutes*
*Cooking Time: 3-4 hours*
*Ideal slow cooker size: 5- to 6-qt.*

3 lbs. ground beef
1 envelope dry onion soup
   mix
14-oz. can sweetened
   condensed milk

**Sauce:**
18-oz. bottle ketchup
½ cup brown sugar
¼ cup Worcestershire sauce

1. Combine beef, soup
mix, and condensed milk in a
large bowl. Form into about 3
dozen meatballs, each about
1½" around.
2. Place meatballs on
baking sheet. Brown in 350°
oven for 30 minutes. Remove
from oven and drain. Place
meatballs in slow cooker.
3. Combine Sauce ingre-
dients in a good-sized bowl.
Pour over meatballs, making
sure all are covered.
4. Cover. Cook on Low 3-4
hours.

**Note:**
*I have made these meatballs
for many different parties and
events, and they are always a
big hit. Everyone asks for the
recipe.*

# Easy Meatballs for a Group

**Penny Blosser**
Beavercreek, OH

*Makes 10-12 main-dish servings*

*Prep. Time: 5 minutes*
*Cooking Time: 4 hours*
*Ideal slow cooker size: 5- to 6-qt.*

80-100 frozen small
   meatballs
16-oz. jar barbecue sauce
16-oz. jar apricot jam

1. Fill slow cooker with
meatballs.
2. Combine sauce and jam
in a bowl. Pour over meatballs, making sure that all are
covered with sauce.
3. Cover. Cook on Low 4
hours, stirring occasionally if
you're home and able to do so.

*Serving suggestion: This
works well as an appetizer
(served with picks), or as a
main dish over **rice**.*

# Sweet 'n' Tangy Meatballs

**Donna Lantgen**
Rapid City, SD

*Makes 8 servings*

*Prep. Time: 45 minutes*
*Cooking Time: 5 hours*
*Ideal slow cooker size: 4-qt.*

1½ lbs. ground beef
¼ cup plain dry bread
   crumbs
3 Tbsp. prepared mustard
1 tsp. Italian seasoning
¾ cup water
¼ cup ketchup
2 Tbsp. honey
1 Tbsp. red-hot cayenne
   pepper sauce
¾-oz. pkg. brown gravy mix

1. Combine ground beef,
bread crumbs, mustard, and
Italian seasoning in a large
bowl. Shape into 1" balls.
2. Bake or microwave
until browned. Drain. Place
Meatballs in slow cooker.
3. Cover. Cook on Low 3
hours.
4. Combine remaining
ingredients in saucepan.
Cook for 5 minutes. Pour over
meatballs, making sure that
all are covered.
5. Cover cooker. Cook 2
more hours on Low.

**Variation:**
For a fuller flavor, use
orange juice instead of water
in sauce.

# Meatballs and Spaghetti Sauce

**Carol Sommers**
Millersburg, OH

*Makes 6-8 servings*

*Prep. Time: 35 minutes*
*Cooking Time: 6-8 hours*
*Ideal slow cooker size: 4-qt.*

**Meatballs:**
1½ lbs. ground beef
2 eggs
1 cup bread crumbs
oil

**Sauce:**
28-oz. can tomato purée
6-oz. can tomato paste
10¾-oz. can tomato soup
¼-½ cup grated Romano,
   or Parmesan, cheese
1 tsp. oil
1 garlic clove, minced
sliced mushrooms, either
   canned, or fresh, *optional*

1. Combine ground beef, eggs and bread crumbs in a large bowl. Form into 16 Meatballs.
2. Brown in batches in oil in skillet.
3. Meanwhile, combine Sauce ingredients in slow cooker.
4. Add Meatballs to slow cooker as you finish browning a batch. Stir gently into Sauce.
5. Cover. Cook on Low 6-8 hours.
6. Add mushrooms 1-2 hours before sauce is finished.

*Serving suggestion: Serve over cooked **spaghetti**.*

# Snappy Meatballs

**Clara Newswanger**
Gordonville, PA

*Makes 6-8 main-dish servings,*
*or 25 appetizer servings*

*Prep. Time: 35 minutes*
*Cooking Time: 4 hours*
*Ideal slow cooker size: 4-qt.*

**Meatballs:**
2 lbs. ground beef
½ cup chopped onions
1 cup bread crumbs
2 eggs
1 tsp. salt

oil

**Sauce:**
3½ cups tomato juice
1 cup brown sugar
¼ cup vinegar
1 tsp. grated onion
12 gingersnap cookies,
   crushed

1. Combine Meatball ingredients in a large bowl. Shape into balls.
2. Brown in batches in skillet in oil. As you finish a batch, drain Meatballs and place in slow cooker.
3. Combine Sauce ingredients in large bowl. Pour over meatballs. Mix gently.
4. Cover. Cook on Low 4 hours.

**Note:**
*Our son married a woman from the West Coast. He brought his new bride "home" on their honeymoon. We held an informal reception for friends who could not attend*

*their wedding. Served with a light lunch, this recipe brought raves! Now we think of our children 3,000 miles away whenever we make these Meatballs.*

# Meatballs and Peppers

**Frances L. Kruba**
Dundalk, MD

*Makes 6-8 servings*

*Prep. Time: 10-15 minutes*
*Cooking Time: 4-6 hours*
*Ideal slow cooker size: 4- to 5-qt.*

2 28-oz. cans diced
   tomatoes with basil,
   garlic, and oregano,
   undrained
6-oz. can tomato paste
1½ lbs. (about 48) frozen
   meatballs
14-oz. pkg. frozen pepper
   strips

1. Combine tomatoes, tomato paste, meatballs, and pepper strips in slow cooker.
2. Cover. Cook on Low 4-6 hours.

# Sweet and Sour Meatballs

**Alice Miller**
Stuarts Draft, VA

*Makes 4 servings*

*Prep. Time: 35 minutes*
*Cooking Time: 3-4 hours*
*Ideal slow cooker size: 4-qt.*

**Meatballs:**
1 lb. ground beef
½ cup dry bread crumbs
¼ cup milk
1 tsp. salt
1 egg, beaten
2 Tbsp. finely chopped
  onions
½ tsp. Worcestershire sauce

oil

**Sauce:**
½ cup packed brown sugar
2 Tbsp. cornstarch
13¼-oz. can pineapple
  chunks, undrained
⅓ cup vinegar
1 Tbsp. soy sauce
1 green bell pepper, chopped

1. Combine Meatball
ingredients in a large bowl.
Shape into 1½″ balls.
2. Brown in batches in oil
in skillet. As you finish a
batch, drain well and place in
slow cooker.
3. Add brown sugar and
cornstarch to drippings in
skillet. Stir in remaining
Sauce ingredients.
4. Heat to boiling, stir-
ring constantly. Pour over
meatballs. Make sure all are
covered with Sauce.

5. Cover cooker. Cook on
Low 3-4 hours.

**Variation:**
If you like pineapples,
use a 20-oz. can of chunks,
instead of a 13¼-oz. can.

# Asian Meatballs

**Evelyn L. Ward**
Greeley, CO

*Makes 6 servings*

*Prep. Time: 40 minutes*
*Cooking Time: 3 hours*
*Ideal slow cooker size: 3-qt.*

1 lb. ground beef
1 egg
5 Tbsp. cornstarch, *divided*
½ tsp. salt
2 Tbsp. minced onions
2 cups pineapple juice
2 Tbsp. soy sauce
½ cup wine vinegar
¾ cup water
½ cup sugar
1 green bell pepper, cut in
  strips
1 can water chestnuts,
  drained

1. Combine beef, egg, 1
Tbsp. cornstarch, salt, and
onions in bowl. Mix well.
2. Shape into 1″ Meatballs.
Place on baking sheet. Brown
on all sides under broiler.
3. Mix remaining corn-
starch with pineapple juice
in saucepan. When smooth,
mix in soy sauce, vinegar,
water, and sugar. Bring to

boil. Simmer, stirring until
thickened.
4. Combine Meatballs and
Sauce in slow cooker.
5. Cover. Cook on Low 2
hours.
6. Stir in green peppers
and water chestnuts.
7. Cover. Cook 1 hour on
Low.

*Serving suggestion: Serve*
*over **chow mein noodles** and*
*garnish with **pineapple slices**.*

# Applesauce Meatballs

**Mary E. Wheatley**
Mashpee, MA

*Makes 6 servings*

*Prep. Time: 40 minutes*
*Cooking Time: 4-6 hours*
*Ideal slow cooker size: 3-qt.*

¾ lb. ground beef
¼ lb. ground pork
1 egg
¾ cup soft bread crumbs
½ cup unsweetened
  applesauce
¾ tsp. salt
¼ tsp. pepper
oil
¼ cup ketchup
¼ cup water

1. Combine beef, pork, egg,
bread crumbs, applesauce,
salt, and pepper in bowl.
Form into 1½″ balls.
2. Brown in oil in batches
in skillet. Transfer meat

to slow cooker as a batch browns, reserving drippings.

3. Combine ketchup and water in skillet. Stir up browned drippings and mix together well. Spoon over meatballs, making sure that all are covered.

4. Cover. Cook on Low 4-6 hours.

*Serving suggestion: Serve with steamed rice and green salad.*

# Holiday Meatballs

**Jean Robinson**
Cinnaminson, NJ

*Makes 20 servings*

**Prep. Time: 10 minutes**
**Cooking Time: 3½-6½ hours**
**Ideal slow cooker size: 5-qt.**

2 15-oz. bottles ketchup
   (spicy, if you can find it)
2 cups blackberry wine
2 12-oz. jars apple jelly
2 lbs. frozen, precooked
   meatballs, *or* your own
   favorite meatballs,
   cooked

1. Heat ketchup, wine, and jelly in slow cooker on High.
2. When hot, stir in frozen meatballs.
3. Cover. Cook on High 4-6 hours. (If the meatballs are not frozen, cook on High 3-4 hours.)

**Variations:**
1. For those who like it hotter and spicier, put a bottle of

hot sauce on the table to add to their individual servings.

2. If you prefer a less winey flavor, use 1 cup water and only 1 cup wine.

# Meatballs with Bounce

**Arlene Leaman Kliewer**
Lakewood, CO

*Makes 8-10 servings,*
*or 60 very small meatballs*

**Prep. Time: 1 hour**
**Ideal slow cooker size: 4-qt.**

**Meatballs:**
2 lbs. ground beef
2 eggs, slightly beaten
1 cup bread crumbs
2 tsp. salt
¼ tsp. pepper

**Sauce:**
12-oz. bottle chili sauce
10-oz. jar grape jelly
½ cup ketchup
1 tsp. Worcestershire sauce

1. Combine ground beef, eggs, bread crumbs, salt, and pepper in bowl. Form into 60 small balls. Place on baking sheet.
2. Bake at 400° for 15-17 minutes. Place in slow cooker.
3. Combine Sauce ingredients in saucepan. Heat and stir until jelly melts. Pour over Meatballs.
4. Heat on Low until ready to serve.

**Note:**
*We often make this recipe for our family's Christmas evening snack.*

**Variations:**
1. Liven up the Meatballs by adding ⅔ cup chopped onions, 2 Tbsp. snipped fresh parsley, and 1 tsp. Worcestershire sauce in Step 1.
    **Joan Rosenberger**
    Stephens City, VA

2. Add juice of half a lemon to the Sauce in Step 3.
    **Linda Sluiter**
    Schererville, IN

3. Use ½ cup crushed cornflakes in place of 1 cup bread crumbs in Meatball mixture.
    Add 1 Tbsp. bottled lemon juice to Sauce in Step 3.
    **Alice Miller**
    Stuarts Draft, VA

# Meatball-Barley Casserole

Marjorie Y. Guengerich
Harrisonburg, VA

*Makes 6 servings*

*Prep. Time: 40 minutes*
*Cooking Time: 4-8 hours*
*Ideal slow cooker size: 4-qt.*

⅔ cup pearl barley
1 lb. ground beef
½ cup soft bread crumbs
1 small onion, chopped
¼ cup milk
¼ tsp. pepper
1 tsp. salt
oil
½ cup thinly sliced celery
½ cup finely chopped
    sweet peppers
10¾-oz. can cream of
    celery soup
⅓ cup water
paprika

1. Cook barley as directed
on package. Set aside.
2. Combine beef, bread
crumbs, onion, milk, pepper,
and salt in a bowl. Shape into
20 balls.
3. Brown in batches on all
sides in oil in skillet. Drain
off drippings as you finish a
batch, and place Meatballs in
slow cooker.
4. Stir in barley, celery, and
peppers.
5. Combine soup and water
in a bowl. Pour into slow
cooker. Mix all together gently.
6. Sprinkle with paprika.
7. Cover. Cook on Low 6-8
hours or on High 4 hours.

# Sloppy Beef Sandwiches

Colleen Konetzni
Rio Rancho, NM

*Makes 6 servings*

*Prep. Time: 30 minutes*
*Cooking Time: 3-4 hours*
*Ideal slow cooker size: 3- to 4-qt.*

1½ lbs. lean ground beef
1 onion, chopped
½ cup water
1 small can sliced black
    olives, drained
1 jar salsa

1. Cook beef and onion in
skillet with ½ cup water until
meat is no longer pink. Stir
with wooden spoon to break
up clumps. Drain off drippings.
2. Place beef mixture into
slow cooker. Add olives and
salsa. Mix well.
3. Cover. Cook on Low 3-4
hours.

*Serving suggestion: Divide
sandwich meat among **buns** and
sprinkle with 2 cups shredded
**cheese** and ½ cup chopped
**lettuce**.*

# Barbecue Sauce and Hamburgers

Dolores Kratz
Souderton, PA

*Makes 6 servings*

*Prep. Time: 25 minutes*
*Cooking Time: 2-3 hours*
*Ideal slow cooker size: 4-qt.*

14¾-oz. can beef gravy
½ cup ketchup
½ cup chili sauce
1 Tbsp. Worcestershire
    sauce
1 Tbsp. prepared mustard
6 grilled hamburger
    patties

1. Combine all ingredients
except hamburger patties in
slow cooker.
2. Add hamburger patties.
3. Cover. Cook on Low 2-3
hours.

*Serving suggestion: Serve in
**buns**, each topped with a slice
of **cheese** if you like.*

Tips:
1. Freeze leftover sauce for
future use.
2. This is both a practical
and a tasty recipe for serving
a crowd (picnics, potlucks,
etc.). You can grill the patties
early in the day, rather than
at the last minute when your
guests are arriving.

# No-More-Bottled Barbecue Sauce

**Lauren Eberhard**
Seneca, IL

*Makes 2-2½ cups sauce*

**Prep. Time: 10 minutes**
**Cooking Time: 3 hours**
**Ideal slow cooker size: 1½-qt.**

1 cup finely chopped
  onions
¼ cup oil
6-oz. can tomato paste
½ cup water
¼ cup brown sugar
¼ cup lemon juice (freshly
  squeezed juice is best)
3 Tbsp. Worcestershire
  sauce
2 Tbsp. prepared mustard
2 tsp. salt
¼ tsp. pepper

1. Combine all ingredients
in slow cooker.
2. Cover. Cook on Low 3
hours.
3. Use on hamburgers,
sausage, pork chops, ribs,
steaks, chicken, turkey, or
fish.

Note:
  Sauce will keep in refrigerator for up to 2 weeks.

# Pizzaburgers

**Deborah Swartz**
Grottoes, VA

*Makes 4-6 servings*

**Prep. Time: 20 minutes**
**Cooking Time: 1-2 hours**
**Ideal slow cooker size: 4-qt.**

1 lb. ground beef
½ cup chopped onions
¼ tsp. salt
⅛ tsp. pepper
8 oz. pizza sauce
10¾-oz. can cream of
  mushroom soup
2 cups shredded cheddar
  cheese

1. Brown ground beef
and onion in skillet. Drain
off drippings. Place in slow
cooker.
2. Stir in remaining
ingredients. Mix well.
3. Cover. Cook on Low 1-2
hours.

*Serving suggestion: Serve on
hamburger buns.*

# Yum-Yums

**Evelyn L. Ward**
Greeley, CO

*Makes 12 servings*

**Prep. Time: 35 minutes**
**Cooking Time: 4-6 hours**
**Ideal slow cooker size: 4-qt.**

3 lbs. ground beef
2 onions, chopped
10¾-oz. can cream of
  chicken soup
1½ cups tomato juice
1 tsp. prepared mustard
1 tsp. Worcestershire sauce
1 tsp. salt
¼ tsp. pepper

1. Brown beef and onions
in skillet. Drain off drippings.
Place in slow cooker.
2. Stir in remaining
ingredients.
3. Cover. Cook on Low 4-6
hours.

*Serving suggestion: Serve on
hamburger buns.*

Note:
  *This is a great recipe for
serving a crowd. A club I am
a part of serves it when we do
fund-raisers. Our menu is Yum-
Yums, marinated bean salad,
and strawberry short cake. We
make the food in our homes and
carry it to the meeting site.*

*Don't apologize if your house is not spotless. Your
guests will feel more relaxed when they invite you.*
*Karen Sauder, Adamstown, PA*

# Dianna's Barbecue

**Lauren Eberhard**
Seneca, IL

*Makes 12 servings*

*Prep. Time: 30 minutes*
*Cooking Time: 1-4 hours*
*Ideal slow cooker size: 5-qt.*

4 lbs. ground beef
oil
24-oz. bottle ketchup
¼ cup prepared mustard
2 Tbsp. vinegar
¼ cup sugar
¾ cup water
1 tsp. pepper
1 Tbsp. paprika
1 cup chopped celery
1 cup chopped onion

1. Brown ground beef in large skillet, in oil if needed. Drain off drippings. Place beef in slow cooker.
2. Stir in all other ingredients.
3. Cover. Cook on High 1-2 hours or on Low 4 hours.

*Serving suggestion: Serve in 12 **sandwich rolls**.*

# Chili Spaghetti

**Clara Newswanger**
Gordonville, PA

*Makes 8-10 servings*

*Prep. Time: 25 minutes*
*Cooking Time: 2-3 hours*
*Ideal slow cooker size: 4-qt.*

1½ lbs. ground beef
12-oz. dry spaghetti
½ cup diced onions
2 cups tomato juice
2 tsp. chili powder
1 tsp. salt
¾ cup grated mild cheese

1. Brown beef in skillet, stirring frequently to break up clumps. When no longer pink, place in slow cooker.
2. Meanwhile, cook spaghetti until just softened in large stockpot. Drain and add to slow cooker.
3. Add all remaining ingredients to slow cooker. Mix together gently and well.
4. Cover. Cook on Low 2-3 hours. Check mixture about halfway through the cooking time. If it's becoming dry, stir in an additional cup of tomato juice.

Variations:
1. Add 8-oz. can sliced mushrooms to Step 3.
2. Use 2 Tbsp. chili powder instead of 2 tsp. chili powder for added flavor.

# Dawn's Spaghetti and Meat Sauce

**Dawn Day**
Westminster, CA

*Makes 6-8 servings*

*Prep. Time: 30 minutes*
*Cooking Time: 4 hours*
*Ideal slow cooker size: 4-qt.*

1 lb. ground beef
1 Tbsp. oil, if needed
½ lb. fresh mushrooms, sliced
1 medium onion, chopped
3 garlic cloves, minced
½ tsp. dried oregano
½ tsp. salt
¼ cup grated Parmesan, *or* Romano, cheese
6-oz. can tomato paste
2 15-oz. cans tomato sauce
15-oz. can chopped, *or* crushed, tomatoes

1. Brown ground beef in skillet, in oil if needed. Stir frequently, breaking up clumps. Continue cooking until meat is no longer pink. Reserve drippings and transfer meat to slow cooker.
2. Sauté mushrooms, onion, and garlic in drippings until onions are transparent. Add to slow cooker.
3. Mix remaining ingredients into cooker.
4. Cover. Cook on Low 4 hours.

*Serving suggestion: Serve with **pasta** and **garlic bread**.*

Tip:
This recipe freezes well.

# Quick and Easy Spaghetti

**Beverly Getz**
Warriors Mark, PA

*Makes 8 servings*

*Prep. Time: 30 minutes*
*Cooking Time: 3-4 hours*
*Ideal slow cooker size: 4-qt.*

1½ lbs. ground beef
2 onions, chopped
26-oz. jar spaghetti sauce
  with mushrooms
10¾-oz. can tomato soup
1, *or* 2, 14½-oz. cans stewed
  tomatoes, depending
  on the consistency you
  prefer
8-oz. can mushrooms,
  undrained
½ tsp. garlic powder
½ tsp. garlic salt
½ tsp. minced dried garlic
½ tsp. onion salt
½ tsp. Italian seasoning

1. Brown beef and onions
in skillet, stirring frequently
to break up clumps. When
meat is no longer pink, drain
off drippings. Place meat and
onions into slow cooker.

2. Stir in all remaining
ingredients.

3. Cover. Cook on Low 3-4
hours.

*Serving suggestion: Serve
over 1 lb. cooked spaghetti.*

# Spaghetti Sauce for a Crowd

**Sue Pennington**
Bridgewater, VA

*Makes 18 cups*

*Prep. Time: 25 minutes*
*Cooking Time: 4-6 hours*
*Ideal slow cooker size: 6-qt.*

1 lb. ground beef
1 lb. ground turkey
1 Tbsp. oil
5 15-oz. cans tomato sauce
3 6-oz. cans tomato paste
1 cup water
½ cup minced fresh, *or* 3
  Tbsp. dried, parsley
½ cup minced fresh, *or* 3
  Tbsp. dried, oregano
4 tsp. salt

1. Brown meat in oil in
skillet. Stir frequently to
break up clumps. When meat
is no longer pink, drain off
dripping. Place meat in 6-qt.
slow cooker. (A 5-qt. cooker
will work, but it will be
brimful.)

2. Stir in remaining
ingredients. Mix together
thoroughly.

3. Cover. Cook on Low 4-6
hours.

Notes:
1. Add 1 medium onion,
chopped, and/or 3 cloves
garlic, minced, to Step 1,
browning along with the
meat.

2. Add 1 can crushed
tomatoes, or 2 cups cut-up
fresh tomatoes, to Step 2 to
add a fresh-tomato taste.
(This will make your cooker
even fuller, so you may want
to switch to two 4- or 5-qt.
cookers.)

3. Make the sauce without
meat if you prefer.

4. Use as a pizza sauce,
especially if you make it
meatless.

5. Sauce can be refrigerated
for a week, or frozen up to 3
months.

Have a balance of meat and no-meat appetizers/dishes
so you're not worried about vegetarian preferences. Veggie
and fruit options allow dieters to enjoy the party as well.
Susan Tjon, Austin, TX

# Beef and Sausage Spaghetti Sauce

**Sherri Grindle**
Goshen, IN

*Makes 10-12 servings*

*Prep. Time: 30 minutes*
*Cooking Time: 6-8 hours*
*Ideal slow cooker size: 5-qt.*

1 lb. ground beef
1 lb. Italian sausage, bulk,
 *or* cut in thin slices
1 large onion, chopped
3 Tbsp. oil, if needed
5 lbs., *or* 3 28-oz. cans,
 tomato purée
6 cloves garlic, minced
2 Tbsp. parsley
1 Tbsp. salt
¼ rounded tsp. pepper
3 bay leaves
1 Tbsp. dried oregano
crushed red pepper, *optional*

1. Brown meat and onion
in skillet in oil, unless they
produce enough of their own
drippings. Stir frequently to
break up clumps. When meat
is no longer pink, drain off
drippings and place meat in
slow cooker.
2. Combine all remaining
ingredients in slow cooker
with meat and onions.
3. Cover. Cook on Low 6-8
hours.

*Serving suggestion: Serve
over your favorite* **pasta***.*

Variation:
 Add 1 box uncooked
spaghetti 1 hour before serving.
Cook on High for last hour.

# Spaghetti Sauce with a Kick

**Andrea O'Neil**
Fairfield, CT

*Makes 4-6 servings*

*Prep. Time: 25 minutes*
*Cooking Time: 4-6 hours*
*Ideal slow cooker size: 4-qt.*

1 lb. ground beef
1 onion, chopped
2 28-oz. cans crushed
 tomatoes
16-oz. can tomato sauce
1-lb. Italian sausage, cut in
 chunks
3 cloves garlic, crushed
1 Tbsp. Italian seasoning
2 tsp. dried basil
red pepper flakes to taste

1. Brown beef and onions
in skillet. Stir frequently to
break up clumps. When meat
is no longer pink, drain off
drippings and place in slow
cooker.
2. Stir remaining ingredients into slow cooker.
3. Cover. Cook on Low 4-6
hours.

*Serving suggestion: Serve
over your favorite* **pasta***.*

Variation:
 Add 1-2 tsp. salt and 1-2
Tbsp. brown sugar or honey
to Step 2, if you wish.

# Slow Cooker Lasagna

**Crystal Brunk**
Singers Glen, VA

*Makes 6-8 servings*

*Prep. Time: 20 minutes*
*Cooking Time: 4-8 hours*
*Ideal slow cooker size: 4-qt.*

1 lb. ground beef
oil
4-5 cups spaghetti sauce,
 depending upon how
 firm *or* how juicy you
 want the finished lasagna
1 egg
24-oz. container cottage
 cheese
8-10 uncooked lasagna
 noodles, *divided*
2-3 cups mozzarella
 cheese, *divided*

1. Brown ground beef
in skillet, in oil if needed.
Stir frequently to break
up clumps. When meat is
no longer pink, drain off
drippings.
2. Stir spaghetti sauce into
beef in skillet.
3. Combine egg and cottage
cheese in a bowl.
4. Layer half of ground
beef mixture into slow
cooker.
5. Layer in half the dry
noodles (break to fit if you
need to), half the cottage
cheese mixture, and half the
mozzarella cheese in slow
cooker. Repeat layers.
6. Cover. Cook on High 4-5
hours or on Low 6-8 hours.

**Variations:**

1. Use ricotta instead of cottage cheese.

2. Add 2 Tbsp. chopped fresh parsley to Step 3.

3. Add 2 Tbsp. grated Parmesan cheese to Step 3, and sprinkle 2 Tbsp. grated Parmesan cheese over top before cooking in Step 5.

**Elaine Rineer**
Lancaster, PA

# Now That's Lasagna

**Shirley Unternahrer**
Wayland, IA

*Makes 10 servings*

*Prep. Time: 20 minutes*
*Cooking Time: 4 hours*
*Ideal slow cooker size: 6-qt.*

1 lb. sausage, *or ground beef (if ground beef, add 1 tsp. dried basil, ½ tsp. salt, and ¼ tsp. pepper)*
1 small onion, chopped
1 small bell pepper, chopped
1 qt. tomato juice, *divided*
15 lasagna noodles, uncooked, *divided*
12 oz. cottage cheese, *divided*
3 cups grated mozzarella cheese
28-oz. jar spaghetti sauce of your choice, *divided*
6 oz. sliced pepperoni
3 cups grated mozzarella cheese

1. Brown sausage or hamburger in skillet. Drain off half the drippings.

2. Add chopped onions and peppers to skillet. Sauté 3 minutes in drippings with meat.

3. Pour 1 cup tomato juice into slow cooker as first layer.

4. Add a layer of 5 uncooked lasagna noodles. Break to fit inside curved edges of slow cooker.

5. Spread with half of cottage cheese as next layer.

6. Spoon half of meat/veggie mix over cottage cheese.

7. Sprinkle with 1 cup mozzarella cheese

8. Spoon half of spaghetti sauce over grated cheese.

9. Add another layer of 5 lasagna noodles.

10. Add remaining cottage cheese, followed by a layer of remaining meat/veggie mix.

11. Add remaining 5 noodles.

12. Top with pepperoni slices, remaining spaghetti sauce, and half of remaining mozzarella cheese.

13. Pour rest of tomato juice slowly around edge of cooker and its ingredients.

14. Cover. Cook on High 3½ hours.

15. Remove lid and top with remaining mozzarella cheese. Cook another 15 minutes.

16. Allow Lasagna to rest 15-20 minutes before serving.

# Easy Ravioli

**Karen Sauder**
Adamstown, PA

*Makes 4 servings*

*Prep. Time: 5 minutes*
*Cooking Time: 4 hours*
*Ideal slow cooker size: 3- to 4-qt.*

25-oz. bag frozen beef ravioli
45-oz. jar spaghetti sauce of your choice
1 cup Monterey Jack, *or* mozzarella, cheese, grated

1. Place all of ravioli into slow cooker.

2. Pour in spaghetti sauce. Stir to distribute sauce evenly.

3. Sprinkle with cheese.

4. Cover. Cook on Low 4 hours.

Note:

This is my favorite recipe for a potluck or fellowship meal, or supper on a busy day.

# Slow Cooker Almost Lasagna

**Jeanette Oberholtzer**
Manheim, PA

*Makes 8-10 servings*

*Prep. Time: 40 minutes*
*Cooking Time: 4-6 hours*
*Ideal slow cooker size: 6-qt.*

1 box rotini, *or* ziti, cooked
2 Tbsp. olive oil
2 28-oz. jars pasta sauce
  with tomato chunks
2 cups tomato juice
½ lb. ground beef
½ lb. bulk sausage,
  crumbled, *or* links cut
  into ¼" slices
2 cups grated Parmesan
  cheese, *divided*
½ cup Italian bread
  crumbs
3 eggs, *divided*
2 cups mozzarella cheese,
  *divided*
2 cups ricotta cheese
1½ tsp. parsley flakes
¾ tsp. salt
¼ tsp. pepper

1. In large bowl, toss pasta with olive oil. Add pasta sauce and tomato juice and mix well. Set aside.
2. Brown beef and sausage together in skillet. Stir frequently to break up clumps. When meat is no longer pink, drain off drippings. Remove skillet from heat; keep meat in skillet.
3. Stir 1 cup Parmesan cheese, bread crumbs, 1 egg, and 1 cup mozzarella cheese

into meat in skillet. Set aside.
4. In separate bowl, beat together ricotta cheese, 2 eggs, 1 cup Parmesan cheese, parsley, salt, and pepper. Set aside.
5. Pour half of pasta-sauce mixture into slow cooker.
6. Spread entire ricotta mixture over pasta. Top with entire meat-cheese mixture. Cover with remaining pasta-sauce mixture.
7. Sprinkle with remaining 1 cup mozzarella cheese.
8. Cover. Cook on Low 4-6 hours.

# Meat Loaf Burgers

**Lafaye M. Musser**
Denver, PA

*Makes 6 servings*

*Prep. Time: 25 minutes*
*Cooking Time: 7-9 hours*
*Ideal slow cooker size: 4-qt.*

1 large onion, sliced
1 rib celery, chopped
2 lbs. ground beef
1 tsp. salt
1¼ tsp. pepper
2 cups tomato juice
4 garlic cloves, minced
1 Tbsp. ketchup
1 tsp. Italian seasoning
½ tsp. salt

1. Place onion and celery in slow cooker.
2. Combine beef, salt, and pepper. Shape into 6 patties. Arrange in slow cooker.

3. In a good-sized mixing bowl, combine tomato juice, garlic, ketchup, Italian seasoning, and salt. Pour over patties.
4. Cover. Cook on Low 7-9 hours.

*Serving suggestion: This makes enough to serve on 6* **hamburger buns**.

# Barbecued Hamburgers

**Martha Hershey**
Ronks, PA

*Makes 4 serving*

*Prep. Time: 20 minutes*
*Cooking Time: 2-6 hours*
*Ideal slow cooker size: 3-qt.*

1 lb. ground beef
¼ cup chopped onions
3 Tbsp. ketchup
1 tsp. salt
1 egg, beaten
¼ cup seasoned bread
  crumbs
oil
18-oz. bottle of your
  favorite barbecue sauce

1. Combine beef, onions, ketchup, salt, egg, and bread crumbs in a good-sized bowl. Form into 4 patties.
2. Brown both sides lightly in oil in skillet. Arrange browned burgers in slow cooker.
3. Cover with barbecue sauce.

4. Cover. Bake on High 2-3 hours or on Low 5-6 hours.

**Note:**

*We first had Barbecued Hamburgers at a 4-H picnic, and they have been a family favorite ever since.*

**Tip:**

Mix the hamburger patties, brown them, and freeze them in advance, and you'll have little to do at the last minute.

# Hamburger-Potato Slow Cooker Dinner

**Lafaye M. Musser**
Denver, PA

*Makes 6-8 servings*

*Prep. Time: 30 minutes*
*Cooking Time: 3-8 hours*
*Ideal slow cooker size: 4-qt.*

1 lb. ground beef
1 cup water
½ tsp. cream of tartar
6 medium potatoes, thinly sliced
1 onion, chopped
¼ cup flour
½ tsp. salt
¼ tsp. pepper
1 cup grated cheddar cheese, *divided*
¼ stick (2 Tbsp.) butter
10¾-oz. can cream of mushroom soup

1. Brown ground beef in skillet, using oil if necessary. Drain off drippings. Set aside.

2. In separate bowl, combine water and cream of tartar. Toss potatoes in water. Drain.

3. In another bowl, mix together onion, flour, salt, pepper, and half of cheese.

4. Place browned beef in bottom of cooker. Top with sliced potatoes. Add onion-cheese mixture.

5. Dot top with butter.

6. Pour soup over all.

7. Cover. Cook on Low 6-8 hours or on High 3-4 hours.

8. Sprinkle remaining cheese over top, 30 minutes before serving.

**Variation:**

Spread 2 4¼-oz. cans chopped green chilies, undrained, over potatoes in Step 4.

**Colleen Konetzni**
Rio Rancho, NM

# 1-2-3-4 Casserole

**Betty K. Drescher**
Quakertown, PA

*Makes 8 servings*

*Prep. Time: 35 minutes*
*Cooking Time: 7-9 hours*
*Ideal slow cooker size: 4-qt.*

1 lb. ground beef
2 onions, sliced
3 carrots, thinly sliced
½ tsp. salt
⅛ tsp. pepper
½ tsp. cream of tartar
1 cup cold water
4 potatoes, thinly sliced
10¾-oz. can cream of mushroom soup
¼ cup milk
½ tsp. salt
⅛ tsp. pepper

1. Layer in greased slow cooker in this order: ground beef, onions, carrots, ½ tsp. salt, and ⅛ tsp. pepper.

2. Dissolve cream of tartar in water in large bowl. Toss sliced potatoes with water. Drain off water.

3. Combine soup and milk in bowl with potatoes. Stir in remaining salt and pepper.

4. Arrange potatoes in slow cooker over top vegetables.

5. Cover. Cook on Low 7-9 hours, or until meat is cooked through and vegetables are as tender as you like them.

**Variations:**

1. Substitute sour cream for the milk.

2. Top potatoes with ½ cup shredded cheese.

# Hamburger Potato Casserole

Sue Pennington
Bridgewater, VA

*Makes 6-10 servings*

*Prep. Time: 30 minutes*
*Cooking Time: 8-10 hours*
*Ideal slow cooker size: 4-qt.*

1 lb. ground beef, *divided*
1 Tbsp. oil
6-8 potatoes, peeled and
  sliced, *divided*
4-6 carrots, sliced, *divided*
2 medium onions, sliced,
  *divided*
1 cup grated cheddar
  cheese, *divided*
1 tsp. salt , *divided*
¼ tsp. pepper, *divided*
10-oz. can cream of
  chicken soup
1 cup peas

1. Brown ground beef in oil in skillet. Drain off drippings.
2. Layer half of beef, potatoes, carrots, onions, and cheese in cooker. Sprinkle with half of salt and pepper.
3. Repeat layers.
4. Pour cream of chicken soup over top.
5. Cover. Cook on Low 8-10 hours.
6. Fifteen minutes before end of cooking time, stir in 1 cup peas.

Note:
*My husband came up with this recipe. Our family loves it and often requests it when I ask them what they want to eat.*

# Hamburger Casserole

Kelly Evenson
Pittsboro, NC

*Makes 6-8 servings*

*Prep. Time: 30 minutes*
*Cooking Time: 8 hours*
*Ideal slow cooker size: 4-qt.*

2 large potatoes, sliced
2-3 medium carrots, sliced
3 medium onions, sliced
2 celery ribs, sliced
garlic salt to taste
pepper to taste
salt to taste
1 lb. ground beef
oil
10¾-oz. can tomato soup
1 soup can of water
1 cup frozen peas, thawed
  and drained

1. Layer potatoes, carrots, onions, and celery in order given into slow cooker.
2. Sprinkle each layer with garlic salt, pepper, and salt.
3. Brown ground beef in oil in skillet. Stir frequently to break up clumps. When meat is no longer pink, drain off drippings.
4. Place meat on top of celery.
5. Combine soup and water in bowl. Pour over all.
6. Cover. Cook on Low 8 hours, or until vegetables are as tender as you like them.
7. Fifteen minutes before end of cooking time, stir in peas.

*Serving suggestion: Serve this nearly complete meal with **applesauce**.*

# Wholesome Hamburger Dinner

Reba Rhodes
Bridgewater, VA

*Makes 6-8 servings*

*Prep. Time: 25 minutes*
*Cooking Time: 3-6 hours*
*Ideal slow cooker size: 4-qt.*

1 lb. ground beef
1 cup sliced carrots
1 cup coarsely chopped
  celery
1 medium onion, sliced
1 cup green beans
1 tsp. salt
¼ tsp. pepper
2 tsp. sugar
2-3 cups tomato juice
½ lb. grated cheese

1. Brown ground beef in skillet. Stir frequently to break up clumps. Continue browning until pink no longer appears.
2. Drain off drippings. Place meat in bottom of slow cooker.
3. Layer remaining ingredients, except cheese, over ground beef in order given.
4. Cover. Cook on High 3-4 hours or on Low 5-6 hours, or until vegetables are done to your liking.
5. Thirty minutes before end of cooking time, layer cheese on top. Cover and resume cooking.

*Serving suggestion: Serve with **cornbread**.*

Tip:
You can double all vegetable amounts, if you wish.

If you do so, increase cooking time to 5-6 hours on High or 9-11 hours on Low, or until vegetables are as tender as you like.

# Stuffed Baked Topping

**Fannie Miller**
Hutchinson, KS

*Makes 12 servings*

**Prep. Time: 35 minutes**
**Cooking Time: 1 hour**
**Ideal slow cooker size: 6- to 7-qt.**

3 lbs. ground beef
1 cup chopped green bell
   peppers
½ cup chopped onions
¾ stick (6 Tbsp.) butter
¼ cup flour
3 cups milk
½ cup pimento, *or* chopped
   sweet red peppers
¾ lb. cheddar cheese,
   grated
¾ lb. your favorite mild
   cheese, grated
½ tsp. hot pepper sauce
¼ tsp. dry mustard
salt to taste

1. Brown ground beef, green peppers, and onions in butter in large skillet. Transfer mixture to slow cooker, reserving drippings.

2. Stir flour into drippings in skillet. Slowly add milk. Stir continually over medium heat until smooth and thickened.

3. Stir pimento, cheeses, and seasonings into white sauce in skillet. Continue stirring until cheese melts and sauce is smooth.

4. Pour sauce over ingredients in slow cooker.

5. Cover. Heat on Low for 1 hour.

*Serving suggestion: Serve over **baked potatoes**, each one split open on an individual dinner plate.*

# Ground Beef Stew

**Ruth Ann Hoover**
New Holland, PA

**Kim Stoltzfus**
New Holland, PA

*Makes 8-10 servings*

**Prep. Time: 25 minutes**
**Cooking Time: 4½-5 hours**
**Ideal slow cooker size: 4-qt.**

1 lb. ground beef
oil
6 medium potatoes, peeled
   if you wish, and cubed
16-oz. pkg. baby carrots
3 cups water
3 Tbsp. dry onion soup mix
1 garlic clove, minced
1½ tsp. Italian seasoning
1-1½ tsp. salt
½ tsp. garlic powder
¼ tsp. pepper
10¾-oz. can tomato soup
6-oz. can Italian tomato
   paste

1. Brown beef in skillet, in oil if needed. Stir frequently, breaking up clumps. Continue cooking until all pink disappears.

2. Remove beef from drippings and place in slow cooker.

3. Combine all remaining ingredients in cooker, except tomato soup and tomato paste.

4. Cover. Cook on High 3½-4 hours, or until carrots are nearly tender.

5. Stir in soup and tomato paste.

6. Cover. Cook on High 1 hour more.

Variation:
If you'd like to add color and more vegetables to the stew, stir in 1½ cups frozen peas in Step 5.

# Prompt

**Mary Martins**
Fairbank, IA

*Makes 6-8 servings*

*Prep. Time: 20 minutes*
*Cooking Time: 1½-2 hours*
*Ideal slow cooker size: 4-qt.*

4-6 medium-sized potatoes, sliced
½-¾ cup uncooked minute rice
1 onion, sliced
1½ lbs. ground beef
1 diced green bell pepper, *optional*
1 qt. tomatoes with juice
salt to taste
pepper to taste

1. Layer ingredients in order given in greased slow cooker. Salt and pepper each layer to taste.
2. Cover. Cook on High 1½-2 hours.

## Variation:

You may substitute 1 qt. V-8 juice for the quart of tomatoes with juice.

# Cheeseburger Casserole

**Erma Kauffman**
Cochranville, PA

*Makes 6 servings*

*Prep. Time: 20 minutes*
*Cooking Time: 3 hours*
*Ideal slow cooker size: 3-qt.*

1 lb. ground beef
1 small onion, chopped
1 tsp. salt
dash of pepper
½ cup bread crumbs
1 egg
tomato juice to moisten
4½ cups mashed potatoes (leftover mashed potatoes work well)
9 slices your favorite cheese

1. Combine beef, onions, salt, pepper, bread crumbs, egg, and tomato juice in a large bowl.
2. Place one-third of mixture in slow cooker.
3. Spread with one-third of mashed potatoes and 3 slices cheese.
4. Repeat layering 2 times.
5. Cover. Cook on Low 3 hours.

# Hamburger/ Green Bean Dish

**Hazel L. Propst**
Oxford, PA

*Makes 4-5 servings*

*Prep. Time: 25 minutes*
*Cooking Time: 5-6 hours*
*Ideal slow cooker size: 4-qt.*

1 lb. ground beef
1 onion, chopped
1 qt. green beans, *or* 2 lbs. frozen green beans, *or* 2 15-oz. cans green beans
10¾-oz. can tomato soup
¾ tsp. salt
¼ tsp. pepper
6-7 cups mashed potatoes
1 egg, beaten

1. Brown meat and onion in skillet. Stir frequently to break up clumps. When meat is no longer pink, drain off drippings and discard.
2. Place meat in slow cooker. Stir in beans, soup, and seasonings.
3. Combine mashed potatoes with egg in large bowl. Spread over meat-vegetable mixture in slow cooker.
4. Cover. Cook on Low 5-6 hours, or until beans are tender.

*Have a recycled Christmas. All gifts can be either handmade or bought from a boutique specializing in used items. All wrappings can be either reused gift bags or homemade gift wrap, using brown paper bags or the comics papers.*

*Katrina Eberly, Wernersville, PA*

# Meal-in-One

**Melanie L. Thrower**
McPherson, KS

*Makes 6-8 servings*

*Prep. Time: 25 minutes*
*Cooking Time: 4 hours*
*Ideal slow cooker size: 4- to 5-qt.*

2 lbs. ground beef
1 onion, diced
1 green bell pepper, diced
1 tsp. salt
¼ tsp. pepper
1 large bag frozen hash
   brown potatoes, *divided*
16-oz. container sour
   cream, *divided*
24-oz. container cottage
   cheese, *divided*
1 cup Monterey Jack
   cheese, shredded

1. Brown ground beef, onion, and green pepper in skillet. Stir frequently to break up clumps. Continue cooking until meat is no longer pink. Drain off drippings and discard.
2. Season meat and vegetable mixture with salt and pepper.
3. In slow cooker, layer one-third of potatoes, then one-third of meat mixture, one-third of sour cream, and one-third of cottage cheese.
4. Repeat layers twice.
5. Cover. Cook on Low 4 hours, sprinkling Monterey Jack cheese over top during last hour.

*Serving suggestion: Serve with **red** or **green salsa**.*

Variation:
For a cheesier dish, prepare another cup of shredded cheese and sprinkle ½ cup over first layer of potatoes, meat, sour cream, and cottage cheese, and another ½ cup over second layer of those ingredients.

# Cedric's Casserole

**Kathy Purcell**
Dublin, OH

*Makes 4-6 servings*

*Prep. Time: 30 minutes*
*Cooking Time: 3-4 hours*
*Ideal slow cooker size: 3-qt.*

1 medium onion, chopped
3 Tbsp. butter
1 lb. ground beef
½-¾ tsp. salt
¼ tsp. pepper
3 cups shredded cabbage,
   *divided*
10¾-oz. can tomato soup

1. Sauté onion in skillet in butter.
2. Add ground beef and brown. Stir frequently, breaking up clumps until pink no longer appears.
3. Season meat and onions with salt and pepper.
4. Layer half of cabbage in slow cooker, followed by half of meat mixture.
5. Repeat layers again.
6. Pour soup over top.
7. Cover. Cook on Low 3-4 hours.

*Serving suggestion: Serve with **garlic bread** and **canned fruit**.*

Note:
*I grew up with this recipe and remember my mother serving it often. It makes a wonderful potluck take-a-long.*

# Beef and Macaroni

**Esther J. Yoder**
Hartville, OH

*Makes 4-5 servings*

**Prep. Time: 20 minutes**
**Cooking Time: 2-2½ hours**
**Ideal slow cooker size: 3-qt.**

1 lb. ground beef
1 small onion, chopped
half a green bell pepper,
    chopped
1 cup cooked macaroni
½ tsp. dried basil
½ tsp. dried thyme
1 tsp. Worcestershire sauce
1 tsp. salt
10¾-oz. can cheddar
    cheese soup

1. Brown beef, onions, and green pepper in skillet. Stir frequently to break up clumps. Cook until no more pink appears in meat. Drain off drippings.
2. Place meat and vegetables in slow cooker.
3. Combine all ingredients in cooker.
4. Cover. Cook on High 2-2½ hours, stirring once or twice, if you're home and able to do so.

*Serving suggestion: Serve with **broccoli** and **applesauce**.*

# Plenty More in the Kitchen

**Jean Robinson**
Cinnaminson, NJ

*Makes 12-16 servings*

**Prep. Time: 30 minutes**
**Cooking Time: 5¼ hours**
**Ideal slow cooker size: 6-qt.**

3 lbs. ground beef
1 cup chopped onions
1 Tbsp. oil
26-oz. jar tomato sauce, *or*
    spaghetti sauce
1 tsp. salt
2 tsp. chili powder
1 tsp. pepper
2 Tbsp. dark brown sugar
16-oz. can whole-kernel
    corn
2 14½-oz. cans beef broth
8-oz. pkg. uncooked elbow
    macaroni
1 cup grated sharp cheese

1. Brown beef and onion in oil in skillet. Stir frequently, breaking up clumps. Continue cooking until meat is no longer pink. Drain off drippings.
2. Place meat in cooker, along with all other ingredients except cheese.
3. Cover. Cook on High 1 hour. Turn to Low and cook 4 more hours.
4. Sprinkle with cheese and cook 10 minutes more.

Variation:
    You can change the balance of ingredients by using only 1-1½ lbs. ground beef

and adding another ½-1 cup uncooked macaroni.

Note:
    *This is a tried and true recipe adapted from an old 1984 Pennsylvania Grange cookbook. It's an easy meal to carry outside to the picnic table or to take to a Little League game.*

# Cheese and Pasta in a Pot

**Cathy Boshart**
Lebanon, PA

*Makes 8 servings*

**Prep. Time: 35-40 minutes**
**Cooking Time: 2-3 hours**
**Ideal slow cooker size: 5-qt.**

2 lbs. ground beef
1 Tbsp. oil
2 medium onions, chopped
1 garlic clove, minced
14-oz. jar spaghetti sauce
16-oz. can stewed tomatoes
4-oz. can sliced
    mushrooms, undrained
8 oz. dry shell macaroni,
    cooked al dente, *divided*
1½ pints sour cream,
    *divided*
½ lb. provolone cheese,
    sliced
½ lb. mozzarella cheese,
    sliced thin, *or* shredded

1. Brown ground beef in oil in large skillet or Dutch oven. Stir frequently to break up clumps. Continue cooking

until all pink disappears. Drain off all but 2 Tbsp. drippings.

2. Add onions, garlic, spaghetti sauce, stewed tomatoes, and undrained mushrooms to beef and remaining drippings in skillet. Mix well.

3. Simmer 10-15 minutes in skillet, or until onions are soft.

4. Pour half of macaroni into slow cooker.

5. Cover with half tomato-meat sauce.

6. Spread half sour cream over sauce.

7. Top with provolone cheese.

8. Repeat macaroni and tomato-meat sauce layers.

9. Top with mozzarella cheese.

10. Cover. Cook on High 2 hours or on Low 3 hours.

# Hamburger Rice Casserole

**Shari Mast**
Harrisonburg, VA

*Makes 6-8 servings*

*Prep. Time: 25 minutes*
*Cooking Time: 4 hours*
*Ideal slow cooker size: 4-qt.*

½ lb. ground beef
1 onion, chopped
1 cup diced celery
1 tsp. dried basil
1 tsp. dried oregano
10¾-oz. can cream of
  mushroom soup

1 soup can water
4 cups cooked rice, *divided*
4-oz. can mushroom
  pieces, drained, *divided*
Velveeta cheese slices

1. Brown ground beef, onion, and celery in skillet. Stir frequently to break clumps of meat. Continue browning until no pink remains in meat. Drain off drippings.

2. Season meat in skillet with basil and oregano.

3. Combine soup and water in bowl.

4. In well greased slow cooker, layer half of rice, half of mushrooms, half of ground-beef mixture, and half of soup mixture.

5. Repeat layers.

6. Cover. Cook on High 4 hours.

7. Top with cheese 30 minutes before serving.

*Serving suggestion: This casserole, served with corn-bread and applesauce, makes a well-rounded meal that is quick and easy to prepare and well-received by children and adults.*

# Hearty Rice Casserole

**Dale Peterson**
Rapid City, SD

*Makes 12-16 servings*

*Prep. Time: 25 minutes*
*Cooking Time: 6-7 hours*
*Ideal slow cooker size: 4-qt.*

1 lb. ground beef
1 lb. loose pork sausage
10¾-oz. can cream of
  mushroom soup
10¾-oz. can creamy onion
  soup
10¾-oz. can cream of
  chicken soup
1 cup water
1 large onion, chopped
1 large green bell pepper,
  chopped
1½ cups uncooked long-
  grain rice
shredded cheese, *optional*

1. Brown beef and sausage in large skillet. Stir frequently to break up clumps. Continue cooking until no more pink remains. Drain off drippings.

2. Place browned meat in slow cooker.

3. Add all ingredients except cheese to slow cooker. Mix well.

4. Cover. Cook on Low 6-7 hours, or until rice is fully cooked.

5. Sprinkling with cheese during last hour if you wish.

# Beef and Pepper Rice

**Liz Ann Yoder**
Hartville, OH

*Makes 4-6 servings*

**Prep. Time: 20 minutes**
**Cooking Time: 3-6 hours**
**Ideal slow cooker size: 3-qt.**

1 lb. ground beef
2 green bell peppers, *or*
   1 green and 1 red bell
   pepper, coarsely chopped
1 cup chopped onions
1 cup uncooked brown rice
2 beef bouillon cubes,
   crushed
3 cups water
1 Tbsp. soy sauce

1. Brown beef in skillet. Stir frequently to break up clumps. Continue cooking until meat is no longer pink. Drain off drippings.

2. Place meat in slow cooker.

3. Add all remaining ingredients to slow cooker. Mix well.

4. Cover. Cook on Low 5-6 hours or on High 3 hours, or until rice is tender and liquid is absorbed.

# Stuffed Green Peppers

**Patricia Howard**
Albuquerque, NM

*Makes 6 servings*

**Prep. Time: 40 minutes**
**Cooking Time: 4-5 hours**
**Ideal slow cooker size: 6- to 7-qt.**

6 green bell peppers
1 lb. ground beef
¼ cup chopped onions
1 tsp. salt
¼ tsp. pepper
1¼ cups cooked rice
1 Tbsp. Worcestershire
   sauce
8-oz. can tomato sauce
¼ cup beef broth

1. Cut stem ends from peppers. Carefully remove seeds and membrane without breaking pepper apart. Parboil in water for 5 minutes. Drain. Set aside.

2. Brown ground beef and onions in skillet. Stir frequently to break up clumps. Continue cooking until meat is no longer pink. Drain off drippings.

3. Place meat and onions in mixing bowl.

4. Add seasonings, rice, and Worcestershire sauce to meat and combine well.

5. Stuff green peppers with mixture. Stand stuffed peppers upright in large slow cooker.

6. Mix together tomato sauce and beef broth in a bowl. Pour over peppers.

7. Cover. Cook on Low 4-5 hours.

**Variation:**
Add ½-¾ cup grated cheddar cheese to Step 4.

**Rosaria Strachan**
Fairfield, CT

---

*Ask for help. It's okay to ask someone to bring a dish, bread, or beverage. It's okay to ask your children to pick up toys and be a "pre-host or hostess," especially if your get-together is for families with children. Have your family help to decorate. I know this can take longer, but if you keep things simple, you will be enjoying family time together and broader ownership of the event. Next time it will be easier for all, and you will have begun traditions that can be carried to the next generation.*

*Carol Findling, Carol Stream, IL*

# Spanish Stuffed Peppers

**Katrine Rose**
Woodbridge, VA

*Makes 4 servings*

*Prep. Time: 20 minutes*
*Cooking Time: 8-10 hours*
*Ideal slow cooker size: 6- to 7-qt.*

1 lb. ground beef
7-oz. pkg. Spanish rice mix
1 egg
¼ cup chopped onions
4 medium-sized green
   bell peppers, halved
   lengthwise, cored, and
   seeded
28-oz. can stewed, *or*
   crushed, tomatoes
10¾-oz. can tomato soup
1 cup water
shredded cheese, *optional*

1. Combine beef, rice mix (reserving seasoning packet), egg, and onions in large bowl.
2. Divide meat mixture among pepper halves.
3. Pour tomatoes into slow cooker. Arrange pepper halves over tomatoes.
4. Combine tomato soup, rice-mix seasoning packet, and water in bowl. Pour over peppers.
5. Cover. Cook on Low 8-10 hours.
6. Twenty minutes before end of the cooking time, top stuffed peppers with cheese if you wish.

# Haystacks

**Judy Buller**
Bluffton, OH

*Makes 10-12 servings*

*Prep. Time: 20 minutes*
*Cooking Time: 1-3 hours*
*Ideal slow cooker size: 5-qt.*

2 lbs. ground beef
oil
1 small onion, chopped
2 8-oz. cans tomato sauce
2 15-oz. cans chili beans
   with chili gravy, *or* red
   beans
2 10-oz. cans mild enchilada
   sauce, *or* mild salsa
½ tsp. chili powder
1 tsp. garlic salt
pepper to taste

Condiments:
raisins
chopped apples
shredded lettuce
chopped tomatoes
shredded cheese
corn chips
rice, *or* baked potatoes

1. Brown beef in skillet, in oil if needed, stirring frequently to break up clumps. Continue cooking until meat is no longer pink. Drain off drippings.
2. Combine beef, onion, tomato sauce, chili beans, enchilada sauce, chili powder, garlic salt, and pepper in slow cooker.
3. Cover. Bake on Low 2-3 hours or on High 1 hour.
4. Serve over baked potatoes or rice and pass dishes of condiments so everyone can choose their own toppings.

Note:
*Because this recipe offers such a wide choice of toppings, all diners are sure to find something they like. Haystacks are easy to serve buffet-style. The wide array of condiments sparks conversation—and becomes an adventure in eating. Members of my family like a little of each topping over the chili.*

*Guests are often surprised to see how large their haystacks are when they're finished serving themselves. They frequently fill their entire plates!*

*The atmosphere can be comfortable when everything is prepared ahead. And with this recipe, the serving time can vary to meet uncertain schedules.*

*Don't forget to do the rice or baked potatoes in a second slow cooker.*

# Mexican Goulash

### Sheila Plock
### Boalsburg, PA

*Makes 8-10 servings*

*Prep. Time: 45 minutes*
*Cooking Time: 3-4 hours*
*Ideal slow cooker size: 5-qt.*

1½-2 lbs. ground beef
2 onions, chopped
1 green bell pepper,
  chopped
½ cup celery, chopped
1 garlic clove, minced
28-oz. can whole tomatoes,
  cut up
6-oz. can tomato paste
4¼-oz. can sliced black
  olives, drained
14½-oz. can green beans,
  drained
15¼-oz. can Mexicorn,
  drained
15-oz. can dark red kidney
  beans, rinsed and
  drained
diced jalapeño peppers to
  taste
1 tsp. salt
¼ tsp. pepper
1 Tbsp. chili powder
3 dashes Tabasco sauce
grated cheddar cheese

1. Brown ground beef in
skillet, stirring frequently to
break up clumps. Continue
cooking until meat is no
longer pink. Reserve drippings and transfer beef to
slow cooker.
2. Sauté onions, pepper,
celery, and garlic in drippings
in skillet. Transfer to slow
cooker.

3. Add remaining ingre-
dients except cheese to slow
cooker. Mix well.
4. Cover. Cook on Low 3-4
hours.
5. Sprinkle individual
servings with grated cheese.

*Serving suggestion: Serve
with **tortilla chips**.*

# Tortilla Bake

### Kelly Evenson
### Pittsboro, NC

*Makes 6-8 servings*

*Prep. Time: 20 minutes*
*Cooking Time: 3-4 hours*
*Ideal slow cooker size: 3-qt.*

1½ lbs. ground beef, *divided*
oil
10¾-oz. can cheddar
  cheese soup
1½-oz. pkg. dry taco
  seasoning mix
8 corn tortillas, *divided*
3 medium tomatoes,
  coarsely chopped, *divided*

**Toppings:**
**sour cream**
**grated cheese**
**thinly sliced green onions**
**cut-up bell peppers**
**diced avocado**
**shredded lettuce**

1. Brown ground beef
in skillet, in oil if needed.
Stir frequently to break up
clumps. Continue cooking
until no pink remains in
meat. Drain off drippings.
Set aside meat in skillet.
2. Combine soup and taco
seasoning in bowl.
3. Cut each tortilla into 6
wedges.
4. Spoon one-quarter of
ground beef into slow cooker.
5. Top with one-quarter of
all tortilla wedges.
6. Spoon one-quarter of
soup mixture over tortillas.
7. Top with one-quarter of
tomatoes.
8. Repeat layers 3 times.
9. Cover. Cook on Low 3-4
hours.
10. To serve, spoon onto
plates and offer toppings as
condiments.

*We call the local assisted-living facility and ask for
names and a list of gift ideas for 3 people who live in the
facility but who don't usually get visitors at Christmas-
time. Then on Christmas Day, our family delivers the
gifts and visits with each person. Our kids are learning that
Christmas is not all about them.*

*Kendra Dreps, Liberty, PA*

# Three-Bean Burrito Bake

**Darla Sathre**
Baxter, MN

*Makes 6 servings*

*Prep. Time: 30 minutes*
*Cooking Time: 4-5 hours*
*Ideal slow cooker size: 4-qt.*

1 onion, chopped
1 green bell pepper, chopped
2 garlic cloves, minced
1 Tbsp. oil
16-oz. can pinto beans, drained
16-oz. can kidney beans, drained
15-oz. can black beans, drained
4-oz. can sliced black olives, drained
4-oz. can green chilies, undrained
2 15-oz. cans diced tomatoes, undrained
1 tsp. chili powder
1 tsp. ground cumin
6-8 6" flour tortillas, *divided*
2 cups shredded Colby Jack cheese, *divided*

1. Sauté onions, green peppers, and garlic in large skillet in oil.
2. Add beans, olives, chilies, tomatoes, chili powder, and cumin to skillet. Stir together well.
3. In greased slow cooker, layer ¾ cup vegetables, followed by a tortilla, followed by ⅓ cup cheese.

4. Repeat layers until all those ingredients are used, ending with vegetable sauce on top.
5. Cover. Cook on Low 4-5 hours.

*Serving suggestion: Serve with dollops of **sour cream** on individual servings.*

# Taco Casserole

**Marcia S. Myer**
Manheim, PA

*Makes 6 servings*

*Prep. Time: 25 minutes*
*Cooking Time: 3-4 hours*
*Ideal slow cooker size: 3-qt.*

1½ lbs. ground beef
oil
14½-oz. can diced tomatoes with chilies
10¾-oz. can cream of onion soup
1 envelope dry taco seasoning mix
¼ cup water
6 corn tortillas, cut in ½" strips
½ cup sour cream
1 cup shredded cheddar cheese
2 green onions, sliced, *optional*

1. Brown beef in skillet, in oil if needed. Stir frequently, breaking up clumps. Continue cooking until no pink remains in meat. Drain off drippings.
2. Place beef in slow cooker.

3. Stir in tomatoes, soup, seasoning mix, and water in slow cooker. Mix together well.
4. Stir in tortilla strips.
5. Cover. Cook on Low 3-4 hours.
6. Spread sour cream over casserole. Sprinkle with cheese.
7. Cover. Let stand 5 minutes until cheese melts.
8. Remove cover. Garnish with green onions. Allow to stand 15 more minutes before serving.

# Casserole Verde

**Julia Fisher**
New Carlisle, OH

*Makes 6 servings*

**Prep. Time: 35 minutes**
**Cooking Time: 2-3 hours**
**Ideal slow cooker size: 4-qt.**

1 lb. ground beef
1 small onion, chopped
⅛ tsp. garlic powder
oil
8-oz. can tomato sauce
⅓ cup chopped black
    olives
4-oz. can sliced
    mushrooms, drained
8-oz. container sour cream
8-oz. container cottage
    cheese
4¼-oz. can chopped green
    chilies, drained
12-oz. pkg. tortilla chips,
    *divided*
8 oz. Monterey Jack cheese,
    grated, *divided*

1. Brown ground beef,
onions, and garlic in skillet, in
oil if needed. Stir frequently
to break up clumps. Continue
cooking until no pink remains
in meat. Drain off drippings.
2. Add tomato sauce,
olives, and mushrooms to
meat in skillet.
3. In a separate bowl,
combine sour cream, cottage
cheese, and green chilies.
4. In slow cooker, layer in
one-third of chips, followed by
half the ground beef mixture.
5. Follow with a layer of
half the sour cream mixture
and half the shredded cheese.

6. Repeat all layers, except
reserve last third of chips to
add just before serving.
7. Cover. Cook on Low 2-3
hours.
8. Ten minutes before
serving time, scatter reserved
chips over top and continue
cooking, uncovered.

# Tiajuana Tacos

**Helen Kenagy**
Carlsbad, NM

*Makes 6 servings*

**Prep. Time: 20 minutes**
**Cooking Time: 2 hours**
**Ideal slow cooker size: 3½-qt.**

3 cups thinly sliced
    uncooked beef steak
oil
1-lb. can refried beans
½ cup chopped onions
½ cup chopped green bell
    peppers
½ cup chopped ripe olives
8-oz. can tomato sauce
3 tsp. chili powder
1 Tbsp. Worcestershire
    sauce
½ tsp. garlic powder
¼ tsp. pepper
¼ tsp. paprika
⅛ tsp. celery salt
⅛ tsp. ground nutmeg
¾ cup water
1 tsp. salt
1 cup crushed corn chips
6 taco shells
shredded lettuce
chopped tomatoes
grated cheddar cheese

1. Sauté beef lightly in
skillet, in oil if needed. Drain
off drippings.
2. Place in slow cooker,
along with all ingredients
except corn chips, taco shells,
lettuce, chopped tomatoes,
and grated cheese.
3. Cover. Cook on Low 2
hours.
4. Just before serving, fold
in corn chips.
5. Spoon mixture into taco
shells.

*Serving suggestion: Top with
lettuce, tomatoes, and cheese.*

126

# Pork and Ham Main Dishes

## Barbecued Ribs

Virginia Bender
Dover, DE

*Makes 6 servings*

**Prep. Time: 10 minutes**
**Cooking Time: 8-10 hours**
**Ideal slow cooker size: 6-qt.**

4 lbs. pork ribs
½ cup brown sugar
12-oz. jar chili sauce
¼ cup balsamic vinegar
2 Tbsp. Worcestershire
   sauce
2 Tbsp. Dijon mustard
1 tsp. hot sauce

1. Place ribs in slow cooker.
2. Combine remaining ingredients in a good-sized bowl.
3. Pour half of sauce over ribs.
4. Cover. Cook on Low 8-10 hours.
5. Serve with remaining sauce.

## Sweet and Sour Ribs

Cassandra Ly
Carlisle, PA

*Makes 8-10 servings*

**Prep. Time: 15 minutes**
**Cooking Time: 8-10 hours**
**Ideal slow cooker size: 6-qt.**

3-4 lbs. boneless country-
   style pork ribs
20-oz. can pineapple
   tidbits, drained
2 8-oz. cans tomato sauce
½ cup thinly sliced onions
½ cup thinly sliced green
   bell peppers
½ cup packed brown sugar
¼ cup cider vinegar

¼ cup tomato paste
2 Tbsp. Worcestershire
   sauce
1 garlic clove, minced
1 tsp. salt
½ tsp. pepper

1. Place ribs in slow cooker.
2. Combine remaining ingredients in a good-sized bowl. Pour over ribs.
3. Cover. Cook on Low 8-10 hours.

*Serving suggestion: Serve over rice.*

*Give a basket filled with a recipe, the ingredients to make it, decorative potholders or towels, and a special utensil for preparing the recipe.*   Maryann Markano, Wilmington, DE

# 1-2-3 Barbecued Country Ribs

**Barbara Walker**
Sturgis, SD

*Makes 4 servings*

*Prep. Time: 10 minutes*
*Cooking Time: 8-10 hours*
*Ideal slow cooker size: 5-qt.*

18-oz. bottle prepared
   barbecue sauce
4 lbs. spareribs, *or* 3 lbs.
   country-style ribs, cut in
   serving-size pieces

1. Pour a little sauce into slow cooker. Put in a layer of ribs, meaty side up. Cover with barbecue sauce.
2. Continue layering until all ribs are in the pot. Submerge them as much as possible in sauce.
3. Cover. Cook on Low 8-10 hours.

Note:
   No need to precook the ribs if they're lean. If they're fattier than you like, parboil in water in stockpot before placing in cooker, to cook off some of the grease. Drain and place in slow cooker. Follow Steps 1-3.

# Tender 'n' Tangy Ribs

**Sherri Grindle**, Goshen, IN

*Makes 2-3 servings*

*Prep. Time: 20 minutes • Cooking Time: 4-6 hours*
*Ideal slow cooker size: 4-qt.*

¾-1 cup vinegar
½ cup ketchup
2 Tbsp. sugar
2 Tbsp. Worcestershire
   sauce
1 clove garlic, minced
1 tsp. ground mustard
1 tsp. paprika
½-1 tsp. salt
⅛ tsp. pepper
2 lbs. pork spareribs, *or*
   country-style ribs
1 Tbsp. oil

1. Combine first nine ingredients in slow cooker.
2. Cut ribs into serving-size pieces. Brown in batches in oil in skillet. Don't crowd the skillet or the ribs will steam and not brown. Transfer to slow cooker as you finish browning them.
3. Stir sauce through ribs.
4. Cover. Cook on Low 4-6 hours.

*Serving suggestion: Serve the ribs with **baked potatoes** or **rice**.*

**Note:** *I often use this recipe if I am having company for Sunday lunch.*

# Country-Style Ribs and Sauerkraut

**Rhonda Burgoon**
Collingswood, NJ

*Makes 4-6 servings*

*Prep. Time: 15 minutes*
*Cooking Time: 8-10 hours*
*Ideal slow cooker size: 5-qt.*

16-oz. bag sauerkraut,
   rinsed and drained
1 onion, diced
1 red-skinned apple,
   chopped
2-3 lbs. country-style
   pork ribs
1 cup beer

1. Combine sauerkraut, onion, and apple in slow cooker.
2. Layer ribs over sauerkraut mixture.
3. Pour beer over ribs just before turning on cooker.
4. Cover. Cook on Low 8-10 hours.

*Serving suggestion: You'll love this served with homemade **cornbread** and **mashed potatoes**, or deboned on **kaiser rolls**.*

# Sauerkraut & Pork Ribs

**Annabelle Unternahrer**
Shipshewana, IN

*Makes 6-8 servings*

*Prep. Time: 15-25 minutes*
*Cooking Time: 6 hours*
*Ideal slow cooker size: 3- to 4-qt.*

2 lbs. country pork ribs
oil
32-oz. jar sauerkraut
1 large apple, chopped
1 cup shredded carrots
1½ cups tomato juice
3 Tbsp. brown sugar
2 tsp. caraway seeds,
    *optional*

1. Cut ribs in 2"-thick pieces. Brown in skillet with small amount of oil.
2. Combine sauerkraut, apple, carrots, juice, brown sugar, and caraway seeds if you wish, in a bowl.
3. Put half of sauerkraut mixture in bottom of slow cooker.
4. Top with browned ribs.
5. Cover with remainder of sauerkraut mixture.
6. Cover cooker. Cook on Low 6 hours, or until meat leaves the bone when pulled with a fork.

# Barbara Jean's Whole Pork Tenderloin

**Barbara Jean Fabel**
Wausau, WI

*Makes 6-8 servings*

*Prep. Time: 25 minutes*
*Cooking Time: 3-5 hours*
*Ideal slow cooker size: 4- to 5-qt.*

½ cup sliced celery
¼ lb. fresh mushrooms,
    quartered
1 medium onion, sliced
half a stick (4 Tbsp.)
    butter, melted
2 1¼-lb. pork tenderloins
1 Tbsp. butter
2 tsp. salt
¼ tsp. pepper
1 Tbsp. butter
½ cup beef broth
1 Tbsp. flour

1. Place celery, mushrooms, onion, and half a stick melted butter in slow cooker.
2. Brown tenderloins in skillet in 1 Tbsp. butter. Layer browned meat over vegetables in slow cooker.
3. Sprinkle with salt and pepper.
4. Combine broth and flour in small bowl until smooth. Pour over tenderloins.
5. Cover. Cook on High 3 hours or on Low 4-5 hours.

# Autumn Harvest Pork Loin

**Stacy Schmucker Stoltzfus**
Enola, PA

*Makes 4-6 servings*

*Prep. Time: 30 minutes*
*Cooking Time: 5-6 hours*
*Ideal slow cooker size: 5-qt.*

1 cup cider, *or* apple juice
1½-2-lb. pork loin
salt
pepper
2 large Granny Smith
    apples, peeled and sliced
1½ whole butternut
    squashes, peeled and
    cubed
½ cup brown sugar
¼ tsp. cinnamon
¼ tsp. dried thyme
¼ tsp. dried sage

1. Heat cider in hot skillet. Sear pork loin on all sides in cider.
2. Sprinkle meat with salt and pepper on all sides. Place in slow cooker, along with pan juices.
3. In a good-sized bowl, combine apples and squash. Sprinkle with sugar and herbs. Stir. Spoon around pork loin in cooker.
4. Cover. Cook on Low 5-6 hours.
5. Remove pork from cooker. Let stand 10-15 minutes. Slice into ½"-thick slices.
6. Serve topped with apples and squash.

# Cranberry Pork

**Barbara Walker**
Sturgis, SD
**Donna Treloar**
Muncie, IN

*Makes 9-12 servings*

*Prep. Time: 15 minutes*
*Cooking Time: 6¼-8¼ hours*
*Ideal slow cooker size: 5-qt.*

3-4-lb. boneless rolled pork
   loin roast
2 Tbsp. canola oil
14-oz. can whole berry
   cranberry sauce
¾ cup sugar
¾ cup cranberry juice
1 tsp. ground mustard
1 tsp. pepper
¼ tsp. ground cloves
¼ cup cornstarch
¼ cup cold water
salt to taste

1. In Dutch oven, brown roast in oil on all sides over medium-high heat. You may need to cut roast in half to fit into your Dutch oven and/or your slow cooker.
2. Place browned roast in slow cooker.
3. In a medium-sized bowl, combine cranberry sauce, sugar, cranberry juice, mustard, pepper, and cloves. Pour over roast.
4. Cover. Cook on Low 6-8 hours, or until a meat thermometer reads 160 degrees in center of roast. Remove roast and keep warm. Keep sauce on Low in slow cooker.
5. In a small bowl, combine cornstarch, water, and salt until smooth.
6. Turn cooker to High. Stir cornstarch-water mixture into cooking juices. Bring to a boil. Cook and stir until sauce thickens. Serve with slices of pork roast.

**Variations:**

1. In place of sugar, use ¼ cup honey.
2. Instead of ¼ tsp. ground cloves, use ⅛ tsp. ground cloves and ⅛ tsp. ground nutmeg.
3. Add 1 tsp. grated orange peel to Step 3.

**Renee Baum**
Chambersburg, PA

4. Create a whole different twist to the Cranberry Pork Loin by dropping the sugar, cranberry juice, ground mustard, pepper, and cloves. Instead, add 2 Tbsp. Dijon mustard, 1 Tbsp. grated horseradish, and 1 cup chicken stock to the cranberry sauce. Continue with Steps 4-6.

**Susan Kasting**
Jenks, OK

# Pork Loin with Spiced Fruit Sauce

**Maricarol Magill**
Freehold, NJ

*Makes 4 servings*

*Prep. Time: 25-40 minutes*
*Cooking Time: 4-6 hours*
*Ideal slow cooker size: 5- to 5-qt.*

8-oz. pkg. dried mixed
   fruit (including plums
   and apricots), chopped
¼ cup golden raisins
2 tsp. minced fresh ginger
1 small onion, chopped
⅓ cup brown sugar
2 Tbsp. cider vinegar
¾ cup water
¼ tsp. ground cinnamon
¼ tsp. curry powder
½ tsp. salt, *divided*
½ tsp. pepper, *divided*
2¼-lb. boneless pork loin
   roast, trimmed of fat
¾ lb. fresh green beans,
   ends nipped off
1 Tbsp. Dijon mustard
1 Tbsp. cornstarch
1 Tbsp. cold water

1. In slow cooker, combine dried fruit, raisins, ginger, onion, sugar, vinegar, water, cinnamon, curry powder, and ¼ tsp. each of salt and pepper. Stir.
2. Season pork with remaining ¼ tsp. salt and pepper. Place pork on top of fruit mixture in slow cooker. Cover. Cook on High 2 hours or on Low 3 hours.
3. Layer green beans over pork. Cover.

4. Cook for 2 more hours on High or for 3 more hours on Low—or until meat is tender and beans are done to your liking.

5. When meat and beans are tender but not dry, remove to separate plates. Cover and keep warm.

6. Stir mustard into sauce in cooker.

7. In a small bowl, mix cornstarch with 1 Tbsp. cold water until smooth. Stir into sauce.

8. Cover. Turn cooker to High and let sauce cook a few minutes until thickened.

9. Slice pork and serve with sauce and green beans.

**Note:**

*We discovered this to be a great Christmas dinner one year when we were remodeling and had limited kitchen facilities. I put the ingredients in the slow cooker, and we played Scrabble all day while it cooked. I served it with microwaved rice pilaf. It was my most stress-free Christmas ever!*

# No Fuss Sauerkraut

**Vera M. Kuhns**
Harrisonburg, VA

*Makes 12 servings*

**Prep. Time: 10-15 minutes**
**Cooking Time: 4-5 hours**
**Ideal slow cooker size: 5-qt.**

3-lb. pork roast
3 2-lb. pkgs. sauerkraut
 (drain off juice from 1 pkg.)
2 apples, peeled and sliced
½ cup brown sugar
1 cup apple juice

1. Place meat in large slow cooker.

2. Place sauerkraut on top of meat.

3. Add apples and brown sugar. Add juice.

4. Cover. Cook on High 4-5 hours.

*Serving suggestion: I think this is made to be eaten with* **mashed potatoes.**

**Tip:**

If your slow cooker isn't large enough to hold all the ingredients, cook one package of sauerkraut and half the apples, brown sugar, and apple juice in another cooker. Mix the ingredients of both cookers together before serving.

**Variations:**

1. Replace brown sugar with ¼ cup honey.

2. Sprinkle 2 Tbsp. dried basil over contents of slow cooker at end of Step 3.
 **Jean Harris Robinson**
 Pemberton, NJ

# Flautas with Pork Filling

**Donna Lantgen**
Rapid City, SD

*Makes 6-8 servings*

**Prep. Time: 20 minutes**
**Cooking Time: 4-6 hours**
**Ideal slow cooker size: 3½-qt.**

1-lb. pork roast, *or* chops, cubed
¼ cup chopped onions
4-oz. can diced green chilies, drained
7-oz. can green chile salsa, *or* chile salsa
1 tsp. cocoa powder
16-oz. can chili

1. Brown cubed pork in non-stick skillet. Drain off any drippings. Place in slow cooker.

2. Stir in remaining ingredients except chili.

3. Cover. Cook on Low 2-3 hours.

4. Add chili. Cook on Low 2-3 hours longer.

**Tip:**

This is especially good served on spinach-herb tortillas with guacamole dip.

# Pork Chops and Gravy

**Barbara Walker**
Sturgis, SD

*Makes 6 servings*

*Prep. Time: 15-20 minutes*
*Cooking Time: 2-2½ hours*
*Ideal slow cooker size: 4-qt.*

½ cup flour
½ tsp. salt
½ tsp. garlic powder
1½ tsp. dry mustard
6 1"-thick lean pork chops
10¾-oz can condensed chicken broth
2 Tbsp. vegetable oil

1. Mix first 4 ingredients in a shallow dish. Dredge pork chops in flour mixture then set aside.
2. Combine remaining flour mixture and chicken broth in slow cooker until thoroughly mixed.
3. Pour oil into large skillet. Place over medium-high heat until hot. Cook chops in hot oil just until browned on both sides. Place in cooker, pushing them down into broth.
4. Cover. Cook on High 2-2½ hours, or just until chops are tender.

# Pork Chops

**Linda Sluiter**
Schererville, IN

*Makes 4 servings*

*Prep. Time: 10 minutes*
*Cooking Time: 5-8 hours*
*Ideal slow cooker size: 3-qt.*

4 boneless pork chops, 1"-thick
½ tsp. dry mustard
¼ cup flour
½ tsp. sugar
1 tsp. vinegar
½ cup water
½ cup ketchup
½ tsp. salt

1. Place pork chops in slow cooker.
2. Combine remaining ingredients in a bowl. Pour over pork chops.
3. Cover. Cook on High 2-3 hours, and then on Low 3-4 hours, or cook on Low 8 hours—just until chops are fork-tender but not dry.
4. Spoon sauce over chops to serve.

# Barbecued Pork Chops

**LaVerne A. Olson**
Lititz, PA

*Makes 6-8 servings*

*Prep. Time: 15 minutes*
*Cooking Time: 2-3 hours*
*Ideal slow cooker size: 5-qt.*

6-8 thin pork chops
½ cup ketchup
1 tsp. salt
1 tsp. celery seed
½ tsp. ground nutmeg
⅓ cup vinegar
½ cup water
1 bay leaf

1. Lightly brown chops on both sides in non-stick skillet. Do it in several batches so chops brown and don't steam each other.
2. Place browned chops in slow cooker.
3. Combine remaining ingredients in a small bowl. Pour over chops.
4. Cover. Cook on Low 2-3 hours, or until chops are tender.
5. Remove bay leaf before serving. Top chops with sauce.

# Pork Chops Pierre

**Genelle Taylor**
Perrysburg, OH

*Makes 6 servings*

*Prep. Time: 30-40 minutes*
*Cooking Time: 4½-6½ hours*
*Ideal slow cooker size: 3-qt.*

6 pork chops, each
    ½"-thick
½ tsp. salt, *optional*
⅛ tsp. pepper
2 medium onions, chopped
2 ribs celery, chopped
1 large green bell pepper,
    sliced
14-oz. can stewed tomatoes
½ cup ketchup
2 Tbsp. cider vinegar
2 Tbsp. brown sugar
2 Tbsp. Worcestershire
    sauce
1 Tbsp. lemon juice
1 beef bouillon cube
2 Tbsp. cornstarch
2 Tbsp. water

1. Place chops in slow
cooker. Sprinkle with salt and
pepper.

2. Spoon onions, celery,
green pepper, and tomatoes
over chops.

3. In a small bowl, com-
bine ketchup, vinegar, sugar,
Worcestershire sauce, lemon
juice, and bouillon cube. Pour
over vegetables.

4. Cover. Cook on Low 4-6
hours, just until chops are
tender but not dry.

5. Remove chops to a
platter and keep warm.

6. In a small bowl, mix
together cornstarch and water
until smooth. Stir into liquid
in slow cooker.

7. Cover. Cook on High
30 minutes or until sauce
thickens.

*Serving suggestion: Serve
over cooked **rice** if you wish.*

# Pork Chops and Potatoes

**Sherry H. Kauffman**
Minot, ND

*Makes 6 servings*

*Prep. Time: 25 minutes*
*Cooking Time: 3½-4½ hours*
*Ideal slow cooker size: 5-qt.*

10¾-oz. can cream of
    mushroom soup
¼ cup chicken broth
¼ cup country-style Dijon
    mustard
1 garlic clove, minced
½ tsp. dried thyme
¼-½ tsp. salt, according to
    your taste preference
¼ tsp. pepper
6 medium red potatoes,
    sliced
1 medium onion, thinly
    sliced
6 5-oz. boneless pork loin
    chops

1. In slow cooker, combine
soup, broth, mustard, garlic,
thyme, salt, and pepper.

2. Stir in potatoes and
onion slices.

3. Top with pork chops.
Push down into sauce as
much as possible.

4. Cover. Cook on Low
3½-4½ hours, or until meat
and potatoes are tender.

*Choose a large vase and stick a small pine branch
down into it head first. Sprinkle a handful of cranberries
or holly berries on top. Fill the vase with a mixture of
evergreens stuck in stem first. Lay a few miniature pine
cones and cranberries or holly berries around the foot of the
vase. Lay some smaller branches around the base, too, if
you like.*

*Juanita Weaver, Johnsonville, IL*

# Pork Chops on Rice

**Hannah D. Burkholder**
Bridgewater, VA

*Makes 4 servings*

**Prep. Time: 30 minutes**
**Cooking Time: 4-9 hours**
**Ideal slow cooker size: 5-qt.**

⅔ cup uncooked converted white rice
½ cup uncooked brown rice
half a stick (4 Tbsp.) butter
½ cup chopped onions
4-oz. can sliced mushrooms, drained
½ tsp. dried thyme
½ tsp. sage
½ tsp. salt
¼ tsp. black pepper
4 boneless pork chops, ¾"-1" thick
10½-oz. can beef consommé
2 Tbsp. Worcestershire sauce
½ tsp. dried thyme
½ tsp. paprika
¼ tsp. ground nutmeg

1. Sauté white and brown rice in butter in skillet until rice is golden brown.
2. Remove from heat and stir in onions, mushrooms, thyme, sage, salt, and pepper. Pour into greased slow cooker.
3. Arrange chops over rice.
4. Combine consommé and Worcestershire sauce in a bowl. Pour over chops.
5. Combine thyme, paprika, and nutmeg in a

small bowl. Sprinkle over chops.
6. Cover. Cook on Low 7-9 hours or on High 4-5 hours.

# Baked Beans and Chops

**John D. Allen**
Rye, CO

*Makes 6 servings*

**Prep. Time: 10 minutes**
**Cooking Time: 4-6 hours**
**Ideal slow cooker size: 5-qt.**

2 16½-oz. cans baked beans
6 rib pork chops, ½" thick
1½ tsp. prepared mustard
1½ Tbsp. brown sugar
1½ Tbsp. ketchup
6 onion slices, ¼" thick

1. Pour baked beans into bottom of greased slow cooker.
2. Layer pork chops over beans.
3. Spread mustard over pork chops. Sprinkle with brown sugar and drizzle with ketchup.
4. Top with onion slices.
5. Cover. Cook on High 4-6 hours.

# Pork Chops in Orange Sauce

**Kelly Evenson**
Pittsboro, NC

*Makes 4 servings*

**Prep. Time: 25 minutes**
**Cooking Time: 5¼-6¼ hours**
**Ideal slow cooker size: 5-qt.**

4 thick, center-cut pork chops
salt to taste
pepper to taste
1 Tbsp. oil
1 orange
¼ cup ketchup
¾ cup orange juice
1 Tbsp. orange marmalade
1 Tbsp. cornstarch
¼ cup water

1. Season pork chops on both sides with salt and pepper.
2. Brown chops lightly on both sides in skillet in oil. Transfer to slow cooker. Reserve 2 Tbsp. drippings and discard the rest.
3. Grate ½ tsp. orange zest from top or bottom of orange (in order to preserve the main part of the orange for later use). Combine zest with ketchup, orange juice, and marmalade in skillet with reserved drippings. Simmer 1 minute, stirring constantly.
4. Pour sauce over chops.
5. Cover. Cook on Low 5-6 hours. Remove chops and keep warm on a platter.
6. In a small bowl, dissolve cornstarch in water. Stir into

# Oxford Canal Chops Deluxe

Willard E. Roth, Elkhart, IN

*Makes 6 servings*

*Prep. Time: 25 minutes • Cooking Time: 4 hours*
*Ideal slow cooker size: 5-qt.*

6 6-oz. boneless pork
  chops
¼ cup flour
1 tsp. powdered garlic
1 tsp. sea salt
1 tsp. black pepper
1 tsp. dried basil and/or
  dried oregano

2 medium onions, sliced
2 Tbsp. oil
1 cup burgundy wine
14½-oz. can beef broth
1 soup can water
6-oz. can tomato sauce
8 oz. dried apricots
½ lb. fresh mushroom caps

1. Shake chops in bag with flour and seasonings.
2. Glaze onions in oil in medium hot skillet. Add chops and brown on both sides.
3. Pour any remaining flour over chops in skillet.
4. In large bowl mix together wine, broth, water, and tomato sauce. Pour over meat. Bring to boil.
5. Remove chops from skillet and place in cooker.
6. Layer in apricots and mushrooms. Pour heated broth over top.
7. Cover. Cook on Low 2½ hours, and then on High 1½ hours, or until chops are just tender.

*Serving suggestion: This is a great dish to serve with the Celtic speciality Bubble and Squeak—Irish potatoes mashed with green cabbage or brussels sprouts.*

Note:
*My favorite memory with this recipe was the time I prepared it in the tiny kitchen of a houseboat on the Oxford Canal and then shared it with five friends. It was a hit!*

sauce in slow cooker until it becomes smooth. Cook on High 15 minutes, or until sauce thickens.

7. Serve chops with orange sauce on top, along with slices of fresh orange.

# Pork Chop Slow Cooker Casserole

Janice Crist
Quinter, KS

*Makes 5 servings*

*Prep. Time: 15 minutes*
*Cooking Time: 4-6 hours*
*Ideal slow cooker size: 5-qt.*

4-5 medium potatoes,
  quartered or sliced
10¾-oz. can cream of
  chicken soup
10¾-oz. can cream of
  celery soup
2 15-oz. cans green beans,
  drained
5 pork chops

1. Layer potatoes in slow cooker.
2. In a medium-sized bowl combine 2 soups until smooth. Spread over potatoes.
3. Cover with green beans.
4. Place chops on top of beans.
5. Cover. Cook on Low 5-6 hours or on High 4 hours.

Variations:
1. Cover soup layer with 4 slices of your favorite cheese.
2. Sprinkle chops with garlic salt.

**Cheryl Hagner**
Montague, MI

# Teriyaki Pineapple Pork Chops

**Kayla Snyder**
North East, PA

*Makes 4 servings*

*Prep. Time: 10-15 minutes*
*Cooking Time: 4-5 hours*
*Ideal slow cooker size: 2- to 3-qt.*

4 8-oz. bone-in pork loin
   chops
1 Tbsp. minced fresh
   rosemary, *or* 1 tsp. dried
   rosemary, crushed
1 tsp. garlic powder
½ tsp. salt
¼ tsp. pepper
1 cup unsweetened
   pineapple juice
½ cup teriyaki sauce

1. Put chops in slow
cooker.
2. Mix remaining ingre-
dients in a small bowl. Pour
over chops. If you've stacked
the chops, lift up the top ones
and ladle sauce over bottom
ones, too.
3. Cover. Cook on High
4-5 hours, or until chops are
tender but still juicy.

**Tip:**
   For added flavor, marinate
chops in sauce 2-3 hours
before cooking.

# Apples, Sauerkraut, and Chops

**Carol Sherwood**
Batavia, NY

*Makes 4 servings*

*Prep. Time: 25 minutes*
*Cooking Time: 4-8 hours*
*Ideal slow cooker size: 5-qt.*

1 onion, sliced and
   separated into rings,
   *divided*
⅛ tsp. garlic flakes, *or*
   garlic powder, *divided*
3 cups sauerkraut,
   drained, *divided*
1 cup unpeeled apple
   slices, *divided*
1½ tsp. caraway seeds,
   *divided*
¼ tsp. salt, *divided*
¼ tsp. dried thyme, *divided*
¼ tsp. pepper, *divided*
4 ½"-thick pork chops
¾ cup apple juice

1. Place half of onion rings,
garlic flakes, sauerkraut,
apple slices, and caraway
seeds in slow cooker.
2. Season with half the
salt, thyme, and pepper.
3. Brown chops in large
non-stick skillet over high heat
on both sides. This takes only
a few minutes since you're
browning and not cooking.
4. Place pork chops on top
of ingredients in slow cooker.
5. Layer remaining ingredients in order given.
6. Pour apple juice over all.
7. Cover. Cook on Low 6-8
hours or on High 4 hours.

# Pork Chops with Stuffing

**Erma Kauffman**
Cochranville, PA

*Makes 2 servings*

*Prep. Time: 15 minutes*
*Cooking Time: 4-5 hours*
*Ideal slow cooker size: 1½-qt.*

4 slices bread, cubed
1 egg
¼ cup grated, *or* finely
   chopped, celery
¼-½ tsp. salt
⅛ tsp. pepper
2 thick pork chops
1 cup water

1. Combine bread cubes,
egg, celery, salt, and pepper
in a good-sized bowl.
2. Cut pork chops part way
through their thick sides,
creating a pocket. Fill with
stuffing, dividing the stuffing
between them.
3. Pour water into slow
cooker. Add chops.
4. Cover. Cook on Low
4-5 hours, or until chops are
tender but not dry.

# Pork Chops and Stuffing with Curry

**Mary Martins**
Fairbank, IA

*Makes 3-4 servings*

**Prep. Time: 10 minutes**
**Cooking Time: 6-7 hours**
**Ideal slow cooker size: 4-qt.**

1 box stuffing mix
1 cup water
10¾-oz. can cream of
　mushroom soup
1 tsp., *or more,* curry
　powder, according to
　your taste preference
3-4 pork chops

1. Combine stuffing mix and water in a large mixing bowl. Place half in bottom of slow cooker.

2. In another bowl, combine soup and curry powder. Pour half over stuffing.

3. Place pork chops on top.

4. Spread remaining stuffing over pork chops. Pour rest of soup on top.

5. Cover. Cook on Low 6-7 hours, or just until chops are tender.

# Moo Shu Pork

**Gwendolyn Chapman**
Gwinn, MI

*Makes 12 servings*

**Prep. Time: 20 minutes**
**Cooking Time: 2-5 hours**
**Ideal slow cooker size: 4- to 5-qt.**

½ cup hoisin sauce
3 large cloves garlic,
　minced
2 Tbsp. dark Asian sesame
　oil
2 Tbsp. soy sauce
1 Tbsp. cornstarch
16-oz. bag shredded cole
　slaw mix
half a 10-oz. bag shredded
　carrots
1 lb. boneless pork loin
　chops
12 6" flour tortillas
scallion strips, *optional*

1. In small bowl, stir together hoisin sauce, garlic, sesame oil, soy sauce, and cornstarch. Set aside.

2. Place cole slaw and carrots into slow cooker.

3. Cut pork into ⅛"-thick slices. Then cut each slice in half lengthwise. Scatter over top of cabbage mixture in slow cooker.

4. Drizzle with ¼ cup hoisin sauce mixture.

5. Cover. Cook on High 2-3 hours or on Low 4-5 hours, or just until vegetables and meat are as tender as you like them.

6. Remove cover. Stir in remaining ½ cup hoisin sauce mixture.

7. Heat tortillas according to package directions.

8. Place ½ cup pork mixture in center of each tortilla. Top with scallion strips if you wish and roll up.

**Tip from Tester:**
　The Moo Shu mixture is also great served over rice instead of rolling it into tortillas.

*Give the gift of time. Give certificates for a trip to the movies, a day at the mall, or a visit to a local historical site, with you, of course. Also, find ways to spread gift-giving throughout the holidays, rather than just on one overwhelming Christmas Day.*

*Sandra Haverstraw, Hummelstown, PA*

# Pork Roast with Applesauce "Pulled Pork"

**Colleen Heatwole**
Burton, MI

*Makes 8-10 servings*

*Prep. Time: 30 minutes*
*Cooking Time: 10-12 hours*
*Ideal slow cooker size: 5- to 6-qt.*

4-6-lb. pork roast, visible fat removed
24-oz. jar unsweetened applesauce
18-24-oz. bottle barbecue sauce of your choice

1. Place meat in slow cooker.
2. Spread applesauce over top.
3. Spoon barbecue sauce over top of applesauce, being careful not to disturb it.
4. Cover. Cook on Low 10-12 hours, or until roast is very tender but not dry.
5. Remove from slow cooker onto platter. Pull apart with forks.
6. Put shredded meat in bowl. Add some of cooking broth so meat is somewhat juicy but not swimming in sauce.

*Serving suggestion: Serve on sandwich or hamburger **buns**.*

**Tip from Tester:**
I cooked rice in the leftover sauce. I mixed some water with it; the proportion of the liquid was about ⅔ roast-pork sauce and ⅓ water. It was delicious rice!

# Zesty Pulled Pork

**Sheila Plock**
Boalsburg, PA

*Makes 10 servings*

*Prep. Time: 5-10 minutes*
*Cooking Time: 4½-10¾ hours*
*Ideal slow cooker size: 4-qt.*

2½-3½ lbs. boneless pork shoulder roast, *or* pork sirloin roast
salt to taste
pepper to taste
½ cup water
3 Tbsp. cider vinegar
2 Tbsp. Worcestershire sauce
1 tsp. cumin
18-oz. bottle barbecue sauce of your choice

1. Trim fat from roast. Fit roast into slow cooker.
2. Season meat with salt and pepper.
3. In a small bowl, combine water, vinegar, Worcestershire sauce, and cumin. Spoon over roast, being careful not to wash off the seasonings.
4. Cover. Cook on Low 8-10 hours or on High 4-5 hours, just until pork is very tender but not dry.
5. Remove meat onto a platter. Discard liquid.
6. Shred meat using 2 forks. Return to slow cooker.
7. Stir in 1-2 cups barbecue sauce to taste.
8. Cover. Cook on High 30-45 minutes.

*Serving suggestion: Serve on split hamburger **buns**.*

**Note:**
*This is a great recipe when having friends over to watch Christmas and New Year's Bowl games.*

# Pulled Pork BBQ

**Marsha Sabus**
Fallbrook, CA

*Makes 4-6 servings*

*Prep. Time: 20 minutes*
*Cooking Time: 8 hours*
*Ideal slow cooker size: 3- to 4-qt.*

2 tsp. salt
2 tsp. pepper
1 Tbsp. paprika
2-lb. pork butt
2 Tbsp. olive oil
1 large onion, chopped
12-oz. can beer
1 bottle Sweet Baby Ray's Hickory and Brown Sugar BBQ Sauce
½ cup ketchup
3-4 drops hot pepper sauce

1. Rub or pat salt, pepper, and paprika on pork butt.
2. In large skillet, brown each side of meat in olive oil. Place browned butt in slow cooker.
3. Add onion to skillet. Sauté just until tender. Add to slow cooker.
4. Mix remaining ingredients in a good-sized bowl. Pour over pork in slow cooker.
5. Cover. Cook on High 2 hours. Turn to Low and cook 6 more hours.

6. Remove pork from slow cooker to platter. Shred meat with 2 forks.

7. Return pulled pork to slow cooker. Mix thoroughly with sauce.

*Serving suggestion: Serve the meat on toasted **buns** with **cole slaw**—either inside the rolls, or alongside.*

**Note:**

This recipe can easily be doubled for a large group.

# Rob's Sweet and Sour Joe

**Sue Hamilton**
Minooka, IL

*Makes 12 servings*

**Prep. Time: 10 minutes**
**Cooking Time: 3-4 hours**
**Ideal slow cooker size: 3- to 4-qt.**

**1 lb. ground lean pork**
**8 oz. cocktail sauce**
**8 oz. orange marmalade**
**¼ tsp. Chinese five spice**
**½ tsp. garlic powder**
**2 cups cole slaw mix,** *or*
  **shredded cabbage**
**ground black pepper to taste**

1. Brown pork in saucepan, stirring frequently to break up clumps. Drain off drippings. Place meat in slow cooker.

2. Add sauce, marmalade, spice, garlic powder, cole slaw mix, and pepper. Mix well.

3. Cover. Cook on High 3-4 hours, or until heated through.

*Serving suggestion: This makes enough to fill 12 **sandwich rolls**.*

**Tip:**

If you can't find Chinese 5 spice in your grocery store, you can make your own:

**2 tsp. fresh peppercorns**
**1 star anise**
**½ Tbsp. ground cloves**
**1 Tbsp. ground cinnamon**
**1 Tbsp. fennel seeds**

Grind all together in a coffee or spice grinder until fine.

Use only ¼ tsp. in Rob's Sweet and Sour Joe, but store the rest in a tightly covered container for the next time.

# Savory Sausage Sandwiches

**Mary Jane Musser**
Manheim, PA

*Makes 8 servings*

**Prep. Time: 25 minutes**
**Cooking Time: 3-6 hours**
**Ideal slow cooker size: 3½-qt.**

**2 lbs. fresh sausage, cut**
  **into bun-length pieces**
**2 pkgs. dry spaghetti sauce**
  **mix**
**12-oz. can tomato paste**
**3 cups water**
**½ cup brown sugar**
**¼ cup vinegar**

1. Cook sausage in skillet in water for 10 minutes.* Drain. Place in slow cooker.

2. Combine remaining ingredients in saucepan. Simmer 5 minutes. Pour over sausage.

3. Cover. Cook on High 3 hours or Low 6 hours.

*Serving suggestion: Serve in **rolls** topped with grated **cheese**.*

*You can skip this step. But pre-cooking the sausages lightly in this way cooks off much of their grease.

**Variation:**

Use 1 qt. spaghetti sauce, either homemade or bought, instead of sauce mix, tomato paste, and water.

# Italian Sausage

**Lauren Eberhard**
Seneca, IL

*Makes 15 servings*

*Prep. Time: 40 minutes*
*Cooking Time: 6-7 hours*
*Ideal slow cooker size: 6-qt., or 2 4-qt. cookers*

5 lbs. Italian sausage in casing
4 large green bell peppers, sliced
3 large onions, sliced
1, *or* 2, garlic cloves, minced
28-oz. can tomato purée
14-oz. can tomato sauce
12-oz. can tomato paste
1 Tbsp. dried oregano
1 Tbsp. dried basil
½ tsp. garlic powder
1½ tsp. salt
2 tsp. sugar

1. Cut sausage into 4″ or 5″ pieces and brown on all sides in batches in skillet.
2. Sauté peppers, onions, and garlic in drippings.
3. Combine tomato purée, sauce, and paste in bowl. Stir in seasonings and sugar.
4. Layer half of sausage, onions, and peppers in 6-qt. slow cooker, or in 2 4-qt. cookers. Cover with half the tomato mixture. Repeat layers.
5. Cover. Cook on High 1 hour and then on Low 5-6 hours.

*Serving suggestion: Serve over **pasta**, or dip mixture with a straining spoon onto **Italian sandwich rolls**.*

# Dawn's Sausage and Peppers

**Dawn Day**
Westminster, CA

*Makes 8-10 servings*

*Prep. Time: 25-30 minutes*
*Cooking Time: 6 hours*
*Ideal slow cooker size: 5-qt.*

3 medium onions, sliced
1 sweet red pepper, sliced
1 sweet green pepper, sliced
1 sweet yellow pepper, sliced
4 garlic cloves, minced
1 Tbsp. oil
28-oz. can chopped tomatoes
1 tsp. salt
½ tsp. crushed red pepper flakes
2-3 lbs. sweet Italian sausage, cut into 3″ pieces

1. Sauté onions, peppers, and garlic in oil in skillet. When just softened, place in slow cooker. (Or skip this step, but check that the vegetables are cooked to your liking at the end of the 6-hour cooking time.)
2. Add tomatoes, salt, and crushed red pepper. Mix well.
3. Add sausage links.
4. Cover. Cook on Low 6 hours.

*Serving suggestion: Serve on **rolls**, or over **pasta** or **baked potatoes**.*

**Variation:**
For a thicker sauce, stir 2 Tbsp. cornstarch into 2 Tbsp. water in a small bowl until smooth. Fifteen minutes before end of cooking time, stir into slow cooker, stirring until well mixed. Cover and cook 15 minutes.

# Super-Simple Sausage and Sauerkraut

**Eileen Lehman**
Kidron, OH

*Makes 12 servings*

*Prep. Time: 10 minutes*
*Cooking Time: 4-8 hours*
*Ideal slow cooker size: 4-qt.*

2-3 lbs. fresh sausage, cut in 3″-lengths, or removed from casings
3 32-oz. cans sauerkraut

1. Brown sausage in large non-stick skillet. (Don't crowd the skillet or the sausages will steam and not brown.)
2. Combine sausage and sauerkraut in slow cooker.
3. Cover. Cook on Low 4-8 hours, or until meat is fully cooked.

**Note:**
*It is traditional to serve sauerkraut with mashed potatoes on New Year's Day in Kidron!*

# Bratwurst in Sauce

### Joyce Shackelford
### Green Bay, WI

*Makes 6-10 servings*

*Prep. Time: 20 minutes*
*Cooking Time: 6-10 hours*
*Ideal slow cooker size: 4-qt.*

2-3 lbs. uncooked
    bratwursts
6-oz. can tomato paste
½ cup ketchup
12-oz. can beer
½ small onion, chopped
    fine
2 cloves garlic, minced

1. Place bratwursts in
saucepan. Barely cover with
water. Bring to a boil and
cook 5-10 minutes. Drain
well. Cut into bite-size pieces.
2. Combine tomato paste,
ketchup, beer, onion, and
garlic in slow cooker. Add
partially cooked brats.
3. Cover. Cook on Low
6-10 hours, or until brats are
cooked through and as hot as
you like them.

*Serving suggestion: Serve
over cooked **rice** or **pasta**.
Or serve with wooden picks,
accompanied with a good **dark
bread**.*

# Brats and Spuds

### Kathi Rogge
### Alexandria, IN

*Makes 6 servings*

*Prep. Time: 35 minutes*
*Cooking Time: 4-6 hours*
*Ideal slow cooker size: 4-qt.*

5-6 bratwurst links, cut
    into 1" pieces
5 medium-sized potatoes,
    peeled and cubed
27-oz. can sauerkraut,
    rinsed and drained
1 medium-sized tart apple,
    chopped
1 small onion, chopped
⅓-½ cup packed brown
    sugar
½ tsp. salt

1. Brown bratwurst on all
sides in skillet.
2. Combine remaining
ingredients in slow cooker.
Stir in bratwurst and pan
drippings.
3. Cover. Cook on High 4-6
hours, or until potatoes and
apples are tender.

**Variation:**
    Add a small amount of
caraway seeds or crisp bacon
pieces, just before serving.

# Sausage and Scalloped Potatoes

### Carolyn Baer
### Conrath, WI

*Makes 5 servings*

*Prep. Time: 25 minutes*
*Cooking Time: 5-10 hours*
*Ideal slow cooker size: 4-qt.*

2½ lbs. potatoes, sliced
    ¼" thick, *divided*
1 lb. fully cooked smoked
    sausage links, sliced
    ½" thick, *divided*
2 medium onions,
    chopped, *divided*
10¾-oz. can cheddar
    cheese soup, *divided*
10¾-oz. can cream of
    celery soup, *divided*

1. Layer one-third of
potatoes, one-third of sausage,
one-third of onions, one-third
of cheddar cheese soup, and
one-third of celery soup into
slow cooker.
2. Repeat 2 times.
3. Cover. Cook on Low 10
hours or on High 5 hours, or
until vegetables are as tender
as you like them.

*Serving suggestion: Serve
with **peas**, a **salad**, and
**dessert**.*

**Note:**
    I like to prepare this
delicious dish when I will be
gone for the day, but know
I will have guests for the
evening meal. When I get
home, the meat and potatoes
are already cooked.

# Sausage-Potato Slow Cooker Dinner

**Deborah Swartz**
Grottoes, VA

*Makes 6-8 servings*

*Prep. Time: 25-30 minutes*
*Cooking Time: 3-9 hours*
*Ideal slow cooker size: 4-qt.*

¾ lb. sausage, casings
  removed, *divided*
1 cup water
½ tsp. cream of tartar
6 medium potatoes, thinly
  sliced, peeled or not,
  *divided*
1 onion, chopped, *divided*
¼ cup flour, *divided*
salt to taste
pepper to taste
1½ cups grated cheddar
  cheese, *divided*
¼ stick (2 Tbsp.) butter
10¾-oz. can cream of
  mushroom soup

1. Brown sausage in skillet.
Drain off drippings.
2. Combine water and
cream of tartar in a good-
sized mixing bowl. Place
potatoes in water as you slice
them. When finished slicing,
toss potatoes in water to keep
them from turning brown.
Drain off water.
3. Layer half of potatoes,
sausage, onion, flour, a
sprinkling of salt and pepper,
and half of cheddar cheese in
slow cooker.
4. Repeat layers of
potatoes, sausage, onion,
flour, salt and pepper until
completely used.
5. Dot butter over top. Pour
soup over all.
6. Cover. Cook on Low 7-9
hours or on High 3-4 hours,
or until potatoes and onions
are tender.
7. Sprinkle reserved cheese
over top just before serving.

# Sausage and Sweet Potatoes

**Ruth Hershey**
Paradise, PA

*Makes 4-6 servings*

*Prep. Time: 25 minutes*
*Cooking Time: 4-10 hours*
*Ideal slow cooker size: 4-qt.*

1 lb. bulk sausage
2 sweet potatoes, peeled
  and sliced
3 apples, peeled and sliced
2 Tbsp. brown sugar
1 Tbsp. flour
¼ tsp. ground cinnamon
¼ tsp. salt
¼ cup water

1. Brown sausage in skillet.
Drain off drippings.
2. Layer sausage, sweet
potatoes, and apples in slow
cooker.
3. Combine remaining
ingredients in a small bowl.
Stir until well mixed.
4. Pour over ingredients in
slow cooker.
5. Cover. Cook on Low 8-10
hours or on High 4 hours.

*As Christmas comes near, my husband and I spend seven different evenings with each one of our seven married children. It's so special to see their reactions as they open their gifts. On Christmas Day we all gather together to eat and sing.*
*Mary B. Sensenig, New Holland, PA*

# Harvest Kielbasa

**Christ Kaczynski**
Schenectady, NY

*Makes 6 servings*

*Prep. Time: 20 minutes*
*Cooking Time: 4-8 hours*
*Ideal slow cooker size: 5-qt.*

2 lbs. smoked kielbasa
3 cups unsweetened
    applesauce
½ cup brown sugar
3 medium onions, sliced

1. Slice kielbasa into ¼" slices. Brown in skillet. Drain off drippings.

2. Combine applesauce and brown sugar in a good-sized mixing bowl.

3. Layer kielbasa, onions, and applesauce mixture in slow cooker.

4. Cover. Cook on Low 4-8 hours.

Note:

The longer it cooks, the better the flavor.

# Kielbasa Stew

**Fannie Miller**
Hutchinson, KS

*Makes 6-8 servings*

*Prep. Time: 40-45 minutes*
*Cooking Time: 8-10 hours*
*Ideal slow cooker size: 5-qt.*

6 strips of bacon
1 onion, chopped
1-1½ lbs. smoked, fully
    cooked kielbasa, thinly
    sliced
2 15½-oz. cans great
    northern beans, drained
2 8-oz. cans tomato sauce
4¼-oz. can chopped green
    chilies, undrained
2 medium carrots, thinly
    sliced
1 medium green bell
    pepper, chopped
½ tsp. Italian seasoning
½ tsp. dried thyme
½ tsp. black pepper

1. Fry bacon in skillet until crisp. Crumble bacon and place in large slow cooker.

2. Add onions and sausage to drippings in skillet. Cook until onions are soft. Drain off drippings.

3. Transfer onions and sausage to slow cooker.

4. Add all remaining ingredients to cooker and stir together well.

5. Cover. Cook on Low 8-10 hours, or until vegetables are as tender as you like them.

# Kielbasa and Cabbage

**Mary Ann Lefever**
Lancaster, PA

*Makes 4 servings*

*Prep. Time: 10-15 minutes*
*Cooking Time: 8 hours*
*Ideal slow cooker size: 4- to 5-qt.*

1 lb. kielbasa cut into 4
    chunks
4 large white potatoes, cut
    into chunks
1-lb. head green cabbage,
    shredded
1 qt. whole tomatoes
    (strained if you don't
    like seeds)
onion, thinly sliced,
    *optional*

1. Layer kielbasa, then potatoes, and then cabbage into slow cooker.

2. Pour tomatoes over top.

3. Top with sliced onions if you wish.

4. Cover. Cook on High 8 hours, or until meat is cooked through and vegetables are as tender as you like them.

143

# Rice and Beans— and Sausage

**Marcia S. Myer**
Manheim, PA

*Makes 8 servings*

**Prep. Time: 25 minutes**
**Cooking Time: 4-6 hours**
**Ideal slow cooker size: 5-qt.**

3 celery ribs, chopped
1 onion, chopped
2 garlic cloves, minced
1¾ cups tomato juice
2 16-oz. cans kidney beans, drained
¾ tsp. dried oregano
¾ tsp. dried thyme
¼ tsp. red pepper flakes
¼ tsp. pepper
½ lb. (*or more*) fully cooked smoked turkey sausage, *or* kielbasa, cut into ¼"-thick slices

1. Combine all ingredients in slow cooker.
2. Cover. Cook on Low 4-6 hours.

*Serving suggestion: Serve over **rice**. Garnish with **shredded cheese** if you wish.*

# Election Lunch

**Alix Nancy Botsford**
Seminole, OK

*Makes 6-12 servings*

**Prep. Time: 30 minutes**
**Cooking Time: 2-4 hours**
**Ideal slow cooker size: 6-qt., or 2 4-qt. cookers**

1 large onion, chopped
1 lb. sausage, cut into thin slices, *or* with casings removed and meat crumbled
1 rib celery, sliced
1 Tbsp. Worcestershire sauce
1½ tsp. dry mustard
¼ cup honey
10-oz. can tomatoes with green chili peppers
1-lb. can lima, *or* butter, beans, drained, with liquid reserved
1-lb. can red kidney beans, drained, with liquid reserved
1-lb. can garbanzo beans, drained, with liquid reserved

1. Brown onion and sausage in skillet. Stir frequently. Continue cooking until pink disappears from meat. Drain off drippings.
2. Place meat and onions in 6-qt. slow cooker, or divide between 2 4-qt. cookers.
3. Stir in all other ingredients, combining well. Add reserved juice from lima, kidney, and garbanzo beans if there's enough room in the cooker(s).
4. Cover. Cook on Low 2-4 hours.

Note:
*I mixed up this hearty stew the night before an Election Day and took it to the voting site the next morning. I plugged it in, and all day long we could smell the Lunch cooking. I work at a very sparsely populated, country poling place and ended up giving out the recipe in little water-cup samples to many voters!*

*I have four different sizes of slow cookers. One is very tiny, with only an on and off switch, for keeping cheese sauce hot. One I use for heating gravy. Another I often use to keep mashed potatoes warm.*

# Sausage Pasta Stew

**Betty K. Drescher**
Quakertown, PA

*Makes 8 servings*

*Prep. Time: 30-35 minutes*
*Cooking Time: 7¼-9¼ hours*
*Ideal slow cooker size: 6-qt.*

1 lb. Italian sausage,
  casings removed
4 cups water
26-oz. jar meatless
  spaghetti sauce
16-oz. can kidney beans,
  rinsed and drained
1 medium yellow summer
  squash, cut in 1" pieces
2 medium carrots, cut in
  ¼" slices
1 medium red, *or* green,
  sweet pepper, diced
⅓ cup chopped onions
1½ cups uncooked spiral
  pasta
1 cup frozen peas
1 tsp. sugar
½ tsp. salt
¼ tsp. pepper

1. Sauté sausage in skillet
until no longer pink. Drain
off drippings. Place sausage
in slow cooker.

2. Add water, spaghetti
sauce, kidney beans, squash,
carrots, pepper, and onions.
Mix well.

3. Cover. Cook on Low 7-9
hours, or until vegetables are
tender.

4. Add remaining ingredi-
ents. Mix well.

# Golden Autumn Stew

**Naomi E. Fast**, Hesston, KS

*Makes 8-10 servings*

*Prep. Time: 30-40 minutes • Cooking Time: 6 hours*
*Ideal slow cooker size: 5-qt.*

2 cups cubed Yukon gold
  potatoes
2 cups cubed, peeled
  sweet potatoes
2 cups cubed, peeled
  butternut squash
1 cup cubed, peeled
  rutabaga
1 cup diced carrots
1 cup sliced celery
1 lb. smoked sausage
2 cups apple juice, *or* cider
1 tart apple, thinly sliced
salt to taste
pepper to taste
1 Tbsp. sugar, *or* honey

1. Combine vegetables in slow cooker.

2. Place ring of sausage on top. Or arrange sausage links
or pieces over top of vegetables.

3. Pour in apple juice. Place apple slices over top.

4. Cover. Cook on High 2 hours, and then on Low 4
hours, or until vegetables are tender. Do not stir.

5. To prepare to serve, remove sausage and keep warm.
Season vegetables with salt, pepper, and sugar as desired.
Place vegetables in bowl. Slice meat into pieces and place
on top.

*Serving suggestion: I like to serve the Stew with hot*
***baking-powder biscuits*** *and* ***honey***, *and a* ***green salad*** *or*
***cole slaw.***

**Tip:**
  Don't omit the rutabaga! Get acquainted with its rich
uniqueness. It will surprise and please your taste buds.

5. Cover. Cook on High
15-20 minutes, or until pasta
is tender.

**Note:**
  Add 1 Tbsp. tapioca in Step
5 if you like a thicker stew.

# Chili Casserole

**Sharon Miller**
Holmesville, OH

*Makes 6 servings*

*Prep. Time: 20-25 minutes*
*Cooking Time: 7 hours*
*Ideal slow cooker size: 5-qt.*

1 lb. bulk pork sausage
2 cups water
15½-oz. can chili beans, drained
14½-oz. can diced tomatoes
¾ cup uncooked brown rice
¼ cup chopped onions
1 Tbsp. chili powder
1 tsp. Worcestershire sauce
1 tsp. prepared mustard
¾ tsp. salt
⅛ tsp. garlic powder
1 cup shredded cheddar cheese

1. Brown sausage in skillet. Stir frequently to break up clumps. When meat is no longer pink, drain off drippings.
2. Spoon meat into slow cooker.
3. Add all other ingredients, except cheese, to slow cooker.
4. Cover. Cook on Low 7 hours.
5. Stir in cheese during last 10 minutes of cooking time.

# Pizza Rigatoni

**Tina Snyder**
Manheim, PA

*Makes 6-8 servings*

*Prep. Time: 25 minutes*
*Cooking Time: 4 hours*
*Ideal slow cooker size: 5-qt.*

1½ lbs. bulk sausage, *divided*
3 cups rigatoni, lightly cooked, *divided*
4 cups shredded mozzarella cheese, *divided*
10¾-oz. can cream of mushroom soup, *divided*
1 small onion, sliced, *divided*
15-oz. can pizza sauce, *divided*
8-oz. can pizza sauce, *divided*
3½-oz. pkg. sliced pepperoni, *divided*
6-oz. can sliced ripe olives, drained, *divided*

1. Brown sausage in skillet. Drain off drippings.
2. Place half the sausage in the slow cooker.
3. Place half of pasta, cheese, soup, onion, pizza sauce, pepperoni, and olives in layers over sausage. Repeat layers.
4. Cover. Cook on Low 4 hours.

**Tip:**
If your store doesn't carry 8-oz. cans pizza sauce, substitute an 8-oz. can tomato sauce with basil, garlic, and oregano.

# Slow-Cooker Pizza

**Sharon Miller**
Holmesville, OH

*Makes 6 servings*

*Prep. Time: 25 minutes*
*Cooking Time: 6-8 hours*
*Ideal slow cooker size: 5-qt.*

1½ lbs. bulk sausage, *divided*
1 small onion, chopped, *divided*
1-lb. pkg. pasta, *or noodles,* uncooked, *divided*
28-oz. jar spaghetti sauce
16-oz. can tomato sauce
¾ cup water
4-oz. can mushrooms, drained
8-oz. pkg. pepperoni, chopped
16-oz. pkg. shredded mozzarella cheese

1. Brown sausage and onion in skillet. Drain.
2. Place one-third of mixture in slow cooker.
3. Layer in one-third of uncooked pasta.
4. Combine spaghetti sauce, tomato sauce, water, and mushrooms in a good-sized bowl. Ladle one-third of that mixture over noodles.
5. Repeat the above layers 2 more times.
6. Top with pepperoni. Top pepperoni with shredded cheese.
7. Cover. Cook on Low 6-8 hours, or until pasta is cooked to your liking and pizza is hot throughout.

# Ham in Foil

**Jeanette Oberholtzer**
Manheim, PA
**Vicki Dinkel**
Sharon Springs, KS
**Janet Roggie**
Lowville, NY

*Makes 8 servings*

*Prep. Time: 5 minutes*
*Cooking Time: 7 hours*
*Ideal slow cooker size: 5-qt.*

½ cup water
3-4-lb. precooked ham
liquid smoke

1. Pour water into slow cooker.
2. Sprinkle ham with liquid smoke. Wrap in foil. Place in slow cooker.
3. Cover. Cook on High 1 hour, and then on Low 6 hours.
4. Cut into thick chunks or ½"-thick slices and serve.

# Easy and Elegant Ham

**Lorraine Pflederer**
Goshen, IN

*Makes 18-20 servings*

*Prep. Time: 10 minutes*
*Cooking Time: 6-7 hours*
*Standing Time: 10-15 minutes*
*Ideal slow cooker size: 5-qt.*

2 20-oz. cans sliced pineapple, *divided*
1 fully cooked boneless ham (about 6 lbs.), halved
6-oz. jar cherries, well drained
12-oz. jar orange marmalade

1. Drain pineapple, reserving juice. Set juice aside.
2. Place half of pineapple in ungreased slow cooker.
3. Top with ham. Add cherries, remaining pineapple, and reserved juice.
4. Spoon marmalade over ham.
5. Cover. Cook on Low 6-7 hours or until heated through. Remove to serving platter and let stand for 10-15 minutes before slicing.
6. Serve pineapple and cherries over sliced ham.

# Honey-Dijon Holiday Ham

**Robin Schrock**
Millersburg, OH

*Makes 10 servings*

*Prep. Time: 15 minutes*
*Cooking Time: 8 hours*
*Ideal slow cooker size: 6-qt.*

5-lb. bone-in fully cooked smoked ham
⅓ cup apple juice
¼ cup packed brown sugar
1 Tbsp. honey
1 Tbsp. Dijon mustard

1. Place ham in slow cooker.
2. In a small bowl, mix juice, brown sugar, honey, and mustard together. Spread over ham.
3. Cover. Cook on Low 8 hours or until ham is hot through.
4. Slice ham and serve.
5. Pass sauce to top ham slices.

*We ask the youngest child present on Christmas Eve to place baby Jesus in the crib or nativity as we all sing "Away in a Manger" and other Christmas carols.*

*Donna Treloar, Muncie, IN*

# Glazed Ham in a Bag

**Eleanor J. Ferreira**
North Chelmsford, MA

*Makes 12 servings*

*Prep. Time: 10 minutes*
*Cooking Time: 6-8 hours*
*Ideal slow cooker size: 6-qt.*

5-lb. cooked ham
3 Tbsp. orange juice
1 Tbsp. Dijon mustard

1. Rinse meat.
2. Combine orange juice and mustard. Spread over ham.
3. Place in cooking bag. Seal bag with twist tie. Poke 4 holes in top of bag. Place in slow cooker.
4. Cover. Cook on Low 6-8 hours.
5. To serve, remove ham from bag, reserving juices. Slice ham and spoon juices over.

**Tip:**
Serve additional juice with ham in small pitcher.

# Raspberry-Glazed Ham

**Gloria Frey**
Lebanon, PA

*Makes 16-20 servings*

*Prep Time: 10-15 minutes*
*Cooking Time: 4 hours*
*Ideal slow-cooker size: 6-qt.*

8-10-lb. boneless ham, fully cooked
¼ cup apple juice
2 Tbsp. lemon juice
2 tsp. cornstarch
⅓ cup seedless raspberry jam, *divided*
1 Tbsp. butter

1. Place ham in slow cooker. Cover. Cook on Low 2 hours.
2. While ham is cooking, blend apple juice, lemon juice, and cornstarch together in saucepan.
3. Stir in about half of jam after liquid is well blended.
4. Cook and stir until hot and bubbly. Add butter. Stir in remaining jam.
5. Spoon glaze over ham after it has cooked 2 hours.
6. Cover. Cook 2 more hours on Low.
7. Slice ham and serve.

**Tip:**
If you wish, double the amount of glaze. Place half in a serving bowl. Pass alongside ham slices so individuals can add more glaze to the meat if they wish.

# Ham with Pineapple Sauce

**Kayla Snyder**
North East, PA

*Makes 14-16 servings*

*Prep. Time: 20-30 minutes*
*Cooking Time: 3 hours*
*Ideal slow cooker size: 5-qt.*

20-oz. can crushed pineapple, undrained
1 tsp. vinegar
1 Tbsp. lemon juice
½ tsp. salt
2 cups brown sugar
¾ tsp. dry mustard
4 Tbsp. flour
7-8-lb. ham, precooked and sliced in ¼"-thick slices

1. Mix together pineapple, vinegar, lemon juice, salt, brown sugar, mustard, and flour in a saucepan. Bring to boil. Cook, stirring frequently until slightly thickened.
2. Layer several slices of ham into slow cooker. Ladle some of sauce over top of each slice. Continue layering until all ham and sauce are stacked in slow cooker.
3. Cover. Cook on High 3 hours, or until heated through.

**Note:**
*We served this recipe at our wedding, so it is especially special to us.*

# New England Boiled Dinner

**Leona M. Slabaugh**
Apple Creek, OH

*Makes 4 servings*

*Prep. Time: 30 minutes*
*Cooking Time: 3-6 hours*
*Ideal slow cooker size: 3- to 5-qt.*

2 lbs. boneless smoked
   ham piece
1 lb. potatoes, halved
1-lb. bag baby carrots
1 lb. cabbage, cut in wedges
¼ cup water

1. Place meat in slow cooker.
Fit vegetables around meat.
2. Add water
3. Cover. Cook on Low 6
hours or on High 3 hours, or
just until meat and vegetables
are as tender as you like.

# Ham, Bean, and Potato Dish

**Hazel L. Propst**
Oxford, PA

*Makes 6-8 servings*

*Prep. Time: 10 minutes*
*Cooking Time: 6-8 hours*
*Ideal slow cooker size: 5-qt.*

8-10 small potatoes
3-4 cans string beans,
   undrained
ham hock, *or* leftover ham

salt to taste
pepper to taste

1. Place potatoes in bottom
of slow cooker.
2. Alternate layers of
beans and ham over potatoes.
Sprinkle with salt and pepper.
3. Cover. Cook on Low 8
hours if using ham hock; 6
hours if using leftover ham,
or until meat and potatoes are
tender but not dry or mushy.

# Schnitz und Knepp

**Jean Robinson**
Cinnaminson, NJ

*Makes 6 servings*

*Prep. Time: 20 minutes*
*Soaking Time: 2-3 hours*
*Cooking Time: 5¼ hours*
*Ideal slow cooker size: 4-qt.*

Schnitz:
¾-1 lb. dried sweet apples
   (also known as "schnitz")
3 lbs. ham slices, cut into
   2" cubes
2 Tbsp. brown sugar
1 cinnamon stick

Knepp (dumplings):
2 cups flour
4 tsp. baking powder
1 egg, well beaten
3 Tbsp. melted butter
scant ½ cup milk
1 tsp. salt
¼ tsp. pepper

1. Cover apples with water
in large bowl and let soak for
a few hours.

2. Place ham cubes in slow
cooker. Cover with water.
3. Cover cooker. Cook on
High 2 hours.
4. Add apples and water
in which they have been
soaking.
5. Add brown sugar and
cinnamon stick. Mix until
sugar dissolves.
6. Cover. Cook on Low 3
hours.
7. Combine dumpling
ingredients in bowl. Drop
into hot liquid in cooker by
tablespoonfuls.
8. Turn cooker to High.
Cover. Do not lift lid for 15
minutes.
9. Serve piping hot on a
large platter.

Note:
*This was my grandmother's
recipe and she had no slow
cooker. I was allowed to drop
in the dumplings. Schnitz und
Knepp cooked on the back of
the woodstove while Grandma
quilted.*

# Ham with Sweet Potatoes and Oranges

**Esther Becker**, Gordonville, PA

*Makes 4 servings*
*Prep. Time: 15 minutes • Cooking Time: 7-8 hours*
*Ideal slow cooker size: 3-qt.*

2-3 sweet potatoes, peeled
  and sliced ¼" thick
1 large ham slice
3 seedless oranges,
  peeled and sliced

3 Tbsp. orange juice
  concentrate
3 Tbsp. honey
½ cup brown sugar
2 Tbsp. cornstarch

1. Place sweet potato slices in slow cooker.
2. Arrange ham and orange slices on top of potatoes.
3. Combine remaining ingredients in a small bowl. Drizzle over ham and oranges.
4. Cover. Cook on Low 7-8 hours.

*Serving suggestion: Delicious served with a **fruit salad**.*

# Ham and Hash Browns

**Evelyn Page**, Riverton, WY
**Anna Stoltzfus**, Honey Brook, PA

*Makes 6-8 servings*
*Prep. Time: 15 minutes*
*Cooking Time: 6-8 hours*
*Ideal slow cooker size: 5-qt.*

28-oz. pkg. frozen hash
  brown potatoes
2½ cups cubed cooked ham
2-oz. jar pimentos, drained
  and chopped
10¾-oz. can cheddar
  cheese soup

¾ cup half-and-half, *or*
  milk
dash of pepper
salt to taste

1. Combine potatoes, ham, and pimentos in slow cooker.
2. In a bowl, combine soup, half-and-half, and seasonings. Pour over potatoes and ham. Stir well.
3. Cover. Cook on Low 6-8 hours. (If you turn the cooker on when you go to bed, you'll have a wonderfully tasty breakfast in the morning.)

Variation:
Add a 4-oz. can of mushrooms, drained, *or* ¼ lb. sliced fresh mushrooms, to Step 1.

# Creamy Ham Topping (for baked potatoes)

**Judy Buller**
Bluffton, OH

*Makes 6 servings*

*Prep. Time: 15 minutes*
*Cooking Time: 1-2 hours*
*Ideal slow cooker size: 3½-qt.*

half a stick (¼ cup) butter
¼ cup flour
2 cups milk
¼ cup half-and-half
1 Tbsp. chopped parsley
1 Tbsp. chicken bouillon
  granules
½ tsp. Italian seasoning
2 cups diced cooked ham
¼ cup Romano cheese,
  grated
1 cup sliced mushrooms
baked potatoes
shredded cheese
sour cream

1. Melt butter in saucepan over medium heat. Stir in flour. Add milk and half-and-half.
2. Continue stirring until sauce thickens and becomes smooth.
3. Stir in remaining ingredients (except baked potatoes, shredded cheese, and sour cream). Pour into slow cooker.
4. Cover. Cook on Low 1-2 hours.
5. Serve over baked potatoes. Top with shredded cheese and sour cream.

# Ham and Lima Beans

**Charlotte Shaffer**
East Earl, PA

*Makes 6 servings*

*Prep. Time: 15 minutes*
*Soaking Time: 8 hours, or overnight*
*Cooking Time: 4-7 hours*
*Ideal slow cooker size: 4-qt.*

1 lb. dry lima beans
1 onion, chopped
1 bell pepper, chopped
1 tsp. dry mustard
1 tsp. salt
1 tsp. pepper
½ lb. ham, finely cubed
1 cup water
10¾-oz. can tomato soup

1. Cover beans with water. Soak 8 hours or overnight. Drain.
2. Combine all ingredients in slow cooker.
3. Cover. Cook on Low 7 hours or on High 4 hours, or until vegetables are as tender as you like them.
4. If mixture begins to dry out, add ½ cup water or more and stir well.

*Serving suggestion: We think this is delicious served with hot **cornbread.***

# Black Beans with Ham

**Colleen Heatwole**
Burton, MI

*Makes 8-10 servings*

*Prep. Time: 20 minutes*
*Soaking Time: 8 hours or overnight*
*Cooking Time: 10-12 hours*
*Ideal slow cooker size: 5-qt.*

4 cups dry black beans
1-2 cups diced ham
1 tsp. salt, *optional*
1 tsp. cumin
½-1 cup minced onion
2 garlic cloves, minced
3 bay leaves
1 qt. diced tomatoes
1 Tbsp. brown sugar

1. Cover black beans with water and soak 8 hours, or overnight, in slow cooker.
2. Drain and pour beans back into slow cooker.
3. Add all remaining ingredients. Stir well. Cover with water.
4. Cover cooker. Cook on Low 10-12 hours, or until beans are as tender as you like them.

Note:
*This is our favorite black bean recipe. We usually serve it over rice. It's good any time of the year, but we make it especially frequently in the winter.*

# Ham 'n' Cabbage Stew

**Dede Peterson**
Rapid City, SD

*Makes 4-5 servings*

*Prep. Time: 25-30 minutes*
*Cooking Time: 4-6 hours*
*Ideal slow cooker size: 4-qt.*

½ lb. cooked ham, cubed
½ cup diced onions
1 garlic clove, minced
4-oz. can sliced mushrooms, undrained
4 cups shredded cabbage
2 cups sliced carrots
¼ tsp. pepper
¼ tsp. caraway seeds
⅔ cup beef broth
1 Tbsp. cornstarch
2 Tbsp. water

1. Combine all ingredients except cornstarch and water in slow cooker.
2. Cover. Cook on Low 4-6 hours, or until vegetables are cooked as you like them.
3. In a small bowl, mix cornstarch into water until smooth. Stir into slow cooker during last hour to thicken Stew slightly.

# Ham and Corn Slow-Cooker Casserole

**Vicki Dinkel**
Sharon Springs, KS

*Makes 8 servings*

*Prep. Time: 30 minutes*
*Cooking Time: 4-8 hours*
*Ideal slow cooker size: 4-qt.*

1 stick (8 Tbsp.) butter
1 small green bell pepper, chopped
1 medium onion, chopped
½ cup flour
½ tsp. paprika
½ tsp. salt
½ tsp. pepper
¼ tsp. dried thyme
1 tsp. dry mustard
4 cups milk
8-oz. can cream-style corn
2 cups diced, slightly cooked potatoes
4 cups diced cooked ham
1 cup shredded cheddar cheese

1. Sauté green pepper and onion in butter in skillet.
2. Stir in flour and seasonings.
3. Gradually stir in milk and cook over medium heat. Stir continually until thickened. Pour into slow cooker.
4. Stir in remaining ingredients.
5. Cover. Cook on Low 8 hours or on High 4 hours.

# Cheesy Ham and Broccoli

**Dolores Kratz**
Souderton, PA

*Makes 6 servings*

*Prep. Time: 25-30 minutes*
*Cooking Time: 6-7 hours*
*Ideal slow cooker size: 4- to 5-qt.*

1 bunch fresh broccoli
1½ cups chopped ham
¾ cup uncooked rice
4-oz. can mushrooms, drained
1 small onion, chopped
10¾-oz. can cheddar cheese soup
¾ cup water
¼ cup half-and-half, *or* milk
dash of pepper
½-1 can chow mein noodles

1. Cut broccoli into pieces and steam for 4 minutes in microwave. Place in slow cooker.
2. Add remaining ingredients to slow cooker except noodles. Mix well.
3. Cover. Cook on Low 6-7 hours.
4. Just before serving, sprinkle with noodles.

*Serving suggestion: This is a good main dish, with a **tossed salad** or **applesauce** as a go-along.*

# Broccoli Casserole

**Rebecca Meyerkorth**
Wamego, KS

*Makes 4 servings*

*Prep. Time: 20 minutes*
*Cooking Time: 4-5 hours*
*Ideal slow cooker size: 4- to 5-qt.*

16-oz. pkg. frozen broccoli cuts, thawed and drained
2-3 cups cubed, cooked ham
10¾-oz. can cream of mushroom soup
4 oz. of your favorite mild cheese, cubed
1 cup milk
1 cup instant rice, uncooked
1 rib celery, chopped
1 small onion, chopped

1. Combine broccoli and ham in slow cooker.
2. In a medium-sized bowl, combine soup, cheese, milk, rice, celery, and onion. Stir into broccoli and ham.
3. Cover. Cook on Low 4-5 hours.

# Ham and Broccoli

**Dede Peterson**
Rapid City, SD

*Makes 6-8 servings*

*Prep. Time: 20 minutes*
*Cooking Time: 3¼-4¼ hours*
*Ideal slow cooker size: 5-qt.*

¾ lb. fresh broccoli, chopped, *or* 10-oz. pkg.

frozen chopped broccoli
10¾-oz. can cream of
   mushroom soup
8-oz. jar cheese sauce
2½ cups milk
1¼ cups long-grain rice,
   uncooked
1 rib celery, sliced
⅛ tsp. pepper
3 cups cooked and cubed
   ham
8-oz. can water chestnuts,
   drained and sliced
½ tsp. paprika

1. Combine all ingredients
except ham, water chestnuts,
and paprika in slow cooker.
2. Cover. Cook on High 3-4
hours.
3. Stir in ham and water
chestnuts. Cook 15-20
minutes, or until heated
through. Let stand 10 minutes
before serving.
4. Sprinkle with paprika
just before serving.

# Underground
# Ham and Cheese

Carol Sommers
Millersburg, OH

Makes 12-16 servings

*Prep. Time: 30-40 minutes*
*Cooking Time: 3-4 hours*
*Ideal slow cooker size: 2 4- to*
   *5-qt. cookers*

half a stick (4 Tbsp.) butter
½ cup chopped onions
4 cups cooked ham, cut
   into chunks

1 Tbsp. Worcestershire
   sauce
2 10¾-oz. cans cream of
   mushroom soup
1 cup milk
2 cups Velveeta cheese,
   cubed
4 qts. mashed potatoes
1 pt. sour cream
browned and crumbled
bacon

1. Combine butter and
onions in saucepan. Cook
until onions are tender.
2. Place sautéed onions,
ham, and Worcestershire
sauce in large slow cooker, or
divide between 2 4- or 5-qt.
cookers.
3. In saucepan, heat
together soup, milk, and
cheese until cheese melts.
Pour into cooker(s).
4. In a large bowl, fold
mashed potatoes and sour
cream together. Spread over
mixture in slow cooker(s).
5. Sprinkle with bacon.
6. Cover. Cook on Low
3-4 hours, or until cheese
mixture comes to top when
done (hence, the name
"Underground").

# Verenike
# (or Creamy Lasagna)

Jennifer Yoder Sommers
Harrisonburg, VA

Makes 8-10 servings

*Prep. Time: 10-15 minutes*
*Cooking Time: 5-6 hours*
*Ideal slow cooker size: 5-qt.*

24 ozs. cottage cheese
3 eggs
1 tsp. salt
½ tsp. pepper
1 cup sour cream
2 cups evaporated milk
2 cups cubed cooked ham
7-9 uncooked lasagna
   noodles

1. Combine all ingredients
except noodles in a good-
sized mixing bowl.
2. Place half of creamy ham
mixture in bottom of cooker.
3. Stack in uncooked
noodles. Break them to fit if
you need to.
4. Cover with remaining
half of creamy ham sauce.
Push noodles down so that
they are fully submerged in
the sauce.
5. Cover. Cook on Low 5-6
hours, or until noodles are
tender but not mushy.

*Serving suggestion: Serve it*
*with **green salad**, **peas**, and*
***zwiebach** (a favorite Mennonite*
*food), or small **dinner rolls**.*

Note:
   *This is an easy way to make*
*the traditional Russian Men-*
*nonite dish—verenike.*

# Shepherd's Pie

**Melanie Thrower**
McPherson, KS

*Makes 3-4 servings*

**Prep. Time: 30-40 minutes**
**Cooking Time: 3 hours**
**Ideal slow cooker size: 4-qt.**

1 lb. ground pork
1 Tbsp. vinegar
1 tsp. salt
¼ tsp. hot pepper
1 tsp. paprika
¼ tsp. dried oregano
¼ tsp. black pepper
1 tsp. chili powder
1 small onion, chopped
15-oz. can whole-kernel
    corn, drained
3 large potatoes
¼ cup milk
1 tsp. butter
¼ tsp. salt
dash of pepper
shredded cheese

1. Combine pork, vinegar, and seasonings in skillet. Cook until meat browns.
2. Add onions and cook until they begin to glaze.
3. Spread mixture into slow cooker.
4. Spread corn over meat.
5. Cook potatoes in water on stovetop until soft. Mash with milk, butter, ¼ tsp. salt, and dash of pepper.
6. Spread mashed potatoes over meat and corn.
7. Cover. Cook on Low 3 hours.
8. Sprinkle top with cheese a few minutes before serving.

**Variation:**
You can substitute ground beef for the pork.

**Note:**
*This is my 9-year-old son's favorite dish!*

# Ham Balls

**Jo Haberkamp**
Fairbank, IA

*Makes 12-16 servings*

**Prep. Time: 30 minutes**
**Cooking Time: 4-5 hours**
**Ideal slow cooker size: 6-qt.**

**Ham Balls:**
3 eggs
3 cups crushed graham
    crackers
2 cups milk
1 tsp. salt
1 tsp. onion salt
¼ tsp. pepper
2 lbs. ground ham
1½ lbs. ground beef
1½ lbs. ground pork

**Topping:**
½ cup ketchup
¼ cup water
1 cup brown sugar
¼ cup, plus 2 Tbsp., apple
    cider vinegar
½ tsp. dry mustard

1. Beat eggs slightly in large bowl. Add graham crackers, milk, salt, onion salt, pepper, and ground meats. Mix well.
2. Form into 24 balls, using ½-cup measuring cup for each ball.
3. In a separate bowl, combine Topping ingredients.
4. Layer Ham Balls and Topping in greased slow cooker. Make sure each layer of Ham Balls is well covered with Topping.
5. Cover. Cook on High 1 hour. Reduce heat to Low and cook 3-4 hours more, or until meat is cooked through but not dried out.

# Ham Loaf or Balls

**Michelle Strite**
Goshen, IN

*Makes 8-10 servings*

**Prep. Time: 30 minutes**
**Cooking Time: 4-6 hours**
**Ideal slow cooker size: 4- to 5-qt.**

**Ham Loaf or Balls:**
1 lb. ground ham
1 lb. ground pork, *or*
    ground beef
1 cup soft bread crumbs
2 eggs, slightly beaten
1 cup milk

*Beside each dish of food on the buffet, place a stack of cards with its recipe written on them. Then guests can take the recipe if they wish.*
Anita Troyer, Fairview, MI

2 Tbsp. minced onions
1¼ tsp. salt
⅛ tsp. pepper

Glaze:
¾ cup brown sugar
1 tsp. dry mustard
1 Tbsp. cornstarch
¼ cup vinegar
½ cup water

1. Combine ingredients
for Ham Loaf or Ham Balls.
Form into Loaf or Balls and
place in slow cooker.
2. Combine dry ingredients
for Glaze in bowl. Mix in
vinegar and water until smooth.
3. Pour Glaze into sauce-
pan. Cook uncovered until
slightly thickened.
4. Pour over meat.
5. Cover. Cook on High 4-6
hours, or until meat is cooked
through.

Variations:
1. For a firmer Loaf, or
Balls, use dry bread crumbs
instead of soft. Use only ¾
cup milk instead of 1 cup.
2. Form meat mixture into
1" balls. Brown lightly by
baking on cookie sheet in
400° oven for 5-10 minutes.
Place browned Balls in slow
cooker. Pour cooked Glaze
over Balls. Cover. Cook on
High 2-4 hours.

**Julia A. Fisher**
New Carlisle, OH

# Pork Barbecue

**Barbara L. McGinnis**
Jupiter, FL

*Makes 6 servings*

**Prep. Time: 5-10 minutes**
**Cooking Time: 8 hours**
**Ideal slow cooker size: 5-qt.**

3-4-lb. pork loin
2 cups cider vinegar
salt to taste
pepper to taste
2 tsp. sugar
½ cup ketchup
crushed red pepper to taste
Tabasco sauce to taste
sandwich rolls

1. Place pork in slow
cooker.
2. Pour vinegar over meat.
Sprinkle salt, pepper and
sugar over top.
3. Cover. Cook on Low 8
hours.
4. Remove pork from
cooker and shred meat.
Reserve drippings.
5. In large mixing bowl,
stir together ketchup, red
pepper, Tabasco sauce, and ½
cup vinegar-sugar drippings
from slow cooker. Stir in
shredded meat.
6. Serve on sandwich rolls.

*Serving suggestion:* **Cole
slaw** *is a good accompaniment
to these sandwiches. Serve it
either alongside them, or pile it
into the rolls with the meat.*

Variation:
To increase the tang, add
1 tsp. dry mustard in Step 5.

Use ¼ cup ketchup and ¼
cup orange juice, instead of ½
cup ketchup.

# Barbecued Pork and Beef Sandwiches

**Sherry L. Lapp**
Lancaster, PA

*Makes 6-8 sandwiches*

**Prep. Time: 15 minutes**
**Cooking Time: 8 hours**
**Ideal slow cooker size: 4-qt.**

1½ lbs. cubed pork
1 lb. stewing beef, cubed
6-oz. can tomato paste
¼ cup vinegar
½ cup brown sugar
1 tsp. salt
1 Tbsp. chili powder
1 large onion, chopped
1 green bell pepper, chopped

1. Combine ingredients in
slow cooker.
2. Cover. Cook on Low 8
hours.
3. Shred meat with fork
before serving on rolls.

*Serving suggestion: Bring to
the table with* **sandwich rolls**
*and creamy* **cole slaw.**

# Ham Barbecue

**Amber Swarey**
Honea Path, SC

*Makes 10-12 servings*

**Prep. Time: 10 minutes**
**Cooking Time: 4-5 hours**
**Ideal slow cooker size: 3-qt.**

2 lbs. thinly sliced deli ham
1 cup water
1 cup ketchup
¼ cup packed brown sugar
¼ cup Worcestershire
   sauce
2 Tbsp. white vinegar
2 tsp. prepared mustard

1. Place ham in greased slow cooker.
2. In bowl, combine water, ketchup, brown sugar, Worcestershire sauce, vinegar, and mustard. Pour over ham and stir well.
3. Cover. Cook on Low 4-5 hours, or until heated through.

*Serving suggestion: This Ham Barbecue will fill 12 **hamburger buns**. They're especially good if you've split and toasted them.*

# Super-Bowl Little Smokies

**Mary Sommerfeld**
Lancaster, PA

**Alicia Denlinger**
Lancaster, PA

*Makes 9-10 main-dish servings,
or 15-20 appetizer servings*

**Prep. Time: 5 minutes**
**Cooking Time: 2 hours**
**Ideal slow cooker size: 4-qt.**

3 1-lb. pkgs. Little Smokies
8-oz. bottle Catalina
   dressing
splash of liquid smoke

1. Combine all ingredients in slow cooker.
2. Cover. Cook on Low 2 hours.
3. Use toothpicks to serve. Or pile into sandwich rolls for a lunch or supper.

Note:
*These are always a hit at parties, whether it's Christmas, New Year's, or the Super Bowl. They are good any time that you'd like to serve food beyond dessert, but you don't want to have a formal sit-down meal.*

# Cranberry Franks

**Loretta Krahn**
Mountain Lake, MN

*Makes 15-20 servings*

**Prep. Time: 10 minutes**
**Cooking Time: 1-2 hours**
**Ideal slow cooker size: 3-qt.**

2 pkgs. cocktail wieners, or
   little smoked sausages
16-oz. can jellied cranberry
   sauce
1 cup ketchup
3 Tbsp. brown sugar
1 Tbsp. lemon juice

1. Combine all ingredients in slow cooker.
2. Cover. Cook on High 1-2 hours.

Note:
*Great picnic, potluck, or buffet food.*

*I have a few antique Christmas ornaments, but they tend to get lost on the tree with everything else. So I put them in a glass bowl with evergreens, and they are noticed and appreciated much more.*

*Carol L. Miller, Lockport, NY*

# Chicken Main Dishes

## Sunday Roast Chicken

**Ruth A. Feister**, Narvon, PA

*Makes 4-5 servings*

**Prep. Time: 30-35 minutes**
**Cooking Time: 6 hours**
**Ideal slow cooker size: 6- to 7-qt.**

**Seasoning Mix:**
1 Tbsp. salt
2 tsp. paprika
1½ tsp. onion powder
1½ tsp. garlic powder
1½ tsp. dried basil
1 tsp. dry mustard
1 tsp. cumin
2 tsp. pepper
½ tsp. dried thyme
½ tsp. savory

¼ stick (2 Tbsp.) butter
2 cups chopped onions
1 cup chopped green bell
    pepper
1 roasting chicken
¼ cup flour
1-2 cups chicken stock

1. Combine Seasoning Mix ingredients in small bowl.

2. Melt butter over high heat in skillet. When butter starts to sizzle, add chopped onions and peppers, and 3 Tbsp. seasoning mix.

3. Cook until onions are golden brown. Cool.

4. Stuff cavity of chicken with cooled vegetables.

5. Sprinkle outside of chicken with 1 Tbsp. seasoning mix. Rub in well so it sticks.

6. Place chicken in large slow cooker.

7. Cover. Cook on Low 6 hours.

8. Empty vegetable stuffing and juices into saucepan. Whisk in flour and 1 cup stock from slow cooker.

9. Cook over high heat until thickened. Add more stock if you prefer a thinner gravy.

Note:

*The first time I served this dish was when we had family visiting us from Mississippi. We had a wonderful time sitting around a large table, sharing many laughs and catching up on the years since our last visit.*

# Old-Fashioned Stewed Chicken

**Bonnie Goering**
Bridgewater, VA

*Makes 6-8 servings*

*Prep. Time: 20 minutes*
*Cooking Time: 8¼ hours*
*Ideal slow cooker size: 5-qt.*

3-4-lb. chicken, cut up
1 small onion, cut into
    wedges
1 rib celery, sliced
1 carrot, sliced
1 Tbsp. chopped fresh
    parsley, *or* 1 tsp. dried
    parsley
1 Tbsp. chopped fresh
    thyme, *or* 1 tsp. dried
    thyme
1 Tbsp. chopped fresh
    rosemary, *or* 1 tsp. dried
    rosemary
3 tsp. salt
¼ tsp. pepper
3-4 cups hot water
⅓ cup flour

1. Place chicken in slow cooker. Scatter vegetables, herbs, and seasonings around it and over top. Pour water down along interior wall of cooker so as not to disturb the other ingredients.
2. Cover. Cook on Low 8 hours.
3. Remove chicken from cooker. When cool enough to handle, debone. Set aside and keep warm.
4. In small bowl, stir ⅓ cup flour into 1 cup chicken broth from slow cooker.

5. When smooth, stir back into slow cooker. Continue cooking on Low until broth thickens, stirring occasionally to prevent lumps from forming.
6. When gravy is bubbly and thickened, stir in chicken pieces.

*Serving suggestion: Serve with **mashed potatoes** or **noodles** and **creamed peas**.*

Note:
  *I cook every Thursday afternoon for a 93-year-old woman who lives by herself. She taught me how to cook with fresh herbs from her garden. I've found they make food taste so much better that I've started an herb garden. And I dry some herbs to use during the winter.*

# One-Pot Easy Chicken

**Jean Robinson**
Cinnaminson, NJ

*Makes 6 servings*

*Prep. Time: 25-30 minutes*
*Cooking Time: 6 hours*
*Ideal slow cooker size: 6-qt.*

6-8 potatoes, quartered
1-2 large onions, sliced
3-5 carrots, cubed
5-lbs. chicken, skin
    removed (quarters, or
    legs and thighs work
    well)
1 small onion, chopped

1 tsp. black pepper
1 Tbsp. whole cloves,
    *optional*
1 Tbsp. garlic salt
1 Tbsp. chopped fresh
    oregano
1 tsp. dried rosemary
½ cup lemon juice, *or*
    chicken broth

1. Layer potatoes, sliced onions, and carrots in bottom of slow cooker.
2. Rinse and pat chicken dry. In shallow dish with sides mix together chopped onions, pepper, cloves, and garlic salt.
3. Dredge chicken in seasonings. Place in cooker over vegetables. Spoon any remaining seasonings over chicken.
4. Sprinkle with oregano and rosemary. Pour lemon juice around chicken.
5. Cover. Cook on Low 6 hours.

Note:
  *This is a lifesaver when the grandchildren come for a weekend. I get to play with them, and dinner is timed and ready when we are.*

# Chicken Cacciatore with Spaghetti

**Phyllis Pellman Good**, Lancaster, PA

*Makes 4-5 servings*

**Prep. Time: 15 minutes • Cooking Time: 4 hours**
*Ideal slow cooker size: 4- to 5-qt.*

2 onions, sliced
2½-3 lbs. chicken legs and
   thighs, skin removed
2 garlic cloves, minced
16-oz. can stewed
   tomatoes
8-oz. can tomato sauce

1 tsp. salt
¼ tsp. pepper
1-2 tsp. dried oregano
½ tsp. dried basil
1 bay leaf
¼ cup white wine

1. Place onions in bottom of slow cooker.
2. Lay chicken over onions.
3. Combine remaining ingredients in a good-sized bowl. Pour over chicken.
4. Cover. Cook on Low 4 hours, or until chicken is tender but not dry.
5. Remove bay leaf before serving.

*Serving suggestion: Serve over hot **buttered spaghetti**, **linguini**, or **fettucini**.*

# Chicken Cacciatore

**Eleanor J. Ferreira**
North Chelmsford, MA

*Makes 8 servings*

**Prep. Time: 40 minutes**
**Cooking Time: 4-5 hours**
**Ideal slow cooker size: 6- to**
   **6½-qt., or 2 4-qt. cookers**

2 chickens, cut into pieces
1 cup flour
2 tsp. salt
½ tsp. pepper

olive oil
2 4-oz. cans sliced
   mushrooms, drained
3 medium onions, sliced
2 celery ribs, chopped
4 large green bell peppers,
   cut into 1″ strips
28-oz. can tomatoes
28-oz. can tomato purée
½ tsp. dried basil
½ tsp. dried oregano
½ tsp. salt
¼ tsp. pepper
½ tsp. dried parsley

1. Shake chicken pieces, one at a time, in bag with flour, salt, and pepper. When well coated, brown chicken pieces on both sides in skillet in oil.
2. Place chicken in large slow cooker, or in two medium-sized cookers, reserving drippings.
3. Sauté mushrooms, onions, celery, and peppers in drippings from chicken. Spread over chicken in cooker.
4. Mix remaining ingredients together in bowl and pour over chicken and vegetables.
5. Cover. Cook on Low 4-5 hours.

*Serving suggestion: Serve over hot **spaghetti**.*

# Chicken and Sausage Cacciatore

**Joyce Kaut**
Rochester, NY

*Makes 4-6 servings*

*Prep. Time: 25-35 minutes*
*Cooking Time: 3-4 hours*
*Ideal slow cooker size: 5-qt.*

1 lb. Italian sausage, cut in
 ½"-thick slices
1 lb. skinless, boneless
 chicken breasts, cut into
 1" pieces
oil
1 large green bell pepper,
 sliced in 1" strips
1 cup sliced fresh
 mushrooms
1 medium onion, sliced in
 rings
½ tsp. dried oregano
½ tsp. dried basil
1½ cups Italian-style
 tomato sauce

1. Lightly brown sausage
and chicken breast pieces in
skillet, in oil if needed. Drain
off drippings.
2. Layer vegetables into
slow cooker.
3. Top with meat.
4. Sprinkle with oregano
and basil.
5. Top with tomato sauce.
6. Cover. Cook on Low 3-4
hours.
7. Remove cover during
last 30 minutes of cooking
time to allow sauce to cook
off and thicken.

*Serving suggestion: Serve
over cooked **spiral pasta**.*

# Basil Chicken

**Sarah Niessen**, Akron, PA

*Makes 4-6 servings*

*Prep. Time: 15 minutes • Cooking Time: 7-10 hours*
*Ideal slow cooker size: 5-qt.*

1 lb. baby carrots
2 medium onions, sliced
1-2 cups celery slices and
 leaves
3-lb. chicken, cut-up
½ cup chicken broth, *or*
 white cooking wine
2 tsp. salt
½ tsp. black pepper
1 tsp. dried basil

1. Place carrots, onions, and celery in bottom of slow cooker.
2. Add chicken.
3. Pour broth over chicken.
4. Sprinkle with salt, pepper, and basil.
5. Cover. Cook on Low 7-10 hours, or until chicken and
vegetables are tender.

# Con Pollo

**Dorothy Van Deest**
Memphis, TN

*Makes 4-6 servings*

*Prep. Time: 10 minutes*
*Cooking Time: 3-5 hours*
*Ideal slow cooker size: 5-qt.*

3-4-lb. chicken, cut-up
salt to taste
pepper to taste
paprika to taste
garlic salt to taste
6-oz. can tomato paste
½ cup beer
3-oz. jar stuffed olives with
 liquid

1. Wash chicken. Sprinkle
all over with salt, pepper,
paprika, and garlic salt. Place
in slow cooker.
2. Combine tomato paste
and beer in small bowl. Pour
over chicken.
3. Scatter olives over
chicken. Pour liquid into
cooker.
4. Cover. Cook on Low 5
hours or on High 3 hours.

*Serving suggestion: Serve
over **rice** or **noodles**, along
with **salad** and **cornbread**,
and **sherbet** for dessert.*

Note:
 *This is chicken with a
Spanish flair. This easy supper
is quick, too, by slow-cooker
standards, if you use the high
temperature. Let your slow
cooker be the chef.*

## Dad's Spicy Chicken Curry

Tom & Sue Ruth
Lancaster, PA

*Makes 8 servings*

*Prep. Time: 25 minutes*
*Cooking Time: 6-8 hours*
*Ideal slow cooker size: 6- to 7-qt.*

4 lbs. chicken pieces, with
bones in
water
2 onions, diced
10-oz. pkg. frozen chopped
spinach, thawed and
squeezed dry
1 cup plain yogurt
2-3 diced red potatoes
3 tsp. salt
1 tsp. garlic powder
1 tsp. ground ginger
1 tsp. ground cumin
1 tsp. ground coriander
1 tsp. pepper
1 tsp. ground cloves
1 tsp. ground cardamom
1 tsp. ground cinnamon
½ tsp. chili powder
1 tsp. red pepper flakes
3 tsp. turmeric

1. Place chicken in large
slow cooker. Cover with
water.
2. Cover. Cook on High 2
hours, or until tender.
3. Drain chicken. Remove
from slow cooker. Cool
briefly and cut/shred into
small pieces.
4. Return chicken to slow
cooker.
5. Stir in all remaining
ingredients.

6. Cover. Cook on Low 4-6
hours, or until potatoes are
tender.

*Serving suggestion: Serve on
rice. Accompany with **fresh
mango slices** or **mango
chutney**.*

Variation:
Substitute 5 tsp. curry
powder for the garlic powder,
ginger, cumin, coriander, and
pepper.

## Delicious Chicken with Curried Cream Sauce

Jennifer J. Gehman
Harrisburg, PA

*Makes 4-6 servings*

*Prep. Time: 25 minutes*
*Cooking Time: 3-5 hours*
*Ideal slow cooker size: 4-qt.*

4-6 boneless, skinless,
chicken breasts, *or* legs
and thighs
oil
salt to taste
pepper to taste
10¾-oz. can cream of
chicken soup
½ cup mayonnaise
1-2 Tbsp. curry powder
½ tsp. salt
⅛ tsp. pepper
1 lb. fresh, *or* 15-oz. can,
asparagus spears
½-1 cup shredded cheddar
cheese

1. Brown chicken on all
sides in skillet in oil. Season
with salt and pepper. Place in
slow cooker.
2. Combine soup, mayon-
naise, curry powder, salt, and
pepper in bowl. Pour over
chicken.
3. Cover. Cook on High 3
hours or on Low 5 hours.
4. If using fresh asparagus,
steam lightly until just tender.
If using canned asparagus,
drain asparagus.
5. Place asparagus in
bottom of serving dish.
6. Cover asparagus with
chicken and sauce.
7. Sprinkle with cheese.

*Serving suggestion: Serve
with **egg noodles** or **white
rice**. Add another **cooked
vegetable**, along with **fruit
salad**, **applesauce**, or **mandarin oranges**, as side dishes.*

# Curried Chicken

**Marlene Bogard**
Newton, KS

*Makes 5 servings*

**Prep. Time: 20 minutes**
**Cooking Time: 4¼-6¼ hours**
**Ideal slow cooker size: 5-qt.**

2½-3½-lb. fryer chicken,
   cut up
salt to taste
pepper to taste
1 Tbsp. curry powder
1 garlic clove, crushed *or*
   minced
1 Tbsp. melted butter
½ cup chicken broth, *or* 1
   chicken bouillon cube
   dissolved in ½ cup water
2 Tbsp. onion, chopped fine
29-oz. can sliced peaches
½ cup pitted prunes
3 Tbsp. cornstarch
3 Tbsp. cold water

1. Sprinkle chicken with salt and pepper. Arrange in slow cooker.
2. Combine curry, garlic, butter, broth, and onions in bowl.
3. Drain peaches, reserving syrup. Add ½ cup syrup to curry mixture. Pour over chicken.
4. Cover. Cook on Low 4-6 hours.
5. Remove chicken pieces from cooker to platter. Keep warm.
6. Turn cooker on High. Stir in prunes.
7. Dissolve cornstarch in cold water in small bowl. Stir into hot sauce in cooker.
8. Cover. Cook on High 10 minutes, or until thickened.
9. Stir in peaches and cooked chicken.

*Serving suggestion: Serve over **rice**. Offer **peanuts**, **shredded coconut**, and **fresh pineapple chunks** as condiments.*

# Lemon Chicken

**Judy Newman**
St. Mary's, Ontario Canada

*Makes 10-12 servings*

**Prep. Time: 25 minutes**
**Cooking Time: 3-4 hours**
**Ideal slow cooker size: 5-qt.**

¼-½ cup flour
1 tsp. salt
5-6 lbs. chicken, cut into
   pieces
2-4 Tbsp. oil, *divided*
1 can frozen lemonade
   concentrate, thawed
3 Tbsp. brown sugar
1 Tbsp. ketchup
1 Tbsp. vinegar
2 Tbsp. cold water
2 Tbsp. cornstarch

1. Combine flour and salt in a shallow bowl. Dredge chicken pieces in it, one at a time.
2. Place 2 Tbsp. oil in large skillet. Brown several pieces of chicken in oil at a time. Be careful not to crowd the skillet, or the chicken will steam and not brown. Continue until all pieces are browned on both sides, adding more oil as necessary.
3. As you finish browning pieces of chicken, place them in slow cooker.
4. In a mixing bowl, whisk together lemonade concentrate, brown sugar, ketchup, and vinegar. Pour over chicken.
5. Cover. Cook on High 3-4 hours.
6. Remove chicken, place on platter, cover with foil, and keep warm.
7. In a small bowl, blend cold water into cornstarch.
8. Stir into juices in slow cooker until well blended. Cover and continue cooking juices several minutes, until thickened and bubbly.
9. Spoon some of thickened juice over chicken to serve.
10. Place remaining juices in serving bowl and pass as topping for chicken and cooked rice.

Tip:
*Put this in the slow cooker and then go wrap your gifts without concern!*

# Garlic Lime Chicken

**Loretta Krahn**
Mountain Lake, MN

*Makes 5 servings*

*Prep. Time: 10 minutes*
*Cooking Time: 4-8 hours*
*Ideal slow cooker size: 4-qt.*

5 skinless chicken breast
   halves
½ cup soy sauce
¼-⅓ cup lime juice,
   according to your taste
   preference
1 Tbsp. Worcestershire
   sauce
2 garlic cloves, minced, *or*
   1 tsp. garlic powder
½ tsp. dry mustard
½ tsp. ground pepper

1. Place chicken in slow cooker.
2. Combine remaining ingredients in a bowl. Pour over chicken.
3. Cover. Cook on High 4-6 hours or on Low 6-8 hours, or until chicken is tender but not dry.

# Herbed Chicken

**LaVerne A. Olson**
Lititz, PA

*Makes 8 serving*

*Prep. Time: 10 minutes*
*Cooking Time: 6¼-8¼ hours*
*Ideal slow cooker size: 6- to 7-qt.*

4 whole chicken breasts,
   halved, with skin
   removed
10¾-oz. can cream of
   mushroom, *or* chicken,
   soup
¼ cup soy sauce
¼ cup oil
¼ cup wine vinegar
¾ cup water
½ tsp. minced garlic
1 tsp. ground ginger
½ tsp. dried oregano
1 Tbsp. brown sugar

1. Arrange chicken in slow cooker.
2. Combine remaining ingredients in bowl. Pour over chicken.
3. Cover. Cook on Low 6-8 hours, or until tender but not dry.
4. Uncover and cook 15 minutes more.

*Serving suggestion: Serve with **rice**.*

Note:
*A favorite with our whole family, even the grandchildren. The gravy is delicious!*

# Teriyaki Chicken

**Colleen Konetzni**
Rio Rancho, NM

*Makes 6 servings*

*Prep. Time: 10 minutes*
*Cooking Time: 6-7 hours*
*Ideal slow cooker size: 4-qt.*

6-8 skinless chicken thighs
½ cup soy sauce
2 Tbsp. brown sugar
2 Tbsp. grated fresh ginger
2 garlic cloves, minced

1. Wash and dry chicken. Arrange in slow cooker.
2. Combine remaining ingredients in bowl. Pour over chicken.
3. Cover. Cook on High 1 hour. Reduce heat to Low and cook 5-6 hours, or until chicken is fork-tender.

*Serving suggestion: Serve over **rice** with a **fresh salad**.*

163

# Barbecued Chicken

**Gladys Longacre**
Susquehanna, PA

*Makes 4-6 servings*

*Prep. Time: 20-25 minutes*
*Cooking Time: 3½-6 hours*
*Ideal slow cooker size: 5-qt.*

3-4 lbs. boneless, skinless, chicken breasts
oil
1 onion, chopped
¼ cup chopped green bell pepper
1 cup ketchup
1-2 Tbsp. hickory-smoked barbecue sauce
1 Tbsp. prepared mustard
1 Tbsp. Worcestershire sauce
1 Tbsp. lemon juice
2 Tbsp. vinegar
3 Tbsp. brown sugar
¼ cup water
½ tsp. salt
⅛ tsp. pepper

1. Lightly brown chicken in oil in skillet. Drain off drippings. Arrange chicken in slow cooker.
2. Layer onions and green pepper over chicken.
3. Combine remaining ingredients in bowl. Pour over chicken.
4. Cover. Cook on Low 6 hours or on High 3½-4 hours, or just until chicken is tender but still moist.

*Serving suggestion: Serve chicken and sauce over cooked **rice**.*

# Barbecued Chicken with Peppers, Onions, and Celery

**Joanne Kennedy**
Plattsburgh, NY

*Makes 4 servings*

*Prep. Time: 15 minutes*
*Cooking Time: 2½-6 hours*
*Ideal slow cooker size: 4-qt.*

2 whole boneless, skinless chicken breasts, cubed
1 medium onion, sliced
1 green bell pepper, sliced
1 cup chopped celery
2 Tbsp. Worcestershire sauce
2 Tbsp. brown sugar
1½ cups ketchup
1½ cups water
½ tsp. pepper

1. Combine all ingredients in slow cooker.
2. Cover. Cook on Low 5-6 hours or on High 2½-3 hours, or until chicken is tender but not dry.

*Serving suggestion: Serve over **rice** with a **tossed salad**.*

# Hawaiian Chicken

**Leona M. Slabaugh**
Apple Creek, OH

*Makes 6-8 servings*

*Prep. Time: 30 minutes*
*Cooking Time: 3-8 hours*
*Ideal slow cooker size: 3- to 5-qt.*

3 lbs. boneless, skinless chicken breast halves
16-oz. can pineapple slices, drained
15-oz. can mandarin oranges, drained
2 Tbsp. cornstarch
3 Tbsp. brown sugar, packed
2 tbsp. lemon juice
¼ tsp. salt
¼ tsp. ground ginger

1. Combine all ingredients in slow cooker. Stir well.
2. Cover. Cook on Low 6-8 hours or on High 3 hours, or until meat is tender but not dry.

*On Christmas Eve we visit our neighbors, just to say "Merry Christmas." If you set aside 30 minutes per house, you can visit six to eight in no time. Those visits really can make a difference during the year if problems arise (like dogs barking or where to shovel unwanted snow).*

*Rose Hankins, Stevensville, MD*

# Chicken Stew with Peppers and Pineapples

**Judi Manos**
West Islip, NY

*Makes 4 servings*

*Prep. Time: 20 minutes*
*Cooking Time: 2¾-6¼ hours*
*Ideal slow cooker size: 4-qt.*

1 lb. boneless, skinless chicken breasts, cut in 1½" cubes
4 medium carrots, sliced into 1" pieces
½ cup chicken broth
2 Tbsp. gingerroot, chopped
1 Tbsp. brown sugar
2 Tbsp. soy sauce
½ tsp. ground allspice
½ tsp. hot pepper sauce
8-oz. can pineapple chunks, drained, with juice reserved
1 Tbsp. cornstarch
1 medium sweet green pepper, cut in 1" pieces

1. Combine chicken, carrots, chicken broth, gingerroot, sugar, soy sauce, allspice, and red pepper sauce in slow cooker.
2. Cover. Cook on Low 5-6 hours or on High 2½-3 hours, or until chicken is tender.
3. Combine pineapple juice and cornstarch in bowl until smooth. Stir into chicken mixture.
4. Add pineapple chunks and green pepper.
5. Cover. Cook on High 15 minutes, or until sauce is slightly thickened.

*Serving suggestion: Serve over cooked rice.*

Variation:

Add 1 cut-up fresh tomato 30 minutes before end of cooking time.

# Pineapple-Glazed Chicken with Sweet Potatoes

**Katrina Eberly**
Wernersville, PA

*Makes 4 servings*

*Prep. Time: 25-30 minutes*
*Cooking Time: 3½-4 hours*
*Ideal slow cooker size: 4- to 5-qt.*

3 medium sweet potatoes, peeled and sliced into 1" chunks
⅔ cup, plus 3 Tbsp., flour, *divided*
1 tsp. salt
1 tsp. onion powder
1 tsp. ground nutmeg
1 tsp. ground cinnamon
1 tsp. pepper
4 5-oz. boneless skinless chicken breast halves
¼ stick (2 Tbsp.) butter
10¾-oz. can cream of chicken soup
¾ cup pineapple juice
2 tsp. brown sugar
1 tsp. grated orange peel

1. Layer sweet potatoes into slow cooker.
2. In a large resealable plastic bag, combine ⅔ cup flour and seasonings. Add chicken, one piece at a time, and shake to coat.
3. In a large skillet over medium heat, cook chicken in butter for 3 minutes on each side, or until lightly browned. Don't crowd the skillet or the chicken will steam rather than brown.) Arrange browned chicken over sweet potatoes.
4. Place remaining flour in a medium-sized mixing bowl. Stir in soup, pineapple juice, brown sugar, and orange peel until blended. Pour over chicken.
5. Cover. Cook on Low 3½-4 hours, or until potatoes are soft and chicken is cooked through but not dry.

*Serving suggestion: Serve over rice if you wish.*

# Maui Chicken

**John D. Allen**, Rye, CO

*Makes 6 servings*

*Prep. Time: 20 minutes • Cooking Time: 3-4 hours*
*Ideal slow cooker size: 4- to 5-qt.*

6 boneless, skinless
   chicken breast halves
2 Tbsp. oil
14½-oz. can chicken broth
20-oz. can pineapple
   chunks
¼ cup vinegar
2 Tbsp. brown sugar
2 tsp. soy sauce
1 garlic clove, minced
1 medium green bell pepper,
   chopped
3 Tbsp. cornstarch
¼ cup water

1. Brown chicken in oil in skillet until lightly browned. Transfer chicken to slow cooker.
2. Combine remaining ingredients, except cornstarch and water, in bowl. Pour over chicken.
3. Cover. Cook on High 3-4 hours, or just until chicken is tender.
4. Ten minutes before end of cooking time, dissolve cornstarch in water in a small bowl. When smooth, stir into slow cooker until dissolved. Continue cooking until sauce thickens.

*Serving suggestion: Serve over **rice**.*

# Chicken in a Hurry

**Yvonne Boettger**
Harrisonburg, VA

*Makes 4-5 servings*

*Prep. Time: 10 minutes*
*Cooking Time: 3-7 hours*
*Ideal slow cooker size: 4- to 5-qt.*

2½-3 lbs. skinless chicken
   drumsticks
½ cup ketchup
¼ cup water
¼ cup brown sugar
1 envelope dry onion soup
   mix

1. Arrange chicken in slow cooker.
2. Combine remaining ingredients in a bowl. Pour over chicken.
3. Cover. Cook on High 3-4 hours or on Low 6-7 hours, or just until chicken is tender.

# Tender Barbecued Chicken

**Betty Stoltzfus**
Honeybrook, PA

*Makes 4-6 servings*

*Prep. Time: 10 minutes*
*Cooking Time: 6-8 hours*
*Ideal slow cooker size: 6-qt.*

3-4-lb. broiler chicken,
   whole, or cut up
1 medium onion, thinly
   sliced
1 medium lemon, thinly
   sliced
18-oz. bottle barbecue
   sauce
¾ cup cola-flavored soda

1. Place chicken in slow cooker.
2. Top with onion and lemon.
3. Combine barbecue sauce and cola in bowl. Pour into slow cooker.
4. Cover. Cook on Low 6-8 hours, or until chicken juices run clear.
5. Cut into serving-sized pieces and serve with barbecue sauce.
6. Slice any leftovers and use in sandwiches.

## Spicy Sweet Chicken

**Carolyn Baer**
Conrath, WI

*Makes 4 servings*

*Prep. Time: 25 minutes*
*Cooking Time: 3½-6¾ hours*
*Ideal slow cooker size: 4-qt.*

2½-3 lbs. chicken breasts, thighs, and/or legs, skinned
1 Tbsp. oil
16-oz. can whole cranberry sauce, *divided*
¼ cup spicy-sweet Catalina salad dressing
2 Tbsp. dry onion soup mix
1 Tbsp. cornstarch

1. Rinse chicken. Pat dry. Brown in hot oil in skillet. Arrange in slow cooker.
2. In a bowl, combine half of cranberry sauce and all of salad dressing and soup mix. Pour over chicken.
3. Cover. Cook on Low 6 hours or on High 3 hours.
4. Stir cornstarch into remaining cranberry sauce in bowl. Stir into chicken mixture.
5. Turn slow cooker to High. Cover and cook 30-45 minutes more, or until thickened and bubbly.

*Serving suggestion: Serve over cooked **noodles** or **rice**.*

## Chicken with Applesauce

**Kelly Evenson**
Pittsboro, NC

*Makes 4 servings*

*Prep. Time: 20 minutes*
*Cooking Time: 2-3 hours*
*Ideal slow cooker size: 4-qt.*

4 boneless, skinless chicken breast halves
salt to taste
pepper to taste
2 Tbsp. oil
2 cups applesauce
¼ cup barbecue sauce
½ tsp. poultry seasoning
2 tsp. honey
½ tsp. lemon juice

1. Season chicken with salt and pepper. Brown in oil in skillet for 5 minutes per side.
2. Allow chicken to cool. Then cut up into 1" chunks. Transfer to slow cooker.
3. Combine remaining ingredients in medium-sized bowl. Pour over chicken and mix together well.
4. Cover. Cook on High 2-3 hours, or just until chicken is tender.

*Serving suggestion: Serve over **rice** or **noodles**.*

## Saucy Apricot Chicken

**Anna Stoltzfus**
Honey Brook, PA

*Makes 6 servings*

*Prep. Time: 5-10 minutes*
*Cooking Time: 4-5 hours*
*Ideal slow cooker size: 4-qt.*

6 boneless, skinless chicken breast halves
2 12-oz. jars apricot preserves
1 pkg. dry onion soup mix

1. Arrange chicken in slow cooker.
2. Combine preserves and onion soup mix in separate bowl. Spoon over chicken.
3. Cover. Cook on Low 4-5 hours.

*Serving suggestion: Serve over **rice**.*

*I put a tea kettle with water, cinnamon, and apple peels on top of my woodstove. It makes the house smell great.*

Kendra Dreps, Liberty, PA

# Chicken ala Orange

**Carlene Horne**
Bedford, NH

*Makes 8 servings*

*Prep. Time: 10 minutes*
*Cooking Time: 6-7 hours*
*Ideal slow cooker size: 4-qt.*

**8 boneless, skinless chicken breast halves**
**½ cup chopped onion**
**12-oz. jar orange marmalade**
**½ cup Russian dressing**
**1 Tbsp. dried parsley, *or* to taste**

1. Arrange chicken and onion in slow cooker.
2. Combine marmalade and dressing in bowl. Pour over chicken.
3. Sprinkle with parsley.
4. Cover. Cook on Low 6-7 hours, or until chicken is just tender.

*Serving suggestion: Serve with **rice**.*

# Scrumptious Chicken

**Kathi Rogge**
Alexandria, IN

*Makes 8 servings*

*Prep. Time: 10 minutes*
*Cooking Time: 6-7 hours*
*Ideal slow cooker size: 6-qt.*

**8 skinned chicken breast halves**
**10¾-oz. can cream of mushroom, *or* cream of chicken, soup**
**16 ozs. sour cream**
**1 envelope dry onion soup mix**
**fresh basil, *or* oregano, chopped**

1. Arrange chicken in slow cooker.
2. Combine all remaining ingredients, except fresh herbs, in good-sized mixing bowl. Pour over chicken.
3. Cover. Cook on Low 6-7 hours, or until chicken is fork-tender. (If convenient for you, stir after 3 hours of cooking.)
4. Sprinkle with fresh herbs just before serving.

*Serving suggestion: Serve with **brown and wild rice, mixed**, or **couscous**.*

Variation:
1. Cut up 4 lightly cooked chicken breast halves. Place in slow cooker.
2. Add 8 ozs. sour cream, 1 envelope dry onion soup mix, and a 10¾-oz. can cream of mushroom soup. Mix together well.
3. Cover and cook on Low 3-4 hours.

**Sherry Conyers**
McPherson, KS

# Angel Chicken Pasta

**Lena Sheatfer**
Port Matilda, PA

*Makes 4 servings*

*Prep. Time: 10 minutes*
*Cooking Time: 5-6 hours*
*Ideal slow cooker size: 4- to 5-qt.*

**half a stick (4 Tbsp.) butter**
**1 pkg. dry Italian-style salad-dressing mix**
**½ cup white wine**
**10¾-oz. can condensed golden mushroom soup**
**half an 8-oz. pkg. cream cheese with chives**
**4 boneless skinless chicken breast halves**

1. In large saucepan, melt butter over low heat. Stir in salad-dressing mix. Blend in wine and soup. Mix in cream cheese and stir until smooth. Do not boil.
2. Arrange chicken in slow cooker. Pour sauce over top.
3. Cover. Cook on Low 5-6 hours, or just until chicken is tender but not dry.

*Serving suggestion: When ready to eat, cook **pasta**. Serve chicken and sauce over pasta.*

# Sunday Chicken

**Leona M. Slabaugh**
Apple Creek, OH

*Makes 6 servings*

*Prep. Time: 30-45 minutes*
*Cooking Time: 2-5 hours*
*Ideal slow cooker size: 3- to 5-qt.*

10½-oz. can cream of
   celery soup
½ cup white wine, *or*
   chicken broth
3½ lbs. chicken, cut-up,
   *divided*
paprika
salt
pepper

1. Combine soup and wine in a small bowl.
2. Rinse chicken in cold water. Pat dry.
3. Sprinkle chicken with paprika, salt, and pepper.
4. Place half of chicken in slow cooker.
5. Pour half of soup mixture over chicken.
6. Repeat layers.
7. Cover. Cook on Low 4-5 hours or on High 2-3 hours, or until chicken is tender but not dry.

# Creamy Chicken Breasts

**Judy Buller**
Bluffton, OH

*Makes 6-8 servings*

*Prep. Time: 5-10 minutes*
*Cooking Time: 6 hours*
*Ideal slow cooker size: 6-qt.*

6-8 skinless chicken breast
   halves
salt to taste
pepper to taste
paprika to taste
10¾-oz. can cream of
   mushroom soup
½ cup sour cream

1. Season chicken breasts with salt, pepper, and paprika. Arrange in slow cooker.
2. Combine mushroom soup and sour cream in bowl. Pour over chicken.
3. Cover. Cook on Low 6 hours, or just until tender but not dry.

*Serving suggestion: Serve with **rice**, **noodles**, or **mashed potatoes**.*

# Miriam's Chicken

**Arlene Leaman Kliewer**
Lakewood, CO

*Makes 6 servings*

*Prep. Time: 10 minutes*
*Cooking Time: 5-6 hours*
*Ideal slow cooker size: 4-qt.*

4 boneless, skinless
   chicken breast halves,
   cut into 1" chunks
8-oz. pkg. cream cheese,
   cubed
2 10¾-oz. cans cream
   soup, your favorite, *or*
   a combination of your
   favorites

1. Place chicken in slow cooker.
2. Combine cream cheese and soups in bowl.
3. Pour over chicken. Stir.
4. Cover. Cook on Low 5-6 hours, or until chicken is cooked through and tender.

*Serving suggestion: Serve over **croissants** split in half. Sprinkle with **paprika** and **parsley**.*

*Involve your guests, whether family or friends, in making your holiday meals. It's a great way to spend time together, learn different cooking tips and tricks from each other, and share recipes.*
*Moreen Weaver, Bath, NY*

# Elegant Chicken with Gravy

**Leesa Lesenski**, South Deerfield, MA

*Makes 6 servings*

*Prep. Time: 10 minutes • Cooking Time: 3-6 hours*
*Ideal slow cooker size: 4-qt.*

6 boneless, skinless chicken breast halves
10¾-oz. can cream of broccoli, *or* broccoli cheese, soup
10¾-oz. can cream of chicken soup
½ cup white wine
4-oz. can sliced mushrooms, undrained, *optional*

1. Arrange chicken breasts in slow cooker.
2. In bowl mix together soups, wine, and mushroom slices if you wish.
3. Pour over chicken.
4. Cover. Cook on High 3 hours or on Low 6 hours, or until chicken is tender but not dry.

*Serving suggestion: Serve over **rice** or **noodles**.*

# Janie's Chicken a La King

**Lafaye M. Musser**
Denver, PA

*Makes 4 servings*

*Prep. Time: 20 minutes*
*Cooking Time: 3½-4½ hours*
*Ideal slow cooker size: 4-qt.*

10¾-oz. can cream of chicken soup
3 Tbsp. flour
½ tsp. salt
¼ tsp. pepper
dash cayenne pepper
1 lb. boneless chicken thighs, uncooked and cut in pieces
1 rib celery, chopped
½ cup chopped green bell pepper
¼ cup chopped onions
9-oz. bag frozen peas, thawed

1. Combine soup, flour, salt, pepper, and cayenne pepper in slow cooker.
2. Stir in chicken, celery, green pepper, and onion.
3. Cover. Cook on Low 3-4 hours, or until chicken and vegetables are as tender as you like them.
4. Stir in peas.
5. Cover. Cook 30 minutes longer.

*Serving suggestion: Serve in **pastry cups** or over **rice**, **waffles**, or **toast**.*

# Savory Chicken, Meal #1

**Shari Mast**
Harrisonburg, VA

*Makes 8-10 servings*

*Prep. Time: 10 minutes*
*Cooking Time: 4-5 hours*
*Ideal slow cooker size: 5-qt.*

4 boneless, skinless chicken breast halves
4 skinless chicken quarters
10¾-oz. can cream of chicken soup
1 Tbsp. water
¼ cup chopped sweet red peppers
1 Tbsp. chopped fresh parsley, *or* 1 tsp. dried parsley
1 Tbsp. lemon juice
½ tsp. paprika

1. Layer chicken in slow cooker.
2. Combine remaining ingredients in bowl. Pour over chicken.
3. Cover. Cook on High 4-5 hours, or until chicken is tender.

# Savory Chicken, Meal #2

**Shari Mast**
Harrisonburg, VA

*Makes 8-10 servings*

*Prep Time: 30 minutes*
*Cooking Time: 3¼-4¼ hours*
*Ideal slow cooker size: 4- to 5-qt.*

leftover chicken and broth
from Savory Chicken,
Meal #1
2 carrots
1 rib celery
2 medium-sized onions
2 Tbsp. flour *or* cornstarch
¼ cup cold water

1 For a second Savory
Chicken Meal, pick leftover
chicken off bone. Set aside.

2. Return remaining broth
to slow cooker. Stir in thinly
sliced carrots and celery, and
onions cut up in chunks.

3. Cover. Cook 3-4 hours
on High.

4. In small bowl, mix flour
or cornstarch with cold water.
When smooth, stir into hot
broth.

5. Stir in cut-up chicken.
Heat 15-20 minutes, or until
broth thickens and chicken
is hot.

*Serving suggestion: Serve
over* **rice** *or* **pasta**.

# Creamy Chicken and Vegetables

**Dawn M. Propst**
Levittown, PA

*Makes 4 servings*

*Prep. Time: 10 minutes*
*Cooking Time: 5-6 hours*
*Ideal slow cooker size: 4-qt.*

10¾-oz. can cream of
mushroom soup, *divided*
4 boneless, skinless
chicken breast halves
16-oz. pkg. frozen vegetable
medley (broccoli,
cauliflower, and carrots),
thawed and drained
½ tsp. salt
⅛-¼ tsp. pepper
1 cup shredded cheddar
cheese, *divided*

1. Pour small amount
of soup in bottom of slow
cooker.

2. Add chicken breasts,
vegetables, and seasonings.

3. Mix in ½ cup cheddar
cheese. Stir in remaining
soup.

4. Cover. Cook on Low
5-6 hours, or until vegetables
are cooked and chicken is no
longer pink.

5. Sprinkle with remaining
cheese 10-15 minutes before
serving.

# Chicken Alfredo

**Dawn M. Propst**
Levittown, PA

*Makes 4-6 servings*

*Prep. Time: 20 minutes*
*Cooking Time: 6 hours*
*Ideal slow cooker size: 4-qt.*

16-oz. jar Alfredo sauce,
*divided*
4-6 boneless, skinless
chicken breast halves
8 ozs. dry noodles, cooked
4-oz. can mushroom pieces
and stems, drained
1 cup shredded mozzarella
cheese, *or* ½ cup grated
Parmesan cheese

1. Pour about one-third of
Alfredo sauce in bottom of
slow cooker.

2. Add chicken and cover
with remaining sauce.

3. Cover. Cook on Low
6 hours, or until chicken is
tender but not dry.

4. Fifteen minutes before
serving, add noodles and
mushrooms to cooker ingredients, mixing well.

5. Sprinkle top with
cheese. Dish is ready to serve
when cheese is melted.

*Serving suggestion: Serve
with* **green salad** *and* **Italian
bread**.

# Creamy Chicken and Noodles

**Rhonda Burgoon**
Collingswood, NJ

*Makes 4-6 servings*

**Prep. Time: 25 minutes**
**Cooking Time: 4¼-9¼ hours**
**Ideal slow cooker size: 4-qt.**

2 cups sliced carrots
1½ cups chopped onions
1 cup sliced celery
2 Tbsp. snipped fresh
　parsley
bay leaf
3 medium-sized chicken
　legs and thighs (about 2
lbs.), skin removed
2 10¾-oz. cans cream of
　chicken soup
½ cup water
1 tsp. dried thyme
1 tsp. salt
¼ tsp. pepper
1 cup peas

1. Place carrots, onions, celery, parsley, and bay leaf in slow cooker.
2. Arrange chicken on top of vegetables.
3. Combine soup, water, thyme, salt, and pepper in bowl. Pour over chicken and vegetables.
4. Cover. Cook on Low 8-9 hours or on High 4-4½ hours.
5. Remove chicken from slow cooker. Cool slightly.
6. Debone chicken, cut into bite-sized pieces, and return to slow cooker.
7. Remove and discard bay leaf.
8. Stir peas into mixture in slow cooker. Cook 5-10 minutes.

*Serving suggestion: Pour over 12-oz. pkg. cooked **noodles**. Toss gently to combine. Serve with **crusty bread** and a **salad**.*

# Szechwan-Style Chicken and Broccoli

**Jane Meiser**, Harrisonburg, VA

*Makes 4 servings*

**Prep. Time: 20 minutes • Cooking Time: 1-3 hours**
**Ideal slow cooker size: 4-qt.**

2 whole boneless, skinless
　chicken breasts
oil
½ cup picante sauce
2 Tbsp. soy sauce
½ tsp. sugar
½ Tbsp. quick-cooking
　tapioca
1 medium onion, chopped
2 garlic cloves, minced
½ tsp. ground ginger
2 cups broccoli florets
1 medium red bell pepper,
　cut into pieces

1. Cut chicken into 1" cubes. Brown lightly in oil in skillet. Place meat in slow cooker.
2. Stir in remaining ingredients.
3. Cover. Cook on High 1-1½ hours or on Low 2-3 hours.

# Chicken Gumbo

**Virginia Bender**
Dover, DE

*Makes 6-8 servings*

**Prep. Time: 25 minutes**
**Cooking Time: 2½-6 hours**
**Ideal slow cooker size: 4-qt.**

1 large onion, chopped
3-4 garlic cloves, minced
1 green bell pepper, diced
2 cups okra, sliced
2 cups tomatoes, chopped
4 cups chicken broth
1 lb. chicken breast, cut
　into 1" pieces
2 tsp. Old Bay Seasoning

1. Combine all ingredients in slow cooker.
2. Cover. Cook on Low 5-6 hours or on High 2½-3 hours.

*Serving suggestion: Serve over **rice**.*

# Gourmet Chicken Breasts

**Sharon Swartz Lambert**
Dayton, VA

**Deborah Santiago**
Lancaster, PA

*Makes 4-6 servings*

**Prep. Time: 15 minutes**
**Cooking Time: 6-8 hours**
**Ideal slow cooker size: 4-qt.**

6-8 slices thinly sliced
   dried beef
4-6 boneless, skinless
   chicken breast halves
2-3 slices bacon, cut in half
   lengthwise
10¾-oz. cream of
   mushroom soup
8 oz. sour cream
½ cup flour

1. Line bottom of slow
cooker with dried beef.
2. Roll up each chicken
breast half and wrap with a
half-slice of bacon. Place in
slow cooker.
3. Combine remaining
ingredients in bowl. Pour
over breasts.
4. Cover. Cook on Low 6-8
hours, or until chicken and
bacon are fully cooked but
not dry.

*Serving suggestion: Serve
with **cooked noodles**, **rice**, or
**mashed potatoes**.*

# Creamy Nutmeg Chicken

**Amber Swarey**
Honea Path, SC

*Makes 6 servings*

**Prep. Time: 25 minutes**
**Cooking Time: 3-4 hours**
**Ideal slow cooker size: 4-qt.**

6 boneless, skinless
   chicken breast halves
oil
¼ cup chopped onions
¼ cup minced parsley
2 10¾-oz. cans cream of
   mushroom soup
½ cup sour cream
½ cup milk
1 Tbsp. ground nutmeg
¼ tsp. sage
¼ tsp. dried thyme
¼ tsp. crushed rosemary

1. Brown chicken in skillet
in oil. Reserve drippings and
place chicken in slow cooker.
2. Sauté onions and parsley
in drippings until onions are
tender.
3. Stir in remaining
ingredients. Mix well. Pour
over chicken.
4. Cover. Cook on Low
3-4 hours, or until juices run
clear.

*Serving suggestion: Serve
over **mashed** or **fried potatoes**, or **rice**.*

# Slow Cooker Creamy Chicken Italian

**Sherri Grindle**
Goshen, IN

*Makes 8 servings*

**Prep. Time: 10-15 minutes**
**Cooking Time: 5-6 hours**
**Ideal slow cooker size: 4- to 5-qt.**

8 boneless, skinless
   chicken breast halves
1 envelope dry Italian
   salad dressing mix
¼ cup water
8-oz. pkg. cream cheese,
   softened
10¾-oz. can cream of
   chicken soup
4-oz. can mushrooms,
   drained

1. Place chicken in greased
slow cooker.
2. Combine salad-dressing
mix and water in bowl. Pour
over chicken.
3. Cover. Cook on Low 4-5
hours.
4. In saucepan, combine
cream cheese and soup. Heat
slightly to melt cream cheese.
Stir in mushrooms. Pour over
chicken.
5. Cover. Cook 1 additional
hour on Low.

*Serving suggestion: Serve
over **noodles** or **rice**.*

Variation:
   Add frozen vegetables along
with the mushrooms in Step 4.

# Mushroom Chicken in Sour Cream Sauce

**Lavina Hochstedler**
Grand Blanc, MI

**Joyce Shackelford**
Green Bay, WI

*Makes 6 servings*

*Prep. Time: 15 minutes*
*Cooking Time: 3-7 hours*
*Ideal slow cooker size: 6-qt.*

1½ tsp. salt
¼ tsp. pepper
½ tsp. paprika
¼ tsp. lemon pepper
1 tsp. garlic powder
6 skinless, bone-in chicken breast halves
10¾-oz. can cream of mushroom soup
8 oz. sour cream
½ cup dry white wine, *or* chicken broth
½ lb. fresh mushrooms, sliced

1. Combine salt, pepper, paprika, lemon pepper, and garlic powder in a small bowl. Rub over chicken. Place meat in slow cooker.
2. Combine soup, sour cream, and wine or broth in bowl. Stir in mushrooms. Spoon over chicken, being careful not to disturb rub.
3. Cover. Cook on Low 5-7 hours or on High 3 hours, or until chicken is fully cooked but not dry.

*Serving suggestion: Serve over **potatoes**, **rice**, or **cous-cous**. Delicious accompanied with **broccoli-cauliflower salad** and **applesauce**.*

# Indonesian Peanut Chicken

**Naomi Ressler**
Harrisonburg, VA

*Makes 6 servings*

*Prep. Time: 15-20 minutes*
*Cooking Time: 4 hours*
*Ideal slow cooker size: 4-qt.*

1½ lbs. boneless, skinless chicken breasts, cut into chunks
⅓ cup chopped onions
⅓ cup water
¼ cup creamy, *or* chunky, peanut butter
3 Tbsp. chili sauce
¼ tsp. salt
¼ tsp. pepper
¼ tsp. cayenne pepper
cooked rice, *or* soba noodles
6 Tbsp. chopped peanuts
6 Tbsp. chopped sweet red peppers

1. Place chicken in slow cooker.
2. In a small bowl, combine onions, water, peanut butter, chili sauce, salt, and peppers. Pour over chicken.
3. Cover. Cook on Low 4 hours, or until chicken is tender.
4. Serve over rice or soba noodles. Sprinkle with peanuts and red peppers.

# Chicken Cashew Dish

**Dorothy Horst**
Tiskilwa, IL

*Makes 6 servings*

*Prep. Time: 15 minutes*
*Cooking Time: 2-4 hours*
*Ideal slow cooker size: 3-qt.*

14-oz. can bean sprouts, drained
3 Tbsp. butter, melted
4 green onions, chopped
4-oz. can mushroom pieces, drained
10¾-oz. can cream of mushroom soup
1 cup sliced celery
12½-oz. can chunk chicken breast, *or* 1 cup cooked chicken, cubed
1 Tbsp. soy sauce
1 cup cashew nuts

1. Combine all ingredients except nuts in slow cooker.
2. Cover. Cook on Low 3-4 hours or on High 2-2½ hours.
3. Stir in cashew nuts before serving.

*Serving suggestion: Serve over **rice**.*

Note:
*I teach English as a Second Language to Vietnamese women. Occasionally they invite us to join them for dinner on Vietnamese New Year. We enjoy the fellowship and Vietnamese traditions immensely. They always have a "Lucky Tree," a tree with yellow flowers which blooms in*

*Vietnam on New Year's. They decorate the tree by hanging red envelopes in it. Each contains a money gift; one is given to each unmarried person present, including the babies.*

# Chicken Azteca

**Katrine Rose**
Woodbridge, VA

*Makes 10-12 servings*

*Prep. Time: 15-20 minutes*
*Cooking Time: 2½-6½ hours*
*Ideal slow cooker size: 6- to 7-qt.*

2 15-oz. cans black beans, drained
4 cups frozen corn kernels
2 garlic cloves, minced
¾ tsp. ground cumin
2 cups chunky salsa, *divided*
10 boneless, skinless chicken breast halves
2 8-oz. pkgs. cream cheese, cubed

1. Combine beans, corn, garlic, cumin, and half of salsa in slow cooker.
2. Arrange chicken breasts over top. Pour remaining salsa over top.
3. Cover. Cook on High 2-3 hours or on Low 4-6 hours, or until chicken is tender but not dry.
4. Remove chicken and cut into bite-sized pieces. Return to cooker.
5. Stir in cream cheese. Cook on High until cream cheese melts.

*Serving suggestion: Spoon chicken and sauce over cooked rice. Top with **shredded cheese**.*

# Tamale Chicken

**Jeanne Allen**
Rye, CO

*Makes 6 servings*

*Prep. Time: 45 minutes*
*Cooking Time: 3-4 hours*
*Ideal slow cooker size: 4-qt.*

1 medium onion, chopped
4-oz. can chopped green chilies, drained
2 Tbsp. oil
10¾-oz. can cream of chicken soup
2 cups sour cream
1 cup sliced ripe olives
1 cup chopped stewed tomatoes
2 cups shredded cheddar cheese
8 boneless, skinless chicken breast halves, cooked* and chopped
16-oz. can beef tamales, chopped
1 tsp. chili powder
1 tsp. garlic powder
1 tsp. pepper
½ cup shredded cheddar cheese, *divided*

1. Sauté onion and chilies in oil in skillet. Place in slow cooker.
2. Combine all remaining ingredients, except ½ cup shredded cheese, in slow cooker.
3. Top with remaining cheese.
4. Cover. Cook on High 3-4 hours.

*Serving suggestion: Pass chopped fresh **tomatoes**, **shredded lettuce**, **sour cream**, **salsa**, and **guacamole** so guests can top their Tamale Chicken with these condiments.*

*You can cook the chicken breasts by placing them in your slow cooker. Sprinkle generously with salt and pepper. Pour 3-4 cups water into cooker, along its interior side so as not to wash the seasonings off the meat. Cover. Cook on Low 6 hours or so, until chicken is fork-tender but not dry.

*Choose a country that has special meaning for your family and plan a holiday menu around the foods of that country. For example, our children grew up in Honduras where tamales were served on Christmas and New Year's Eve. These foods bring back special memories.*

*Elena Yoder, Albuquerque, NM*

## Tex-Mex Chicken and Rice

**Kelly Evenson**
Pittsboro, NC

*Makes 8 servings*

*Prep. Time: 25 minutes*
*Cooking Time: 4-4½ hours*
*Ideal slow cooker size: 5-qt.*

1 cup uncooked converted
white rice
28-oz. can diced peeled
tomatoes
6-oz. can tomato paste
3 cups hot water
1 envelope dry taco
seasoning mix
4 whole boneless, skinless
chicken breasts,
uncooked and cut into
½" cubes
2 medium onions, chopped
1 green bell pepper,
chopped
4-oz. can diced green
chilies
1 tsp. garlic powder
½ tsp. pepper

1. Combine all ingredients
except chilies and seasonings
in large slow cooker.
2. Cover. Cook on Low
4-4½ hours, or until rice is
tender and chicken is cooked.
3. Stir in green chilies and
seasonings and serve.

*Serving suggestion: Serve
with **mixed green leafy salad**
and **refried beans**.*

## Red Pepper Chicken

**Sue Graber**
Eureka, IL

*Makes 4 servings*

*Prep. Time: 10 minutes*
*Cooking Time: 4-6 hours*
*Ideal slow cooker size: 4-qt.*

4 boneless, skinless
chicken breast halves
15-oz. can black beans,
drained
12-oz. jar roasted red
peppers, undrained
14½-oz. can Mexican
stewed tomatoes,
undrained
1 large onion, chopped
½ tsp. salt
pepper to taste

1. Place chicken in slow
cooker.
2. Combine beans, red
peppers, stewed tomatoes,
onion, salt, and pepper in a
good-sized mixing bowl. Pour
over chicken.
3. Cover. Cook on Low
4-6 hours, or until chicken is
tender and no longer pink.

*Serving suggestion: Serve
over **rice**.*

## Chicken and Seafood Gumbo

**Dianna Milhizer**
Brighton, MI

*Makes 12 servings*

*Prep. Time: 40-45 minutes*
*Cooking Time: 8-10 hours*
*Ideal slow cooker size: 6-qt.*

1 cup chopped celery
1 cup chopped onions
½ cup chopped green bell
peppers
¼ cup olive oil
¼ cup, plus 1 Tbsp., flour
6 cups chicken stock
2 lbs. chicken, skin
removed and cut up
3 bay leaves
1½ cups sliced okra
12-oz. can diced tomatoes
1 tsp. Tabasco sauce
salt to taste
pepper to taste
1 lb. ready-to-eat shrimp
½ cup snipped fresh parsley

1. Sauté celery, onions, and
peppers in oil in skillet.
2. Blend in flour and chicken
stock until smooth. Cook 5
minutes. Pour into slow cooker.
3. Stir remaining ingre-
dients, except seafood and
parsley, into slow cooker.
4. Cover. Cook on Low
8-10 hours, or until chicken is
tender but not dry.
5. One hour before serving
add shrimp and parsley.
6. Remove bay leaves
before serving.

*Serving suggestion: Serve
over **white rice**.*

# Chicken Rice Special

**Jeanne Allen**
Rye, CO

*Makes 6-8 servings*

*Prep. Time: 40 minutes*
*Cooking Time: 4-6 hours*
*Ideal slow cooker size: 4-qt.*

1 lb. pork, *or* turkey, sausage
6 chicken breast halves, cooked* and chopped (save 4 cups broth)
half a large sweet green pepper, chopped
1 medium onion, chopped
4 ribs celery, chopped
1 cup uncooked rice
2-oz. pkg. dry noodle-soup mix
½ cup sliced almonds
1-2 oz. jar pimentos, chopped

1. Brown sausage in skillet. Drain off any drippings. Place meat in slow cooker.
2. Add all other ingredients, except almonds and pimentos, to slow cooker. Stir well.
3. Top with almonds and pimentos.
4. Cover. Cook on High 4-6 hours, or until rice is done and liquid has been absorbed.
5. Stir well 1 hour before serving.

*See page 175, at end of recipe for Tamale Chicken, for instructions about cooking chicken in your slow cooker.

# Company Casserole

**Vera Schmucker**
Goshen, IN

*Makes 4-6 servings*

*Prep. Time: 15-20 minutes*
*Cooking Time: 3-8 hours*
*Ideal slow cooker size: 5-qt.*

1¼ cups uncooked long-grain rice
1 stick (8 Tbsp.) butter, melted
3 cups chicken broth
3-4 cups cut-up cooked chicken breast
2 4-oz. cans sliced mushrooms, drained
⅓ cup soy sauce
12-oz. pkg. shelled frozen shrimp, thawed
8 green onions, chopped, 2 Tbsp. reserved
⅔ cup slivered almonds

1. Combine rice and butter in slow cooker. Stir to coat rice well.
2. Add remaining ingredients, except almonds and 2 Tbsp. green onions.
3. Cover. Cook on Low 6-8 hours or on High 3-4 hours, until rice is tender.
4. Thirty minutes before end of cooking time, stir in thawed shrimp.
5. Sprinkle almonds and green onions over top before serving.

*Serving suggestion: Serve with **green beans**, **tossed salad**, and **fruit salad**.*

# Chicken Broccoli Rice Casserole

**Gloria Julien**
Gladstone, MI

*Makes 4-6 servings*

*Prep. Time: 30 minutes*
*Cooking Time: 2-3 hours*
*Ideal slow cooker size: 5-qt.*

1 onion, chopped
3 Tbsp. oil
2-3 cups uncooked chicken, cut in 1" pieces
10¾-oz. can cream of chicken soup
12-oz. can evaporated milk
2 cups cubed Velveeta cheese
3 cups cooked rice
2 cups frozen broccoli cuts, thawed
¼ tsp. pepper
4-oz. can mushrooms, drained

1. Sauté onion in oil in skillet.
2. Add chicken and sauté until no longer pink.
3. Combine all ingredients in slow cooker.
4. Cover. Cook on Low 2-3 hours.

Notes:
*1. This is an ideal dish for people who are not big meat-eaters.*
*2. This is good carry-in for potluck or fellowship meals. I put the ingredients together the night before.*

# Baked Chicken and Rice

**Fannie Miller**
Hutchinson, KS

*Makes 10-12 servings*

*Prep. Time: 15 minutes*
*Cooking Time: 4-6 hours*
*Ideal slow cooker size: 6- to 7-qt.*

2 cups dry instant rice
10¾-oz. can cream of chicken soup
10¾-oz. can cream of mushroom soup
10¾-oz. can cream of celery soup
1 stick (8 Tbsp.) butter
1 soup can water
10 skinless chicken breast halves, *or* 1 large chicken, cut into 10-12 pieces
1 envelope dry onion soup mix

1. Place rice in large slow cooker.
2. Combine soups, butter, and water in large bowl. Pour half over rice.
3. Lay chicken over rice. Pour remaining soup mixture over chicken.
4. Sprinkle with dry onion soup mix.
5. Cover. Cook on Low 4-6 hours, or until chicken is done but not dry, and rice is tender but not mushy.

# Chicken Pasta

**Evelyn L. Ward**
Greeley, CO

*Makes 4 servings*

*Prep. Time: 25-30 minutes*
*Cooking Time: 4 hours and 20 minutes*
*Ideal slow cooker size: 4-qt.*

1½-lb. boneless, skinless chicken breast
1 large zucchini, diced
1 envelope chicken gravy mix
2 Tbsp. water
2 Tbsp. evaporated milk, *or* cream
1 large tomato, chopped
4 cups cooked macaroni
8 ozs. smoked Gouda cheese, grated

1. Cut chicken into 1" cubes. Place in slow cooker.
2. Add zucchini, gravy mix, and water, and stir together.
3. Cover. Cook on Low 4 hours.
4. Add milk and tomato. Cook an additional 20 minutes.
5. Stir in pasta. Top with cheese. Serve immediately.

# Our Favorite Chicken and Stuffing

**Kim Stoll**
Abbeville, SC

*Makes 6 servings*

*Prep. Time: 10-15 minutes*
*Cooking Time: 3-5 hours*
*Ideal slow cooker size: 5-qt.*

6 boneless, skinless chicken breast halves
6 slices Swiss cheese
¼ cup milk
10¾-oz. can cream of mushroom, *or* chicken, soup
2 cups stuffing mix
1 stick (8 Tbsp.) butter, melted

1. Grease slow cooker with nonstick cooking spray.
2. Top each breast half with slice of cheese. Arrange cheese-covered chicken in slow cooker.
3. In a mixing bowl, combine milk and soup until smooth. Pour over chicken. (If you've stacked the breasts, lift the ones on top to make sure the ones on the bottom are topped with sauce, too.)

*Depending on the number of guests you may do formal or informal. Thanksgiving with 40 has me using disposables. Christmas with seven adults calls for fine china and crystal at our house.*
*Colleen Heatwole, Burton, MI*

4. Sprinkle stuffing mix evenly over sauced chicken, including those on the bottom.

5. Drizzle with melted butter.

6. Cover. Cook on High 3 hours or on Low 5 hours, or just until meat is tender but not dry.

**Variation:**

Use cornbread stuffing instead of regular stuffing mix.
**Betty Moore**
Plano, IL

# Chicken Dressing

**Lydia A. Yoder**
London, ON

*Makes 20 servings*
*Prep. Time: 40-45 minutes*
*Cooking Time: 3-4 hours*
*Ideal slow cooker size: 6-qt.*

1½ sticks (12 Tbsp.) butter
1 cup chopped onions
2 cups chopped celery
2 Tbsp. parsley flakes
1½ tsp. salt
½ tsp. pepper
3½-4 cups chicken broth
12-14 cups dried bread cubes
4 cups cut-up, cooked chicken*
2 eggs, beaten
1 tsp. baking powder

1. Sauté onion and celery in butter in skillet.

2. Combine seasonings and broth in large bowl. Mix in bread cubes.

3. Fold in chicken and sautéed onions and celery.

4. Add eggs and baking powder.

5. Lightly pack into large slow cooker.

6. Cover. Cook on Low 3-4 hours.

*Serving suggestion: Serve with turkey or chicken, mashed potatoes, a vegetable, and lettuce salad.*

*For instructions about how to cook chicken in your slow cooker, see page 175, at end of recipe for Tamale Chicken. (Or use leftover chicken.)

**Tip:**
The longer the dressing cooks, the drier it will become. Keep that in mind if you do not care for moist stuffing.

# Chicken and Stuffing Dinner

**Trudy Kutter**
Corfu, NY

*Makes 4-6 servings*
*Prep. Time: 20 minutes*
*Cooking Time: 6¾-7 hours*
*Ideal slow cooker size: 6-qt.*

4-6 skinless chicken breast halves
10¾-oz. can cream of chicken, *or* celery, soup
4-6 potatoes, peeled and sliced
6-oz. pkg. stuffing mix
1¼ cups water
¼ stick (2 Tbsp.) melted butter
1-1½ cups frozen green beans, thawed

1. Arrange chicken in slow cooker.

2. Spoon soup over chicken.

3. Top with potatoes.

4. Combine stuffing mix, water, and butter in bowl. Spoon over potatoes.

5. Cover. Cook on Low 6 hours.

6. Sprinkle green beans over stuffing.

7. Cover. Cook on Low 45-60 minutes, or until beans are just tender.

*Serving suggestion: Serve with a salad.*

# Chicken and Dumplings

**Bonnie Miller**
Louisville, OH

*Makes 4 servings*

**Prep. Time:** *20 minutes*
**Cooking Time:** *3½-8½ hours*
**Ideal slow cooker size:** *4-qt.*

**2 lbs. boneless, skinless chicken breast halves**
**1¾ cups chicken broth**
**2 chicken bouillon cubes**
**2 tsp. salt**
**1 tsp. pepper**
**1 tsp. poultry seasoning**
**2 celery ribs, cut into 1" pieces**
**6 small carrots, cut into 1" chunks**

Biscuits:
**2 cups buttermilk biscuit mix**
**½ cup, plus 1 Tbsp., milk**
**1 tsp. parsley**

1. Arrange chicken in slow cooker.
2. Dissolve bouillon in broth in bowl. Stir in salt, pepper, and poultry seasoning.
3. Pour over chicken.
4. Spread celery and carrots over top.
5. Cover. Cook on Low 6-8 hours or on High 3-3½ hours, or until chicken is tender but not dry.
6. Combine Biscuit ingredients in a bowl until just moistened. Drop by spoonfuls over steaming chicken.
7. Cover. Cook on High 35

minutes. Do not remove cover while dumplings are cooking. Serve immediately.

# Scalloped Chicken

**Brenda Joy Sonnie**
Newton, PA

*Makes 4-6 servings*

**Prep. Time:** *15-30 minutes*
**Cooking Time:** *2-3 hours*
**Ideal slow cooker size:** *5-qt.*

**4 cups cooked chicken***
**1 box stuffing mix for chicken**
**2 eggs**
**1 cup water**
**1½ cups milk**
**1 cup frozen peas**

1. In large bowl, combine chicken and dry stuffing mix. Place in slow cooker.
2. In same bowl, beat together eggs, water, and milk. Pour over chicken and stuffing.
3. Cover. Cook on High 2-3 hours.
4. Add frozen peas during last hour of cooking.

Variation:
For more flavor use chicken broth instead of water.

*If you don't have leftover cooked chicken, turn to page 175, at end of recipe for Tamale Chicken, for instructions about how to cook chicken in your slow cooker.

# Brunswick Stew

**Violette Denney**
Carrollton, GA

*Makes 8-10 servings*

**Prep. Time:** *30-60 minutes*
**Cooking Time:** *4 hours*
**Ideal slow cooker size:** *8-qt.*

**3 lbs. boneless, skinless chicken breasts**
**reserved chicken broth (from cooking chicken breasts)**
**2 lbs. lean ground beef**
**2 cans creamed corn**
**1 can whole-kernel corn, drained**
**2 cups ketchup**
**1 cup mild barbecue sauce**
**2 Tbsp. Worcestershire sauce**
**2 large sweet onions, chopped**
**15-oz. can English peas, drained**
**1 qt. stewed tomatoes**
**salt and pepper to taste**

1. In good-sized stockpot, cook chicken in 2" of water. Cover and cook slowly, just until meat is tender but not at all dry.
2. Remove chicken to platter and allow to cool. (Reserve broth.) When cool enough to handle, cut chicken into small chunks.
3. Meanwhile, brown ground beef in large skillet. Stir occasionally with wooden spoon, breaking up clumps. Brown until meat is no longer pink.
4. Place 1 cup chicken

broth in slow cooker. (Reserve rest of broth.)

5. Drain drippings off browned ground beef. Add beef to slow cooker.

6. Stir all other ingredients into slow cooker.

7. Cover. Cook on Low 4 hours.

**Notes:**

1. Add more broth if the Stew gets thicker than you like. Use canned broth if you need to.

2. If you have leftovers, this Stew freezes well and is welcome on any cold day when you want something hot.

3. Serve this as soup, or over pasta as a topping.

# Hot Chicken Sandwiches

**Glenna Fay Bergey**
Lebanon, OR

*Makes 6-8 servings*

*Prep. Time: 5 minutes*
*Cooking Time: 6-7 hours*
*Ideal slow cooker size: 6-qt.*

**1 large chicken, whole or cut up**
**1 cup water**

1. Place chicken in slow cooker. Add water.

2. Cover. Cook on Low 6-7 hours.

3. Debone chicken. Mix cut-up chicken with broth.

4. Spoon into dinner rolls with straining spoon to make small hot sandwiches.

*Serving suggestion: Top with your favorite **condiments**.*

**Tip:**

This is also a great way to prepare cooked chicken for soups or casseroles. Save the broth if you think you might make soup.

# Barbecued Chicken Sandwiches

**Brittany Miller**
Millersburg, OH

*Makes 10 servings*

*Prep. Time: 25-30 minutes*
*Cooking Time: 6 hours*
*Ideal slow cooker size: 5-qt.*

**3 lbs. boneless, skinless chicken thighs**
**1 cup ketchup**
**1 small onion, chopped**
**¼ cup water**
**¼ cup cider vinegar**
**2 Tbsp. Worcestershire sauce**
**1 Tbsp. brown sugar**
**1 garlic clove, minced**
**1 bay leaf**
**2 tsp. paprika**
**1 tsp. dried oregano**
**1 tsp. chili powder**
**½ tsp. salt**
**½ tsp. pepper**

1. Place chicken in slow cooker.

2. In a medium-sized mixing bowl, combine ketchup, onion, water, vinegar, Worcestershire sauce, brown sugar, garlic, bay leaf, and seasonings. Pour over chicken.

3. Cover. Cook on Low 5 hours, or until meat is tender.

4. Discard bay leaf.

5. Remove chicken to large bowl. Shred meat with 2 forks. Return chicken to slow cooker.

6. Stir shredded chicken and sauce together thoroughly.

7. Cover. Cook on Low 30 minutes. Remove lid. Continue cooking 30 more minutes, allowing sauce to cook off and thicken.

*Serving suggestion: This is enough chicken and sauce to fill up to 10 **sandwich rolls**.*

# Levi's Sesame Chicken Wings

**Shirley Unternahrer**
Wayland, IA

*Makes 16 appetizer servings,*
*or 6-8 main-dish servings*

**Prep. Time: 35-40 minutes**
**Cooking Time: 2½-5 hours**
**Ideal slow cooker size: 4-qt.**

3 lbs. chicken wings
salt to taste
pepper to taste
1¾ cups honey
1 cup soy sauce
½ cup ketchup
2 Tbsp. canola oil
2 Tbsp. sesame oil
2 garlic cloves, minced
toasted sesame seeds

1. Rinse wings. Cut at joint. Sprinkle with salt and pepper. Place on broiler pan.
2. Broil 5 inches from broiler flame, 10 minutes on each side. Place chicken in slow cooker.
3. Combine remaining ingredients in bowl, except sesame seeds. Pour over chicken.

4. Cover. Cook on Low 5 hours or on High 2½ hours.
5. Sprinkle sesame seeds over top just before serving.
6. Serve as appetizer, or with white or brown rice and shredded lettuce to turn this appetizer into a meal.

Note:

*My husband and his co-workers have a pot-luck-lunch at work. It's a good way to break the monotony of the week or month. And it gives them a chance to share with each other.*

*What better way to have the food ready than in a slow cooker!*

# Chicken Wings Colorado

**Nancy Rexrode Clark**
Woodstock, MD

*Makes 6-8 servings*

**Prep. Time: 40 minutes**
**Cooking Time: 6½-7½ hours**
**Ideal slow cooker size: 4-qt.**

1½ cups sugar
¼ tsp. salt
1 chicken bouillon cube
1 cup cider vinegar
½ cup ketchup
2 Tbsp. soy sauce
12-16 chicken wings
¼ cup cornstarch
½ cup cold water
red hot sauce to taste,
    *optional*

1. Combine sugar, salt, bouillon cube, vinegar, ketchup, and soy sauce in slow cooker. Turn to High and bring sauce to a boil.
2. Add chicken wings, pushing them down into sauce.
3. Cover. Cook on Low 6-7 hours.
4. Combine cornstarch and cold water in small bowl. Stir into slow cooker.
5. Cover. Cook on High until liquid thickens, about 30 minutes.
6. Season with red hot sauce, or let each diner add to his or her own serving.

*A loaf of homemade bread is an excellent gift. What comfort comes from a warm loaf, knowing that someone slowed down enough to make it and share it. My mother did this often. Her baking was a way of making the kitchen a comfortable place to be. She was so encouraging when teaching me to bake or cook.*

*Shirley Unternahrer, Wayland, IA*

# Turkey Main Dishes

## Herb-Roasted Turkey Breast

**Kristi See**
Weskan, KS

*Makes 6 servings*

*Prep. Time: 15 minutes*
*Cooking Time: 4-6 hours*
*Ideal slow cooker size: 5- to 6-qt.*

5 tsp. lemon juice
1 Tbsp. olive oil
1-2 tsp. pepper
1 tsp. dried rosemary, crushed
1 tsp. dried thyme
1 tsp. garlic salt
6-7-lb. bone-in turkey breast
1 medium onion, cut into wedges
1 celery rib, cut into 2"-thick pieces
½ cup white wine, *or* chicken broth

1. Spray slow cooker with nonstick cooking spray.

2. In a small bowl, combine lemon juice and olive oil. In another bowl, combine pepper, rosemary, thyme, and garlic salt.

3. With your fingers, carefully loosen skin from both sides of breast. Brush oil mixture under skin. Rub herb-seasoning mixture under and on top of skin.

4. Arrange onion and celery in slow cooker. Place turkey breast, skin-side up, on top of vegetables.

5. Pour wine around breast.

6. Cover. Cook on Low 4-6 hours, or until meat is tender but not dry.

### Note:

*I made this turkey recipe for our first Thanksgiving after we were married. We really enjoyed the taste. Clean-up was easy, and because I prepared the turkey in the slow cooker, I wasn't short on oven space.*

### Variations:

1. Add carrot chunks to Step 4 to add more flavor to the turkey broth.

2. Reserve broth for soups, or thicken with flour-water paste and serve as gravy over sliced turkey.

3. Freeze broth in pint-sized containers for future use.

4. Debone turkey and freeze in pint-sized containers for future use. Or freeze any leftover turkey.

**Liz Ann Yoder**
Hartville, OH

5. See Turkey Cacciatore, page 188, for a great dish with cut-up cooked turkey!

# Turkey Breast with Orange Sauce

**Jean Butzer**
Batavia, NY

*Makes 4-6 servings*

*Prep. Time: 10 minutes*
*Cooking Time: 7-8 hours*
*Ideal slow cooker size: 6-qt.*

1 large onion, chopped
3 garlic cloves, minced
1 tsp. dried rosemary
½ tsp. pepper
2-3-lb. boneless, skinless
  turkey breast
1½ cups orange juice

1. Place onions in slow cooker.
2. Combine garlic, rosemary, and pepper in a small bowl.
3. Make gashes in turkey, about ¾ of the way through at 2" intervals. Stuff with herb mixture. Place turkey in slow cooker.
4. Pour juice over turkey.
5. Cover. Cook on Low 7-8 hours, or until turkey is no longer pink in center.

Note:
This very easy, impressive-looking and -tasting recipe is perfect for company.

# Turkey Slow Cooker

**Arlene Leaman Kliewer**
Lakewood, CO

*Makes 8 servings*

*Prep. Time: 5 minutes*
*Cooking Time: 8 hours*
*Ideal slow cooker size: 6-qt.*

5-lb. turkey breast
1 envelope dry onion soup
  mix
16-oz. can whole cranberry
  sauce

1. Place turkey in slow cooker.
2. Combine soup mix and cranberry sauce in bowl. Spread over turkey.
3. Cover. Cook on Low 8 hours.

# Stuffed Turkey Breast

**Jean Butzer**
Batavia, NY

*Makes 8 servings*

*Prep. Time: 25 minutes*
*Cooking Time: 7-9 hours*
*Ideal slow cooker size: 6-qt.*

half a stick (¼ cup) butter,
  melted
1 small onion, finely
  chopped
½ cup finely chopped
  celery
2½-oz. pkg. croutons with
  real bacon bits
1 cup chicken broth
2 Tbsp. fresh minced
  parsley
½ tsp. poultry seasoning
1 whole uncooked turkey
  breast, *or* 2 halves,
  about 5 lbs. total
salt to taste
pepper to taste
24" x 26" piece of
  cheesecloth for each
  breast half
dry white wine

1. Combine butter, onion, celery, croutons, broth, parsley, and poultry seasoning in a bowl.
2. Cut turkey breast in thick slices from breastbone to rib cage, leaving slices attached to bone (crosswise across breast).
3. Sprinkle turkey with salt and pepper.
4. Soak cheesecloth in wine. Place turkey on cheese-

*Before guests are scheduled to arrive I take the lids off whatever's cooking and allow the fragrances to fill the kitchen. Very inviting!*
            *Barbara Yoder, Angola, IN*

cloth. Stuff bread mixture into slits between turkey slices.

5. Fold one end of cheese-cloth over the other to cover meat. Place on metal rack or trivet in 6-qt. slow cooker.

6. Cover. Cook on Low 7-9 hours or until tender. Pour additional wine over turkey during cooking.

7. Remove turkey from cooker and remove cheesecloth immediately. (If you prefer a browner result, remove from cooker, discard cheesecloth, and brown turkey in 400° oven for 15-20 minutes.)

8. Let turkey stand 10 minutes before slicing through and serving.

9. Thicken the drippings, if you wish, for gravy. Mix together 3 Tbsp. cornstarch and ¼ cup cold water in small bowl.

10. When smooth, stir into broth (with turkey removed from cooker). Turn cooker to High and stir until cornstarch paste is dissolved. Allow to cook about 10 minutes, until broth is thickened and smooth.

# Slow Cooker Turkey and Dressing

**Carol Sherwood**
Batavia, NY

*Makes 4-6 servings*

*Prep. Time: 10-15 minutes*
*Cooking Time: 5-6 hours*
*Ideal slow cooker size: 5- to 6-qt.*

8-oz. pkg., *or* 2 6-oz. pkgs., stuffing mix
½ cup hot water
¼ stick (2 Tbsp.) butter, softened
1 onion, chopped
½ cup chopped celery
¼ cup dried cranberries
3-lb. boneless turkey breast
¼ tsp. dried basil
½ tsp. salt
½ tsp. pepper

1. Spread dry stuffing mix in greased slow cooker.

2. Add water, butter, onion, celery, and cranberries. Mix well.

3. Sprinkle turkey breast with basil, salt, and pepper. Place over stuffing mixture.

4. Cover. Cook on Low 5-6 hours, or until turkey is done but not dry.

5. Remove turkey. Slice and set aside.

6. Gently stir stuffing and allow to stand 5 minutes before serving.

7. Place stuffing on platter, topped with sliced turkey.

# Zucchini and Turkey Dish

**Dolores Kratz**
Souderton, PA

*Makes 6 servings*

*Prep. Time: 15 minutes*
*Cooking Time: 4-5 hours*
*Ideal slow cooker size: 4-qt.*

3 cups zucchini, sliced
1 small onion, chopped
¼ tsp. salt
1 cup cubed cooked turkey
2 fresh tomatoes, sliced, *or* 14½-oz. can diced tomatoes
½ tsp. dried oregano
1 tsp. dried basil
¼ cup grated Parmesan cheese
½ cup shredded provolone cheese
¾ cup dry stuffing mix

1. Combine zucchini, onion, salt, turkey, tomatoes, oregano, and basil in slow cooker. Mix well.

2. Top with cheeses and stuffing.

3. Cover. Cook on Low 4-5 hours.

## Slow-Cooked Turkey Dinner

**Miriam Nolt**
New Holland, PA

*Makes 4-6 servings*

***Prep. Time:** 15 minutes*
***Cooking Time:** 7½ hours*
***Ideal slow cooker size:** 4-qt.*

1 onion, diced
6 small red potatoes, quartered
2 cups sliced carrots
1½-2 lbs. boneless, skinless turkey thighs
¼ cup flour
2 Tbsp. dry onion soup mix
10¾-oz. can cream of mushroom soup
⅔ cup chicken broth, *or* water

1. Place vegetables in bottom of slow cooker.
2. Place turkey thighs over vegetables.
3. Combine remaining ingredients in bowl. Pour over turkey.
4. Cover. Cook on High 30 minutes. Reduce heat to Low and cook 7 hours, or until vegetables and meat are tender but not dry.

**Variation:**
Use 1 cup uncooked long-grain rice instead of potatoes.
Increase water to 1⅔ cups.
Increase dry onion soup to ¼ cup.
Continue with Step 4 above.

## Turkey Thighs, Acorn Squash, and Apples

**Mary E. Wheatley**
Mashpee, MA

*Makes 6-8 sevings*

***Prep. Time:** 35 minutes*
***Cooking Time:** 6-8 hours*
***Ideal slow cooker size:** 6-qt.*

2 lbs. acorn squash, peeled, seeded, and cut into 1"- thick rings
6 medium-sized Granny Smith, *or* other tart, apples cored and cut into ½"-thick rings
4 turkey thighs, skin and excess fat removed
salt and pepper to taste
1 shallot, *or* small onion, chopped
½ cup apple juice, *or* cider
1 Tbsp. apple brandy
3 Tbsp. brown sugar
1 tsp. ground cinnamon
½ tsp. ground allspice

1. Spray inside of slow cooker with non-stick spray. Layer in squash, followed by apple rings.
2. Place turkey thighs on top. Sprinkle with salt, pepper, and onion or shallot.
3. In a small bowl, combine apple juice, brandy, brown sugar, cinnamon, and allspice. Pour over turkey.
4. Cover. Cook on Low 6-8 hours, or just until turkey and squash are tender.

## Barbecued Turkey Legs

**Barbara Walker**
Sturgis, SC

*Makes 4-6 servings*

***Prep. Time:** 10 minutes*
***Cooking Time:** 4-6 hours*
***Ideal slow cooker size:** 4- to 5-qt.*

4 turkey drumsticks
1-2 tsp. salt
¼-½ tsp. pepper
⅓ cup molasses
¼ cup vinegar
½ cup ketchup
3 Tbsp. Worcestershire sauce
¾ tsp. hickory smoke
2 Tbsp. instant minced onion

1. Sprinkle turkey with salt and pepper. Place in slow cooker.
2. Combine remaining ingredients in bowl. Pour over turkey.
3. Cover. Cook on Low 4-6 hours, or until turkey is tender.

# Turkey Barbecue

**Mary B. Sensenig**
New Holland, PA

*Makes 8 servings*

*Prep. Time: 10-20 minutes*
*Cooking Time: 9 hours*
*Ideal slow cooker size: 3- to 4-qt.*

4 cups boneless skinless
  turkey thighs, *uncooked*,
  cut in 1" lengths
½ cup chopped onion
½ cup chopped celery
1 cup ketchup
½ cup water
1 tsp. dried mustard
2 Tbsp. brown sugar
½ tsp. salt
2 Tbsp. vinegar
2 Tbsp. Worcestershire
  sauce

1. Mix all ingredients
together in slow cooker.
2. Cover. Cook on High 1
hour.
3. Turn cooker to Low and
cook 8 more hours.

*Serving suggestion: This
Barbecue will fill at least 8
sandwich rolls.*

# Barbecued Turkey Cutlets

**Maricarol Magill**, Freehold, NJ

*Makes 6-8 servings*

*Prep. Time: 10 minutes • Cooking Time: 3 hours*
*Ideal slow cooker size: 4- to 5-qt.*

6-8 (1½-2 lbs.) turkey
  cutlets
¼ cup molasses
¼ cup cider vinegar
¼ cup ketchup

3 Tbsp. Worcestershire
  sauce
1 tsp. garlic salt
3 Tbsp. chopped onion
2 Tbsp. brown sugar
¼ tsp. pepper

1. Place turkey cutlets in slow cooker.
2. Combine remaining ingredients in bowl. Pour over turkey.
3. Cover. Cook on Low 3 hours.

*Serving suggestion: Serve over **white** or **brown** rice.*

# Fruited Turkey and Yams

**Jean M. Butzer**
Batavia, NY

*Makes 4 servings*

*Prep. Time: 30-40 minutes*
*Cooking Time: 3-10 hours*
*Ideal slow cooker size: 5- to 6-qt.*

¼ stick (2 Tbsp.) butter
2-3 lbs. (3-4) turkey thighs,
  cut in half lengthwise
2 medium (2 cups) yams,
  *or* sweet potatoes, cut
  crosswise into ½"-thick
  slices
1 cup mixed chopped dried
  fruit
1 tsp. chopped garlic
½ tsp. salt

¼ tsp. pepper
¾ cup orange juice
¼ cup chopped fresh
  parsley

1. Melt butter in 12-inch
skillet. Add turkey thighs,
skin-side down. Brown over
medium-high heat, turning
once. Drain off drippings.
2. Meanwhile, place yams
in slow cooker. Top with
turkey thighs.
3. Sprinkle with dried
fruit, garlic, salt, and pepper.
4. Gently pour orange juice
into cooker, being careful not
to disturb fruit and seasonings.
5. Cover. Cook on Low 8-10
hours or on High 3-4 hours,
just until turkey is tender.
6. Slice; then sprinkle with
parsley before serving.

187

# Turkey Fajitas

**Carol Ambrose**
McMinnville, OR

*Makes 8 servings*

**Prep. Time: 10-15 minutes**
**Cooking Time: 3-4 hours**
**Ideal slow cooker size: 2½-qt.**

2½ lbs. turkey tenderloins
1¼-oz. envelope taco
   seasoning mix
1 celery rib, chopped
1 onion, chopped
14½-oz. can mild diced
   tomatoes and green
   chilies, undrained
1 cup (4 oz.) shredded
   cheddar cheese
8 (7½") flour tortillas

Toppings:
   lettuce
   sour cream
   sliced olives
   chopped tomatoes

1. Cut turkey into 2½"-long
strips. Place in zip-top plastic
bag.
2. Add taco seasoning to bag.
Seal and shake to coat meat.
3. Empty seasoned turkey
into slow cooker. Add celery,
onion, and tomatoes. Stir
together gently.
4. Cover. Cook on High 3-4
hours, or just until turkey is
cooked through and tender.
5. Stir in cheese.
6. Warm tortillas according
to package directions. Spoon
turkey mixture evenly into
center of each tortilla, and
roll up.
7. Serve with Toppings.

**Tip:**
   *Put this recipe in your
cooker. Then take your kids
or grandkids out to cut down
the tree or to do their holiday
shopping. When you get back,
your meal is ready!*

# Turkey Sloppy Joes

**Marla Folkerts**
Holland, OH

*Makes 6 servings*

**Prep. Time: 20 minutes**
**Cooking Time: 4½-6 hours**
**Ideal slow cooker size: 4-qt.**

1 red onion, chopped
1 sweet pepper, chopped
1½ lbs. boneless turkey,
   finely chopped
1 cup chili sauce, *or*
   ketchup
¼ tsp. salt
1 garlic clove, minced
1 tsp. Dijon-style mustard
⅛ tsp. pepper

1. Place onion, sweet
pepper, and turkey in slow
cooker.
2. Add chili sauce, salt,
garlic, mustard, and pepper to
cooker. Mix together well.
3. Cover. Cook on Low
4½-6 hours, or until turkey
and vegetables are tender.

*Serving suggestion: Serve
on thickly sliced **homemade
bread** or fill up 6 **sandwich
rolls**.*

# Turkey Cacciatore

**Dorothy VanDeest**
Memphis, TN

*Makes 6 servings*

**Prep. Time: 20 minutes**
**Cooking Time: 4 hours**
**Ideal slow cooker size: 4-qt.**

2½ cups cut-up *cooked*
   turkey
1 tsp. salt
dash of pepper
1 Tbsp. dried onion flakes
1 green bell pepper, seeded
   and finely chopped
1 clove garlic, finely
   chopped
15-oz. can whole tomatoes,
   mashed
4-oz. can sliced
   mushrooms, drained
2 tsp. tomato paste
1 bay leaf
¼ tsp. dried thyme
2 Tbsp. finely chopped
   pimento

1. Combine all ingredients
well in slow cooker.
2. Cover. Cook on Low 4
hours.

*Serving suggestion: Serve
over **rice** or **pasta**. Or drain off
most liquid and serve in **taco
shells**.*

# Turkey Lasagna

**Rhoda Atzeff**
Lancaster, PA

*Makes 8-10 servings*

*Prep. Time: 20-30 minutes*
*Cooking Time: 5 hours*
*Ideal slow cooker size: 5-qt.*

1 lb. lean ground turkey
1 onion, chopped
⅛ tsp. garlic powder
2 15-oz. cans tomato sauce
6-oz. can tomato paste
½-1 tsp. salt
1 tsp. dried oregano, *or*
    ½ tsp. dried oregano and
    ½ tsp. dried basil
12 oz. fat-free cottage
    cheese
½ cup grated Parmesan
    cheese
12 oz. shredded non-fat
    mozzarella cheese
12 oz. lasagna noodles,
    uncooked, *divided*

1. Brown ground turkey and onions in skillet. Drain off any drippings.

2. Stir garlic powder, tomato sauce, tomato paste, salt, and herbs into browned turkey in skillet.

3. In a good-sized mixing bowl, blend together cottage cheese, Parmesan cheese, and mozzarella cheese.

4. Spoon ⅓ of meat sauce into slow cooker.

5. Add ⅓ of uncooked lasagna noodles, breaking them to fit.

6. Top with ⅓ of cheese mixture. You may have to use a knife to spread it.

7. Repeat layers two more times.

8. Cover. Cook on Low 5 hours.

9. Allow to stand 10 minutes before serving.

**Note:**

*I tried this on my brothers. It is a delicious dish, but I thought their raves were maybe a bit overdone. But it was a good feeling to know it pleased them. I overheard my one brother calling another brother in Virginia and telling him about it!*

# Savory Turkey Meatballs in Italian Sauce

**Marla Folkerts**
Holland, OH

*Makes 8 servings*

*Prep. Time: 30 minutes*
*Cooking Time: 3-4 hours*
*Ideal slow cooker size: 4-qt.*

28-oz. can crushed
    tomatoes
1 Tbsp. red wine vinegar
1 medium onion, finely
    chopped
2 garlic cloves, minced
¼ tsp. Italian herb
    seasoning
1 tsp. dried basil
1 lb. ground turkey
⅛ tsp. garlic powder
⅛ tsp. black pepper
⅓ cup dried parsley
2 egg whites
¼ tsp. dried minced onion
½ cup dry quick oats
¼ cup grated Parmesan
    cheese
¼ cup flour
oil

1. Combine tomatoes, vinegar, onions, garlic, Italian seasoning, and basil in slow cooker. Turn to Low.

2. Combine remaining ingredients, except flour and oil, in large bowl. Form into 1" balls.

3. Dredge each ball in flour.

4. Brown balls in batches in oil in skillet over medium heat. As you finish a batch, transfer it to slow cooker. Stir into sauce in cooker.

5. When all balls are browned and in cooker, cover. Cook on Low 3-4 hours, or until Meatballs are cooked through.

*Serving suggestion: Serve over pasta or rice.*

**Tip:**
The meatballs and sauce freeze well.

# Tricia's Cranberry Turkey Meatballs

**Shirley Unternahrer**
Wayland, IA

*Makes 12 servings*

**Prep. Time: 25 minutes**
**Cooking Time: 3½ hours**
**Ideal slow cooker size: 3-qt.**

16-oz. can jelled cranberry
　sauce
½ cup ketchup, *or* barbecue
　sauce
1 egg
1 lb. ground turkey
half a small onion,
　chopped
1 tsp. salt
¼ tsp. black pepper
1-2 tsp. grated orange peel,
　*optional*
oil

1. Combine cranberry sauce and ketchup in slow cooker.
2. Cover. Cook on High until cranberry sauce is melted and well blended with ketchup, about 30 minutes.
3. Combine remaining ingredients, except oil, in bowl. Shape into 24 balls.
4. Cook in batches over medium heat in skillet, in oil if you need it, for 8-10 minutes, or just until browned. As you finish a batch, add it to sauce in slow cooker.
5. Cover. Cook on Low 3 hours.

*Serving suggestion: Serve with **rice** and a **steamed vegetable**.*

# Turkey Meatballs and Gravy

**Betty Sue Good**
Broadway, VA

*Makes 8 servings*

**Prep. Time: 30 minutes**
**Cooking Time: 2-4 hours**
**Ideal slow cooker size: 4-qt.**

2 eggs, beaten
¾ cup bread crumbs
½ cup finely chopped
　onions
½ cup finely chopped
　celery
2 Tbsp. chopped fresh
　parsley
¼ tsp. pepper
⅛ tsp. garlic powder
1 tsp. salt
2 lbs. ground raw turkey
1½ Tbsp. cooking oil
10¾-oz. can cream of
　mushroom soup
1 cup water
⅞-oz. pkg. turkey gravy
　mix
½ tsp. dried thyme
2 bay leaves

1. Combine eggs, bread crumbs, onions, celery, parsley, pepper, garlic powder, salt, and meat in a large bowl. Shape into 1½" balls.
2. Brown meat balls in oil in skillet. Don't crowd skillet, or Meatballs will steam and not brown. As you finish a batch, drain off drippings. Place meatballs into slow cooker.
3. Combine soup, water, dry gravy mix, thyme, and bay leaves in bowl. Pour over browned Meatballs in cooker.
4. Cover. Cook on Low 4 hours or on High 2 hours.
5. Discard bay leaves before serving.

*Serving suggestion: Serve over **mashed potatoes** or **buttered noodles**.*

*I'm beginning to notice more and more slow cookers at our family potluck gatherings. Old favorite recipes are being converted for slow-cooker use, and new ones are being introduced. Take a copy of the recipe you prepared, plus some blank cards, just in case you want to swap recipes with others.*
　　　　　　　　　　Shirley Unternahrer, Wayland, IA

# Meat and Bean Main Dishes

## "Famous" Baked Beans

**Katrine Rose**
Woodbridge, VA

*Makes 10 servings*

*Prep. Time: 20 minutes*
*Cooking Time: 3-6 hours*
*Ideal slow cooker size: 4-qt.*

1 lb. ground beef
¼ cup minced onions
1 cup ketchup
4 15-oz. cans pork and beans
1 cup brown sugar
2 Tbsp. liquid smoke
1 Tbsp. Worcestershire sauce

1. Brown beef and onions in skillet. Stir frequently to break up clumps of meat. Continue cooking until no pink remains in meat. Drain off drippings.

2. Spoon meat and onions into slow cooker.

3. Add remaining ingredients and stir well.

4. Cover. Cook on High 3 hours or on Low 5-6 hours.

Note:
*There are many worthy baked bean recipes, but these are both easy and absolutely delicious. The secret to this recipe is the liquid smoke. I get many requests for this recipe, and some friends have added the word "famous" to its name.*

## Barbecued Beans

**Esther J. Yoder**
Hartville, OH

*Makes 10 servings*

*Prep. Time: 20 minutes*
*Cooking Time: 2-3 hours*
*Ideal slow cooker size: 3-qt.*

1 lb. ground beef
½ cup chopped onions
½ tsp. salt
¼ tsp. pepper

28-oz. can pork and beans
   (your favorite variety)
½ cup ketchup
1 Tbsp. Worcestershire sauce
1 Tbsp. vinegar
¼ tsp. Tabasco sauce

1. Brown beef and onions together in skillet. Stir frequently to break up clumps of meat. Continue cooking until meat is no longer pink. Drain off drippings.

2. Spoon meat and onions into cooker.

3. Add all other ingredients to cooker.

4. Cover. Cook on High 2-3 hours, stirring once or twice, if you're home and able to do so.

Tip:
   These beans' flavor gets better on the second and third days.

# Cowboy Beans

**Reba Rhodes**
Bridgewater, VA

*Makes 8 servings*

*Prep. Time: 20-25 minutes*
*Cooking Time: 1-2 hours*
*Ideal slow cooker size: 3-qt.*

1 lb. ground beef
1 large onion, finely chopped
1 small green bell pepper, finely chopped
28-oz. can pork and beans
1½ cups ketchup
1 tsp. vinegar
3 Tbsp. brown sugar
2 tsp. prepared mustard
2 tsp. salt
1 tsp. pepper

1. Brown ground beef, onion, and bell pepper in skillet. Stir often to break up clumps of meat. Continue cooking until meat is no longer pink. Drain off drippings.
2. Spoon meat and vegetables into slow cooker.
3. Add all other ingredients to slow cooker. Mix well.
4. Cover. Cook on Low 1-2 hours.

Note:
*This travels well to a potluck or holiday buffet.*

# Hamburger Beans

**Joanne Kennedy**
Plattsburgh, NY

*Makes 6 servings*

*Prep. Time: 20-25 minutes*
*Cooking Time: 2-3 hours*
*Ideal slow cooker size: 3-qt.*

1 lb. ground beef
1 onion, chopped
2 15-oz. cans pork and beans
15-oz. can butter beans, drained
15-oz. can kidney beans, drained
½ tsp. garlic powder
1 cup ketchup
¾ cup molasses
½ cup brown sugar

1. Brown ground beef and onion in skillet. Stir frequently to break up clumps. Continue cooking until meat is no longer pink. Drain off drippings.
2. Spoon beef and onion into slow cooker.
3. Add remaining ingredients. Mix well.
4. Cover. Cook on Low 2-3 hours.

# Pasta Bean Pot

**Donna Conto**
Saylorsburg, PA

*Makes 8 servings*

*Prep. Time: 10-15 minutes*
*Cooking Time: 4-5 hours*
*Ideal slow cooker size: 4-qt.*

1 Tbsp. olive oil
1 medium onion, chopped
1 garlic clove, minced
½ tsp. vinegar
8 oz. uncooked elbow macaroni
28-oz. can stewed, or diced, tomatoes
15-oz. can cannellini beans, undrained
15-oz. can kidney beans, undrained
12-oz. can chicken broth
1 tsp. dried oregano
1 tsp. parsley
dash red pepper

1. Put all ingredients in slow cooker. Mix well.
2. Cover. Cook on Low 4-5 hours, or until macaroni are tender but not mushy.

Note:
*I like to have this soup cooking as my granddaughter and I bake cookies. That frees us from worrying about making dinner.*

*Keep a bowl of ornaments by the door throughout the season and let guests help themselves when they leave.*
*Carol L. Miller, Lockport, NY*

# One-Pot Dinner

**Vicki Dinkel**
Sharon Springs, KS

*Makes 4 servings*

*Prep. Time: 30 minutes*
*Cooking Time: 3-9 hours*
*Ideal slow cooker size: 4- to 5-qt.*

½-1 lb. ground beef,
   according to your
   preference
½ lb. bacon, cut in pieces
1 cup chopped onions
2 31-oz. cans pork and
   beans
16-oz. can kidney beans,
   drained
1 cup ketchup
16-oz. can butter beans,
   drained
¼ cup brown sugar
1 Tbsp. liquid smoke
3 Tbsp. white vinegar
1 tsp. salt
dash of pepper

1. Brown ground beef in
skillet. Stir frequently to
break up clumps of meat.
Continue cooking until meat
is no longer pink. Drain off
drippings.
2. Place beef in slow
cooker.
3. Brown bacon and
onions in same skillet. Stir
frequently to brown evenly.
Drain off drippings.
4. Add bacon and onions to
slow cooker.
5. Stir remaining ingredients into cooker.
6. Cover. Cook on Low 5-9
hours or on High 3 hours.

# Calico Beans

**Mary Rogers**
Waseca, MN

*Makes 12-15 servings*

*Prep. Time: 30-40 minutes*
*Cooking Time: 3-4 hours*
*Ideal slow cooker size: 4- to 5-qt.*

1 lb. bacon
1 lb. ground beef
½ cup chopped onions
½ cup chopped celery
½ cup ketchup
1 Tbsp. prepared mustard
16-oz. can kidney beans,
   undrained
16-oz. can great northern
   beans, undrained
½ cup brown sugar
1 Tbsp. vinegar
16-oz. can butter beans,
   undrained
28-oz. can Bush's Baked
   Beans

1. Cut bacon in small
squares. Brown in skillet,
stirring often to brown evenly.
Drain off drippings.
2. Spoon bacon into slow
cooker.
3. Brown ground beef in
skillet, stirring frequently
to break up clumps of meat.
Continue cooking until meat
is no longer pink.
4. Using a slotted spoon,
lift beef from drippings and
place in slow cooker. Reserve
drippings.
5. Sauté onions and celery
in drippings until soft. Place
vegetables in cooker.
6. Combine all ingredients in
slow cooker. Stir together well.

7. Cover. Simmer on Low
3-4 hours.

Note:
*This is a favorite dish that
we serve at neighborhood and
family gatherings any time of
the year. Our children especially
enjoy it.*

# Trio Bean Casserole

**Stacy Schmucker Stoltzfus**
Enola, PA

*Makes 4-6 servings*

*Prep. Time: 15-20 minutes*
*Cooking Time: 2-4 hours*
*Ideal slow cooker size: 3½-qt.*

16-oz. can kidney beans,
   drained
16-oz. can green beans,
   drained
16-oz. can pork and beans
   with tomato sauce
½ cup chopped onions
½ cup brown sugar
½ cup ketchup
1 Tbsp. vinegar
1 tsp. prepared mustard
1 lb. bacon, fried and
   crumbled, *or* 1 lb.
   cooked ham, cubed
1 Tbsp. barbecue sauce

1. Combine all ingredients
in slow cooker. Stir well.
2. Cover. Cook on High 2
hours or on Low 3-4 hours.

# Galloping Beans

**Sharon Timpe**
Mequon, WI

*Makes 10-12 servings*

*Prep. Time: 15-20 minutes*
*Cooking Time: 3-7 hours*
*Ideal slow cooker size: 3½-qt.*

6 slices bacon, cut in pieces
½ cup onions, chopped
1 garlic clove, minced
16-oz. can baked beans
16-oz. can kidney beans, drained
15-oz. can butter, *or* pinto, beans, drained
2 Tbsp. dill pickle relish, *or* chopped dill pickles
⅓ cup chili sauce, *or* ketchup
2 tsp. Worcestershire sauce
½ cup brown sugar
⅛ tsp. hot pepper sauce, *optional*

1. Lightly brown bacon, onions, and garlic in skillet. Stir frequently. Drain off drippings.
2. Lift bacon and vegetables into slow cooker with slotted spoon.
3. Add all other ingredients to slow cooker. Mix well.
4. Cover. Cook on Low 5-7 hours or on High 3-4 hours.

# Deb's Baked Beans

**Deborah Swartz**
Grottoes, VA

*Makes 4-6 servings*

*Prep. Time: 20 minutes*
*Cooking Time: 1½-2 hours*
*Ideal slow cooker size: 3-qt.*

4 slices bacon
2 Tbsp. reserved drippings
½ cup chopped onions
2 15-oz. cans pork and beans
½ tsp. salt, *optional*
2 Tbsp. brown sugar
1 Tbsp. Worcestershire sauce
1 tsp. prepared mustard

1. Fry bacon in skillet until crisp. Drain off all but 2 Tbsp. drippings.
2. Remove bacon from skillet and crumble into cooker.
3. Cook onions in reserved drippings until just tender.
4. Add onions to slow cooker.
5. Mix in all additional ingredients.
6. Cover. Cook on High 1½-2 hours.

# Lotsa-Beans Pot

**Dorothy Van Deest**
Memphis, TN

*Makes 15-20 servings*

*Prep. Time: 30 minutes*
*Cooking Time: 3-4 hours*
*Ideal slow cooker size: 5-qt.*

8 bacon strips, diced
2 onions, thinly sliced
1 cup packed brown sugar
½ cup cider vinegar
1 tsp. salt
1 tsp. ground mustard
½ tsp. garlic powder
28-oz. can baked beans
16-oz. can kidney beans, rinsed and drained
15½-oz. can pinto beans, rinsed and drained
15-oz. can lima beans, rinsed and drained
15½-oz. can black-eyed peas, rinsed and rained
1 cup ketchup
2 Tbsp. barbecue sauce
1 Tbsp. liquid smoke

1. Cook bacon in skillet until crisp. Remove bacon to paper towels.
2. Drain off drippings, reserving 2 Tbsp.
3. Sauté onions in drippings until tender.
4. Add brown sugar, vinegar, salt, mustard, and garlic powder to skillet. Bring to boil.
5. Combine beans and peas in slow cooker.
6. Add onion mixture, ketchup, barbecue sauce, liquid smoke, and bacon. Mix well.

*Set your table early. Have ready any soup, salad or dessert plates. Clear well after each entrée. Do dishes the next day—enjoy your guests.*
*Karen Ceneviva, Seymour, CT*

7. Cover. Cook on High 3-4 hours.

**Note:**

*This hearty bean concoction tastes especially yummy when the gang comes in from an evening of sledding or skating or Christmas carolling. Keep the beans warm to hot and serve them from the pot.*

# Auntie Ginny's Baked Beans

**Becky Harder**
Monument, CO

*Makes 8 servings*

*Prep. Time: 15 minutes*
*Cooking Time: 4-5 hours*
*Ideal slow cooker size: 3-qt.*

**4 slices bacon, diced**
**28-oz. can pork and beans**
**1 tsp. dark molasses**
**1 Tbsp. brown sugar**
**1 cup dates, cut up**
**1 medium onion, chopped**

1. Partially fry bacon in skillet. Drain off drippings.
2. Place bacon in slow cooker.
3. Add all other ingredients to slow cooker.
4. Cover. Cook on Low 4-5 hours.

**Tip:**

There are many varieties of canned baked beans available. Choose a flavor that fits your guests—from vegetarian

(you'll want to leave out the bacon if this is important to your diners) to country-style to onion.

**Note:**

*Written down at the bottom of my copy of this recipe is this note: "Harder picnic—1974." Notations like that help us remember special family get-togethers or reunions.*

*This recipe was shared almost 20 years ago as we gathered cousins and aunts together in our hometown. Today no one from our family lives in the hometown, and we cousins are scattered over six states, but one way to enjoy fond memories is to record dates or events on recipes we share with each other.*

# Creole Black Beans

**Joyce Kaut**
Rochester, NY

*Makes 6-8 servings*

*Prep. Time: 30 minutes*
*Cooking Time: 4-8 hours*
*Ideal slow cooker size: 4-qt.*

**1½-2 lbs. smoked sausage, sliced in ½"-thick pieces**
**3 15-oz. cans black beans, drained**
**1½ cups chopped onions**
**1½ cups chopped green bell peppers**
**1½ cups chopped celery**
**4 garlic cloves, minced**
**2 tsp. dried thyme**
**1½ tsp. dried oregano**
**1½ tsp. pepper**
**1 chicken bouillon cube**
**3 bay leaves**
**8-oz. can tomato sauce**
**1 cup water**

1. Brown sausage in non-stick skillet.
2. Place in slow cooker.
3. Stir in all other ingredients and mix well.
4. Cover. Cook on Low 8 hours or on High 4 hours.
5. Remove bay leaves before serving.

*Serving suggestion: Serve over **rice**, with a **salad** and **fresh fruit** for dessert.*

**Variation:**

You may substitute a 14½-oz. can of stewed tomatoes for the tomato sauce.

# Pizza Beans

**Kelly Evenson**
Pittsboro, NC

*Makes 6 servings*

*Prep. Time: 30 minutes*
*Cooking Time: 7-9 hours*
*Ideal slow cooker size: 4-qt.*

16-oz. can pinto beans,
    drained
16-oz. can kidney beans,
    drained
2¼-oz. can ripe olives,
    sliced, drained
28-oz. can stewed, *or*
    whole, tomatoes
¾ lb. bulk Italian sausage
1 Tbsp. oil
1 green bell pepper,
    chopped
1 medium onion, chopped
1 garlic clove, minced
1 tsp. salt
1 tsp. dried oregano
1 tsp. dried basil
Parmesan cheese, grated

1. Combine beans, olives,
and tomatoes in slow cooker.
2. Brown sausage in oil
in skillet. Stir frequently,
breaking up clumps of meat.
Continue cooking until meat
is no longer pink. Drain,
reserving drippings.
3. Transfer sausage to slow
cooker.
4. Sauté green pepper in
drippings 1 minute, stirring
constantly. Add onions and
continue stirring until onions
start to become translucent.
Add garlic and cook 1 more
minute. Transfer vegetables
to slow cooker.

5. Stir in seasonings.
6. Cover. Cook on Low 7-9
hours.
7. To serve, sprinkle with
Parmesan cheese.

**Variation:**

For a thicker dish, 20
minutes before serving
remove ¼ cup liquid from
cooker. Place in small bowl.
Add 1 Tbsp. cornstarch to it.
Stir until dissolved. Return
to soup. Cook on High 15
minutes, or until thickened.

# Pioneer Beans

**Kay Magruder**
Seminole, OK

*Makes 4-6 servings*

*Prep. Time: 10 minutes*
*Soaking Time: 8 hours, or*
    *overnight*
*Cooking Time: 8-9 hours*
*Ideal slow cooker size: 4-qt.*

1 lb. dry lima beans
1 bunch green onions,
    chopped
3 beef bouillon cubes
6 cups water
1 lb. smoked sausage, cut
    in ½"-thick slices
½ tsp. garlic powder
¾ tsp. Tabasco sauce

1. Place dry lima beans
in slow cooker. Cover with
water. Let soak 8 hours, or
overnight.
2. Drain off water.
3. Add all other ingredients

to beans in slow cooker. Mix
together well.
4. Cover. Cook on Low 8-9
hours, or until beans are soft
but not mushy.

# Dawn's Special Beans

**Dawn Day**
Westminster, CA

*Makes 8-10 servings*

*Prep. Time: 10-15 minutes*
*Cooking Time: 6 hours*
*Ideal slow cooker size: 4-qt.*

16-oz. can kidney beans
16-oz. can small white
    beans
16-oz. can butter beans
16-oz. can small red beans
1 cup chopped onions
2 tsp. dry mustard
½ tsp. hickory-smoke
    flavoring
½ cup dark brown sugar
½ cup honey
1 cup barbecue sauce
2 Tbsp. apple cider vinegar

1. Combine all ingredients
in slow cooker.
2. Cover. Cook on Low 6
hours.

**Tip:**

If you like soupy beans,
do not drain the beans before
adding them to the cooker. If
you prefer a drier outcome,
drain all beans before pouring into cooker.

## Partytime Beans

**Beatrice Martin**
Goshen, IN

*Makes 14-16 servings*

*Prep. Time: 15-20 minutes*
*Cooking Time: 5-7 hours*
*Ideal slow cooker size: 4-qt.*

1½ cups ketchup
1 onion, chopped
1 green bell pepper,
    chopped
1 sweet red pepper,
    chopped
½ cup water
½ cup packed brown sugar
2 bay leaves
2-3 tsp. cider vinegar
1 tsp. ground mustard
⅛ tsp. pepper
16-oz. can kidney beans,
    rinsed and drained
15½-oz. can great northern
    beans, rinsed and
    drained
15-oz. can lima beans,
    rinsed and drained
15-oz. can black beans,
    rinsed and drained
15½-oz. can black-eyed
    peas, rinsed and drained

1. Combine first 10 ingredients in slow cooker. Mix well.
2. Add remaining ingredients. Mix well.
3. Cover. Cook on Low 5-7 hours, or until onion and peppers are tender.
4. Remove bay leaves before serving.

## Red Beans and Pasta

**Naomi E. Fast**, Hesston, KS

*Makes 6-8 servings*

*Prep. Time: 10-15 minutes • Cooking Time: 3½-4½ hours*
*Ideal slow cooker size: 5-qt.*

3 15-oz. cans chicken, *or* vegetable, broth
½ tsp. ground cumin
1 Tbsp. chili powder
1 garlic clove, minced
8 oz. uncooked spiral pasta
half a large green bell pepper, diced
half a large red bell pepper, diced
1 medium onion, diced
15-oz. can red beans, rinsed and drained
chopped fresh parsley
chopped fresh cilantro

1. Combine broth, cumin, chili powder, and garlic in slow cooker.
2. Cover. Cook on High until mixture comes to boil.
3. Add pasta, vegetables, and beans. Stir together well.
4. Cover. Cook on Low 3-4 hours.
5. Add parsley and cilantro before serving.

## Slow-Cooker Kidney Beans

**Jeanette Oberholtzer**
Manheim, PA

*Makes 12 servings*

*Prep. Time: 10-15 minutes*
*Cooking Time: 6-7 hours*
*Ideal slow cooker size: 5-qt.*

2 30-oz. cans kidney beans, rinsed and drained
28-oz. can diced tomatoes
2 medium-sized red bell peppers, chopped
1 cup ketchup
½ cup brown sugar
¼ cup honey
¼ cup molasses
1 Tbsp. Worcestershire sauce
1 tsp. dry mustard
2 medium red apples, cored, unpeeled, cut into pieces

1. Combine all ingredients, except apples, in slow cooker.
2. Cover. Cook on Low 4-5 hours.
3. Stir in apples.
4. Cover. Cook 2 more hours on Low.

Note:
Tasty, meatless eating!

# Zesty Calico Beans

**Gloria Julien**
Gladstone, MI

*Makes 10 servings*

*Prep. Time: 20-30 minutes*
*Cooking Time: 2-3 hours*
*Ideal slow cooker size: 5-qt.*

1 lb. hamburger
½ cup chopped onion
½ lb. bacon
1 can kidney beans, drained
1 can great northern white beans, drained
1 cup brown sugar
1 cup ketchup
2 large cans baked beans, undrained
4 drops Tabasco sauce
2 tsp. dry mustard
1 tsp. chili powder

1. Brown hamburger and onion together in skillet. Stir frequently to break up clumps of meat. When meat is no longer pink, drain off drippings.
2. Spoon beef and onions into slow cooker.
3. Brown bacon in same skillet until crispy. Remove from drippings and drain. Place bacon in slow cooker.
4. Stir remaining ingredients into slow cooker until well mixed.
5. Cover. Cook on Low 2-3 hours.

# Edna's Baked Beans

**Sharon Easter**
Yuba City, CA

*Makes 6 servings*

*Prep. Time: 5-10 minutes*
*Cooking Time: 4 hours*
*Ideal slow cooker size: 3½-qt.*

1 cup applesauce (not chunky)
¼ cup brown sugar
¼ cup ketchup
½ tsp. prepared mustard (or use small pkg. hot mustard from Chinese take-out)
21-oz. can pork & beans, *or* 2 15-oz. cans
6 hot dogs, sliced ¼"-thick, *optional*

1. Stir all ingredients together in slow cooker.
2. Cover. Cook on Low 4 hours.

**Variation:**
Substitute ½ lb. thinly sliced smoked sausage for hot dogs.

**Note from Tester:**
This recipe was as good, if not better, the second day. Next time I'll double the recipe so we're sure to have leftovers!

# Vegetarian Baked Beans

**Janice Muller**
Derwood, MD

*Makes 4 servings*

*Prep. Time: 10-15 minutes*
*Cooking Time: 4-5 hours*
*Ideal slow cooker size: 4-qt.*

1 cup picante sauce
¼ cup molasses
2 Tbsp. packed brown sugar
2 tsp. prepared mustard
1 tsp. onion powder
16-oz. can black beans, rinsed and drained
16-oz. can white beans, rinsed and drained
1 Tbsp. lime juice

1. Mix all ingredients together in slow cooker.
2. Cover. Cook on Low 4-5 hours.

*Make more than enough food so you can send a small amount home with your guests. This is especially nice for older friends who find it hard to cook, but any guest will enjoy eating good leftovers.*

*Leona M. Slabaugh, Apple Creek, OH*

# Other Main Dish Favorites

## Lamb Stew

**Dottie Schmidt**
Kansas City, MO

*Makes 6 servings*

*Prep Time: 35 minutes*
*Cooking Time: 8-10 hours*
*Ideal slow cooker size: 5-qt.*

2 lbs. lamb, cubed
½ tsp. sugar
2 Tbsp. oil
2 tsp. salt
¼ tsp. pepper
¼ cup flour
2 cups water
¾ cup red wine
¼ tsp. powdered garlic
2 tsp. Worcestershire sauce
6-8 carrots, sliced
4 small onions, quartered
4 ribs celery, sliced
3 medium potatoes, diced

1. Sprinkle lamb with sugar. Brown in oil in skillet.
2. Remove lamb and place in cooker, reserving drippings. Stir salt, pepper, and flour into drippings until smooth. Stir in water and wine until smooth, stirring until broth simmers and thickens.
3. Pour into cooker. Add remaining ingredients and stir until well mixed.
4. Cover. Cook on Low 8-10 hours.

*Serving suggestion: We like this served with **crusty bread**.*

## Lamb Chops

**Shirley Sears**
Tiskilwa, IL

*Makes 4-6 servings*

*Prep. Time: 10 minutes*
*Cooking Time: 4-6 hours*
*Ideal slow cooker size: 5-qt.*

1 medium onion, sliced
1 tsp. dried oregano
½ tsp. dried thyme
½ tsp. garlic powder
¼ tsp. salt
⅛ tsp. pepper
8 loin lamb chops (1¾-2 lbs.)
2 garlic cloves, minced
¼ cup water

1. Place onion in slow cooker.
2. In a small bowl, combine oregano, thyme, garlic powder, salt, and pepper. Rub over lamb chops. Place chops in slow cooker.
3. Top chops with garlic.
4. Pour water down along side of cooker, so as not to disturb rub and garlic on chops.
5. Cover. Cook on Low 4-6 hours, or until Chops are tender but not dry.

# Venison Roast

**Colleen Heatwole**
Burton, MI

*Makes 6-8 servings*

**Prep. Time: 15 minutes**
**Marinating Time: at least 8 hours**
**Cooking Time: 8-12 hours**
**Ideal slow cooker size: 5-qt.**

3-4-lb. venison roast
¼ cup vinegar
2 garlic cloves, minced
2 Tbsp. salt
½ cup chopped onions
15-oz. can tomato sauce
1 Tbsp. ground mustard
1 pkg. brown gravy mix
½ tsp. salt
¼ cup water

1. Place venison in deep bowl. Combine vinegar, garlic, and salt in a small bowl. Pour over venison.
2. Add enough cold water to cover venison. Cover. Marinate for at least 8 hours in refrigerator.
3. Rinse and drain venison. Place in slow cooker.
4. Combine remaining ingredients in a bowl. Pour over venison.
5. Cover. Cook on Low 8-12 hours, or until fork-tender but not dry.

*Serving suggestion: Serve this with a green salad, potatoes, and rolls to make complete meal.*

Notes:
1. The sauce on this Roast works well for any meat.
2. This is an easy meal to have for a Saturday dinner with guests or extended family. There is usually a lot of sauce, so make plenty of potatoes, noodles, or rice.

# Venison in Sauce

**Anona M. Teel**
Bangor, PA

*Makes 12 sandwiches*

**Prep. Time: 20 minutes**
**Marinating Time: 8 hours**
**Cooking Time: 8-10 hours**
**Ideal slow cooker size: 5-qt.**

3-4-lb. venison roast
½ cup vinegar
2 garlic cloves, minced
2 Tbsp. salt
cold water
oil
large onion, sliced
half a green bell pepper, sliced
2 ribs celery, sliced
1-2 garlic cloves, minced
1½-2 tsp. salt
¼ tsp. pepper
½ tsp. dried oregano
¼ cup ketchup
1 cup tomato juice

1. Place venison in a large bowl. Combine vinegar, garlic cloves, and 2 Tbsp. salt, and pour over venison. Add water until meat is covered. Marinate 8 hours.
2. Cut meat into pieces. Brown in oil in skillet. Place in slow cooker.
3. Mix remaining ingredi-ents together; then pour into cooker. Stir together well.
4. Cover. Cook on Low 8-10 hours.
5. Using two forks, pull meat apart and stir it through Sauce.

*Serving suggestion: Serve on sandwich rolls, or over rice or pasta.*

# Beef-Venison Barbecue

**Gladys Longacre**
Susquehanna, PA

*Makes 8 servings*

**Prep. Time: 25 minutes**
**Cooking Time: 1-3 hours**
**Ideal slow cooker size: 4-qt.**

1½ lbs. ground beef
½ lb. ground venison
oil, if needed
1 onion, chopped
½ cup chopped green bell peppers
1 garlic clove, minced
1 tsp. salt
¼ tsp. pepper
½ tsp. dried thyme
1 tsp. dried oregano
1 tsp. dried basil
¼ cup brown sugar
¼ cup vinegar
1 Tbsp. dry mustard
1 cup ketchup
½-1 Tbsp. hickory-smoked barbecue sauce

1. Brown meat in skillet, in oil if needed. Drain off

drippings. Place meat in slow cooker.

2. Add remaining ingredients. Mix well.

3. Cover. Cook on High 1 hour or on Low 2-3 hours.

*Serving suggestion: Serve Barbecue in* **hamburger rolls.**

Tip:

This recipe can be made in larger quantities to freeze and then reheat when needed.

Note:

*This Barbecue recipe was made in large quantities and served at the concession stand for our farm machinery sale in 1987. The servers used ice-cream dippers to scoop the meat into sandwich rolls.*

# Company Seafood Pasta

**Jennifer Yoder Sommers**
Harrisonburg, VA

*Makes 4-6 servings*

*Prep. Time: 15 minutes*
*Cooking Time: 1-2 hours*
*Ideal slow cooker size: 4-qt.*

2 cups sour cream
3 cups shredded Monterey Jack cheese
¼ stick (2 Tbsp.) butter, melted
½ lb. crabmeat, *or* imitation flaked crabmeat
⅛ tsp. pepper
½ lb. bay scallops, lightly cooked
1 lb. medium shrimp, cooked and peeled

1. Combine sour cream, cheese, and butter in slow cooker.

2. Stir in remaining ingredients.

3. Cover. Cook on Low 1-2 hours.

*Serving suggestion: Serve immediately over* **linguine.** *Garnish with* **fresh parsley.**

# Oyster and Potato Filling Yuletide

**Jane Geigley**
Honey Brook, PA

*Makes 3-4 servings*

*Prep. Time: 10 minutes if mashed potatoes are prepared; 50 minutes if you need to make the mashed potatoes*
*Cooking Time: 1½-3 hours*
*Ideal slow cooker size: 2-qt.*

1 small onion, minced
½ cup celery, diced
¼ stick (2 Tbsp.) butter, melted
2 cups very moist mashed potatoes
1 egg, well beaten
1 Tbsp. minced parsley
1-1½ tsp. salt
dash of black pepper
1 qt. stale bread, cubed
1 doz. oysters with liquid
milk, *if needed*

1. Sauté onion and celery in butter in skillet.

2. Blend together mashed potatoes and egg in slow cooker. Pour in sautéed onion and celery. Mix together well.

3. Stir in parsley, salt, pepper, bread cubes, and oysters with their liquid. If mixture is stiff, add several Tbsp. milk.

4. Cover cooker.

5. Cook on High 1½ hours, or on Low 3 hours.

*Invite an elderly person, or someone with limited mobility, to help you bake. If they are unable to stand for long periods they can use bar stools at the kitchen counter or even work at the table from a wheelchair. This offers great fellowship and conversation.* Orpha Herr, Andover, NY

# Curried Shrimp

**Charlotte Shaffer**
East Earl, PA

*Makes 4-5 servings*

**Prep. Time:** *5-10 minutes*
**Cooking Time:** *2 hours*
**Ideal slow cooker size:** *3-qt.*

1 small onion, chopped
2 cups cooked shrimp
1 tsp. curry powder
10¾-oz. can cream of
    mushroom soup
1 cup sour cream

1. Place chopped onion in non-stick skillet over medium heat. Stir until onion wilts.
2. Place in slow cooker along with all other ingredients, except sour cream.
3. Cover. Cook on Low 2 hours.
4. Ten minutes before serving, stir in sour cream.

*Serving suggestion: Serve over **rice** or **puff pastry**.*

**Variation:**
Add another ½ tsp. curry for some added flavor.

# Tuna Noodle Casserole

**Ruth Hofstetter**
Versailles, Missouri

*Makes 8 servings*

**Prep. Time:** *5-10 minutes*
**Cooking Time:** *2-4 hours*
**Ideal slow cooker size:** *3-qt.*

2½ cups dry noodles
1 tsp. salt
½ cup finely chopped
    onion
6- *or* 12-oz. can tuna,
    according to your taste
    preference
10¾-oz. can cream of
    mushroom soup
half a soup can of water
¼ cup almonds, *optional*
½ cup shredded Swiss, *or*
    sharp cheddar, cheese
1 cup frozen peas

1. Combine all ingredients in slow cooker, except peas.
2. Cover. Cook on High 2-3 hours or on Low 4 hours, stirring occasionally.
3. Twenty minutes before end of cooking time, stir in peas and reduce heat to Low if cooking on High.

# Macaroni and Cheese

**Sherry L. Lapp**
Lancaster, PA

*Makes 8 servings*

**Prep. Time:** *20 minutes*
**Cooking Time:** *3 hours*
**Ideal slow cooker size:** *4-qt.*

8-oz. pkg. elbow macaroni,
    cooked al dente
12-oz. can evaporated milk
1 cup whole milk
half a stick (4 Tbsp.) butter,
    melted
2 large eggs, slightly beaten
4 cups grated sharp
    cheddar cheese, *divided*
¼-½ tsp. salt, according to
    your taste preference
⅛ tsp. white pepper
¼ cup grated Parmesan
    cheese

1. In slow cooker, combine lightly cooked macaroni, evaporated milk, whole milk, melted butter, eggs, 3 cups cheddar cheese, salt, and pepper.
2. Top with remaining cheddar and Parmesan cheeses.
3. Cover. Cook on Low 3 hours.

**Variations:**
1. Add 12-oz. can drained tuna in Step 1.

**Janice Muller**
Derwood, MD

2. Add ½ tsp. paprika and 2-4 Tbsp. minced onion in Step 1.

**Kaye Taylor**
Florissant, MO

*I make a list of small jobs and ask each grandchild to do one of them. They love to help get everything on the table.*
*Carol Duree, Salina, KS*

# Slow and Easy Macaroni and Cheese

**Janice Muller**
Derwood, MD

*Makes 6-8 servings*

*Prep. Time: 20 minutes*
*Cooking Time: 4¼ hours*
*Ideal slow cooker size: 3½-qt.*

1 lb. dry macaroni
1 stick (8 Tbsp.) butter
2 eggs
12-oz. can evaporated milk
10¾-oz. can cheddar
   cheese soup
1 cup whole milk
4 cups shredded cheddar
   cheese, *divided*
⅛ tsp. paprika

1. Cook macaroni al dente. Drain off cooking water. Pour hot macaroni into slow cooker.
2. Slice butter into chunks and add to macaroni. Stir until melted.
3. In large mixing bowl, combine eggs, evaporated milk, soup, and whole milk. Add 3 cups cheese. Pour over macaroni and mix well.
4. Cover. Cook on Low 4 hours
5. Sprinkle with remaining cheese. Cook 15 minutes, or until cheese melts.
6. Sprinkle with paprika before serving.

**Variation:**
   Add 12-oz. can drained tuna in Step 3.

# Easy Stuffed Shells

**Rebecca Plank Leichty**
Harrisonburg, VA

*Makes 4-6 servings*

*Prep. Time: 5 minutes*
*Cooking Time: 3-8 hours*
*Ideal slow cooker size: 3½- to 4-qt.*

20-oz. bag frozen stuffed
   shells
15-oz. can marinara, *or*
   spaghetti, sauce
15-oz. can green beans,
   drained

1. Place shells around inside edge of greased slow cooker.
2. Cover with marinara sauce.
3. Pour green beans in center.
4. Cover. Cook on Low 8 hours, or on High 3 hours.

*Serving suggestion: Serve with **garlic toast** and **salad** for a complete meal.*

**Variation:**
   Reverse Steps 2 and 3. Double the amount of marinara sauce and pour over both shells and beans.

# Cheese Souffle Casserole

**Vicki Dinkel**
Sharon Spring, KS

*Makes 4 servings*

*Prep. Time: 15 minutes*
*Cooking Time: 4-6 hours*
*Ideal slow cooker size: 5-qt.*

14 slices fresh bread, crusts
   removed, *divided*
3 cups grated sharp cheese,
   *divided*
¼ stick (2 Tbsp.) butter,
   melted, *divided*
6 eggs
3 cups milk, scalded
2 tsp. Worcestershire sauce
½ tsp. salt
paprika

1. Tear bread into small pieces. Place half in well-greased slow cooker.
2. Add half the grated cheese and half the butter. Repeat layers.
3. In a good-sized bowl, beat together eggs, milk, Worcestershire sauce, and salt.
4. Pour over bread and cheese. Push bread and cheese down into liquid. Sprinkle top with paprika.
5. Cover. Cook on Low 4-6 hours, or until Souffle sets up.

# Arroz Con Queso

### Nadine L. Martinitz
Salina, KS

*Makes 6-8 servings*

*Prep. Time: 15 minutes*
*Cooking Time: 6-9 hours*
*Ideal slow cooker size: 4-qt.*

14½-oz. can whole
    tomatoes, mashed
15-oz. can Mexican-style
    beans, undrained
1½ cups uncooked long-
    grain rice
1 cup grated Monterey Jack
    cheese
1 large onion, finely
    chopped
1 cup cottage cheese
4¼-oz. can chopped green
    chili peppers, drained
1 Tbsp. oil
3 garlic cloves, minced
1 tsp. salt
1 cup grated Monterey Jack
    cheese

1. Combine all ingredients
except final cup of cheese in
well greased slow cooker.
2. Cover. Cook on Low 6-9
hours, or until rice is fully
cooked but dish is not dry.
3. Sprinkle with remaining
cheese before serving.

*Serving suggestion: We eat
this with **salsa** on the side.*

# Minestra Di Ceci

### Jeanette Oberholtzer
Manheim, PA

*Makes 4-6 servings*

*Prep. Time: 25 minutes*
*Soaking Time: 8 hours, or
overnight*
*Cooking Time: 5½-6 hours*
*Ideal slow cooker size: 4-qt.*

1 lb. dry chickpeas
1 sprig fresh rosemary
10 leaves fresh sage
2 Tbsp. salt
1-2 large garlic cloves, minced
olive oil
1 cup uncooked small pasta,
    your choice of shape, *or*
    uncooked penne

1. Wash chickpeas. Place in
slow cooker. Cover with water.
Stir in rosemary, sage, and salt.
Soak 8 hours, or overnight.
2. Drain water. Remove
herbs.
3. Refill slow cooker with
peas and fresh water to 1"
above peas.
4. Cover. Cook on Low 5
hours.
5. Sauté garlic in olive oil
in skillet until clear.
6. Purée half of peas, along
with several cups of broth
from cooker, in blender.
Return purée to slow cooker.
7. Add garlic and oil.
8. Boil pasta in saucepan
until al dente, about 5
minutes. Drain. Add to beans.
9. Cover. Cook on High
30-60 minutes, or until pasta
is tender and heated through,
but not mushy.

**Variation:**
Add ½ tsp. black pepper in
Step 1, if you like.

# Easy Wheatberries

### Elaine Vigoda
Rochester, NY

*Makes 4-6 servings*

*Prep. Time: 10 minutes*
*Soaking Time: 2 hours*
*Cooking Time: 2 hours*
*Ideal slow cooker size: 4-qt.*

1 cup uncooked
    wheatberries
1 cup couscous, *or* small
    pasta like orzo
14½-oz. can broth
½-1 broth can of water
½ cup dried craisins

1. Place wheatberries in
slow cooker. Cover with
water. Soak 2 hours before
cooking.
2. Drain off soaking water.
Add remaining ingredients
to slow cooker. Stir together
well.
3. Cover. Cook on Low
until liquid is absorbed and
berries are soft, about 2 hours.

**Notes:**
1. If craisins are unavail-
able, use raisins.
2. This is a satisfying
vegetarian main dish, if you
use vegetable broth.

# Vegetables

## Easy Flavor-Filled Green Beans

**Paula Showalter**
Weyers Cave, VA

*Makes 10 servings*

*Prep. Time: 5-10 minutes*
*Cooking Time: 2-4 hours*
*Ideal slow cooker size: 3- to 3½-qt.*

2 qts. *or* 4 14½-oz. cans, green beans, drained
⅓ cup chopped onions
4-oz. can mushrooms, drained
2 Tbsp. brown sugar
3 Tbsp. butter
pepper to taste

1. Combine beans, onions, and mushrooms in slow cooker.
2. Sprinkle with brown sugar.
3. Dot with butter.
4. Sprinkle with pepper.
5. Cover. Cook on Low 2-4 hours, or until onions are tender.
6. Stir just before serving.

## Creamy Green Bean Casserole

**Jena Hammond**
Traverse City, MI

*Makes 10 servings*

*Prep. Time: 10 minutes*
*Cooking Time: 3 hours*
*Ideal slow cooker size: 5- to 6-qt.*

3 qts., *or* 6 14½-oz. cans, green beans
2 10¾-oz. cans mushroom soup
1 tsp. black pepper
1 tsp. Lawry's seasoned salt

Topping:
3-oz. can French-fried onions
1 cup Colby cheese, shredded

1. Drain half of liquid off green beans. (Find another use for it or discard.)
2. Mix beans, soup, pepper, and seasoned salt together in the slow cooker.
3. Cover. Cook on Low 3 hours.
4. Twenty minutes before serving, top beans with French-fried onions and shredded cheese.

**Variations:**

1. Instead of canned green beans, use 2 lbs. frozen French-cut green beans, thawed. Extend cooking time to 4-5 hours if you like soft green beans.
**Rhonda Freed**
Croghan, NY

2. Replace one can of mushroom soup with 16 oz. sour cream. Drop Topping above and replace with 2 cups cheddar cheese, shredded, and ½ cup crisp bacon pieces.
**Jennifer A. Crouse**
Mt. Crawford, VA

# Green Bean Casserole

**Jane Meiser**
Harrisonburg, VA

*Makes 4 servings*

*Prep. Time: 10-15 minutes*
*Cooking Time: 3-4 hours*
*Ideal slow cooker size: 3-qt.*

14½-oz. can green beans, drained, *divided*
3½-oz. can French-fried onions, *divided*
1 cup grated cheddar cheese, *divided*
8-oz. can water chestnuts, drained, *divided*
10¾-oz. can cream of chicken soup
¼ cup white wine, *or* water
½ tsp. curry powder
¼ tsp. pepper

1. Alternate layers of half the beans, half the onions, half the cheese, and half the water chestnuts in slow cooker. Repeat.
2. Combine remaining ingredients in a bowl. Pour over vegetables in slow cooker.
3. Cover. Cook on Low 3-4 hours.

# Au Gratin Green Beans

**Donna Lantgen**
Rapid City, SD

*Makes 6 servings*

*Prep. Time: 10 minutes*
*Cooking Time: 3-4 hours*
*Ideal slow cooker size: 2-qt.*

2 14½-oz. cans green beans, drained
¼ cup diced onions
½ cup cubed Velveeta cheese
¼ cup evaporated milk
1 tsp. flour
½ tsp. salt
dash of pepper
sliced almonds, *optional*

1. Combine all ingredients, except almonds, in slow cooker.
2. Cover. Cook on Low 3-4 hours.
3. Garnish with sliced almonds at serving time, if you wish.

# Brookville Hotel Creamed Corn

**Melanie Thrower**
McPherson, KS

*Makes 3-4 servings*

*Prep. Time: 10-15 minutes*
*Cooking Time: 3-8 hours*
*Ideal slow cooker size: 5-qt.*

16-oz. pkg. frozen whole-kernel corn
¾ cup heavy cream
1 tsp. salt
dash of pepper
1 Tbsp. sugar
1 Tbsp. cornstarch

1. Combine all ingredients in slow cooker.
2. Cook on High 3-4 hours or on Low 6-8 hours.

Note:
The corn needs to boil to thicken.

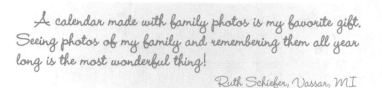

*A calendar made with family photos is my favorite gift. Seeing photos of my family and remembering them all year long is the most wonderful thing!*

*Ruth Schiefer, Vassar, MI*

# Super Creamed Corn

**Ruth Ann Penner**
Hillsboro, KS

**Alix Nancy Botsford**
Seminole, OK

*Makes 8-12 servings*

*Prep. Time: 5-10 minutes*
*Cooking Time: 4 hours*
*Ideal slow cooker size: 3- to 4-qt.*

2-3 lbs. frozen corn
8-oz. pkg. cream cheese, cubed
half a stick (4 Tbsp) butter, melted
2-3 Tbsp. sugar, *or* honey
2-3 Tbsp. water, *optional*

1. Combine all ingredients in slow cooker.
2. Cover. Cook on Low 4 hours

*Serving suggestion: Serve with meat loaf, turkey, or hamburgers.*

**Variation:**
1. Add ¼ lb. mild cheese, shredded to Step 1.
**Marlene Weaver**
Lititz, PA

**Note:**
*A great addition to a holiday that is easy and requires no last-minute preparation. It also frees the stove and oven for other food preparation.*

# Baked Corn

**Velma Stauffer**, Akron, PA

*Makes 8 servings*

*Prep. Time: 5-10 minutes • Cooking Time: 3¾ hours*
*Ideal slow cooker size: 2-qt.*

1 qt. fresh, *or* 2 1-lb. bags frozen, corn
2 eggs, beaten
1 tsp. salt
1 cup milk
⅛ tsp. pepper
2 tsp. oil
3 Tbsp. sugar
3 Tbsp. flour

1. Combine all ingredients well in greased slow cooker.
2. Cover. Cook on High 3 hours and then on Low 45 minutes.

**Tip:**
If you use home-grown sweet corn, you could reduce the amount of sugar.

# Corn and Macaroni

**Kristine Martin**
Newmanstown, PA

*Makes 3-4 servings*

*Prep. Time: 5 minutes*
*Cooking Time: 2½ hours*
*Ideal slow cooker size: 3-qt.*

15½-oz. can whole-kernel corn, drained
15½-oz. can creamed corn
1 cup uncooked macaroni
1 cup mild cheese of your choice, shredded
1 stick (8 Tbsp.) butter, cut in pieces
1 Tbsp. onion powder
1 tsp. salt
¾ cup milk

1. Spray interior of slow cooker with cooking spray.
2. Mix all ingredients together in slow cooker.
3. Cover. Cook on High 2½ hours, or until macaroni is soft but not mushy.

**Variation from Tester:**
Add 1 cup of cubed, fully cooked ham to Step 2 to add flavor and substance.

**Tip:**
*This helps children to eat their vegetables!*

# Dried Corn

**Julia Burkholder**
Robesonia, PA

*Makes 20 servings*

*Prep. Time: 15 minutes*
*Chilling Time: 8 hours, or*
*overnight*
*Cooking Time: 3-4 hours*
*Ideal slow cooker size: 4- to 5-qt.*

22½ oz. dried corn*
half a stick (4 Tbsp.)
   butter, melted
1½ tsp. salt
¼ cup sugar
2 cups half-and-half
¾ cup water
5 cups whole milk

1. Mix all ingredients in
slow cooker.
2. Cover. Refrigerate 8
hours, or overnight.
3. Cook on High 3-4 hours,
or until corn is soft but not
mushy. Stir occasionally.

*Found in canned vegetable
section in 7½-oz. plastic bags.

# Confetti Scalloped Corn

**Rhoda Atzeff**
Harrisburg, PA

*Makes 6-8 servings*

*Prep. Time: 15 minutes*
*Cooking Time: 2-2½ hours*
*Ideal slow cooker size: 3-qt.*

2 eggs, beaten
1 cup sour cream
half a stick (¼ cup) butter,
   melted
1 small onion, finely
   chopped, *or* 2 Tbsp.
   dried chopped onion
11-oz. can Mexicorn,
   drained
14-oz. can cream-style corn
2-3 Tbsp. green jalapeño
   salsa, regular salsa, *or*
   chopped green chilies
8½-oz. pkg. cornbread mix

1. Combine all ingredients
in lightly greased slow
cooker.
2. Cover. Bake on High
2-2½ hours, or until corn is
fully cooked.

# Mexican Corn

**Betty K. Drescher**
Quakertown, PA

*Makes 4-6 servings*

*Prep. Time: 10 minutes*
*Cooking Time: 2¾-4¾ hours*
*Ideal slow cooker size: 2-qt.*

2 10-oz. pkgs. frozen corn,
   partially thawed
4-oz. jar chopped
   pimentos, drained
⅓ cup chopped green bell
   peppers
⅓ cup water
1 tsp. salt
¼ tsp. pepper
½ tsp. paprika
½ tsp. chili powder

1. Combine all ingredients
in slow cooker.
2. Cover. Cook on High 45
minutes, and then on Low
2-4 hours. Stir occasionally
if you're home and able to do
so.

**Variations:**

For more fire, add ⅓ cup
salsa to ingredients, and
increase amounts of pepper,
paprika, and chili powder to
match your taste.

208

# Spicy Corn Casserole

**Beth Nafziger**
Lowville, NY

*Makes 10 servings*

*Prep. Time: 10-15 minutes*
*Cooking Time: 2-3 hours*
*Ideal slow cooker size: 4-qt.*

1 stick (8 Tbsp.) butter
1 large onion, chopped
2 medium green bell
   peppers, chopped
¼ cup flour
2 cups fresh, *or* frozen,
   corn
2 cups cooked long-grain
   rice (I use brown rice)
14½-oz. can diced tomatoes
   with liquid
4 hard-cooked eggs,
   chopped
2½ cups shredded sharp
   cheese
2 Tbsp. Worcestershire
   sauce
2-3 tsp. hot pepper sauce
1 tsp. salt
½ tsp. pepper

1. In large skillet, melt butter. Sauté onion and pepper until tender.
2. Stir in flour and remove from heat.
3. Place sautéed vegetables in slow cooker. Add all remaining ingredients. Mix together gently.
4. Cover. Cook on Low 2-3 hours. If the corn becomes drier than I like while cooking, I add tomato juice.

Note:
*I serve this casserole when I'm looking for a spicy, meatless meal. This recipe is a family favorite that we enjoy over and over and never tire of.*

# Cornbread Casserole

**Arlene Groff**
Lewistown, PA

*Makes 8 servings*

*Prep. Time: 10 minutes*
*Cooking Time: 3¼-4 hours*
*Ideal slow cooker size: 3½- to 4-qt.*

1 qt., *or* 2 14½-oz. cans,
   whole-kernel corn
1 qt., *or* 2 14½-oz. cans,
   creamed corn
1 pkg. corn muffin mix
1 egg
¼ stick (2 Tbsp.) butter
¼ tsp. garlic powder
2 Tbsp. sugar
¼ cup milk
½ tsp. salt
¼ tsp. pepper

1. Combine all ingredients in greased slow cooker.
2. Cover. Cook on Low 3½-4 hours, stirring once halfway through.

Variation:
   You can replace 1 egg and ¼ cup milk with 8 oz. sour cream

**Kendra Dreps**
Liberty, PA

# Cheesy Hominy

**Michelle Showalter**
Bridgewater, VA

*Makes 12-14 servings*

*Prep. Time: 10 minutes*
*Cooking Time: 3½-9 hours*
*Ideal slow cooker size: 5- to 6-qt.*

2 cups dry cracked hominy
6 cups water
2 Tbsp. flour
1½ cups milk
4 cups sharp cheddar
   cheese, grated
1-2 tsp. salt
¼ tsp. pepper
half a stick (4 Tbsp.)
   butter, cut in chunks, *or*
   melted

1. Combine hominy and water in 5-6 qt. slow cooker.
2. Cover. Cook on High 3-4 hours or on Low 6-8 hours.
3. Stir in remaining ingredients.
4. Cover. Cook 30-60 minutes.

Note:
   *Cheesy Hominy is a nice change if you're tired of the same old thing. It's wonderful with ham, slices of bacon, or meatballs. Add a green vegetable and you have a lovely meal. Hominy is available at bulk-food stores.*

# Southwest Posole

**Becky Harder**
Monument, CO

*Makes 6 servings*

*Prep. Time: 5-10 minutes*
*Soaking Time: 4-8 hours*
*Cooking Time: 5 hours*
*Ideal slow cooker size: 4-qt.*

2 12-oz. pkgs. dry posole
1 garlic clove, minced
2 14-oz. cans vegetable, *or*
chicken, broth
2 10-oz. cans Rotel
Mexican diced tomatoes
4¼-oz. can diced green
chilies, drained, *optional*
salt to taste

1. Place dry posole in slow cooker. Cover with water. Soak 4-8 hours.
2. Drain water.
3. Add all remaining ingredients to posole in slow cooker.
4. Cover. Cook on High 3 hours and then on Low 2 hours.

*Serving suggestion: Serve with **enchiladas**, **black beans**, **Spanish rice**, and chopped **lettuce** with **black olives** and **tomatoes**.*

Tip:
*Dry posole can be found in the Mexican food department of the grocery store. If you cannot find dry posole, you can used canned hominy and skip to Step 3.*

# Cheesy Broccoli Casserole

**Dorothy Van Deest**
Memphis, TN

*Makes 3-4 servings*

*Prep. Time: 10-15 minutes*
*Cooking Time: 3-5 hours*
*Ideal slow cooker size: 3-qt.*

10-oz. pkg. frozen chopped
broccoli
6 eggs, beaten
24 oz. small-curd cottage
cheese
6 Tbsp. flour
8 oz. mild cheese of your
choice, diced
half a stick (4 Tbsp.)
butter, melted
2 green onions, chopped
salt to taste

1. Place frozen broccoli in colander. Run cold water over it until it thaws. Separate into pieces. Drain well.
2. Combine broccoli and all other ingredients in greased slow cooker. Mix together gently but well.
3. Cover. Cook on High 1 hour. Stir well, then continue cooking on Low 2-4 hours.

# Broccoli and Rice Casserole

**Deborah Swartz**
Grottoes, VA

*Makes 4-6 servings*

*Prep. Time: 15-20 minutes*
*Cooking Time: 5-6 hours*
*Ideal slow cooker size: 3½-qt.*

1 lb. chopped broccoli,
fresh *or* frozen, thawed
1 medium onion, chopped
half a stick (4 Tbsp.)
butter, cut in chunks
1 cup minute rice, uncooked,
*or* 1½ cups cooked rice
10¾-oz. can cream of
chicken, *or* mushroom,
soup
¼ cup milk
1⅓ cups Velveeta cheese,
cubed, *or* cheddar
cheese, shredded
1 tsp. salt

1. Combine all ingredients in lightly greased slow cooker.
2. Cover. Cook on Low 5-6 hours.

*Don't forget your pastor and his or her family. They may enjoy being included in one of your holiday gatherings.*
*Leona M. Slabaugh, Apple Creek, OH*

# Quick Broccoli Fix

Willard E. Roth, Elkhart, IN

*Makes 6 servings*

*Prep. Time: 15 minutes • Cooking Time: 5-6 hours*
*Ideal slow cooker size: 3½-qt.*

1 lb. fresh, *or* frozen, broccoli, cut up
10¾-oz. can cream of mushroom soup
½ cup mayonnaise
½ cup plain yogurt
½ lb. sliced fresh mushrooms
1 cup shredded cheddar cheese, *divided*
1 cup crushed saltine crackers
sliced almonds, *optional*

1. Microwave broccoli for 3 minutes. Place in greased slow cooker.
2. Combine soup, mayonnaise, yogurt, mushrooms, and ½ cup cheese in mixing bowl. Pour over broccoli. Stir together gently but well
3. Cover. Cook on Low 5-6 hours.
4. Top with remaining cheese and crackers for last half hour of cooking time.
5. If you wish, top with sliced almonds, for a special touch, before serving.

# Christmas Carrots

Lindsey Spencer
Marrow, OH

*Makes 8 servings*

*Prep. Time: 10-15 minutes*
*Cooking Time: 3 hours*
*Ideal slow cooker size: 3-qt.*

2 lbs. carrots
half a stick (4 Tbsp.) butter, melted
½ cup brown sugar
8-oz. can crushed pineapple, undrained
½ cup shredded coconut

1. Peel carrots and cut into strips ½" wide and 2" long.
2. For extra flavor, brown carrots in skillet in butter before placing in slow cooker. Or skip doing that and place carrots and butter straight into slow cooker.
3. Add all other ingredients to slow cooker. Mix together gently but well
4. Cover. Cook on Low 3 hours.
5. Add coconut as garnish to carrots when serving.

# Orange-Glazed Carrots

Barbara Smith
Bedford, PA

*Makes 3-4 servings*

*Prep. Time: 15 minutes*
*Cooking Time: 2½ -3½ hours*
*Ideal slow cooker size: 2½-qt.*

3 cups thinly sliced carrots
2 cups water
¼ tsp. salt
2-3 Tbsp. butter
3 Tbsp. orange marmalade
2 Tbsp. chopped pecans, *optional*

1. Combine carrots, water, and salt in slow cooker.
2. Cover. Cook on High 2-3 hours, or until carrots are as tender as you like them.
3. Drain. Stir in butter and marmalade.
4. Cover. Cook on High 30 minutes.

# Glazed Carrots

**Sharon Timpe**
Jackson, WI

*Makes 6-8 servings*

**Prep. Time:** *15-25 minutes*
**Cooking Time:** *3-3½ hours*
**Ideal slow cooker size:** *3½-qt.*

18 small carrots, cleaned
    and peeled, *or* 2 lbs.
    baby carrots, cleaned
5⅔ Tbsp. (⅓ cup) butter
½ tsp. salt
⅓ cup sugar
½ tsp. cinnamon
⅓ cup water

1. Place carrots in slow cooker.
2. Heat butter, salt, sugar, cinnamon, and water together in a small pan.
3. Pour mixture over carrots in slow cooker. Mix together gently but well.
4. Cover. Cook on Low 3-3½ hours, or until carrots are tender.

Note:

*I've often prepared these Glazed Carrots by baking them in the oven. One year my oven was full and whenever that happens, I bring out my slow cooker and quickly adapt the recipe to it. Slow cooker to the rescue!*

*One of our favorite holiday meals for guests includes these carrots, along with beef rouladen, riced boiled potatoes with gravy, and green beans with browned butter and basil.*

# Sweet-Sour Red Cabbage

**Kaye Taylor**
Florissant, MO

*Makes 6-8 servings*

**Prep. Time:** *30-45 minutes*
**Cooking Time:** *3-4 hours*
**Ideal slow cooker size:** *3½-qt.*

4 slices bacon, diced
¼ cup brown sugar
2 Tbsp. flour
1 tsp. salt
⅛ tsp. pepper
½ cup water
¼ cup vinegar
1 medium head red cabbage
    shredded (6-8 cups)
1 small onion, finely
    chopped

1. Sauté bacon in skillet until crisp. Set bacon aside. Reserve 1 Tbsp. drippings.
2. Combine 1 Tbsp. bacon drippings in slow cooker with sugar, flour, salt, and pepper. Stir in water and vinegar.
3. Add cabbage and onion. Mix together well.
4. Cover. Cook on Low 3-4 hours, or until cabbage and onion are as tender as you like them.
5. Sprinkle cooked bacon on top just before serving.

# Black-Eyed Peas and Ham

**Susan Tjon**
Austin, TX

*Makes 6-8 servings*

**Prep. Time:** *20 minutes*
**Soaking Time:** *8 hours, or overnight*
**Cooking Time:** *8-9 hours*
**Ideal slow cooker size:** *5-qt.*

1 lb. dry black-eyed peas
4 cups water
2 tsp. salt
¼ tsp. pepper
1 large onion, chopped
2 ribs celery, chopped
2 ham hocks

1. Place beans in cooker. Cover with water. Allow to soak overnight or for 8 hours.
2. Drain. Return beans to slow cooker.

*Take your grandkids shopping for their parents and siblings, and then take them to lunch.*

*Carol Ambrose, McMinnville, OR*

3. Add 4 cups water, salt, pepper, onion, and celery. Stir to combine.

4. Place ham hocks in cooker, pushing them down into liquid as much as possible.

5. Cover. Cook on Low 8-9 hours, or until peas are tender but not mushy and ham is tender but not dried out.

6. When finished cooking, remove ham hocks from cooker. Allow to cool until you can handle them without burning your fingers.

7. Debone ham and cut meat into small chunks. Stir into soup. Serve immediately, or turn cooker on High for 30 minutes, or until heated through.

**Note:**

*We always serve this on New Year's Day. It's our good luck dish.*

*On Christmas Eve we always watch "Christmas Vacation" after dinner. Even if a family member is far away, we synchronize the movie start time so we still feel like we're together.*

# Squash Medley

Evelyn Page
Riverton, WY

*Makes 8 servings*

Prep. Time: 20 minutes
Cooking Time: 4-6 hours
Ideal slow cooker size: 3½-qt.

8 summer squash, *or* zucchini, each about 4" long, peeled or not, thinly sliced, *divided*
½ tsp. salt
2 tomatoes, peeled and chopped, *or* 14½-oz. can diced tomatoes, *divided*
¼ cup sliced green onions, *divided*
half a small sweet green pepper, chopped, *divided*
1 chicken bouillon cube
¼ cup hot water
4 slices bacon, fried and crumbled
¼ cup fine dry bread crumbs

1. Sprinkle squash with salt.
2. In slow cooker, layer half the squash, tomatoes, onions, and pepper.
3. Repeat layers.
4. Dissolve bouillon in hot water. Pour into slow cooker.
5. Top with bacon. Sprinkle bread crumbs over top.
6. Cover. Cook on Low 4-6 hours.

**Variation:**

For a sweeter touch, sprinkle 1 Tbsp. brown sugar over half the layered vegetables. Repeat over second half of layered vegetables.

# Baked Acorn Squash

Dale Peterson
Rapid City, SD

*Makes 4 servings*

Prep. Time: 15 minutes
Cooking Time: 5-6 hours
Ideal slow cooker size: 5- to 6-qt., or 2 4- to 6-qt., depending on size of squash

2 acorn squash
⅔ cup cracker crumbs
½ cup coarsely chopped pecans
5⅓ Tbsp. (⅓ cup) butter, melted
4 Tbsp. brown sugar
½ tsp. salt
¼ tsp. ground nutmeg
2 Tbsp. orange juice

1. Cut squash in half through the middle. Remove seeds.
2. Combine remaining ingredients in a bowl. Spoon into squash halves.
3. Place squash halves in slow cooker side by side.
4. Cover. Cook on Low 5-6 hours, or until squash is tender.

# Apple Walnut Squash

**Michele Ruvola**
Selden, NY

*Makes 4 servings*

*Prep. Time: 15 minutes*
*Cooking Time: 3-4 hours*
*Ideal slow cooker size: 5- to 6-qt., or 2 4- to 6-qt., depending on size of squash*

¼ cup water
2 small acorn squash
¼ cup packed brown sugar
half a stick (4 Tbsp.) butter, melted
3 Tbsp. apple juice
1½ tsp. ground cinnamon
¼ tsp. salt
1 cup toasted walnuts
1 apple, chopped

1. Pour water into slow cooker.
2. Cut squash in half through the middle. Remove seeds.
3. Combine brown sugar, butter, apple juice, cinnamon, and salt in bowl.
4. Spoon mixture into squash. Place in slow cooker, side by side.
5. Cover. Cook on High 3-4 hours, or until squash is tender.
6. Combine walnuts and chopped apple in bowl. Add spoonfuls to center of each squash half and mix lightly with sauce.

# Stuffed Acorn Squash

**Jean Butzer**
Batavia, NY

*Makes 6 servings*

*Prep. Time: 15 minutes*
*Cooking Time: 2½ hours*
*Ideal slow cooker size: 5- to 6-qt.*

3 small carnival, *or* acorn, squash
5 Tbsp. instant brown rice, uncooked
3 Tbsp. dried cranberries
3 Tbsp. diced celery
3 Tbsp. minced onion
pinch of ground, *or* dried, sage
1 Tbsp. butter, *divided*
3 Tbsp. orange juice
½ cup water

1. Slice off points on bottoms of squash so they will stand in slow cooker. Slice off tops and discard. Scoop out seeds. Place squash side by side in slow cooker.
2. Combine rice, cranberries, celery, onion, and sage in bowl. Stuff into squash centers.
3. Dot with butter.
4. Pour 1 Tbsp. orange juice into each squash center.
5. Pour water into bottom of slow cooker.
6. Cover. Cook on Low 2½ hours.

*Serving suggestion: Serve with cooked **turkey breast** or **pork** or **ham**.*

Tip:
To make squash easier to slice, microwave whole squash on High 5 minutes to soften skin.

# Tzimmes

**Elaine Vigoda**
Rochester, NY

*Makes 6-8 servings*

*Prep. Time: 25-30 minutes*
*Cooking Time: 10 hours*
*Ideal slow cooker size: 6-qt. or 2 4- to 5-qt.*

1-2 sweet potatoes, sliced
6 carrots, sliced
1 potato, peeled and diced
1 onion, chopped
2 apples, peeled and sliced
1 butternut squash, peeled and sliced
¼ cup dry white wine, *or* apple juice
½ lb. dried apricots
1 Tbsp. ground cinnamon
1 Tbsp. apple pie spice
1 Tbsp. maple syrup, *or* honey
1 tsp. salt
1 tsp. ground ginger

1. Combine all ingredients in large slow cooker, or mix all ingredients in large bowl and then divide between 2 4- or 5-qt. cookers.
2. Cover. Cook on Low 10 hours.

Note:
*This is a special dish served primarily on Jewish holidays*

*such as Rosh Hashana and Passover. The sweetness of the vegetables and fruit signifies wishes for a sweet year.*

# Stewed Tomatoes

### Michelle Showalter
### Bridgewater, VA

*Makes 10-12 servings*

*Prep. Time: 10 minutes*
*Cooking Time: 3-4 hours*
*Ideal slow cooker size: 3-qt.*

2 qts. canned, *or* 4 14½-oz. cans diced *or* stewed, tomatoes
⅓ cup sugar
1½ tsp. salt
dash of pepper
3 Tbsp. butter
2 cups soft bread cubes

1. Place tomatoes in slow cooker.
2. Sprinkle with sugar, salt, and pepper.
3. Lightly toast bread cubes in melted butter on baking sheet in oven, or in large skillet.
4. Spread over tomatoes.
5. Cover. Cook on High 3-4 hours.

Variation:

If you prefer bread that is less moist and soft, add bread cubes 15 minutes before serving and continue cooking without lid.

# Stuffed Mushrooms

### Melanie L. Thrower
### McPherson, KS

*Makes 4-6 servings*

*Prep. Time: 15-20 minutes*
*Cooking Time: 2-4 hours*
*Ideal slow cooker size: 5-qt.*

8-10 large mushrooms
¼ tsp. minced garlic
1 Tbsp. oil
dash of salt
dash of pepper
dash of cayenne pepper
¼ cup grated Monterey Jack cheese

1. Remove stems from mushrooms and dice.
2. Heat oil in skillet. Sauté diced stems with garlic until softened. Remove skillet from heat.
3. Stir in seasonings and cheese. Stuff into mushroom caps.
4. Place in slow cooker.
5. Cover. Heat on Low 2-4 hours.

Variations:
1. Add 1 Tbsp. minced onion to Step 2.
2. Use Monterey Jack cheese with jalapeños.

# Easy Olive Bake

### Jean Robinson
### Cinnaminson, NJ

*Makes 8 servings*

*Prep. Time: 15 minutes*
*Cooking Time: 3 hours*
*Ideal slow cooker size: 3½-qt.*

1 cup uncooked long-grain rice
2 medium onions, chopped
1 stick (8 Tbsp.) butter, melted
2 cups, or 1 14½-oz. can, stewed tomatoes
2 cups water
1 cup black olives, quartered
½-¾ tsp. salt
½ tsp. chili powder
1 Tbsp. Worcestershire sauce
4-oz. can mushrooms with juice
½ cup grated cheese of your choice

1. Place rice in slow cooker.
2. Add all remaining ingredients, except cheese. Mix well.
3. Cover. Cook on High 1 hour, and then on Low 2 hours, or until rice is tender but not mushy.
4. Stir in cheese just before serving.

*Serving suggestion: This is a good accompaniment to **baked ham**.*

# Caponata

**Katrine Rose**
Woodbridge, VA

*Makes 8-10 servings*

*Prep. Time: 20 minutes*
*Cooking Time: 7-8 hours*
*Ideal slow cooker size: 3½- to 4-qt.*

1 medium eggplant, peeled and cut into ½" cubes
14½-oz. can diced tomatoes
1 medium onion, chopped
1 red bell pepper, cut into ½" pieces
¾ cup salsa, your choice of heat
¼ cup olive oil
2 Tbsp. capers, drained
3 Tbsp. balsamic vinegar
3 garlic cloves, minced
1¼ tsp. dried oregano
⅓ cup chopped fresh basil, packed in measuring cup
toasted, sliced French bread

1. Combine all ingredients except basil and bread in slow cooker.
2. Cover. Cook on Low 7-8 hours, or until vegetables are tender.
3. Stir in basil. Serve on toasted bread.

# Candied Sweet Potatoes

**Jean M. Butzer**
Batavia, NY

*Makes 8 servings*

*Prep. Time: 5-10 minutes*
*Cooking Time: 2¼-3¼ hours*
*Ideal slow cooker size: 5-qt.*

2 29-oz. cans cut sweet potatoes, drained
½ cup chopped pecans
¾ stick (6 Tbsp.) butter, cut in pieces
2 Tbsp. frozen orange juice concentrate, thawed
⅓ cup brown sugar
2 tsp. pumpkin pie spice
¼ tsp. cayenne pepper, *optional*
3 cups miniature marshmallows

1. Stir together sweet potatoes, pecans, butter, and orange juice concentrate in lightly greased slow cooker.
2. In a small bowl, combine brown sugar, pumpkin pie spice, and cayenne pepper if you wish. Sprinkle over sweet potato mixture and stir.
3. Cover. Cook on Low 2-3 hours, or until potatoes are heated through.
4. Sprinkle marshmallows over top of sweet potatoes.
5. Cover. Cook on Low 15 minutes, or until marshmallows are melted.

# Orange Candied Sweet Potatoes

**Robin Schrock**
Millersburg, OH

*Makes 10-12 servings*

*Prep. Time: 20-30 minutes*
*Cooking Time: 7¼ hours*
*Ideal slow cooker size: 4-qt.*

4 lbs. (8-10) sweet potatoes, peeled and cut into 1" chunks
1½ sticks (¾ cup) butter, melted
2 cups brown sugar
½ cup orange juice
1 Tbsp. ground cinnamon
1 Tbsp. grated lemon peel
1½ tsp. salt
½ tsp. nutmeg
2½ cups miniature marshmallows

1. Place potato chunks in slow cooker.
2. Mix butter, brown sugar, juice, cinnamon, lemon peel, salt, and nutmeg together in small bowl. Pour over potatoes and stir to coat potatoes.
3. Cover. Cook on Low 7 hours, or until potatoes are tender.
4. Sprinkle marshmallows over mixture and cook on Low until marshmallows are melted, about 15 minutes.

# Orange Yams

**Gladys Longacre**
Susquehanna, PA

*Makes 6-8 servings*

*Prep. Time: 15 minutes*
*Cooking Time: 3 hours*
*Ideal slow cooker size: 3½-qt.*

40-oz. can yams, *or* sweet
  potatoes, drained
2 apples, peeled if you
  wish and thinly sliced
3 Tbsp. butter, melted
2 tsp. orange zest
1 cup orange juice
2 Tbsp. cornstarch
½ cup brown sugar
1 tsp. salt
dash of ground cinnamon
  and/or nutmeg

1. Place yams and apples in slow cooker.
2. Stir in butter and orange zest.
3. Combine remaining ingredients in small bowl. Pour over yams and apples.
4. Cover. Cook on High 1 hour and on Low 2 hours, or until apples are tender.

### Variation:

Substitute 6-8 medium-sized cooked sweet potatoes, or approximately 4 cups cubed butternut squash, for yams.

# Sweet Potatoes That Can Wait

**Alix Nancy Botsford**
Seminole, OK

*Makes 6-8 servings*

*Prep. Time: 15-20 minutes*
*Cooking Time: 3 hours*
*Ideal slow cooker size: 2-qt.*

3-4 medium-sized sweet
  potatoes
½-¾ cup packed brown
  sugar, *or* maple syrup
half a stick (4 Tbsp.)
  butter, cut into pieces
¼-½ tsp. salt
1 cup apple juice, *or* cider

1. Peel and dice sweet potatoes. Put into slow cooker.
2. Add brown sugar, butter, and salt.
3. Pour apple juice or cider over all.
4. Cover. Cook on High 3 hours, or until potatoes are tender.

### Notes:

*When we lived in western New York, I liked to make this recipe with maple syrup from the local area.*

*For our 50th Anniversary, I cooked 6 large briskets. Our daughter and granddaughter made 3 large salads and tripled this potato dish. We fed our whole church that Sunday!*

*The great thing about making a Christmas meal in slow cookers is that when the meal is ready, it can wait until we're ready! There is no pressure. We can sit and visit and wait for the stragglers to arrive.*

# "Baked" Sweet Potatoes

**Shari Mast**
Harrisonburg, VA

*Makes 6-8 servings*

*Prep. Time: 10 minutes*
*Cooking Time: 4-8 hours*
*Ideal slow cooker size: 5-qt.*

6-8 medium-sized sweet
  potatoes

1. Scrub and prick sweet potatoes with fork. Wrap each in tin foil and arrange in slow cooker.
2. Cover. Cook on Low 6-8 hours or on High 4-5 hours, or until each potato is soft.
3. Remove from foil and serve with butter and salt.

# Apples 'n' Yams

**Rebecca Plank Leichty**
Harrisonburg, VA

*Makes 8-10 servings*

*Prep. Time: 20-25 minutes*
*Cooking Time: 4-6 hours*
*Ideal slow cooker size: 4- to 5-qt.*

1 Tbsp. lemon juice, *or*
  lemonade
6 apples, peeled if you
  wish and sliced
6 large yams, *or* sweet
  potatoes, peeled and
  thinly sliced
¼ cup apple juice
1 Tbsp. butter, melted

1. Toss sliced apples and
yams in lemon juice in lightly
greased slow cooker.

2. Combine apple juice
and butter in small bowl.
Pour over apples and sweet
potatoes. Mix well together.

3. Cover. Cook on High 4
hours or on Low 6 hours.

Note:
*This is a tasty vegetable
dish to add to a meal when
serving children. The apples
smell wonderful when cooking
and truly moisten the potatoes
when served together. It is a
well-rounded and easy way to
serve sweet potatoes.*

# Sweet Potatoes and Apples

**Bernita Boyts**
Shawnee Mission, KS

*Makes 8-10 servings*

*Prep. Time: 10-15 minutes*
*Cooking Time: 6-8 hours*
*Ideal slow cooker size: 3-qt.*

3 large sweet potatoes,
  peeled and cubed, *divided*
3 large tart and firm
  apples, peeled if you
  wish and sliced, *divided*
½-¾ tsp. salt
⅛-¼ tsp. pepper
1 tsp. sage
1 tsp. ground cinnamon
half a stick (4 Tbsp.)
  butter, melted
¼ cup maple syrup
toasted sliced almonds, *or*
  chopped pecans, *optional*

1. Place half the sweet
potatoes in slow cooker.
Layer in half the apple slices.

2. Mix together salt, pepper,
sage, and cinnamon in a small
bowl. Sprinkle half over apples.

3. Mix together butter and
maple syrup in a small bowl.
Spoon half over seasonings.

4. Repeat layers.

5. Cover. Cook on Low 6-8
hours, or until potatoes are
soft, stirring occasionally if
you're home and able to do so.

6. To add a bit of crunch,
sprinkle with toasted
almonds or pecans when
serving if you wish.

*Serving suggestion: Serve
with pork or **poultry**.*

# Sweet Potatoes with Applesauce

**Judi Manos**
West Islip, NY

*Makes 6-8 servings*

*Prep. Time: 10 minutes*
*Cooking Time: 6-7 hours*
*Ideal slow cooker size: 3- to 3½-qt.*

6 medium-sized sweet
  potatoes, *or* yams
1½ cups applesauce
⅔ cup packed brown sugar
3 Tbsp. butter, melted
1 tsp. ground cinnamon
½ cup chopped toasted nuts

1. Peel sweet potatoes and
cut into ½" cubes. Place in
slow cooker.

2. Combine remaining
ingredients, except nuts, in a
bowl. Stir into potatoes.

3. Cover. Cook on Low 6-7
hours, or until potatoes are
very tender.

4. Sprinkle with nuts just
before serving.

Variation:
If you prefer a less sweet
dish, cut the sugar back to ⅓
cup.

# Pineapple Sweet Potatoes

**Renee Baum**
Chambersburg, PA

*Makes 12-14 servings*

*Prep. Time: 20-30 minutes, if potatoes are cooked already*
*Cooking Time: 4-5 hours*
*Ideal slow cooker size: 5-qt.*

**6-6½ cups mashed sweet potatoes, without milk and butter added**
**4 eggs**
**1 cup milk**
**1 stick (8 Tbsp.) butter, softened**
**1 tsp. vanilla**
**½ tsp. lemon extract**
**1 tsp. salt**
**1 tsp. cinnamon**
**½ tsp. nutmeg**
**8-oz. can pineapple slices, drained**
**¼ cup chopped pecans**

1. Combine mashed sweet potatoes, eggs, milk, butter, vanilla, lemon extract, salt, cinnamon, and nutmeg in slow cooker.
2. Top with pineapple slices and pecans.
3. Cover. Cook on Low 4-5 hours or until thermometer reaches 160 degrees in middle of potatoes.

**Tips:**

1. If you need to cook the sweet potatoes, scrub 4-5 large potatoes. Peel them. Cut into chunks. Place in stockpot. Add about 2 inches of water.

2. Cover and cook over medium heat.
3. Check every 10 minutes or so to make sure they don't cook dry. Cook until very soft.
4. Mash with electric mixer or potato masher.
5. Drain off water. Then proceed with Step 1 above.

*or*

Follow recipe for "'Baked' Sweet Potatoes" on page 217 of this cookbook. When potatoes are finished cooking, and when they're cool enough to handle, peel. Then proceed with Steps 4 and 5 immediately above.

# Sweet Potato-Cranberry Casserole

**Mary E. Wheatley**
Mashpee, MA

*Makes 6-8 servings*

*Prep. Time: 20-30 minutes*
*Cooking Time: 3-4 hours*
*Ideal slow cooker size: 4- to 6-qt.*

**¼ cup orange juice**
**1 stick (8 Tbsp.) butter**
**2-3 Tbsp. brown sugar**
**1 tsp. ground cinnamon**
**1 cup dried cranberries**
**salt**
**4 lbs. sweet potatoes, *or* yams, peeled and cut into 1" pieces**

1. Place all ingredients except sweet potatoes in slow cooker. Mix together.
2. Cover. Cook on High while preparing potatoes.
3. Add potato pieces to warm mixture.
4. Cover. Cook on High 3-4 hours.
5. When potatoes are soft, stir until they're mashed and then serve.

# Barbecued Black Beans with Sweet Potatoes

**Barbara Jean Fabel**
Wausau, WI

*Makes 4-6 servings*

*Prep. Time: 10-15 minutes*
*Cooking Time: 2-4 hours*
*Ideal slow cooker size: 3-qt.*

**4 large sweet potatoes, peeled and cut into 8 chunks each**
**15-oz. can black beans, rinsed and drained**
**1 medium onion, diced**
**2 ribs celery, sliced**
**9 oz. Sweet Baby Ray's Barbecue Sauce**

1. Place sweet potatoes in slow cooker.
2. Stir in additional ingredients.
3. Cover. Cook on High 2-3 hours, or on Low 4 hours.

# Mashed Potatoes

**Mrs. Audrey L. Kneer**
Williamsfield, IL

*Makes 1 serving, multiplied*

**Prep. Time: 15 minutes**
**Cooking Time: 2 hours**
**Ideal slow cooker size: large**
**enough to hold desired**
**number of servings**

1-2 medium-sized potatoes
  per person
3 Tbsp. milk per potato
½ Tbsp. butter per potato,
  melted
⅛ tsp. salt per potato

1. Peel potatoes. Place in stockpot. Add at least an inch of water to stockpot. Cover. Cook on stovetop over medium heat until soft.

2. Check after about 20 minutes to make sure potatoes aren't cooking dry. If nearly dry, add another inch of water or so.

3. When potatoes are falling-apart-soft, mash with electric mixer or hand-held potato masher.

4. While mashing potatoes, heat milk to scalding. Then add hot milk, butter, and salt to mashed potatoes, stirring in well.

5. Put in slow cooker a couple of hours before serving. Set cooker on Low. Stir once in a while. These will be the same as fresh mashed potatoes when you're ready to serve the meal.

**Tip:**
This saves needing to mash potatoes at the last minute.

# Garlic Mashed Potatoes

**Katrine Rose**
Woodbridge, VA

*Makes 6 servings*

**Prep. Time: 10 minutes**
**Cooking Time: 4-7 hours**
**Ideal slow cooker size: 4-qt.**

2 lbs. baking potatoes,
  unpeeled and cut into
  ½" cubes
¼ cup water
3 Tbsp. butter, sliced
1 tsp. salt
¾ tsp. garlic powder
¼ tsp. black pepper
1 cup milk

1. Combine all ingredients, except milk, in slow cooker. Toss to combine.

2. Cover. Cook on Low 7 hours, or on High 4 hours.

3. Add milk to potatoes during last 30 minutes of cooking time.

4. Mash potatoes with potato masher or electric mixer until fairly smooth.

# Make Ahead Mixed Potatoes Florentine

**Becky Frey**
Lebanon, PA

*Makes 10-12 servings*

**Prep. Time: 45-60 minutes**
**Cooking Time: 8-10 hours**
**Ideal slow cooker size: 4-qt.**

6 medium-sized white
  potatoes
3 medium-sized sweet
  potatoes
¼ stick (2 Tbsp.) butter
2 Tbsp. olive oil
1 large onion, chopped
1-2 cloves garlic, pressed
8 oz. low-fat, *or* non-fat,
  cream cheese, at room
  temperature
½ cup non-fat sour cream
½ cup non-fat plain yogurt
1 tsp. salt, *or* to taste
1-1½ tsp. dill weed
¼ tsp. black pepper
10-oz. pkg. frozen, chopped
  spinach, thawed and
  squeezed dry

1. Peel and quarter both white and sweet potatoes. Place in slow cooker. Barely cover with water.

2. Cover. Cook on Low 6-8 hours, or until potatoes are falling-apart-tender.

*Stockings are one tradition we all love. I shop all year for special treats for the youngest to the oldest. It is super fun!*

*Carol Duree, Salina, KS*

3. Meanwhile, in a saucepan sauté onion and garlic in butter and olive oil, on low heat, until soft and golden.

4. In an electric mixer bowl, combine sautéed onion and garlic with cream cheese, sour cream, yogurt, salt, dill weed, and pepper. Whip until well blended. Set aside.

5. Drain off some of the potato cooking water, but reserve. Mash potatoes in some of their cooking water until soft and creamy. Add more cooking water if you'd like a creamier result.

6. Stir onion-cheese mixture into mashed potatoes.

7. Fold spinach into potato mixture.

8. Turn into greased 4-qt. slow cooker. Cook for 2 hours on Low, or until heated through.

9. If you've made the potatoes a day or so in advance of serving them, refrigerate them until the day of your gathering. Then heat potatoes in slow cooker for 3-4 hours on Low, or until heated through.

**Variation:**

You can use 1 cup plain yogurt and omit the sour cream, or vice versa. The more yogurt, the greater the savory tang.

# Refrigerator Mashed Potatoes

### Deborah Swartz
Grottoes, VA

*Makes 8-10 servings*

*Prep. Time: 30 minutes*
*Cooking Time: 2 hours*
*Ideal slow cooker size: 6-qt.*

5 lbs. potatoes
8-oz. pkg. cream cheese, softened
1 cup sour cream
1 tsp. salt
¼ tsp. pepper
¼ cup crisp bacon, crumbled
¼ stick (2 Tbsp.) butter

1. Cook and mash potatoes.*
2. Place mashed potatoes in lightly greased slow cooker.
3. Stir in all remaining ingredients except butter.
4. Dot with butter.
5. Cover. Cook on Low 2 hours.

**Variations:**

1. These potatoes can be made several days ahead and refrigerated.

2. Cook cold, refrigerated potatoes on Low 5 hours, or until heated through.

3. If you wish, sprinkle 1 cup cheddar cheese over top of potatoes during their last half hour in slow cooker.

4. Substitute chopped ham for bacon.

5. Add 2 Tbsp. chopped fresh chives to Step 2.

*For instructions for cooking and mashing potatoes, see recipe for "Mashed Potatoes" on page 220 of this Cookbook.

# Creamy Mashed Potatoes

### Brenda S. Burkholder
Port Republic, VA

*Makes 10-12 servings*

*Prep. Time: 10-15 minutes*
*Cooking Time: 3-5 hours*
*Ideal slow cooker size: 6-qt.*

2 tsp. salt
¾ stick (6 Tbsp.) butter, melted
2¼ cups milk
6⅞ cups potato flakes
6 cups water
1 cup sour cream
4-5 oz. (approximately half a large pkg.) cream cheese, softened

1. Combine first five ingredients as directed on potato flakes box.

2. Whip cream cheese with electric mixer until creamy. Blend in sour cream.

3. Fold potatoes into cheese and sour cream. Beat well. Place in slow cooker.

4. Cover. Cook on Low 3-5 hours.

# Creamy Red Potatoes

**Kayla Snyder**
North East, PA

*Makes 8 servings*

*Prep. Time: 20-30 minutes*
*Cooking Time: 3½ hours*
*Ideal slow cooker size: 3-qt.*

3 Tbsp. butter
3 Tbsp. flour
1 cup milk
½ tsp. garlic powder
¾ tsp. salt
1 Tbsp. dried onion flakes
1 tsp. parsley flakes
2 3-oz. pkgs. cream cheese, at room temperature
2 lbs. red potatoes

1. Make a white sauce in a saucepan by melting butter, stirring in flour, and adding milk. Whisk and stir until smooth and thickened.
2. Add seasonings. Beat in cream cheese until smooth.
3. Cut up unpeeled potatoes into 1"-2" cubes.
4. Layer potatoes and sauce in slow cooker.
5. Cover. Cook on High 3½ hours, or until potatoes are as soft as you like them.

**Tips:**
1. 5 lbs. of potatoes fills up a 3-qt. slow-cooker nicely.
2. Mix up the sauce ahead of time and refrigerate it. Then when you're ready, cut up the potatoes, and put them and the sauce in your slow cooker.

# Sunday Dinner Potatoes

**Ruth Ann Penner**
Hillsboro, KS

*Makes 8 servings*

*Prep. Time: 15 minutes*
*Cooking Time: 2-5 hours*
*Ideal slow cooker size: 3-qt.*

4 cups cooked, sliced potatoes
5⅔ Tbsp. (⅓ cup) butter
¼ cup flour
2 cups milk
1 tsp. salt
pepper to taste
1 tsp. onion powder

1. Place potatoes in slow cooker.
2. Melt butter in small skillet. Add flour and stir. Slowly add milk, stirring constantly.
3. Add salt, pepper, and onion powder. When smooth and thickened, pour over potatoes.
4. Cover. Cook on High 2-3 hours or on Low 4-5 hours.

# Swiss-Irish Hot Sauce— A Great Potato Topping!

**Jo Haberkamp**
Fairbank, IA

*Makes 6-8 servings*

*Prep. Time: 15 minutes*
*Cooking Time: 4 hours*
*Ideal slow cooker size: 3-qt.*

2 medium onions, diced
5 garlic cloves, minced
¼ cup oil
14½-oz. can puréed tomatoes
15-oz. can tomato sauce
12-oz. can tomato paste
2 Tbsp. parsley, fresh or dried
½ tsp. red pepper
½ tsp. black pepper
1 tsp. chili powder
1 tsp. dried basil
2 tsp. Worcestershire sauce
2 tsp. Tabasco sauce
¼ cup red wine

1. Sauté onions and garlic in oil in skillet.
2. Combine all ingredients in slow cooker.
3. Cover. Cook on Low 4 hours.
4. This is a flavorful sauce for eating over baked potatoes or pasta.

# Herbed Potatoes

**Jo Haberkamp**
Fairbank, IA

*Makes 6 servings*

*Prep. Time: 10 minutes*
*Cooking Time: 2½-3 hours*
*Ideal slow cooker size: 3-qt.*

1½ lbs. small new potatoes
¼ cup water
half a stick (4 Tbsp.)
   butter, melted
3 Tbsp. chopped fresh
   parsley
1 Tbsp. lemon juice
1 Tbsp. chopped fresh
   chives
1 Tbsp. dill weed
¼-½ tsp. salt, according to
   your taste preference
⅛-¼ tsp. pepper, according
   to your taste preference

1. Wash potatoes. Peel a strip around the middle of each potato. Place prepared potatoes in slow cooker.
2. Add water.
3. Cover. Cook on High 2½-3 hours. Drain well.
4. In saucepan, heat butter, parsley, lemon juice, chives, dill, salt, and pepper.
5. Pour over potatoes.

*Serving suggestion: Serve with **ham** or any **meat dish** that does not make its own gravy.*

# Onion Potatoes

**Donna Lantgen**
Rapid City, SD

*Makes 6 servings*

*Prep. Time: 5-10 minutes*
*Cooking Time: 3-6 hours*
*Ideal slow cooker size: 3-qt.*

6 medium potatoes, peeled
   or unpeeled, diced
⅓ cup olive oil
1 envelope dry onion soup
   mix

1. Combine potatoes and olive oil in plastic bag. Shake well.
2. Add onion soup mix. Shake well.
3. Pour into slow cooker.
4. Cover. Cook on Low 6 hours or on High 3 hours.

**Variations:**
Add more zest to the potatoes by stirring in 1 small onion, chopped; 1 bell pepper, chopped; ½ tsp. salt; and ¼ tsp. black pepper, after pouring the potatoes into the slow cooker. Then continue with Step 4.

# Potatoes Perfect

**Naomi Ressler**
Harrisonburg, VA

*Makes 4-6 servings*

*Prep. Time: 15 minutes*
*Cooking Time: 3-10 hours*
*Ideal slow cooker size: 3½-qt.*

¼ lb. bacon, diced and
   browned in a skillet
   until crisp, *divided*
2 medium-sized onions,
   thinly sliced, *divided*
6-8 medium-sized potatoes,
   thinly sliced, *divided*
½ lb. cheddar cheese,
   thinly sliced, *divided*
salt to taste
pepper to taste
¼-½ stick (2-4 Tbsp.)
   butter

1. Layer half of bacon, onions, potatoes, and cheese in greased slow cooker. Season to taste.
2. Dot with butter. Repeat layers.
3. Cover. Cook on Low 8-10 hours or on High 3-4 hours, or until potatoes are soft.

# Pete's Scalloped Potatoes

**Dede Peterson**
Rapid City, SD

*Makes 8-10 servings*

**Prep. Time: 15 minutes**
**Cooking Time: 6-7 hours**
**Ideal slow cooker size: 6-qt.**

**5 lbs. red potatoes, peeled or unpeeled and sliced,** *divided*
**2 cups water**
**1 tsp. cream of tartar**
**¼ lb. bacon, cut in 1" squares, browned until crisp, and drained,** *divided*
**dash of salt**
**½ pt. whipping cream**
**1 pt. half-and-half**

1. In large bowl, toss sliced potatoes in water and cream of tartar. Drain.
2. Layer half of potatoes and half of bacon in large slow cooker. Sprinkle each layer with salt.
3. Repeat layers using all remaining potatoes and bacon.
4. Mix whipping cream and half-and-half in bowl. Pour over potatoes.
5. Cover. Cook on Low 6-7 hours.

**Variations:**
For added flavor, cut one large onion into thin rings. Sauté in bacon drippings; then layer onion along with potatoes and bacon into slow cooker. Sprinkle each layer of potatoes with salt and pepper. Continue with Step 4.

# Lotsa Scalloped Potatoes

**Fannie Miller**
Hutchinson, KS

*Makes 20-25 servings*

**Prep. Time: 25 minutes**
**Cooking Time: 2-3 hours**
**Ideal slow cooker size: 6-qt. or 2 4-qt. cookers**

**5 lbs. potatoes, cooked\* and sliced**
**2 lbs. cooked ham, cubed**
**half a stick (4 Tbsp.) butter**
**½ cup flour**
**2 cups cream,** *or* **milk**
**¼ lb. mild cheese, your favorite, shredded**
**1½ tsp. salt**
**¼-½ tsp. pepper**

1. Place layers of sliced potatoes and ham in very large, or two smaller, slow cooker(s).
2. Melt butter in saucepan on stove. Stir in flour. Gradually add milk to make a white sauce, stirring constantly until smooth and thickened.
3. Stir cheese, salt, and pepper into white sauce.
4. Continue stirring until cheese is melted. Pour over potatoes and ham.
5. Cover. Cook on Low 2-3 hours.

Tip:
A great way to free up oven space.

\*To prepare cooked potatoes for Step 1, peel them if you wish. Place whole potatoes, peeled or unpeeled, in stockpot. Add at least an inch of water to stockpot. Cover. Cook on stovetop over medium heat until soft.
Check frequently to make sure potatoes aren't cooking dry. Add more water if needed.
Allow potatoes to cool enough to handle. Then slice thin, using a knife or mandolin.
Proceed with Step 1 above.

*My extended family usually meets at our home for a Christmas season gathering. Now, instead of preparing a lot of food, we provide hot sandwiches, and guests bring either a salad or a dessert. The 40-50 guests enjoy the more relaxed atmosphere, and the pressure to prepare many dishes is taken off the host and guests alike.*

*Sharon Miller, Holmesville, OH*

# Company Potatoes

**Deborah Swartz**
Grottoes, VA
**Julia A. Fisher**
New Carlisle, OH

*Makes 6-8 servings*

*Prep. Time: 20 minutes*
*Cooking Time: 4 hours*
*Ideal slow cooker size: 3½- to 4-qt.*

6 medium-sized potatoes, cooked,* cooled, and shredded
2 cups shredded cheddar cheese
⅓ cup finely chopped onions
half a stick (4 Tbsp.) butter, melted
1 tsp. salt
¼ tsp. pepper
1½-2 cups sour cream
butter

1. Combine potatoes, cheese, onions, melted butter, salt, pepper, and sour cream in slow cooker. Dot with butter.
2. Cover. Cook on Low 4 hours.

*To prepare cooked potatoes for Step 1, first peel potatoes. Place whole potatoes in stockpot. Add at least an inch of water to stockpot. Cover. Cook on stovetop over medium heat until soft.

Check frequently to make sure potatoes aren't cooking dry. Add water if needed.

Cool potatoes to room temperature. Then refrigerate 4-8 hours, or until thoroughly chilled. Shred into slow cooker.

Continue with Step 1 above.

**Variations:**

1. Use garlic salt instead of regular salt.
2. Add ½ tsp. chopped parsley to Step 1.
3. Use 1 cup milk and 1 cup sour cream instead of 1½-2 cups sour cream.
   **Kim Stoltzfus**
   New Holland, PA

# Cheese Potatoes

Joyce Shackelford, Green Bay, WI

*Makes 10 servings*

*Prep. Time: 10-15 minutes • Cooking Time: 8¼ hours*
*Ideal slow cooker size: 5-qt.*

6 potatoes, peeled and cut into ¼" strips
2 cups sharp cheddar cheese, shredded
10¾-oz. can cream of chicken soup
1 small onion, chopped
half a stick (4 Tbsp.) butter, melted
1 tsp. salt
1 tsp. pepper
1 cup sour cream
2 cups seasoned stuffing cubes
3 Tbsp. butter, melted

1. Toss together potatoes and cheese in slow cooker.
2. In a bowl, combine soup, onion, 4 Tbsp. melted butter, salt, and pepper. Pour over potatoes. Mix together gently.
3. Cover. Cook on Low 8 hours.
4. Stir in sour cream. Cover and heat 10 more minutes.
5. Meanwhile, toss together stuffing cubes and 3 Tbsp. butter in bowl. Sprinkle over potatoes just before serving.

# Christmas Potatoes with Cheese

**Jean Turner**
Williams Lake, B.C.

*Makes 6 servings*

*Prep. Time: 30 minutes*
*Cooking Time: 3-7 hours*
*Ideal slow cooker size: 2½-qt.*

5 Tbsp. butter, *divided*
2 Tbsp. flour
½ tsp. dry mustard
½ tsp. Worcestershire sauce
1½ tsp. salt
⅛ tsp. pepper
3 cups milk
1 cup shredded Swiss cheese
6 medium potatoes, peeled and thinly sliced (6 cups)
4-oz. jar sliced pimento, chopped and drained
¼ cup finely chopped onion
1½ cups soft bread crumbs

1. Melt 3 Tbsp. butter in saucepan. Blend in flour, mustard, Worcestershire sauce, salt, pepper, and milk. Cook and stir until thickened and bubbly. (I do this in the microwave.)
2. Add cheese. Stir to melt.
3. Place potatoes, pimento, and onion in slow cooker. Stir in cheesy sauce and blend well.
4. Cover. Cook on Low 5½-6½ hours or on High 2½-3½ hours, or until potatoes are as soft as you wish.
5. Melt remaining butter in saucepan. Toss with bread crumbs. Sprinkle over potatoes. Cook 30 minutes more, uncovered.

# Creamy Potatoes

**Lena Sheafer**
Port Matilda, PA

**Gloria Julien**
Gladstone, MI

**Jena Hammond**
Traverse City, MI

*Makes 8-10 servings*

*Prep. Time: 20-30 minutes*
*Cooking Time: 4-5 hours*
*Ideal slow cooker size: 5-qt.*

2 lbs. frozen cubed hash browns, thawed, *or* parboiled* fresh potato cubes
2 cups sharp cheddar, *or* mozzarella, cheese, shredded
2 cups sour cream
10¾-oz. can cream of celery soup
10¾-oz. can cream of chicken soup
1 large onion, chopped
half a stick (4 Tbsp.) butter, melted
¼ tsp. pepper
1 lb. cooked ham, *or* crispy bacon pieces, *or* other cooked meat, cut up

1. Place potatoes in slow cooker.
2. Combine cheese, sour cream, soups, onion, butter, and pepper in large mixing bowl. Pour over potatoes and mix well.
3. Cover. Cook on Low 4-5 hours.
4. Thirty minutes before end of the cooking time, stir in meat.

*To parboil potatoes, cut peeled or unpeeled potatoes into cubes. Place in stockpot. Add at least an inch of water to stockpot. Cover.
Cook on stovetop over medium heat until potatoes are no longer crispy, but are not yet soft. Drain.
Proceed with Step 1.

Tips:
1. This is a great way to use up leftovers: extra potatoes in that 5-lb. bag, hashbrowns in the freezer, leftover meat, extra veggies.
2. This works equally well as a main dish or a side dish.

Variation:
You can skip the meat if you wish.

**Jena Hammond**
Traverse City, MI

# Shredded Potatoes with Canadian Bacon

**Carol Eberly**
Harrisonburg, VA

*Makes 8 serving*

*Prep. Time: 10 minutes*
*Cooking Time: 5 hours*
*Ideal slow cooker size: 4-qt.*

32-oz. bag frozen hash
   browns, *divided*
6-8 thin slices Canadian
   bacon, *or* fully cooked
   ham, *divided*
1 cup shredded sharp
   cheese, *divided*
2 cups shredded mild
   cheddar cheese, *divided*
¾ cup chopped onions,
   *divided*
salt to taste
pepper to taste
10¾-oz. can cream of
   mushroom soup
10¾-oz. can cream of
   chicken soup

1. Layer half of potatoes,
meat, cheeses, and onions in
slow cooker. Season with salt
and pepper.
2. Repeat layers.
3. Combine soups in bowl.
Pour over top of mixture in
slow cooker.
4. Cover. Cook on Low 5
hours.

Note:
   *We used this recipe, minus
the meat, for our daughter's
wedding reception meal.*
   *We made 12 slow-cookers-
full. We put the recipe together
the night before, put the mixture
in the refrigerator overnight,
and got up at 4 a.m. to plug in
the cookers. They were ready
for lunch.*

# Hot German Potato Salad

**Judi Manos**
West Islip, NY

*Makes 6 servings*

*Prep. Time: 15 minutes*
*Cooking Time: 8-10 hours*
*Ideal slow cooker size: 3-qt.*

5 medium-sized potatoes,
   cut ¼" thick
1 large onion, chopped
⅓ cup water
⅓ cup vinegar
2 Tbsp. flour
2 Tbsp. sugar
1 tsp. salt
½ tsp. celery seed
¼ tsp. pepper
4 slices bacon, cooked
   crisp and crumbled
chopped fresh parsley

1. Combine potatoes and
onions in slow cooker.
2. Combine remaining
ingredients, except bacon and
parsley, in bowl. Pour over
potatoes.
3. Cover. Cook on Low 8-10
hours, or until potatoes are
tender.
4. Stir in bacon and parsley.
5. Serve warm or at room
temperature.

   *Serving suggestion: Prepare
a full German meal and serve
this with grilled **bratwurst** or
**Polish sausage**, **dill pickles**,
**pickled beets**, and **sliced
apples**.*

*Get out your serving dishes before your guests arrive.
Place a piece of paper in each one, designating what goes
in or on it, along with its serving utensil. When your guests
ask if they may help you, they can follow your plan.*
*Linda Sluiter, Schereville, IN*

# Rudolph's Nose Wild Rice

**Darla Sathre**
Baxter, MN

*Makes 8 servings*

*Prep. Time: 15 minutes*
*Cooking Time: 3 hours*
*Ideal slow cooker size: 3-qt.*

6 cups cooked wild rice, *or*
  3 15-oz. cans wild rice,
  drained
3.8-oz. can sliced black
  olives, drained
4-oz. can sliced button
  mushrooms, rinsed and
  drained
1 large onion chopped
  (about 2 cups)
1 pint (2 cups) grape, *or*
  cherry, tomatoes,
  halved
8-oz. pkg. cheddar cheese,
  cubed
¼ cup olive oil
black pepper, to taste

1. Mix all ingredients
together gently in slow
cooker.
2. Cover. Cook on Low 3
hours.

Tips:
1. The proportions of this
recipe can be adjusted to your
personal preferences quite
easily.
2. When we have just a
small amount of leftovers
of this recipe, we use it as
a pizza topping, and it is
delicious!

# Holiday Wild Rice

**Susan Kasting**, Jenks, OK

*Makes 4 servings*

*Prep. Time: 10 minutes • Cooking Time: 2½-3 hours*
*Ideal slow cooker size: 4-qt.*

1½ cups wild rice,
  uncooked
3 cups chicken stock
3 Tbsp. orange zest
2 Tbsp. orange juice
½ cup raisins (I like
  golden raisins)

1½ tsp. curry powder
1 Tbsp. butter, softened
½ cup fresh parsley
½ cup chopped pecans
½ cup chopped green onion

1. Mix rice, chicken stock, orange zest, orange juice,
raisins, curry powder, and butter in slow cooker.
2. Cover and cook on High 2½-3 hours, or until rice is
tender and has absorbed most of the liquid, but is not dry.
3. Stir in parsley, pecans, and green onion just before
serving.

Note:
*Dear family friends gave
us this to use as an oven
recipe years ago. We have since
adapted it for a slow cooker.
While eating it one Christmas
Eve, someone commented that
the cut tomatoes resembled the
reindeer Rudolph's red nose.
From then on, we changed the
name from Wild Rice Hot Dish
to Rudolph's Nose Wild Rice.*

# Fruited Wild Rice with Pecans

**Dottie Schmidt**
Kansas City, MO

*Makes 4 servings*

*Prep. Time: 15 minutes*
*Cooking Time: 2-2½ hours*
*Ideal slow cooker size: 3-qt.*

½ cup chopped onions
¼ stick (2 Tbsp.) butter, cut
  in chunks
6-oz. pkg. long-grain and
  wild rice, uncooked
seasoning packet from
  wild rice pkg.
1½ cups hot water

⅔ cup apple juice
1 large tart apple, chopped
¼ cup raisins
¼ cup coarsely chopped
  pecans

1. Combine all ingredients except pecans in greased slow cooker.
2. Cover. Cook on High 2-2½ hours, or until rice is fully cooked.
3. Stir in pecans. Serve.

# Mjeddrah

**Dianna Milhizer**
Brighton, MI

*Makes 20-24 servings*

**Prep. Time: 10 minutes**
**Cooking Time: 10 hours**
**Ideal slow cooker size: 6-qt.**

10 cups water
4 cups dried lentils, rinsed
2 cups uncooked brown
  rice
¼ cup olive oil
2 tsp. salt

1. Combine all ingredients in large slow cooker
2. Cover. Cook on High 8 hours and then on Low 2 hours.
3. Check after cooking 8 hours on High. Add 2 more cups water, if needed, to allow rice to continue cooking and to prevent dish from drying out.

*Serving suggestion: This is traditionally eaten with a*

*salad with an **oil-and-vinegar dressing** over the lentil-rice mixture, similar to a tostada without the tortilla.*

# Mushroom Stuffing

**Laverne Stoner**
Scottdale, PA

*Makes 7-8 cups stuffing*

**Prep. Time: 15 minutes**
**Cooking Time: 2-3 hours**
**Ideal slow cooker size: 5-qt.**

1 stick (8 Tbsp.) butter
1 cup finely chopped
  onions
1 cup finely chopped celery
8-oz. can sliced mushrooms,
  drained
¼ cup chopped parsley
1½-2 tsp. poultry seasoning
½ tsp. salt
⅛ tsp. pepper
12 cups toasted bread
  cubes*
2 eggs, well beaten
1½ cups chicken broth

1. Sauté onions and celery in butter in skillet until cooked. Stir in mushrooms and parsley.
2. Combine seasonings and sprinkle over bread cubes in large mixing bowl.
3. Gently add remaining ingredients. Spoon lightly into slow cooker.
4. Cover. Cook on High 1 hour, and then reduce to Low and cook 1-2 hours.

*Lay 18-22 slices of bread on baking sheets. Toast in oven for 15 minutes at 300°.

Tip:
*This is not as much a time-saver as it is a space-saver. If your oven is full, make your stuffing in your slow cooker.*

Variations:
1. Add extra flavor to your stuffing by adding 1 tsp. dried sage, ¾ tsp. dried thyme, and ¼ tsp. dried marjoram to Step 2.
  **Mary H. Nolt**, East Earl, PA
**Jean Turner**, Williams Lake, BC
  **Mary Rogers**, Waseca, MN
  **Kristi See**, Weskan, KS

2. Add 1 lb. loose sausage, browned and drained, to Step 3.
  **Dede Peterson**
Rapid City, SD

# Slow-Cooker Stuffing

**Allison Ingels**
Maynard, IA

*Makes 10-12 servings*

**Prep. Time: 15 minutes**
**Cooking Time: 3 hours**
**Ideal slow cooker size: 5-qt.**

12-13 cups dry bread cubes
(equal to a 20-oz. loaf of
bread)
¼ cup dried parsley
2 eggs, beaten
giblets, cooked and chopped,
broth reserved*
1 tsp. salt
¼ tsp. pepper
½ tsp. sage
1½ tsp. poultry seasoning
3½-4½ cups turkey broth
(from cooking giblets)
2 chicken bouillon cubes
2 cups finely chopped
celery
1 cup finely chopped onion
2 sticks (16 Tbsp.) butter

1. Combine bread cubes
and parsley in slow cooker.
2. Stir in eggs, giblets, and
seasonings.
3. Dissolve bouillon in
heated turkey broth in
stockpot. Add to slow cooker.
4. Sauté celery and onion
in butter in stockpot. Stir into
bread mixture in slow cooker.
5. Cover. Cook on High
1 hour and then on Low 2
hours, stirring occasionally if
you're home and able to do so.

*Place giblets in 3½-4½

cups water in stockpot. Cover.
Cook over medium heat until
giblets are tender.
Remove giblets from
broth and allow them to cool
enough to handle. Then cut
up giblets and proceed with
Step 2.
Reserve broth and keep
warm in stockpot for Step 3.

**Variations:**

1. Add 1 lb. loose sausage,
browned and drained, to Step 2.
**Dorothy VanDeest**
Memphis, TN

2. Use 6 cups cubed day-
old white bread and 6 cups
cubed day-old wheat bread to
add flavor and fiber.
**Jean M. Butzer**
Batavia, NY

**Tip:**

*A convenient way to free
up oven space—or keep your
kitchen cool.*

# Slow-Cooker Dressing

**Marie Shank**
Harrisonburg, VA

*Makes 16 servings*

**Prep. Time: 10 minutes, plus
baking time for cornbread**
**Cooking Time: 2-8 hours**
**Ideal slow cooker size: 6-qt., or
2 4-qt. cookers**

2 boxes Jiffy Cornbread mix
8 slices day-old bread
4 eggs

1 onion, chopped
½ cup chopped celery
2 10¾-oz. cans cream of
chicken soup
2 cups chicken broth
1 tsp. salt
½ tsp. pepper
1½ Tbsp. sage, *or* poultry
seasoning
1-1½ sticks (8-12 Tbsp.)
butter

1. Prepare cornbread
according to package instructions.
2. Crumble cornbread and
bread together in large bowl.
3. Stir in all other ingredients, except butter.
4. Spoon into 6-qt. greased
cooker, or into 2 greased
4-qt. cookers. Dot top(s) with
butter.
5. Cover. Cook on High 2-4
hours or on Low 3-8 hours.

**Variations:**

1. Prepare your favorite
cornbread recipe in an
8"-square baking pan instead
of using cornbread mix.
2. For a more moist
Dressing, use 2 14½-oz. cans
chicken broth instead of 2
cups chicken broth.
3. You may reduce butter
to 2 Tbsp.

**Helen Kenagy**
Carlsbad, NM

# Old-Fashioned Stuffing

**Elaine Rineer**
Lancaster, PA
**Rhonda Freed**
Croghan, NY

*Makes 6 servings*

*Prep. Time: 20-30 minutes*
*Cooking Time: 5 hours*
*Ideal slow cooker size: 4-qt.*

1 stick (8 Tbsp.) butter
1½ cups chopped celery
1 small onion, chopped
12-oz. pkg. bread cubes, *or*
    about 15 slices stale bread
½-¾ tsp. salt
⅛ tsp. pepper
1-2 Tbsp. fresh parsley,
    chopped
2 eggs
1½ cups milk

1. Melt butter in skillet.
Sauté celery and onion in it.
2. Meanwhile, spray
interior of slow cooker with
non-stick cooking spray. Place
bread cubes, salt, pepper, and
parsley in cooker.
3. Pour in sautéed
vegetables, eggs, and milk.
Stir together gently until well
mixed.
4. Cover. Cook on High 1
hour. Stir.
5. Cover. Cook on High 4
more hours.

Tip:
*This is delicious and an easy
way to free up oven space for
the rest of your meal.*

# Corn Stuffing Balls

**Mable Shirk**
Mt. Crawford, VA

*Makes 4-5 servings*

*Prep. Time: 30 minutes*
*Cooking Time: 3-4 hours*
*Ideal slow cooker size: 2- to 4-qt.*

½ cup celery with leaves,
    chopped
1 small onion, chopped
2 cups cream-style corn,
    canned, *or* frozen
¼ cup water
⅛ tsp. pepper
1 tsp. poultry seasoning
8-oz. pkg. herb-seasoned
    stuffing mix
2 slightly beaten eggs
half a stick (4 Tbsp.)
    melted butter

1. In mixing bowl, combine
celery, onion, corn, water,
pepper, poultry seasoning,
stuffing mix, and eggs.
2. Shape into 7 or 8 balls.
Arrange in slow cooker. Pour
butter over top.
3. Cover. Cook on Low 3-4
hours.

*Serving suggestion: Serve
with **gravy** and alongside
**broiled meats** or **roasts**,
or use as extra stuffing with
**turkey**.*

# Mashed Potato Filling

**Betty K. Drescher**
Quakertown, PA

*Makes 8-10 servings*

*Prep. Time: 15-20 minutes*
*Cooking Time: 4 hours*
*Ideal slow cooker size: 5-qt.*

½ cup diced onions
1 cup diced celery
1 stick (8 Tbsp.) butter
2½ cups milk
4 large eggs, beaten
8 oz. bread cubes
4 cups mashed potatoes
1½ tsp. salt
¼ tsp. pepper

1. Sauté onions and celery
in butter in skillet for 5-10
minutes, or until vegetables
are tender.
2. Combine onions and
celery, milk, and eggs in
mixing bowl.
3. Place bread cubes in
large mixing bowl. Pour
vegetable-milk-egg mixture
over bread cubes. Mix lightly.
4. Stir in potatoes and
seasonings.
5. Spoon into greased slow
cooker.
6. Cover. Cook on Low 4
hours.

# Sweet Potato Stuffing

Tina Snyder
Manheim, PA

*Makes 8 servings*

**Prep. Time: 15 minutes**
**Cooking Time: 4 hours**
**Ideal slow cooker size: 4-qt.**

½ **cup chopped celery**
½ **cup chopped onions**
**half a stick (4 Tbsp.) butter**
**6 cups dry bread cubes**
**1 large sweet potato, cooked,***
    **peeled, and cubed**
½ **cup chicken broth**
¼ **cup chopped pecans**
½ **tsp. poultry seasoning**
½ **tsp. rubbed sage**
½ **tsp. salt**
¼ **tsp. pepper**

1. Sauté celery and onions in skillet in butter until tender. Pour into greased slow cooker.
2. Add remaining ingredients. Toss gently.
3. Cover. Cook on Low 4 hours.

*To prepare a cooked sweet potato, wash, dry, and prick it at about 4 different places with a sharp fork. Lay on a paper towel in the microwave. Cook on High 1½ minutes. Turn over. Cook on High another minute. Jag with fork to see if it's tender. If not, continue cooking for 30-second intervals on High, turning over each time, until tender.

Allow to cool. When you're able to handle it, gently peel and cube.

# Scalloped Pineapple

June Groff
Denver, PA

*Makes 8 servings*

**Prep. Time: 10 minutes**
**Cooking Time: 3 hours**
**Ideal slow cooker size: 2- to 3-qt.**

**1 stick (8 Tbsp.) butter,**
    **softened**

½ **cup sugar**
**4 eggs**
**20-oz. can crushed**
    **pineapple, drained**
**5 slices fresh bread, cubed**

1. Cream butter and sugar together in a medium-sized mixing bowl.
2. Add eggs. Mix well.
3. Add drained pineapple. Blend.
4. Fold bread into mixture.
5. Pour into slow cooker.
6. Cover. Cook on High 2 hours and then on Low 1 hour.

*Serving suggestion: This is a good accompaniment to **turkey**, **ham**, and **chicken**, especially at holiday-time. Small individual servings add a bright sweetness to special meals.*

Back in the 1930s, a doctor and his wife lived in Wausau, WI, where the local hospital served a large, mostly rural region. Many children in the area were pretty confined during the holidays. This couple baked and frosted cookies by the hundreds. Walking into their house was like going to Mrs. Claus' kitchen; there were cookies everywhere. They distributed the cookies to the children on Christmas Day.

My aunt lived with them and shared the recipe with our family. This year my 7 grandchildren continue the tradition of baking these cookies into the 5th generation. It's not Christmas until those cookies are decorated.

Carol Findling, Carol Stream, IL

# Beverages

## Cider Snap

**Cathy Boshart**
Lebanon, PA

*Makes 12-16 servings*

**Prep. Time: 5-10 minutes**
**Cooking Time: 2 hours**
**Ideal slow cooker size: 3½-qt.**

**2 qts. apple cider,** *or* **apple juice**
**4 Tbsp. red cinnamon candies**
**at least 16 apple slices**
**at least 16 cinnamon sticks**

1. Combine cider and cinnamon candies in slow cooker.
2. Cover. Cook on High 2 hours, or until candies dissolve and cider is hot.
3. Ladle into mugs and serve with apple-slice floaters and cinnamon-stick stirrers.

**Note:**
This is a cold-winter-night luxury. Make it in the morning and keep it on Low throughout the day so its good fragrance can fill the house.

**Variation:**
Use cran-apple juice instead of apple cider or juice.
**Anita Troyer**
Fairview, MI

## Maple Mulled Cider

**Leesa Lesenski**
Wheatley, MA

*Makes 8-10 servings*

**Prep. Time: 5-10 minutes**
**Cooking Time: 2 hours**
**Ideal slow cooker size: 3½-qt.**

**½ gallon cider**
**3-4 cinnamon sticks**
**2 tsp. whole cloves**
**2 tsp. whole allspice**
**1-2 Tbsp. orange juice concentrate,** *optional*
**1-2 Tbsp. maple syrup,** *optional*

1. Combine ingredients in slow cooker.
2. Cover. Heat on Low 2 hours. Serve warm.

**Note:**
Serve at Halloween, after Christmas caroling, or for sledding parties.

# Matthew's Hot Mulled Cider

**Shirley Unternahrer**, Wayland, IA

*Makes 12 servings*

*Prep. Time: 5 minutes • Cooking Time: 5 hours*
*Ideal slow cooker size: 3½-qt.*

2 qts. apple cider
¼ cup brown sugar
½ tsp. vanilla

1 cinnamon stick
4 cloves

1. Combine ingredients in slow cooker.
2. Cover. Cook on Low 5 hours. Stir.

Note:

*Our kids just tried hot mulled cider for the first time this past Christmas. They loved it. It's fun to try new old things.*

# Deep Red Apple Cider

**Judi Manos**
West Islip, NY

*Makes 8-9 servings*

*Prep. Time: 5-10 minutes*
*Cooking Time: 3-4 hours*
*Ideal slow cooker size: 3½-qt.*

5 cups apple cider
3 cups dry red wine
¼ cup brown sugar
½ tsp. whole cloves
¼ tsp. whole allspice
1 stick cinnamon

1. Combine all ingredients in slow cooker.
2. Cover. Cook on Low 3-4 hours.

3. Remove cloves, allspice, and cinnamon before serving.

Variation:

You can use 8 cups apple cider and no red wine.

# Orange Cider Punch

**Naomi Ressler**
Harrisonburg, VA

*Makes 9-12 6-oz. servings*

*Prep. Time: 5-10 minutes*
*Cooking Time: 2-10 hours*
*Ideal slow cooker size: 3½-qt.*

1 cup sugar
2 cinnamon sticks
1 tsp. whole nutmeg
2 cups apple cider, *or* apple juice
6 cups orange juice
fresh orange thinly sliced

1. Combine all ingredients except orange slices in slow cooker.
2. Cover. Cook on Low 4-10 hours or on High 2-3 hours, until heated through.
3. Float thin slices of orange in cooker before serving.

*I like to sit down a couple of weeks before the holidays and write an outline of what needs to be done and how many days I need to do the work. I try to plan enough time so I don't run out of time on the last day.*

*Jane Geigley, Honey Brook, PA*

# Wassail

**Virginia Bender**
Dover, DE

*Makes 16-18 servings*

*Prep. Time: 10 minutes*
*Cooking Time: 2-8 hours*
*Ideal slow cooker size: 6-qt.*

1 gallon cider
6-oz. container frozen
    orange juice concentrate
6-oz. container frozen
    lemonade concentrate
½-1 cup brown sugar,
    according to your taste
    preference
1 tsp. whole nutmeg
1 Tbsp. whole cloves
1 Tbsp. whole allspice
orange slices
cinnamon sticks

1. Combine cider, orange
juice and lemonade concen-
trates, and brown sugar in
slow cooker. Mix well.
2. Place nutmeg, cloves,
and allspice in cheesecloth
bag or spice ball. Add to
juices in slow cooker.
3. Cover. Cook on Low 2-8
hours, until the Wassail is as
hot as you like it.
4. Float orange slices and
cinnamon sticks on top. Ladle
from slow cooker to serve.

# Hot
# Cranberry Cider

**Kristi See**
Weskan, KS

*Makes 10-12 servings*

*Prep. Time: 10 minutes*
*Cooking Time: 5-9 hours*
*Ideal slow cooker size: 4-qt.*

½ gallon apple cider, *or*
    apple juice
2 cups cranberry juice
½-¾ cup sugar, according
    to your taste preference
2 cinnamon sticks
1 tsp. whole allspice
whole orange studded with
    cloves

1. Put all ingredients
except orange studded with
cloves in slow cooker.
2. Cover. Cook on High 1
hour, and then on Low 4-8
hours, until thoroughly hot.
3 Float clove-studded
orange in cooker. Serve hot.

*Serving suggestion: To*
*garnish Cider with an **orange**,*
*insert 10-12½"-long **whole***
***cloves** halfway into orange.*
*Place studded orange in flat*
*baking pan with sides. Pour in*
*¼ cup water. Bake at 325° for*
*30 minutes. Just before serving,*
*float orange on top of hot Cider.*

Note:
    I come from a family of eight
children, and every Christmas
we all get together. We eat
dinner, and then play games
while drinking Hot Cranberry
Cider.

# Pomegranate
# Punch

**Lindsey Spencer**
Marrow, OH

*Makes 8 servings*

*Prep. Time: 5-7 minutes*
*Cooking Time: 1-2 hours*
*Ideal slow cooker size: 3-qt.*

3 cups pomegranate juice
1-1½ cups cranberry juice
    cocktail, according to
    your taste preference
½ cup orange juice
3"-long cinnamon stick
1 tsp. grated ginger

1. Put all ingredients in
slow cooker.
2. Cover. Cook on Low
1-2 hours, or until heated
through.

# Christmas Wassail

**Dottie Schmidt**
Kansas City, MO

*Makes 6-8 servings*

*Prep. Time: 5-10 minutes*
*Cooking Time: 1 hour*
*Ideal slow cooker size: 3-qt.*

2 cups cranberry juice
3¼ cups hot water
⅓ cup sugar
6-oz. can frozen lemonade
　concentrate
1 stick cinnamon
5 whole cloves
2 oranges, cut in thin slices

1. Combine all ingredients except oranges in slow cooker. Stir until sugar is dissolved.
2. Cover. Cook on High 1 hour. Strain out spices.
3. Serve hot with an orange slice floating in each cup.

# Fruity Hot Punch

**Evelyn L. Ward**
Greeley, CO

*Makes 12 servings*

*Prep. Time: 10 minutes*
*Cooking Time: 4 hours*
*Ideal slow cooker size: 5-qt.*

2 16-oz. cans jellied
　cranberry sauce
4 cups water
1 qt. pineapple juice
¾ cup brown sugar
¼ tsp. salt
¼ tsp. ground nutmeg
¾ tsp. ground cloves
½ tsp. ground allspice
12 cinnamon sticks
**butter,** *optional*

1. Place cranberry sauce in slow cooker and mash with a potato masher.
2. Add all remaining ingredients to slow cooker except cinnamon sticks and butter. Mix well.
3. Cover. Heat on Low 4 hours.
4. Serve in mugs with cinnamon-stick stirrers. Dot each serving with butter if you wish.

## Note:

*My daughter is a teacher and has served this at faculty meetings when it's her turn to treat.*

# Fruity Wassail

**Kelly Evenson**
Pittsboro, NC

*Makes 20 cups*

*Prep. Time: 10 minutes*
*Cooking Time: 1-2 hours*
*Ideal slow cooker size: 5-qt.*

6 cups apple cider
1 cinnamon stick
¼ tsp. ground nutmeg
¼ cup honey
3 Tbsp. lemon juice
1 tsp. grated lemon rind
46-oz. can pineapple juice

1. Combine ingredients in slow cooker.
2. Cover. Cook on Low 1-2 hours, or until hot.
3. Serve warm from slow cooker.

## Variation:

Use 3 cups cranberry juice, and reduce the amount of pineapple juice by 3 cups, to add more color and to change the flavor of the Wassail.

# Spicy Citrus Warmer

**Jean Butzer**
Batavia, NY

**Barbara Walker**
Sturgis, SD

*Makes 12 servings*

*Prep. Time: 5-10 minutes*
*Cooking Time: 2-3 hours*
*Ideal slow cooker size: 5-qt.*

2½ qts. water
1½ cups sugar
1½ cups orange juice (with pulp is great!)
⅔ cup freshly squeezed lemon juice
⅓ cup pineapple juice
6"-long cinnamon stick, *or* two 3" sticks
1 tsp. whole cloves

1. Combine water, sugar, and juices in slow cooker. Stir until sugar is dissolved.
2. Add cinnamon stick to cooker. Place cloves in a tea ball. Close tightly and place in slow cooker.
3. Cover. Cook on Low 2-3 hours, or until heated through.

**Tester Idea:**
Add a half slice of orange or lime on the edge of each individual cup before serving.

# Golden Wassail Punch

**Susan Segraves**
Lansdale, PA

*Makes 9 cups*

*Prep. Time: 10 minutes*
*Cooking Time: 1-3 hours*
*Ideal slow cooker size: 3- to 4-qt.*

3 cups apricot nectar
3 cups orange juice
3 cups white grape juice
¼ cup lemon juice
2 Tbsp. brown sugar
8"-long stick cinnamon, broken
½ tsp. cardamom, coarsely crushed

1. Combine juices and brown sugar in slow cooker. Stir until sugar is dissolved.
2. Lay stick cinnamon and cardamom on a square of cheesecloth. Tie shut securely. Place in slow cooker and push down into liquid.
3. Cover. Cook on High 1 hour, or on Low 2-3 hours. Remove spice bag before serving.

# Hot Buttered Lemonade

**Janie Steele**
Moore, OK

*Makes 5-6 servings*

*Prep. Time: 5-10 minutes*
*Cooking Time: 2½ hours*
*Ideal slow cooker size: 2-qt.*

4½ cups water
¾ cup sugar
1½ tsp. grated lemon peel
¾ cup lemon juice
2 Tbsp. butter
6 cinnamon sticks

1. Combine water, sugar, lemon peel, lemon juice, and butter in slow cooker.
2. Cover. Cook on High 2½ hours, or until well heated through.
3. Serve very hot with a cinnamon stick in each mug.

*When juicing a lemon, let it come to room temperature. You'll get more juice if you do. Then, using some pressure, roll it under your hand on the counter before juicing it so that it releases its juice more easily. Freeze any extra juice in 1 Tbsp. amounts in an ice cube tray.*

*Becky Frey, Lebanon, PA*

# Hot Fruit Tea

**Kelly Evenson**
Pittsboro, NC

*Makes 20 servings*

*Prep. Time: 20 minutes*
*Ideal slow cooker size: 5-qt.*

5-6 tea bags, fruit flavor of
   your choice
2 cups boiling water
1¾ cups sugar
2 cinnamon sticks
2½ qts. water
1¼ tsp. vanilla
1¼ tsp. almond extract
juice of 3 lemons
juice of 3 oranges

1. Steep tea bags in 2 cups
boiling water for 5 minutes.
2. Bring tea water, sugar,
cinnamon sticks, and 2½ qts.
water to boil in saucepan.
3. Pour into slow cooker.
Stir in remaining ingredients.
4. Turn slow cooker to
Low. Keep tea warm on Low
while serving.

*Serving suggestion: Float
thinly cut fresh **lemon** and/or
**orange** slices in tea.*

# Johnny Appleseed Tea

**Sheila Plock**
Boalsburg, PA

*Makes 8-9 cups*

*Prep. Time: 15 minutes*
*Cooking Time: 1-2 hours*
*Ideal slow cooker size: 3½-qt.*

2 qts. water, *divided*
6 tea bags of your favorite
   flavor
6 ozs. frozen apple juice,
   thawed
¼ cup, plus 2 Tbsp., firmly
   packed brown sugar

1. Bring 1 qt. water to
boil in large saucepan. Add
tea bags. Remove from heat.
Cover and let steep 5 minutes. Pour into slow cooker.
2. Add remaining ingredi-
ents and mix well.
3. Cover. Heat on Low
until hot. Continue on Low
while serving from slow
cooker.

Note:

*I serve this wonderful hot
beverage with cookies at our
Open House Tea and Cookies
afternoon, which I host at
Christmas-time for friends and
neighbors.*

# Ginger Tea

**Evelyn Page**
Gillette, WY

*Makes 8 cups*

*Prep. Time: 5-15 minutes*
*Cooking Time: 2 hours*
*Ideal slow cooker size: 3-qt.*

4 cups boiling water
15 single green tea bags
4 cups white grape juice
1-2 Tbsp. honey, according
   to your taste preference
1 Tbsp. minced fresh
   gingerroot
candied ginger pieces,
   *optional*

1. Place boiling water and
tea bags in slow cooker. Cover
and let stand 10 minutes.
Discard tea bags.
2. Stir in juice, honey, and
gingerroot.
3. Cover. Cook on Low
2 hours, or until heated
through.
4. Strain if you wish before
pouring into individual cups.
5. Garnish each cup with
candied ginger, if you wish.

# Triple Delicious Hot Chocolate

**Jennifer Freed**
Harrisonburg, VA

*Makes 6 servings*

*Prep. Time: 15 minutes*
*Cooking Time: 2¼ hours*
*Ideal slow cooker size: 2- to 3-qt.*

⅓ cup sugar
¼ cup unsweetened cocoa powder
¼ tsp. salt
3 cups milk, *divided*
¾ tsp. vanilla
1 cup heavy cream
1 square (1 oz.) bittersweet chocolate
1 square (1 oz.) white chocolate
¾ cup whipped topping
6 tsp. mini-chocolate chips, *or shaved bittersweet chocolate*

1. Combine sugar, cocoa powder, salt, and ½ cup milk in medium-sized bowl. Stir until smooth. Pour into slow cooker.
2. Add remaining 2½ cups milk and vanilla to slow cooker. Cover. Cook on Low 2 hours.
3. Stir in cream. Cover. Cook on Low 10 minutes.
4. Stir in bittersweet and white chocolates until melted.
5. Pour hot chocolate into 6 mugs. Top each with 2 Tbsp. whipped topping and 1 tsp. chocolate chips or shavings.

# Crockery Cocoa

**Betty Hostetler**, Allensville, PA

*Makes 9-12 servings, depending on size of mugs*

*Prep. Time: 10 minutes*
*Cooking Time: 1-4 hours*
*Ideal slow cooker size: 3½-qt.*

½ cup sugar
½ cup unsweetened cocoa powder
2 cups boiling water
3½ cups nonfat dry milk powder
6 cups water
1 tsp. vanilla
mini-marshmallows
1 tsp. ground cinnamon

1. Combine sugar and cocoa powder in slow cooker. Add 2 cups boiling water. Stir well to dissolve.
2. Add dry milk powder, 6 cups water, and vanilla. Stir well to dissolve.
3. Cover. Cook on Low 4 hours or on High 1-1½ hours.
4. Before serving, beat with rotary beater to make frothy. Ladle into mugs. Top with marshmallows and sprinkle with cinnamon.

**Variations:**
1. Add ⅛ tsp. ground nutmeg, along with ground cinnamon in Step 4.
2. Mocha-style—Stir ¾ tsp. instant coffee crystals into each serving in Step 4.
3. Coffee-Cocoa—Pour half-cups of freshly brewed, high quality coffee. Top with half-cups of Crockery Cocoa.

# Hot Chocolate with Stir-Ins

**Stacy Schmucker Stoltzfus**
Enola, PA

*Makes 12 6-oz. servings*

*Prep. Time: 5 minutes*
*Cooking Time: 1-2 hours*
*Ideal slow cooker size: 4-qt.*

9½ cups water
1½ cups hot chocolate mix

Stir-ins:
smooth peanut butter
chocolate-mint candies, chopped
candy canes, broken
assorted flavored syrups: hazelnut, almond, raspberry, Irish creme
instant coffee granules
cinnamon
nutmeg

whipped topping
candy sprinkles

1. Pour water into slow cooker. Heat on High 1-2 hours. (Or heat water in tea kettle and pour into slow cooker.) Turn cooker to Low to keep hot for hours.
2. Stir in hot chocolate mix until blended.
3. Arrange stir-ins in small bowls.
4. Instruct guests to place approximately 1 Tbsp. of their choice of stir-ins in their mugs before ladling in hot chocolate. Stir well.
5. Top each filled mug with whipped topping and candy sprinkles.

# Vanilla Steamer

**Anita Troyer**, Fairview, MI

*Makes 8 servings*

*Prep. Time: 5-10 minutes • Cooking Time: 2-3 hours*
*Ideal slow cooker size: 3-qt.*

8 cups milk
⅛ tsp. cinnamon, *or*
  2 3"-long cinnamon
  sticks
3 Tbsp. sugar
2 Tbsp. vanilla

pinch of salt
pinch of nutmeg
whipped topping, *optional*
sprinkling of ground
  cinnamon, *optional*

1. Put all ingredients except whipped topping and sprinkling of ground cinnamon in slow cooker.

2. Cover. Cook on Low 2-3 hours, taking care to make sure it doesn't boil.

3. Garnish individual servings with whipped topping and a sprinkling of cinnamon if you wish.

**Tip:**

*I usually make a larger recipe than I will need, and then refrigerate the leftovers. We like it either reheated, or as creamer in our coffee. This drink is very soothing and helps everyone relax!*

# Viennese Coffee

**Evelyn Page**
Gillette, WY

*Makes 4 servings*

*Prep. Time: 15 minutes*
*Cooking Time: 3 hours*
*Ideal slow cooker size: 1½- to 2-qt.*

3 cups strong brewed
  coffee
3 Tbsp. chocolate syrup
1 tsp. sugar
⅓ cup heavy whipping
  cream
¼ cup crème de cacao, *or*
  Irish cream liqueur
whipped cream, *optional*
chocolate curls, *optional*

1. In a slow cooker, combine coffee, chocolate syrup, and sugar.

2. Cover. Cook on Low 2½ hours.

3. Stir in heavy cream and crème de cacao.

4. Cover. Cook 30 minutes more, or until heated through.

5. Ladle into mugs. Garnish if you wish with whipped cream and chocolate curls.

# Desserts and Sweets

## Holiday Cherry Cobbler

**Colleen Heatwole**
Burton, MI

*Makes 5-6 servings*

*Prep. Time: 15 minutes*
*Cooking Time: 2½-3½ hours*
*Ideal slow cooker size: 4-qt.*

**16-oz. can cherry filling
(light *or* regular)**
**1 pkg. cake mix for 1 layer
white, *or* yellow, cake**
**1 egg**
**3 Tbsp. evaporated milk**
**½ tsp. cinnamon**
**½ cup walnuts, chopped**

1. Spray slow cooker with cooking spray.
2. Spread pie filling in bottom of cooker.
3. Cover. Cook on High 30 minutes.
4. Meanwhile, in a medium-sized mixing bowl mix together cake mix, egg, evaporated milk, cinnamon, and walnuts.
5. Spoon over hot pie filling. Do not stir.
6. Cover. Cook on Low 2-3 hours, or until toothpick inserted in cake layer comes out clean.

*Use a special holiday kitchen tool. I use my grandmother's 100-year-old tin cookie cutters to make sugar cookies from her recipe box. The angel and lady cutters are my favorite. They make the best "dunking" shapes.*

*Susan J. Heil, Strasburg, PA*

# Gingerbread Pudding Cake

**Katrina Eberly**
Wernersville, PA

*Makes 6-8 servings*

**Prep. Time: 20 minutes**
**Cooking Time: 2-2½ hours**
**Standing Time: 15 minutes**
**Ideal slow cooker size: 3-qt.**

half a stick (4 Tbsp.)
  butter, softened
¼ cup sugar
1 egg white
1 tsp. vanilla extract
½ cup molasses
1 cup water
1¼ cups flour
¾ tsp. baking soda
½ tsp. ground cinnamon
½ tsp. ground ginger
¼ tsp. salt
¼ tsp. ground allspice
⅛ tsp. ground nutmeg
½ cup chopped pecans
6 Tbsp. brown sugar

**Topping:**
¾ cup hot water
5⅔ Tbsp. (⅓ cup) butter,
  melted

1. Spray interior of slow cooker with cooking spray.

2. In a large mixing bowl, cream 4 Tbsp. butter and sugar until light and fluffy. Beat in egg white and vanilla.

3. In a separate bowl, combine molasses and water until blended.

4. In another bowl, combine flour, baking soda, and spices. Add to creamed mixture alternately with molasses mixture, beating well after each addition.

5. Fold in pecans. Spoon into slow cooker. Sprinkle with brown sugar

6. In a small bowl, combine hot water and 5⅔ Tbsp. butter. Pour over batter. Do *not* stir.

7. Cover. Cook on High 2-2½ hours, or until toothpick inserted in center of cake comes out clean.

8. Turn off cooker. Let stand 15 minutes. Serve cake warm.

### Note from Tester:

I used blackstrap molasses, and the flavor didn't overpower the cake.

# Christmas Apple Date Pudding

**Colleen Heatwole**
Burton, MI

*Makes 8 servings*

**Prep. Time: 30 minutes**
**Cooking Time: 3-4 hours**
**Ideal slow cooker size: 2-qt.**

4-5 apples, peeled, cored,
  and diced
½ cup sugar
½ cup chopped dates
½ cup toasted, chopped
  pecans
1 Tbsp. flour
1 tsp. baking powder
⅛ tsp. salt
½ tsp. cinnamon
2 Tbsp. melted butter
1 beaten egg

1. In a greased slow cooker, mix together apples, sugar, dates, and pecans.

2. In a separate bowl, mix together flour, baking powder, salt, and cinnamon. Stir into apple mixture.

3. Drizzle melted butter over batter and stir.

4. Stir in egg.

5. Cover. Cook on Low 3-4 hours. Serve warm.

---

*At the end of our Christmas meal we serve chocolate cake. I write "Happy Birthday, Jesus" on it in yellow frosting. I use extra frosting to make a hay bed for a small baby figurine to rest on. We have one candle for each grandchild to blow out after we sing Happy Birthday to Baby Jesus. Usually amid laughter, we relight some accidentally blown-out candles.*

*Anne Townsend, Albuquerque, NM*

# Date and Nut Loaf

### Jean Butzer
Batavia, NY

*Makes 16 servings*

*Prep. Time: 20 minutes*
*Cooking Time: 3½-4 hours*
*Ideal slow cooker size: large*
*enough to hold 2 coffee cans,*
*or your baking insert*

**1½ cups boiling water**
**1½ cups chopped dates**
**1¼ cups sugar**
**1 egg**
**2 tsp. baking soda**
**½ tsp. salt**
**1 tsp. vanilla**
**1 Tbsp. melted butter**
**2½ cups flour**
**1 cup walnuts, chopped**
**2 cups hot water**

1. In a large mixing bowl, pour 1½ cups boiling water over dates. Let stand 5-10 minutes.

2. Stir in sugar, egg, baking soda, salt, vanilla, and butter.

3. In a separate bowl, combine flour and nuts. Stir into date mixture and combine well.

4. Pour into 2 greased 11½-oz. coffee cans, or one 8-cup baking insert.

5. If using coffee cans, cover with foil and tie securely with kitchen twine. If using baking insert, cover with its lid.

6. Place cans or insert on rack in slow cooker. (If you don't have a rack, use rubber jar rings instead.)

7. Pour 2 cups hot water around cans or insert, up to half their/its height.

# Banana Loaf

### Sue Hamilton, Minooka, IL

*Makes 6-8 servings*

*Prep. Time: 5-10 minutes • Cooking Time: 2-2½ hours*
*Ideal slow cooker size: large enough to hold*
*2-lb. coffee can upright, or a baking insert*

| | |
|---|---|
| **3 very ripe bananas** | **1 tsp. vanilla** |
| **1 stick (8 Tbsp.) butter, softened** | **1 cup sugar** |
| | **1 cup flour** |
| **2 eggs** | **1 tsp. baking soda** |

1. Combine all ingredients in an electric mixing bowl. Beat 2 minutes, or until well blended. Pour into well greased 2-lb. coffee can or baking insert.

2. Place can or insert in slow cooker. Cover can with 6 layers of paper towels between cooker lid and bread. Or cover with baking insert lid.

3. Cover cooker. Bake on High 2-2½ hours, or until toothpick inserted in center comes out clean. Cool 15 minutes before removing from pan.

8. Cover slow cooker tightly. Cook on High 3½-4 hours. Insert toothpick into loaves of bread to see if it comes out clean. If it does, the bread is finished. If it doesn't, allow to cook 30 more minutes. Check again to see if bread is done. If not, continue cooking in 30-minute intervals.

9. When bread is finished, remove cans or insert from cooker. Let bread stand in coffee cans or baking insert for 10 minutes. Turn out onto cooling rack.

10. When thoroughly cooled, slice. Spread with butter, cream cheese, or peanut butter.

# Slow-Cooker Spoon Peaches

**Jeanette Oberholtzer**
Manheim, PA

*Makes 6 servings*

*Prep. Time: 10 minutes*
*Cooking Time: 6-8 hours*
*Ideal slow cooker size: 1½-qt.*

⅓ cup sugar
½ cup brown sugar
¾ cup buttermilk baking
   mix
2 eggs
2 tsp. vanilla
1 Tbsp. butter, melted
half a 12-oz. can
   evaporated milk
2 cups mashed peaches,
   fresh, frozen, *or* canned
   (if canned, drain slightly)
¾ tsp. cinnamon

1. Combine sugar, brown sugar, and baking mix in a good-sized mixing bowl.
2. Add eggs and vanilla. Mix well.
3. Add butter and milk. Mix well.
4. Add peaches and cinnamon. Mix well. Pour into greased slow cooker.
5. Cover. Cook on Low 6-8 hours.

*Serving suggestion: Serve warm with **whipped cream** or **vanilla ice cream**.*

Note:
*This is a great warm dessert for a cold winter evening.*

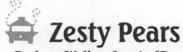

# Zesty Pears

**Barbara Walker**, Sturgis, SD

*Makes 6 servings*

*Prep. Time: 15 minutes • Cooking Time: 4-6 hours*
*Ideal slow cooker size: 2- to 3-qt.*

6 fresh pears
½ cup raisins
¼ cup brown sugar
1 tsp. grated lemon peel
¼ cup brandy
½ cup sauterne wine
½ cup macaroon crumbs
sour cream, *optional*

1. Peel and core pears. Cut into thin slices and place in bowl.
2. In a separate small bowl, combine raisins, sugar, and lemon peel. Layer alternately with pear slices in slow cooker.
3. Pour brandy and wine over top.
4. Cover. Cook on Low 4-6 hours.
5. Spoon into serving dishes. Cool. Sprinkle with macaroons. Serve plain or topped with sour cream.

# Cranberry Sauce with Red Wine and Oranges

**Donna Treloar**
Muncie, IN

*Makes 3-4 servings*

*Prep. Time: 5-10 minutes*
*Cooking Time: 2-2½ hours*
*Ideal slow cooker size: 2-qt.*

12-oz. bag fresh
   cranberries, rinsed
1½ cups sugar
1 cup dry red wine
1 cinnamon stick
grated zest of one orange,
   then cut orange in half
4 whole cloves

1. Combine cranberries, sugar, wine, cinnamon, and zest in slow cooker.
2. Place 2 cloves in each orange half. Push down into cranberry mixture.
3. Cover. Cook on High 2-2½ hours, or until cranberries have popped. Turn off cooker.
4. Discard cinnamon stick and orange halves with cloves.
5. Remove lid and let Sauce cool to room temperature.

*Serving suggestion: Serve chilled or at room temperature over **ice cream** or **pound cake**.*

# Apple Cranberry Compote

**Charlotte Shaffer**
East Earl, PA

*Makes 8 servings*

*Prep. Time: 15-20 minutes*
*Cooking Time: 3-4 hours*
*Ideal slow cooker size: 3- to 4-qt.*

6 apples, peeled and sliced
1 cup fresh cranberries
1 cup sugar
½ tsp. grated orange peel
½ cup water
¼ cup port wine
sour cream

1. Combine apples and cranberries in slow cooker. Sprinkle evenly with sugar. Stir in orange peel, water, and wine.
2. Cover. Cook on Low 3-4 hours.
3. Serve with dollops of sour cream on individual servings.

# Warmed Spiced Fruit

**Susan Segraves**
Lansdale, PA

*Makes 6-8 servings*

*Prep. Time: 20 minutes*
*Cooking Time: 2 hours*
*Ideal slow cooker size: 6-qt.*

3 Golden Delicious, *or* Granny Smith, apples, peeled, cored, and sliced
3 pears, peeled, cored, and sliced
11-oz. can mandarin oranges, drained
1 cup fresh cranberries, rinsed, and coarsely chopped
¼ cup firmly packed brown sugar
2 Tbsp. cornstarch
¼ tsp. ground cinnamon
¼ tsp. ground ginger
⅛ tsp. ground cloves
1 cup apple, white grape, *or* cranberry juice

1. Layer fruit in order given in slow cooker.
2. In a medium-sized bowl, stir together brown sugar, cornstarch, and spices. Slowly stir in juice. Pour over fruit.
3. Cover. Cook on High 2 hours. Serve warm or chilled.

**Note from Tester:**
*Cranberries were out of season when I tested the recipe, so I used 1 cup craisins instead. Excellent results!*

# Fruit Compote

**Janet Batdorf**
Harrisburg, PA

*Makes 5 servings*

*Prep. Time: 15 minutes*
*Cooking Time: 6 hours*
*Ideal slow cooker size: 5-qt.*

1 qt. canned peach slices with juice
1 cup dried apricots
½ cup brown sugar
¼ cup water
1 tsp. grated orange peel
⅓ cup orange juice
½ tsp. grated lemon peel
2 Tbsp. lemon juice
16-oz. can pitted dark sweet cherries, drained

1. Combine peaches with their juice, apricots, brown sugar, water, orange peel, orange juice, lemon peel, and lemon juice in slow cooker.
2. Cover. Cook on Low 6 hours.
3. Fifteen minutes before end of cooking time, stir in cherries. Cover. Cook 15 more minutes.

*Serving suggestion: Serve over **ice cream** or **pound cake**, or alongside a plate of **cookies**.*

# Festive Fruit Compote

**Maryann Markano**
Wilmington, DE

*Makes 10-12 servings*

***Prep. Time: 10-15 minutes***
***Cooking Time: 3-8 hours***
***Ideal slow cooker size: 4- to 5-qt.***

1 lb. dried prunes
1⅓ cups dried apricots
13½-oz. can pineapple
  chunks, undrained
16-oz. can pitted dark
  sweet cherries,
  undrained
¼ cup dry white wine
2 cups water

1. Place all ingredients in slow cooker.
2. Cover. Cook on Low 7-8 hours or on High 3-4 hours.
3. Serve warm.

Note:

You can substitute other dried fruits in place of the prunes and apricots.

---

# Fruit Dessert Topping

**Lavina Hochstedler**
Grand Blanc, MI

*Makes 6 cups*

***Prep. Time: 20 minutes***
***Cooking Time: 3½-4¾ hours***
***Ideal slow cooker size: 3½-qt.***

3 tart apples, peeled and
  sliced
3 pears, peeled and sliced
1 Tbsp. lemon juice
½ cup packed brown sugar
½ cup maple syrup
half a stick (4 Tbsp.)
  butter, melted
½ cup chopped pecans
¼ cup raisins
2 cinnamon sticks
1 Tbsp. cornstarch
2 Tbsp. cold water

1. Toss apples and pears in lemon juice in slow cooker.
2. In a small bowl, combine brown sugar, maple syrup, and butter. Pour over fruit.
3. Stir in pecans, raisins, and cinnamon sticks.
4. Cover. Cook on Low 3-4 hours.
5. In a small bowl, combine cornstarch and water until smooth. Gradually stir into slow cooker.
6. Cover. Cook on High 30-40 minutes, or until fruit thickens.
7. Discard cinnamon sticks.

*Serving suggestion: Serve over **pound cake** or **ice cream**.*

---

Note:
*We also like this served along with pancakes or an egg casserole. We always use Fruit Topping for our breakfasts at church camp.*

# Wagon Master Apple-Cherry Sauce

**Sharon Timpe**
Mequon, WI

*Makes 12-15 servings*

***Prep. Time: 5-10 minutes***
***Cooking Time: 3-4 hours***
***Ideal slow cooker size: 3½-qt.***

2 21-oz. cans apple pie
  filling
2-3 cups frozen tart red
  cherries
1 Tbsp. butter
½ tsp. ground cinnamon
½ tsp. ground nutmeg
⅛ tsp. ground ginger
⅛ tsp. ground cloves

1. Combine all ingredients except whipped cream in slow cooker.
2. Cover. Heat on Low 3-4 hours, or until mixture is hot and bubbly. Stir occasionally.

*Serving suggestion: Serve warm over **vanilla ice cream**, **pudding**, **pound cake**, or **shortcake biscuits**. Top with **whipped cream** or **whipped topping** if you wish.*

# Curried Fruit

**Jane Meiser**
Harrisonburg, VA

*Makes 8-10 servings*

**Prep. Time: 10 minutes**
**Marinating Time: 2-8 hours**
**Cooking Time: 8-10 hours**
**Ideal slow cooker size: 3½- to 4-qt.**

1 can peaches, cut into chunks and undrained
1 can apricots, cut into chunks and undrained
1 can pears, cut into chunks and undrained
1 large can pineapple chunks, undrained
1 can black cherries, undrained
½ cup brown sugar
1 tsp. curry powder
3-4 Tbsp. quick-cooking tapioca, depending upon how thick you'd like the finished dish to be
butter, *optional*

1. Combine fruit in slow cooker. Let stand without heating for at least 2 hours, or up to 8 hours, to allow flavors to blend.
2. Drain off juices.
3. Add remaining ingredients. Mix well. Top with butter chunks, if you wish.
4. Cover. Cook on Low 8-10 hours.
5. Serve warm or at room temperature.

# Southwest Cranberries

**Bernita Boyts**
Shawnee Mission, KS

*Makes 8 servings*

**Prep. Time: 5 minutes**
**Cooking Time: 2-3 hours**
**Ideal slow cooker size: 1½- to 2-qt.**

16-oz. can whole berry cranberry sauce
10½-oz. jar jalapeño jelly
2 Tbsp. chopped fresh cilantro

1. Combine all ingredients in slow cooker.
2. Cover. Cook on Low 2-3 hours.

*Serving suggestion: Cool. Serve at room temperature as a side dish or as a **marinade** for poultry or pork.*

# Cranberry Applesauce

**Susan Segraves**
Lansdale, PA

*Makes 12 servings*

**Prep. Time: 20 minutes**
**Cooking Time: 3-8 hours**
**Ideal slow cooker size: 4- to 5-qt.**

10 cups peeled, cubed apples (about 3 lbs. Granny Smith, *or* McIntosh)
2 cups fresh cranberries
½ cup sugar
½ cup maple-flavored pancake syrup
⅓ cup water
½ tsp. cinnamon
¼ tsp. nutmeg

1. Mix all ingredients in slow cooker.
2. Cover. Cook on High 3-4 hours or on Low 6-8 hours.
3. In cooker, mash apples and cranberries with potato masher.
4. Reduce heat to warm. Hold in slow cooker until serving time. Or chill if you prefer until ready to serve.

*Serving suggestion: Use this as is for dessert, or as a topping for **ice cream** or **pound cake**. Or serve warm as **an accompaniment** to a turkey dinner.*

*For Christmas Eve I prepare plain sugar cookies. I also put out bowls of sprinkles and frosting for the kids to use to decorate the cookies.* Michele Ruvola, Vestal, NY

# Homemade Applesauce

**Renita Denlinger**
Denver, PA

*Makes 7-8 servings*

*Prep. Time: 10-20 minutes*
*Cooking Time: 3½ hours*
*Ideal slow cooker size: 5- to 6-qt.*

**10 large apples, halved, cored, and peeled**
**½ tsp. cinnamon**
**dash of nutmeg**
**dash of ground cloves**
**1 Tbsp. water**

1. Spray slow cooker with non-stick spray.
2. Put apples in slow cooker.
3. Sprinkle cinnamon, nutmeg, cloves, and water over apples. Stir.
4. Cover. Cook on Low 3½ hours, or until apples are soft. If you're home and available, stir the apples after they've cooked for 2 hours. It's okay to mash them up a bit as you stir.
5. Serve warm or chilled.

**Note:**
*This makes the whole house smell wonderful.*

# Cranberry Baked Apples

**Judi Manos**
West Islip, NY

*Makes 4 servings*

*Prep. Time: 15 minutes*
*Cooking Time: 4-6 hours*
*Ideal slow cooker size: 4- to 5-qt.*

**⅓ cup packed brown sugar**
**¼ cup dried cranberries**
**4 large cooking apples**
**½ cup cran-apple juice cocktail**
**¼ stick (2 Tbsp.) butter, melted**
**½ tsp. ground cinnamon**
**¼ tsp. ground nutmeg**
**chopped nuts,** *optional*

1. In a small bowl, mix brown sugar and cranberries together.
2. Core apples but leave whole. Fill centers with brown sugar and cranberry mixture.
3. Set apples upright in slow cooker. (Don't stack them.)
4. In the same small bowl, combine cran-apple juice and butter. Pour over apples.
5. Sprinkle with cinnamon and nutmeg.
6. Cover. Cook on Low 4-6 hours.
7. To serve, spoon sauce over apples and sprinkle with nuts.

*Serving suggestion: A great accompaniment to* **vanilla ice cream.**

**Note:**
*This was one of our favorite recipes while growing up. When it's cooking, the house smells delicious. I'm suddenly full of memories of days gone by and a much more relaxing time. My mother passed away in October, and I re-found this recipe among her collection of favorites.*

# Apple Schnitz

**Betty Hostetler**
Allensville, PA

*Makes 6-8 servings*

*Prep. Time: 5 minutes*
*Cooking Time: 2½-6 hours*
*Ideal slow cooker size: 3-qt.*

**16 oz. dried apples**
**3 cups water**
**1 cup sugar**
**1 tsp. ground cinnamon**
**1 tsp. salt**

1. Combine apples, water, sugar, cinnamon, and salt in slow cooker.
2. Cover. Cook on Low 6 hours, or on High 2½ hours.
3. Serve warm as a side dish with bean soup, or as filling for Half Moon Pies (see below).
4. For pie filling, remove apples from slow cooker. Mash until smooth with potato masher, or put through food mill. Cool.

## Pie Crust:

**4 cups flour**
**2 tsp. salt**
**4 Tbsp. shortening**
**¼ cold water,** *or more*

1. Combine flour and salt in large bowl. Cut in shortening until mixture resembles small peas.

2. Add ¼ cup cold water to dough, adding more by tablespoonfuls as needed to make a soft pie dough.

3. Pinch off small pieces of dough, each about the size of a large walnut. Roll into round pieces, each about 8" in diameter.

4. Jag one half of the circle a few times with a sharp fork to create holes for the steam to escape while baking. On the other half, place a heaping tablespoon of Apple Schnitz.

5. Fold one-half of dough up over the half holding the Apple Schnitz, shaping the pie like a half moon. Press edges of dough together. Cut off remaining dough and crimp edges.

6. Bake at 350° for 30 minutes.

Note:

*On a cold winter day, Mother would prepare dried beans to make soup. After the beans were soft, she added milk to the soup pot. She heated the mixture to the boiling point, then added rivels. While the beans were cooking, she cooked dried apples until they were soft. She served these Half Moon Pies as a side dish/dessert with the soup.*

 # Caramel Apples

**Becky Harder**, Monument, CO
**Jeanette Oberholtzer**, Manheim, PA

*Makes 8-10 servings*
*Prep. Time: 20-30 minutes • Cooking Time: 1-1½ hours*
*Ideal slow cooker size: 2-qt.*

**2 14-oz. bags of caramels**
**¼ cup water**
**8-10 medium apples**
**12-15 sticks, in case a few break**

**granulated sugar in a dish**
**waxed paper, lightly greased**

1. Remove wrapping from caramels. Combine candies and water in slow cooker.

2. Cover. Cook on High 1-1½ hours, stirring every 5 minutes. (This is a good job for a child who's tall enough to take the lid off and stir without steaming him/herself.)

3. Meanwhile, wash and dry apples. Insert a stick into stem end of each apple. Turn cooker to Low.

4. Dip apple into hot caramel, turning to coat entire surface. (This is definitely a task for children, if adults are nearby to help.)

5. Holding apple above cooker, scrape off excess accumulation of caramel from bottom of apple.

6. Then dip bottom of caramel-coated apple in granulated sugar to keep it from sticking. Place apple on greased waxed paper to cool.

Note:

*This is a good recipe for Fall/Harvest/Halloween parties. Children won't forget the hands-on experience of dipping their own apples. Room mothers can make the caramel mix ahead of time and bring it into the classroom. This recipe is also a fun intergenerational activity for church groups or family reunions.*

*In the late 1950s and early 1960s, my sister and I were rewarded with a store-bought caramel apple, only after our Saturday night baths and our Sunday school lessons had been completed. I remember that the waxed paper wrapped around each apple had colorful clowns printed on it, and they sold for less than 50¢ each.*

**Becky Harder**

# Apple Caramel Dessert

**Jeanette Oberholtzer**
Manheim, PA

*Makes 7 servings*

*Prep. Time: 15 minutes*
*Cooking Time: 6 hours*
*Ideal slow cooker size: 2-qt.*

½ cup apple juice
7 ozs. caramels, unwrapped
1 tsp. vanilla
⅛ tsp. ground cardamom
½ tsp. ground cinnamon
⅓ cup creamy peanut butter
2 medium apples, peeled, cored, and cut in wedges

1. Combine apple juice, caramel candies, vanilla, and spices in slow cooker.
2. Drop peanut butter, 1 Tbsp. at a time, into slow cooker. Stir well after each addition.
3. Gently stir in apple wedges.
4. Cover. Cook on Low 5 hours.
5. Stir well.
6. Cover. Then cook 1 more hour on Low.

*Serving suggestion: Serve about ⅓ cup warm mixture over each slice of **angel food cake**, and then top each with **ice cream**.*

# Apple Crisp

**Michelle Strite**
Goshen, IN

*Makes 6-8 servings*

*Prep. Time: 5-10 minutes*
*Cooking Time: 2-3 hours*
*Ideal slow cooker size: 2-qt.*

2 21-oz. cans apple pie filling, *or*
⅔ cup sugar
1¼ cups water
3 Tbsp. cornstarch
4 cups sliced, peeled apples
½ tsp. ground cinnamon
¼ tsp. ground allspice
¾ cup uncooked quick oatmeal
½ cup brown sugar
½ cup flour
half a stick (4 Tbsp.) butter, at room temperature

1. Place pie filling in slow cooker. If not using prepared filling, combine ⅔ cup sugar, water, cornstarch, apples, cinnamon, and allspice in cooker. Stir until well mixed.
2. In a mixing bowl, combine remaining ingredients until crumbly. Sprinkle over apple filling.
3. Cover. Cook on Low 2-3 hours.

# Dried Cranberry Pudding

**Evelyn L. Ward**
Greeley, CO

*Makes 8 servings*

*Prep. Time: 10-15 minutes*
*Cooking Time: 3 hours*
*Ideal slow cooker size: large enough to hold your baking insert*

half a stick (4 Tbsp.) butter, softened
½ cup brown sugar
½ cup molasses
1 egg
½ tsp. baking soda
½ cup hot water
1½ cups flour, *divided*
1 tsp. baking powder
½ cup dried cranberries

**Butter Sauce:**
½ cup sugar
1 Tbsp. flour
½ cup water
pinch salt
1 Tbsp. butter
2 tsp. vanilla

1. To make Pudding, cream together butter, sugar, and molasses in a good-sized mixing bowl.
2. Add egg. Beat well.
3. In a small bowl, dissolve baking soda in hot water. Stir into creamed mixture until well mixed.
4. Beat in 1 cup flour and baking powder.
5. In a small bowl, combine cranberries with ½ cup flour. Stir into batter.

6. Pour into well-greased baking insert or coffee can. Cover tightly with lid or double layer of foil.

7. Place upright on rack in slow cooker.

8. Pour boiling water into cooker, until halfway up sides of insert.

9. Cover cooker. Cook 3 hours on High.

10. Remove insert or can from cooker. Cool 2 minutes on baking rack. Run knife around edge of insert or can, and then turn upside down to unmold onto plate.

11. Serve with hot Butter Sauce.

12. To make Butter Sauce, combine sugar, flour, water, and salt in saucepan until well blended. Cook over medium heat, stirring constantly until thickened. Remove from heat. Stir in butter and vanilla. Serve hot with slices of Pudding.

Tips:

1. A coffee can that stands upright in your slow cooker works as a good pudding mold.

2. You can use a jar ring as a rack under the mold.

# Steamed Chocolate Pudding
**Evelyn L. Ward**
Greeley, CO

*Makes 8 servings*

*Prep. Time: 10 minutes*
*Cooking Time: 2½ hours*
*Ideal slow cooker size: large enough to hold your baking insert or a coffee can standing upright*

1 stick (8 Tbsp.) butter, softened
¾ cup sugar
¾ cup flour
3 Tbsp. cocoa powder
¼ tsp. salt
3 eggs
½ tsp. vanilla
¼ cup half-and-half

1. Cream together butter and sugar with electric mixer.

2. In a separate bowl, sift together flour, cocoa powder, and salt.

3. Add alternately with eggs to creamed mixture. Beat well.

4. Add vanilla and half-and-half. Beat well.

5. Spoon into greased and floured slow cooker baking insert.* Cover tightly with lid or double layer of foil.

6. Place insert on a rack in slow cooker. Add boiling water to slow cooker, halfway up sides of insert.

7. Cover slow cooker. Cook on High 2½ hours.

8. Remove insert from cooker. Cool 2 minutes. Unmold.

*Serving suggestion: Cut into wedges. Serve with **frozen whipped topping, thawed**, or **ice cream**.*

Tips:
* 1. A coffee can that stands upright inside your slow cooker serves as a good pudding mold.

2. You can use a jar ring for a rack under the can or baking insert.

# Slow-Cooker Rice Pudding
**Dede Peterson**
Rapid City, SD

*Makes 5 servings*

*Prep. Time: 10 minutes*
*Cooking Time: 3-4 hours*
*Cooling Time: 2-5 hours*
*Ideal slow cooker size: 2-qt.*

1 pkg. vanilla cook-and-serve pudding mix
1 cup cooked white rice
1 cup raisins
1 tsp. cinnamon
2 tsp. vanilla
3 cups half-and-half, *or* milk

1. Combine ingredients in slow cooker.

2. Cover. Cook on Low 3-4 hours.

3. Serve warm, at room temperature, or chilled.

# Rice Pudding

**Vera Schmucker**
Goshen, IN

*Makes 4-6 servings*

*Prep. Time: 10 minutes*
*Cooking Time: 2-6 hours*
*Chilling Time: 2-5 hours*
*Ideal slow cooker size: 1½- to 2-qt.*

2½ cups cooked rice
1½ cups evaporated, *or*
   scalded, milk
⅔ cup sugar
1 Tbsp. butter, melted
½-1 tsp. ground nutmeg

1. Combine all ingredients in lightly greased slow cooker.
2. Cover. Cook on High 2 hours, or on Low 4-6 hours.
3. Stir after first hour.
4. Cool to slightly warm or to room temperature before serving. Or chill until cold if you wish.

*Serving suggestion: Serve topped with **whipped cream** and/or **maraschino cherries**, if you wish.*

# Chocolate Rice Pudding

**Michele Ruvola**
Selden, NY

*Makes 4 servings*

*Prep. Time: 10 minutes*
*Cooking Time: 2½-3½ hours*
*Chilling Time: 2-5 hours*
*Ideal slow cooker size: 3-qt.*

4 cups cooked white rice
¾ cup sugar
¼ cup baking cocoa
   powder
3 Tbsp. butter, melted
1 tsp. vanilla
2 12-oz. cans evaporated
   milk

1. Combine first 6 ingredients in greased slow cooker.
2. Cover. Cook on Low 2½-3½ hours, or until liquid is absorbed.

*Serving suggestion: Serve warm or chilled. Top individual servings with a dollop of **whipped cream**, **sliced toasted almonds**, and/or a **maraschino cherry** if you wish.*

# Deluxe Tapioca Pudding

**Michelle Showalter**
Bridgewater, VA

*Makes 16 servings*

*Prep. Time: 10 minutes*
*Cooking Time: 3½ hours*
*Chilling Time: 4-5 hours, or*
   *longer*
*Ideal slow cooker size: 4-qt.*

2 qts. milk
¾ cup dry small pearl
   tapioca
1½ cups sugar
4 eggs, beaten
2 tsp. vanilla
3-4 cups whipped cream,
   *or* frozen whipped
   topping, thawed
chocolate candy bar

1. Combine milk, tapioca, and sugar in slow cooker.
2. Cook on High 3 hours.
3. In a medium-sized mixing bowl, add a little hot milk mixture to beaten eggs. Stir.
4. Whisk eggs into milk mixture in slow cooker. Stir in vanilla.
5. Cover. Cook on High 20-30 minutes.
6. Cool to room temperature. Chill in refrigerator.
7. When fully chilled, beat with hand mixer to fluff Pudding.
8. Fold in whipped cream or whipped topping. Garnish with chopped candy bar.

*Our neighborhood has a cookie exchange, and we try to surprise each other with interesting containers to take them home in. We bring as many dozen cookies (of the same kind of cookie) as there are people attending, and we go home with that many different ones.*

*Donna Conto, Saylorsburg, PA*

# Lemon Pudding

**Jean M. Butzer**
Batavia, NY

*Makes 4 servings*

*Prep. Time: 10-15 minutes*
*Cooking Time: 1½-2 hours*
*Standing/Cooling Time:*
*  30 minutes-3 hours*
*Ideal slow cooker size: 3-qt.*

1 cup sugar
¼ cup flour
¼ tsp. salt
1 cup buttermilk
¼ cup lemon juice
3 eggs, separated

1. Spray slow cooker with cooking spray.
2. Combine sugar, flour, and salt in a good-sized mixing bowl.
3. Make a well in the center and add buttermilk and lemon juice. Stir until smooth. Stir in egg yolks.
4. In a separate bowl, beat egg whites until stiff and able to hold a peak. Fold into batter. Pour into slow cooker.
5. Cover. Cook on High 1½-2 hours, or until top is set and pudding is brown around the edges.
6. Turn off cooker. Let stand at least 30 minutes before serving. Serve warm or cold.

Note:

*This recipe is similar to an old-fashioned lemon soufflé that has been a favorite of my family for years. I use a lot of buttermilk when baking for the holiday season. This recipe helps use up any extra I might have.*

# Eggnog Gingersnap Custard

**Sue Hamilton**, Minooka, IL

*Makes 4-6 servings*

*Prep. Time: 5 minutes • Cooking Time: 3½-4 hours*
*Cooling/Chilling Time: 20 minutes-4 hours*
*Ideal slow cooker size: 3- to 4-qt.*

24 small gingersnaps          1 qt. eggnog
4 eggs

1. Spray interior of slow cooker with cooking spray.
2. Lay all cookies on bottom of slow cooker.
3. In a large mixing bowl, beat eggs. Stir in eggnog.
4. Slowly pour into slow cooker. The cookies will rise in a layer to the top.
5. Cover. Cook on Low 3½-4 hours, or until Custard is set.
6. Remove cover. Let cool 20 minutes for a warm Custard, or chill 4 or more hours for a cold Custard.

# Slow-Cooker Pumpkin Pie

**Colleen Heatwole**
Burton, MI

*Makes 5-6 servings*

*Prep. Time: 10 minutes*
*Cooking Time: 3-4 hours*
*Cooling Time: 2-4 hours*
*Ideal slow cooker size: 3-qt.*

15-oz. can solid-pack
  pumpkin
12-oz. can evaporated milk
¾ cup sugar
½ cup low-fat buttermilk
  baking mix
2 eggs, beaten
¼ stick (2 Tbsp.) butter,
  melted

1½ tsp. cinnamon
¾ tsp. ground ginger
¼ tsp. ground nutmeg
whipped topping

1. Spray slow cooker with cooking spray.
2. Mix all ingredients together in slow cooker, except whipped topping.
3. Cover. Cook on Low 3-4 hours, or until a toothpick inserted in center comes out clean.
4. Allow to cool to warm, or chill, before serving with whipped topping.

Variation:

You can substitute 2½ Tbsp. pumpkin pie spice in place of cinnamon, ginger, and nutmeg.

# White Chocolate Bread Pudding

**Linda E. Wilcox**
Blythewood, SC

*Makes 5-6 servings*

**Prep Time: 30 minutes**
**Cooking Time: 1¾ hours**
**Cooling Time: 30 minutes, and**
**then 1-2 hours**
**Ideal slow-cooker size: 3- to 4-qt.**

½ cup dried cranberries, *or*
  dried cherries
3 Tbsp. apple cider, *or*
  brandy
3-oz. white chocolate bar
¼ stick (2 Tbsp.) butter
6 cups stale French bread,
  cubed, *divided*
4 eggs
½ cup sugar
1 cup half-and-half
1 tsp. vanilla

1. Combine dried fruit with cider or brandy in a microwave-safe bowl.
2. Microwave on High for 30 seconds. Set aside to cool (about 30 minutes).
3. Coarsely chop the chocolate. Set aside.
4. Drain the dried fruit. Set aside.
5. Spray interior of slow cooker with cooking spray.
6. Cover bottom of slow cooker with half the bread cubes.
7. Sprinkle half the chocolate and half the fruit over bread cubes.
8. Layer in remaining bread cubes. Top with a layer of remaining fruit and a layer of remaining chocolate.
9. In a bowl beat eggs with whisk. Add sugar, half-and-half, and vanilla to eggs. Mix together thoroughly.
10. Pour over bread mixture and press to make sure egg mixture covers all bread.
11. Cover and cook on High 1¾ hours.
12. Cool until warm or at room temperature.

Note:
*My grandchildren love this dessert.*

# Apple-Nut Bread Pudding

**Ruth Ann Hoover**
New Holland, PA

*Makes 6-8 servings*

**Prep. Time: 15 minutes**
**Cooking Time: 3-4 hours**
**Cooling Time: 3-4 hours**
**Ideal slow cooker size: 4-qt.**

8 slices raisin bread, cubed
2-3 medium-sized tart
  apples, peeled and sliced
1 cup chopped pecans,
  toasted
1 cup sugar
1 tsp. ground cinnamon
½ tsp. ground nutmeg
3 eggs, lightly beaten
2 cups half-and-half
¼ cup apple juice
half a stick (4 Tbsp.)
  butter, melted

1. Place bread cubes, apples, and pecans in greased slow cooker and mix together gently.
2. Combine sugar, cinnamon, and nutmeg in a good-sized mixing bowl.
3. Add remaining ingredients. Mix well.
4. Pour over bread mixture. Stir gently to mix thoroughly.
5. Cover. Cook on Low 3-4 hours, or until knife inserted in center comes out clean.
6. Serve warm (but not hot) or at room temperature.

*Serving suggestion: **Ice cream** is a great accompaniment.*

# Simple Bread Pudding

**Melanie L. Thrower**
McPherson, KS

*Makes 6-8 servings*

**Prep. Time: 5-10 minutes**
**Cooking Time: 2-2½ hours**
**Chilling Time: 2-5 hours**
**Ideal slow cooker size: 1½- to 2-qt.**

6-8 slices of bread, cubed
2 cups milk
2 eggs
¼ cup sugar
1 tsp. ground cinnamon
1 tsp. vanilla

Sauce:
6-oz. can concentrated
  grape juice
1 Tbsp. cornstarch

1. Place cubed bread in slow cooker.

2. In a good-sized bowl, whisk together milk, eggs, sugar, cinnamon, and vanilla. Pour over bread. Press bread down into liquid to dampen.

3. Cover. Cook on High 2-2½ hours, or until mixture is set.

4. Allow Pudding to cool to warm or to room temperature before serving. Or chill until cold.

5. Combine cornstarch and concentrated juice in saucepan. Heat until boiling, stirring constantly, until sauce is thickened. Serve drizzled over bread pudding.

**Tip:**

This is a fine dessert with a cold salad main dish.

# Home-Style Bread Pudding

**Lizzie Weaver**
Ephrata, PA

*Makes 4-6 servings*

*Prep. Time: 10 minutes*
*Cooking Time: 2-3 hours*
*Chilling Time: 1-4 hours*
*Ideal slow cooker size: large enough to hold your baking insert*

2 eggs, beaten
2¼ cups milk
½ tsp. cinnamon
¼ tsp. salt
½ cup brown sugar

1 tsp. vanilla
2 cups 1" bread cubes
½ cup raisins *or* dates

1. Combine all ingredients in good-sized mixing bowl. Pour into slow cooker baking insert.

2. Cover baking insert. Place on metal rack (or rubber jar rings) in bottom of slow cooker.

3. Pour ½ cup hot water into cooker around sides of insert.

4. Cover slow cooker. Cook on High 2-3 hours.

*Serving suggestion: Serve Pudding warm or cold, topped with **cherry pie filling** and/or **whipped topping** if you wish.*

# Pineapple Upside Down Cake

**Vera M. Kuhns**
Harrisonburg, VA

*Makes 10 servings*

*Prep. Time: 20 minutes*
*Cooking Time: 4-5 hours*
*Cooling Time: 10 minutes*
*Ideal slow cooker size: 4-qt.*

1 stick (8 Tbsp.) butter, melted
1 cup brown sugar

1 medium-sized can pineapple slices, drained, juice reserved
6-8 maraschino cherries
1 box yellow cake mix

1. Combine butter and brown sugar in well-greased slow cooker. Spread over cooker bottom.

2. Lay pineapple slices over top. Place a cherry in the center of each slice.

3. In a good-sized mixing bowl, prepare cake according to package directions, using pineapple juice for part of liquid.

4. Spoon cake batter into cooker over top fruit.

5. Cover cooker with 2 tea towels and then with its own lid. Cook on High 1 hour, and then on Low 3-4 hours.

6. Insert toothpick in center of cake. If it comes out clean, cake is finished. If it doesn't, continue to cook in 15-minute increments, checking after each one, until pick comes out clean.

7. Allow cake to cool for 10 minutes. Then run knife around edge and invert cake onto large platter.

*Make your favorite Christmas cookies and have a bag ready to send home with each guest.*
*Leona M Slabaugh, Apple Creek, OH*

# Low-Fat Apple Cake

**Sue Hamilton**
Minooka, IL

*Makes 8 servings*

*Prep. Time: 15 minutes*
*Cooking Time: 2½-3 hours*
*Cooling Time: 1 hour*
*Ideal slow cooker size: 3-qt.*

1 cup flour
1 cup sugar
2 tsp. baking powder
1 tsp. ground cinnamon
¼ tsp. salt
4 medium-sized cooking
   apples, chopped
2 eggs, beaten
2 tsp. vanilla

1. Combine flour, sugar, baking powder, cinnamon, and salt in lightly greased slow cooker.
2. Add apples, stirring gently to coat.
3. In a small bowl, combine eggs and vanilla. Add to apple mixture. Stir until just moistened.
4. Cover. Bake on High 2½-3 hours. Insert toothpick in center of Cake. If tester comes out clean, Cake is finished. If it doesn't, continue cooking for 15-minute intervals, checking after each one with pick until it comes out clean.

*Serving suggestion: Serve warm. Top with **whipped topping** or **ice cream** and a sprinkle of **cinnamon**.*

**Variation:**

Stir ½ cup broken English or black walnuts, or ½ cup raisins, into Step 2.

**Note:**

*The slow cooker is great for "baking" desserts. Your guests will be pleasantly surprised to see a cake coming from your slow cooker.*

# Creamy Orange Cheesecake

**Jeanette Oberholtzer**
Manheim, PA

*Makes 10 servings*

*Prep. Time: 15 minutes*
*Cooking Time: 2½-3 hours*
*Standing Time: 1-2 hours*
*Chilling Time: 2-4 hours*
*Ideal slow cooker size: large enough to hold your baking insert*

**Crust:**

¾ cup graham cracker
   crumbs
2 Tbsp. sugar
3 Tbsp. melted butter

**Filling:**

2 8-oz. pkgs. cream cheese,
   at room temperature
⅔ cup sugar
2 eggs
1 egg yolk
¼ cup frozen orange juice
   concentrate
1 tsp. orange zest
1 Tbsp. flour
½ tsp. vanilla

1. Combine crust ingredients in a small bowl. Pat into 7" or 9" springform pan, whichever size fits into your slow cooker.
2. In a large mixing bowl, cream together cream cheese and sugar. Add eggs and yolk. Beat 3 minutes.
3. Add juice, zest, flour, and vanilla. Beat 2 more minutes.
4. Pour batter into crust. Place on rack (or jar rings) in slow cooker.
5. Cover. Cook on High 2½-3 hours. Turn off and let stand 1-2 hours, or until cool enough to remove from cooker.
6. Cool completely before removing sides of pan. Chill before serving.

*Serving suggestion: Serve with thawed **frozen whipped topping** and **fresh or mandarin orange slices**.*

*Invest in a microplane wand. They are wonderful for zesting citrus. Freeze amounts of lemon or orange zest to use in any given recipe. Orange zest is great in blueberry muffins or sweet potato casserole. Anything that calls for lemon juice will be even better if you also add some lemon zest.*

*Becky Frey, Lebanon, PA*

# Orange Slice Cake

### Steven Lantz
### Denver, CO

*Makes 10-12 servings*

**Prep. Time: 20 minutes**
**Cooking Time: 2-3 hours**
**Cooling Time: 3-4 hours**
**Ideal slow cooker size: 3-qt.**

**1 cup chopped dates**
**½ lb. candied orange slices, cut into thirds**
**½ cup chopped walnuts**
**1 cup flaked, unsweetened coconut**
**1 Tbsp. grated orange rind,** *optional*
**1¾ cups flour,** *divided*
**1 stick (8 Tbsp.) butter, at room temperature**
**1 cup sugar**
**2 eggs**
**½ tsp. baking soda**
**¼ cup buttermilk**

1. In a good-sized mixing bowl, combine dates, orange slices, nuts, coconut, and orange rind if you wish.

2. Pour ¼ cup flour over mixture and stir together.

3. In a separate big bowl, cream butter and sugar together. Add eggs and beat well.

4. In a small bowl, dissolve baking soda in buttermilk.

5. Add remaining 1½ cups flour and buttermilk, in which soda has been dissolved, to creamed mixture.

6. Stir in fruit and nut mixture.

7. Pour into greased slow cooker.

8. Cover. Cook on High 2-3 hours, or until toothpick inserted in center comes out clean.

9. Allow cake to cool completely before removing from slow cooker.

**Tip:**

*This cake is perfect with coffee in the morning or later in the day as dessert.*

**Note from Tester:**

I chopped the dates and nuts in my food processor. I spooned them into a mixing bowl where I combined them with the other ingredients in Steps 1 and 2.

Then I continued using my food processor for Steps 3 and 5. No need to wash it in between.

I believe in saving time whenever I can.

# Carrot Cake

### Colleen Heatwole
### Burton, MI

*Makes 6-8 servings*

**Prep. Time: 20 minutes**
**Cooking Time: 3-4 hours**
**Ideal slow cooker size: large enough to hold your baking insert**

**½ cup vegetable oil**
**2 eggs**
**1 Tbsp. hot water**
**½ cup grated raw carrots**
**¾ cup flour**
**¾ cup sugar**
**½ tsp. baking powder**
**⅛ tsp. salt**
**¼ tsp. ground allspice**
**½ tsp. ground cinnamon**
**⅛ tsp. ground cloves**
**½ cup chopped nuts**
**½ cup raisins,** *or* **chopped dates**
**2 Tbsp. flour**

1. In large bowl, beat oil, eggs, and water for 1 minute.

2. Add carrots. Mix well.

3. In a separate bowl, stir together flour, sugar, baking powder, salt, allspice, cinnamon, and cloves. Add to creamed mixture.

4. Toss nuts and raisins in bowl with 2 Tbsp. flour. Add to creamed mixture. Mix well.

5. Pour into greased and floured 3-lb. shortening can or slow-cooker baking insert. Place can or baking insert in slow cooker.

6. Cover insert with its lid, or cover can with 8 paper towels, folded down over edge of slow cooker to absorb moisture. Cover paper towels with cooker lid. Cook on High 3-4 hours, or until toothpick inserted in center of cake comes out clean.

7. Remove can or insert from cooker and allow to cool on rack for 10 minutes. Run knife around edge of cake. Invert onto serving plate.

# Easy Easy Cake

**Janice Muller**
Derwood, MD

*Makes 8-10 servings*

*Prep. Time: 10 minutes*
*Cooking Time: 2-3 hours*
*Ideal slow cooker size: 3½-qt.*

20-oz. can crushed
   pineapple, undrained
21-oz. can blueberry, *or*
   cherry, pie filling
18½-oz. pkg. yellow cake
   mix
cinnamon
1 stick (8 Tbsp.) butter
1 cup chopped nuts
vanilla ice cream

1. Grease bottom and sides of interior of slow cooker.
2. Spread a layer of pineapple in bottom.
3. Top with a layer of blueberry pie filling.
4. Top that with a layer of dry cake mix. Be careful not to mix the layers!
5. Sprinkle with cinnamon.
6. Top with thin layers of butter chunks and nuts.
7. Cover cooker. Cook on High 2-3 hours, or until toothpick inserted in center comes out clean.
8. Serve warm with vanilla ice cream.

## Variation:
Substitute a pkg. of spice cake mix and apple pie filling.

# Fudgy Peanut Butter Cake

**Betty Moore**
Plano, IL

*Makes 4 servings*

*Prep. Time: 15 minutes*
*Cooking Time: 1½ hours*
*Ideal slow cooker size: 2- to 3-qt.*

¾ cup sugar, *divided*
½ cup flour
¾ tsp. baking powder
⅓ cup milk
¼ cup peanut butter
1 Tbsp. oil
½ tsp. vanilla
2 Tbsp. dry cocoa powder
1 cup boiling water

1. Butter or spray interior of slow cooker.
2. Mix ¼ cup sugar, flour, and baking powder together in a small bowl.
3. In another larger bowl, mix milk, peanut butter, oil, and vanilla together. Beat well.
4. Stir dry ingredients into milk-peanut butter mixture just until combined. Spread in buttered slow cooker.
5. In bowl, combine cocoa powder and remaining ½ cup sugar. Add water, stirring until well mixed. Pour slowly into slow cooker. Do *not* stir.
6. Cover. Cook on High 1½ hours, or until toothpick inserted in center of cake comes out clean.

*Serving suggestion: Serve warm with **vanilla ice cream**.*

**Note:**
*I take this to potlucks and it is always a hit.*

**Notes from Tester:**
1. I was pretty sure my kids would love this, so I doubled the recipe. I cooked that larger recipe for 2 hours. The kids came back for second and third helpings!
2. This is a pretty sturdy cake. I kept one of my test cakes for over an hour before serving it, and it was just as good, if not better, than the one we ate right away.

# Lemon Poppy Seed Upside-Down Cake

**Jeanette Oberholtzer**
Manheim, PA

*Makes 8-10 servings*

*Prep. Time: 10-15 minutes*
*Cooking Time: 2-2½ hours*
*Cooling Time: 2 hours*
*Ideal slow cooker size: 2-qt.*

1 pkg. lemon poppy seed
   bread mix
1 egg
8 oz. light sour cream
½ cup water

## Sauce:
1 Tbsp. butter
¾ cup water
½ cup sugar
¼ cup lemon juice

1. Combine first four ingredients until well moistened in

lightly greased slow cooker.

2. Combine Sauce ingredients in small saucepan. Bring to boil. Pour boiling mixture over batter. Do not stir.

3. Cover. Cook on High 2-2½ hours, or until toothpick inserted in center of Cake comes out clean. Edges will be slightly brown. Turn heat off and leave Cake in cooker for 30 minutes with lid slightly ajar.

4. When cool enough to handle, hold a large plate over top of cooker, then invert.

5. Allow to cool before slicing.

# Graham Cracker Cookies

**Cassandra Ly**
Carlisle, PA

*Makes 8 dozen cookies*

*Prep. Time: 10 minutes*
*Cooking Time: 1½ hours*
*Ideal slow cooker size: 4-qt.*

12-oz. pkg. (2 cups) semi-sweet chocolate chips
2 1-oz. squares unsweetened baking chocolate, shaved
2 14-oz. cans sweetened condensed milk
3¾ cups crushed graham cracker crumbs, *divided*
1 cup finely chopped walnuts

1. Place chocolate in slow cooker.

2. Cover. Cook on High 1 hour, stirring every 15 minutes. Continue to cook on Low, stirring every 15 minutes, or until chocolate is melted (about 30 minutes more).

3. Stir milk into melted chocolate.

4. Add 3 cups graham cracker crumbs, 1 cup at a time, stirring after each addition.

5. Stir in nuts. Mixture should be thick but not stiff.

6. Stir in remaining graham cracker crumbs until batter is consistency of cookie dough.

7. Drop by heaping teaspoonfuls onto lightly greased cookie sheets. Keep remaining mixture warm by covering and turning slow cooker to Warm.

8. Bake at 325° for 7-9 minutes, or until tops of cookies begin to crack. Remove from oven. Cool 1-2 minutes on rack before transferring to waxed paper.

Tip:
These cookies freeze well.

Note:
*This delectable fudge-like cookie is a family favorite. The original recipe (from my maternal grandmother) was so involved and yielded so few cookies that my mom and I would get together to make a couple of batches only at Christmas-time. Adapting the recipe for a slow cooker, rather than a double boiler, allows me to prepare a double batch without help.*

# Chocolate Fondue

**Vera Schmucker**
Goshen, IN
**Vicki Dinkel**
Sharon Springs, KS

*Makes 8-10 servings*

*Prep. Time: 10 minutes*
*Cooking Time: 3-7 hours*
*Ideal slow cooker size: 3½-qt.*

1 Tbsp. butter
16 1-oz. chocolate candy bars with almonds, unwrapped and broken
30 large marshmallows
1⅓ cups milk, *divided*
angel food cake cubes; strawberries; chunks of pineapple, bananas, apples, oranges; pretzel pieces

1. Grease slow cooker with butter. Turn to High for 10 minutes.

2. Add chocolate, marshmallows, and ⅓ cup milk.

3. Cover. Turn cooker to Low. Stir after 30 minutes.

4. Continue cooking for another 30 minutes, or until mixture is melted and smooth.

5. Gradually add remaining milk.

5. Cover. Cook on Low 2-6 hours.

6. Bring cooker to table, along with angel food cake, fruit chunks, and pretzels for dipping.

# Chocolate Covered Pretzels

**Beth Maurer**
Harrisonburg, VA

*Makes 10-12 servings*

*Prep. Time: 10 minutes*
*Cooking Time: 30-60 minutes*
*Ideal slow cooker size: 2-qt.*

1 lb. white chocolate bark
    coating
2 blocks chocolate bark
    coating
1 bag pretzel rods

1. Chop white chocolate into small chunks. Place in slow cooker.
2. Cover. Heat on Low setting, stirring occasionally until melted, about 30 minutes. Turn off cooker.
3. Using a spoon, coat ¾ of each pretzel rod with chocolate. Place on waxed paper to cool.
4. Chop chocolate bark into small chunks. Microwave on High in a microwave-safe bowl for 1½ minutes. Stir. Microwave on High 1 more minute. Stir.
5. Microwave on High in 30-second intervals until chocolate is smooth when stirred. (Do not allow chocolate to get too hot or it will scorch.)
6. Put melted chocolate in small bag. Snip off corner of bag. Drizzle chocolate over white chocolate covered pretzels.

# Hot Fudge Sauce

**Beth Nafziger**, Lowville, NY

*Makes 1½ cups*

*Prep. Time: 15 minutes*
*Ideal slow cooker size: 1-qt.*

¾ cup semi-sweet
    chocolate chips
half a stick (4 Tbsp.)
    butter
⅔ cup sugar
5-oz. can (⅔ cup)
    evaporated milk

1. In a small heavy saucepan melt chocolate and butter together.
2. Add sugar. Gradually stir in evaporated milk.
3. Bring mixture to a boil, and then reduce heat. Boil gently over low heat for 8 minutes, stirring frequently.
4. Remove pan from heat. Pour sauce into slow cooker.
5. Set cooker control to Warm—the ideal temperature for serving.

*Serving suggestion: Use as a dipping sauce for **angel food cake cubes**, **banana chunks**, **pineapple chunks**, and **mini-pretzels**.*

Note:
*I have served this for many years as part of our family Christmas-Eve celebration.*

Tip:
*These are easy to make. They also taste wonderful and are good holiday gifts when thoroughly cooled and placed in small gift bags!*

*Our grandchildren come to help me cut out and decorate sugar cookies during the holidays. They each have their own rolling pins—not toys, but smaller versions than mine. We began this tradition when they had to sit on our laps to help. It's a very messy but enjoyable time!*

*Naomi Ressler, Harrisonburg, VA*

# Equivalent Measurements

dash = little less than ⅛ tsp.

3 teaspoons = 1 Tablespoon

2 Tablespoons = 1 oz.

4 Tablespoons = ¼ cup

5 Tablespoons plus 1 tsp. = ⅓ cup

8 Tablespoons = ½ cup

12 Tablespoons = ¾ cup

16 Tablespoons = 1 cup

1 cup = 8 ozs. liquid

2 cups = 1 pint

4 cups = 1 quart

4 quarts = 1 gallon

1 stick butter = ¼ lb.

1 stick butter = ½ cup

1 stick butter = 8 Tbsp.

Beans, 1 lb. dried = 2-2½ cups (depending upon the size of the beans)

Bell peppers, 1 large = 1 cup chopped

Cheese, hard (for example, cheddar, Swiss, Monterey Jack, mozzarella), 1 lb. grated = 4 cups

Cheese, cottage, 1 lb. = 2 cups

Chocolate chips, 6-oz. pkg. = 1 scant cup

Crackers (butter, saltines, snack), 20 single crackers = 1 cup crumbs

Herbs, 1 Tbsp. fresh = 1 tsp. dried

Lemon, 1 medium-sized = 2-3 Tbsp. juice

Lemon, 1 medium-sized = 2-3 tsp. grated rind

Mustard, 1 Tbsp. prepared = 1 tsp. dry or ground mustard

Oatmeal, 1 lb. dry = about 5 cups dry

Onion, 1 medium-sized = ½ cup chopped

## Pasta

Macaronis, penne, and other small or tubular shapes, 1 lb. dry = 4 cups uncooked

Noodles, 1 lb. dry = 6 cups uncooked

Spaghetti, linguine, fettucine, 1 lb. dry = 4 cups uncooked

Potatoes, white, 1 lb. = 3 medium-sized potatoes = 2 cups mashed

Potatoes, sweet, 1 lb. = 3 medium-sized potatoes = 2 cups mashed

Rice, 1 lb. dry = 2 cups uncooked

Sugar, confectioners, 1 lb. = 3½ cups sifted

Whipping cream, 1 cup unwhipped = 2 cups whipped

Whipped topping, 8-oz. container = 3 cups

Yeast, dry, 1 envelope (¼ oz.) = 1 Tbsp.

# Assumptions about Ingredients

**flour** = unbleached *or* white, and all-purpose

**oatmeal or oats** = dry, quick *or* rolled (old-fashioned), unless specified

**pepper** = black, finely ground

**rice** = regular, long-grain (not minute or instant unless specified)

**salt** = table salt

**shortening** = solid, not liquid

**sugar** = granulated sugar (not brown and not confectioners)

# Three Hints

1  If you'd like to cook more at home—without being in a frenzy—go off by yourself with your cookbook some evening and make a week of menus. Then make a grocery list from that. Shop from your grocery list.

2  Thaw frozen food in a bowl in the fridge (not on the counter-top). If you forget to stick the food in the fridge, put it in a microwave-safe bowl and defrost it in the microwave just before you're ready to use it.

3  Let roasted meat, as well as pasta dishes with cheese, rest for 10-20 minutes before slicing or dishing. That will allow the juices to re-distribute themselves throughout the cooked food. You'll have juicier meat, and a better presentation of your pasta dish.

# Substitute Ingredients
## for when you're in a pinch

For one cup **buttermilk**—use 1 cup plain yogurt; or pour 1⅓ Tbsp. lemon juice or vinegar into a 1-cup measure. Fill the cup with milk. Stir and let stand for 5 minutes. Stir again before using.

For 1 oz. **unsweetened baking chocolate**—stir together 3 Tbsp. unsweetened cocoa powder and 1 Tbsp. butter, softened.

For 1 Tbsp. **cornstarch**—use 2 Tbsp. all-purpose flour; or 4 tsp. minute tapioca.

For 1 **garlic clove**—use ¼ tsp. garlic salt (reduce salt in recipe by ⅛ tsp.); or ⅛ tsp. garlic powder.

For 1 Tbsp. **fresh herbs**—use 1 tsp. dried herbs.

For ½ lb. **fresh mushrooms**—use 1 6-oz. can mushrooms, drained.

For 1 Tbsp. **prepared mustard**— use 1 tsp. dry or ground mustard.

For 1 **medium-sized fresh onion**— use 2 Tbsp. minced dried onion; or 2 tsp. onion salt (reduce salt in recipe by 1 tsp.); or 1 tsp. onion powder. Note: These substitutions will work for meat balls and meat loaf, but not for sautéing.

For 1 cup **sour milk**—use 1 cup plain yogurt; or pour 1 Tbsp. lemon juice or vinegar into a 1-cup measure. Fill with milk. Stir and then let stand for 5 minutes. Stir again before using.

For 2 Tbsp. **tapioca**—use 3 Tbsp. all-purpose flour.

For 1 cup canned **tomatoes**—use 1⅓ cups diced fresh tomatoes, cooked gently for 10 minutes.

For 1 Tbsp. **tomato paste**—use 1 Tbsp. ketchup.

For 1 Tbsp. **vinegar**—use 1 Tbsp. lemon juice.

For 1 cup **heavy cream**—add ⅓ cup melted butter to ¾ cup milk. *Note: This will work for baking and cooking, but not for whipping.*

For 1 cup **whipping cream**—chill thoroughly ⅔ cup evaporated milk, plus the bowl and beaters, then whip; or use 2 cups bought whipped topping.

For ½ cup **wine**—pour 2 Tbsp. wine vinegar into a ½-cup measure. Fill with broth (chicken, beef, or vegetable). Stir and then let stand for 5 minutes. Stir again before using.

# Kitchen Tools and Equipment You Really Ought to Have

1 Make sure you have a little electric vegetable chopper, the size that will handle 1 cup of ingredients at a time.

2 Don't try to cook without a good paring knife that's sharp (and holds its edge) and fits in your hand.

3 Almost as important—a good chef's knife (we always called it a "butcher" knife) with a wide, sharp blade that's about 8 inches long, good for making strong cuts through meats.

4 You really ought to have a good serrated knife with a long blade, perfect for slicing bread.

5 Invest in at least one broad, flexible, heat-resistant spatula. And also a narrow one.

6 You ought to have a minimum of 2 wooden spoons, each with a 10-12 inch-long handle. They're perfect for stirring without scratching.

7 Get a washable cutting board. You'll still need it, even though you have an electric vegetable chopper (#1 above).

8 A medium-sized whisk takes care of persistent lumps in batters, gravies, and sauces when there aren't supposed to be any.

9 Get yourself a salad spinner.

# Index

# Index

# Index

# Index

# Index

# Index

# Index

# Index

# Index

# Index